Susanne Epple (Ed.)

Creating and Crossing Boundaries in Ethiopia

Afrikanische Studien
African Studies

Band/Volume 53

LIT

Creating and Crossing Boundaries in Ethiopia

Dynamics of social categorization and differentiation

edited by

Susanne Epple

LIT

Cover image:
Bayso and Haro fishermen crossing Lake Abbaya together on a traditional boat (Susanne Epple 2012).

Recent cultural change and adaptation to a changing environment has led the Bayso people (agropastoralists) and the Haro people (formerly exclusive hippo hunters) to engage in fishing. The strict social boundaries between the two groups have in course of time been more and more blurred so that nowadays cooperation is the norm and social relations range from neighbourhood to bondfriendship and even intermarriage.

This book is printed on acid-free paper.

Bibliografische Information der Deutschen Nationalbibliothek
Die Deutsche Nationalbibliothek verzeichnet diese Publikation in der Deutschen Nationalbibliografie; detaillierte bibliografische Daten sind im Internet über http://dnb.d-nb.de abrufbar.

ISBN 978-3-643-90534-5

Klosbachstr. 107
CH-8032 Zürich
Tel. +41 (0) 44-251 75 05
Fax +41 (0) 44-251 75 06
E-Mail: zuerich@lit-verlag.ch
http://www.lit-verlag.ch

LIT VERLAG Dr. W. Hopf
Berlin 2014
Verlagskontakt:
Fresnostr. 2
D-48159 Münster
Tel. +49 (0) 2 51-62 03 20
Fax +49 (0) 2 51-23 19 72
E-Mail: lit@lit-verlag.de
http://www.lit-verlag.de

Auslieferung:
Deutschland: LIT Verlag Fresnostr. 2, D-48159 Münster
Tel. +49 (0) 2 51-620 32 22, Fax +49 (0) 2 51-922 60 99, E-Mail: vertrieb@lit-verlag.de
Österreich: Medienlogistik Pichler-ÖBZ, E-Mail: mlo@medien-logistik.at
E-Books sind erhältlich unter www.litwebshop.de

CONTENTS

Acknowledgements vii

Introduction 1
Susanne Epple

Part I: Alteration and Crossing of Boundaries

When Physical Boundaries Express Social Differentiation: The gated communities of inner city Addis Ababa 19
Yeraswork Admassie

The Nyangatom Circle of Trust: Criteria for ethnic inclusion and exclusion 49
Gebre Yntiso

Reclaiming Lost Identity: Redemption of slave descendants among the Ganta, Gamo highlands 73
Bosha Bombe

Part II: Status Change and Interdependencies across Intra-ethnic Divides

Adolescence, Bridehood and Marriage: Local perspectives on female status change in South Omo 91
Susanne Epple

"Time has brought it!": Narrating female identities and change in Maale 115
Sophia Thubauville

Daasanech Notions on Social Causation of Well-being and Misfortune 127
Yvan Houtteman

Giving Birth to an Ancestor: Boundaries and bridges between life and death among the Konso 147
Nicole Poissonnier

Material Culture and Identity in South Omo: Convergence and divergence 163
Tina Brüderlin

Part III: Differential Perception of Social Boundaries

Knowledge, Identity and Epistemological Choices: Competing theoretical trends in Oromo studies **189**
Thomas Osmond

The Way to Shashamane: The Rastafari return to a fictive Ethiopia **213**
Wolfgang Bender

External Designation versus Self-identification: The case of the Bayso and the Haro people on Gidiccho Island, Lake Abbaya. **233**
Susanne Epple and Fabienne Braukmann

Contributors **255**

ACKNOWLEDGEMENTS

First and foremost I want to thank the authors for their scholarly contribution to this book and for their limitless patience and loyalty during the delay of the publication process.

Second, I would like to express my gratitude to different institutions who contributed to the research done on which some of the chapters in this book are based. Four of the chapters are an outcome of research done in the years 2000-2005 in the context of the Special Research Program (SFB) 295 on *Cultural and Linguistic Contacts in North East Africa and West Asia* at the Johannes-Gutenberg University Mainz, Germany. The SFB 295 was financed by the German Research Foundation (DFG), and therefore our thanks are due to the DFG. Within this project, two intercultural workshops were organized and hosted at the South Omo Research Center (SORC) in Jinka, Ethiopia and their outcomes are presented in two chapters of this book. The SORC facilities were also used by several authors and their informants to conduct interviews in a quiet and friendly environment and to analyze their data not far from the field. I would therefore like to express my gratefulness to the SORC, both to the institution and its staff.

On behalf of the authors I would like to thank all the informants for their unreserved cooperation in sharing their knowledge and experiences with the researchers. I am indebted to Christopher Bernard for proofreading the final manuscript for language. Last but not least, I thank my husband, Gebre Yntiso, for his valuable comments and his encouragement, and my children for their patience and lovely company.

INTRODUCTION

Susanne Epple

This collection of essays is meant to shed light on how and why in contemporary Ethiopia social boundaries are created, manipulated, redefined and crossed. The focus lies on the characterizing features and dynamics of both, inter- and intra-group boundary formation, alteration and crossing.

Social boundaries are understood as social limits that human beings create to differentiate each other based on certain parameters. The social boundaries discussed in this book are articulated, among others, along linguistic lines, ethnic identification, aesthetic codes, socio-economic backgrounds, generational differences, and mythical and historical narratives. They are recognized and enforced through social demarcations, adherence to religious values, observation of cultural prohibitions, and the erection of physical barriers. However, as the different chapters reveal, social boundaries are permeable, and rather dynamic than static.

The book is the outcome of the work of different scholars with rich research experiences in Ethiopia. The initial book idea and some of the contributions (namely, Bender, Brüderlin, Epple, Thubauville) are the result of an interdisciplinary research project based in Mainz University, Germany,[1] while the other authors joined later. Originally, it was planned to appear under a different title as the third in a series on cultural contact in Ethiopia, following the edited volumes: *The Perils of Face: Cultural contact, respect, and self-esteem in southern Ethiopia* (Strecker/Lydall 2006) and *To Live with Others: Essays on cultural neighborhood in southern Ethiopia* (Gabbert/Thubauville 2010). However, in the course of its making, things unexpectedly changed and the book finally took its present shape. Unlike the previous two volumes that focused on small groups in Southern Ethiopia alone, this book covers many regions in Ethiopia, including the capital Addis Ababa. Yet, it is thematically linked to the preceding volumes, which also dealt with local perceptions of cultural differences.

The diversity of social boundaries in Ethiopia

Ethiopia is best understood as a country with multiple internal divides, but also endless interconnections.[2] When looking at the divides, one can identify, ethnic, religious, linguistic, political and a multitude of other differences. Geographically,

1 The project was part of the Special Research Program *295 Cultural and Linguistic Contacts in North East Africa and West Asia* at the Johannes Gutenberg University Mainz, Germany. The anthropological subprojects were called *Cultural* Contact, *Respect and Self-Esteem in Southern Ethiopia* (from 2000-2002) and *Alliances and Cultural Neighborhood* (from 2003-2005).

2 In 2007, there were 95 officially recognized ethnic groups (Central Statistical Agency 2008). The number of individual languages listed for Ethiopia is 90. Of those, 85 are living languages and 5 have no known speakers (Lewis 2009).

one can distinguish between highland and lowland groups, and urban and rural communities, categories that are partly overlapping with the political categories of center and periphery (Markakis 2011).

Within these categories one can find sub-categories and sub-sub-categories that further differentiate people into smaller groupings. Common in many Ethiopian societies, for example, is the differentiation and also discrimination of individuals based on occupation, such as potters, tanners, weavers, blacksmiths, hunters (Freeman and Pankhurst 2001; Amborn 2000) or on descent from slaves (Bosha, in this volume). Internal differentiation of statuses related to sex and age are strongly emphasized in many ethnic groups with age- and generation-sets and status change clearly expressed during initiation and marriage. Many of these relationships are nowadays subject to change in various parts of the country, either through contact with modernity, or through government intervention. New differences are also emerging through urban development, which creates disparities in livelihood/occupation, education and wealth, among others.

The way diversity is handled in Ethiopia has also been changing. In the past, in the interest of a unified nation, ethnic, religious and other differences between the various groups were rather downplayed; governance was highly centralized by regimes that tried to emphasize the cultural unity of the country, focusing on the highland Christian 'great tradition' (Clapham 2002:11).[3] Since 1991, ethnicity is the defining principle of state organization and the division into federal states and in some cases their subdivisions into smaller units are largely ethnic-based. However, as Ethiopia has officially more than 90 divergent ethnic groups, none of the nine federal states consists of a homogenous population. Still, most of the states have been established based on a majority group living within its boundaries, such as the Tigray, Amhara, Afar, Somali and Oromia regional states. Others, such as Gambella, Benishangul/Gumuz, Harari and the Southern Nations Nationalities and Peoples Region (SNNPR) are conglomerates of several groups. Especially the SNNPR stands out from the others as it consists of 56 different ethnic groups[4] brought together based on physical proximity rather than on common ethnic identity.

Independent of their size, all ethnic groups are granted equality by the new Ethiopian Constitution of 1995, and ethnic and cultural difference are now not only officially recognized, but also publicly celebrated.[5] One of the consequences of the ethnic federalism has been the proliferation of ethnic identities where formerly suppressed groups claim independent existence and seek political representation. As a result, the official number of ethnic groups in Ethiopia has increased from 58 between 1995 and 2000 to 74 between 2001 and 2008 (Fekadu 2011: 776). In the

3 For a description of the change from the socialist Derg regime to the contemporary Ethiopian political system see for example James et al. (2002); for a critical examination of 'ethnic federalism' see Turton (2006) and Markakis (2011).

4 See http://www.snnprs.gov.et/about.html (last accessed on 10.09.2013).

5 See Epple/Thubauville (eds., 2012) for a discussion of the handling of cultural diversity and some related problems in Ethiopia today.

ethnically very diverse Southern Nations Nationalities and Peoples' Region the number has increased from 45 to 56.[6]

In the study of ethnic identity, local narratives of ethnogenesis can be of great interest. In Ethiopia, many groups explain their ethnogenesis in terms of an amalgamation of migrants from various other groups.[7] In Southern Ethiopia, for example, the Hamar and the Bashada trace their ancestry to migrants from the neighboring Aari, Maale, Tsamai (also: Ts'amakko), Mursi (also: Mun), and others, the descendants of which are nowadays represented by their clans (Lydall/Strecker 1979; Epple 2010).[8] Such clans of different ethnic origins may keep some of their originally assigned qualities (Epple 2010), or may serve as cross-cutting ties with the original group and possibly lead to a prohibition of killing each other (Schlee 1989; Sagawa 2010).The same prohibition exists often for groups who believe to have common roots, such as for the Bayso living on Gidiccho Island and the surrounding neighbours living at the shore (Epple/Braukmann, in this volume), or for the Arbore and Karmet (also: Wata Wando) (Gabbert 2010). The variety of ways of absorbing individuals or splinters of other groups and the differing degrees to which strangers can be integrated has also been the theme of different publications (Girke 2008; Epple 2010; Thubauville 2010), and has proven to be rather unpredictable (Gebre, in this volume).

Ethiopia is also known as a multi-religious country. Besides ethnic identity, religion has always played a major role for drawing boundaries in many parts of the country. The dominant religions are Orthodox Christianity and Islam, and–increasingly in the 20th Century—Protestant Christianity with a variety of local adaptations. Much fewer in numbers are the members of the Catholic Church and Ethiopian Judaism and the traditional belief systems that have continued to exist in various parts of the country.[9]

The spread of new belief systems can lead not only to the redefinition, but also to a reconfiguration of identities. In South Omo, for example, the introduction of Protestant Christianity, has led to new demarcations between members of different

6 Some of the recent literature on SNNPR speaks of the revitalization and creation of ethnic identity in the context of ethnic federalism. Especially minority groups were able to enhance their local status or achieve acknowledgement as an independent "nationality". See for example Matsuda (2002) on the Muguji, Ismagilova (2006) and Nishi (2003) on the Siltie. There are also cases of boundary contraction. For example the Gewada and Dobasse used to be considered as two distinct ethnic groups but were recently reunified as Ale.

7 This process is said to be typical for most African societies that consist of "bits and pieces—human and cultural—of existing societies" (Kopytoff 1987: 3).

8 The same is true for the neighbours of the Hamar and Bashada who likewise claim to be amalgamations of splinters of neighbouring groups, for example the Aari (Gebre 1995), Jensen 1959: 51), the Arbore (Ayalew 1997), the Bodi (Fukui 1994),the Daassanech (Houtteman, in this volume) the Kara (Girke 2008) and the Mursi (Turton 1994).

9 For the history of the different religions in Ethiopia see the bibliography by Abbink (2003) on Orthodox Christianity, Trimingham (1965 and Braukämper (2002) on Islam, Kaplan (1995) on Judaism and Boell et al. (2005) on Catholic and Protestant Missionary Activities.

ethnic groups. Converted individuals of different origins (such as Banna, Kara, Arbore, migrants from highland Ethiopia) consider themselves as belonging to a common category locally called *sabaki* (literal translation from Amharic: 'preacher', locally meaning 'convert'). Besides sharing a common new belief, the members of the *sabaki* group are allowed to freely intermarry, even with people who come from groups that were originally prohibited. At the same time, the ties of the converts to their original ethnic group are weakened (Epple 2005). Also in the context of inherited membership in occupational and other caste groups whose boundaries have been perceived as rather impermeable, changes have be observed. Ellison (2006) describes how among the Konso the categories of Etenta (cultivators) and Xauta (craftworkers perceived as polluted) have been questioned and redefined, boundaries blurred and subcategories created in the context of economic change after the period of socialism, e.g. since 1991. Intensified tourism has recently provided remarkable income to Konso craftworkers (blacksmiths, weavers, potters), so that some cultivators have decided to become Xauta for economic benefit (Belete 2014). Based on the existing literature it can thus be argued that ethnic identities and other internal differentiations in Ethiopia have always been dynamic, and movements across ethnic, religious, class, caste and other boundaries have always taken place.

The aims of this volume are threefold. First, an attempt is made to look at sociocultural differentiation in Ethiopia in a comprehensive manner by bringing together boundary perspectives related to different social groupings in Ethiopia. Thematically, the creation, crossing and manipulation of and communication across different boundaries are covered. These include territorial and spatial, ethnic, religious, and class, caste and status boundaries. Second, the focus of this book is not on ethnic identities per se. Rather, it explores the existing dynamics and movements around social boundaries, i.e. how people invent, affirm and emphasize their differences; how they downplay, ignore, manipulate or eliminate them; and finally when and how boundaries are transgressed or crossed. Third, with the intention to understand layers of boundaries, this book brings together the perspectives on inter-group and intra-group boundary dynamics. It is believed that through this approach parallels and commonalities of dealing with differences in diverse contexts can be illuminated.

The study of boundaries in different academic fields

Boundaries as cognitive adaptation to natural and social environment

> The diversity of ways to distinguish individuals from one another is the result of a universal human activity, the definition of social borders… (Ross 1975: 53)

The classification of the natural and social environment is part of the cognitive functions of the human brain. Social psychologists argue that humans adapt to their environment through cognitive categorizing and stereotyping (Fiske 1998 cf. in Lemont and Molnar 2002: 170). Sociologist Eviatar Zerubavel (1996) calls this process "Lumping and Splitting", referring to the active construction of similarity, and the simultaneous creation of difference between things that are neither inherently similar nor different from one another. The categorization of the environment leads to the creation of social clusters in people's minds. Once these have been established in a specific "thought community" (Fleck 1935 cf. Zerubavel 1996: 427), all members of one category are perceived as similar and those of others as different. Differences within the same category and similarities between two categories are downplayed or ignored. Though contributing to the creation of simplified stereotypes, it is only this generalizing process that enables humans to make sense of the complex world around them (Schutz und Luckmann 1973, Berger and Luckmann 1966, cf. Zerubavel 1996: 423). Individuals adopt these categories and perceive their (natural and social) environment accordingly during their cognitive socialization (Zerubavel 1996: 423). The categorization of people into distinct groups serves the same purpose, in that it helps define how people relate to each other thereby providing orientation to those who are part of a group, but also to those who are outside of it (Donahoe et al. 2009: 12).[10]

The criteria used by a given social or ethnic group to form its identity can neither be predicted nor do they remain the same through time or in different contexts. Often they are based on one or several aspects such as a perceived or claimed common race, language, religion, political boundaries, historical experience, social classes, castes, gender, generation, age-grades or social movements (Donahoe et al. 2009: 2).

Boundary research in social science and related fields

The concept of boundaries has been a focus of research in different disciplines, such as anthropology, history, political science, sociology and social psychology. In the literature, different issues have been looked at, including research on cognition; social and collective identity; divisions based on class, gender, ethnicity, religion and physical boundaries and border issues. (Lamont & Molnar, 2002: 167).

In social anthropology, the term "boundary" became most prominent with Fredrik Barth's seminal work on "Ethnic Groups and Boundaries" (1969). Ethnic groups, Barth (1969: 9f) argued, are socially constructed and ethnic boundaries can be strategically manipulated so that individuals can be included and excluded according to group interests. This idea has been extended and refined in the study of interethnic conflict, for example by Georg Elwert (2002) or by Günther Schlee (2008, 2009), who focused on strategies of inclusion and exclusion in conflict situations. Besides manipulating or redefining a group's own boundary, there is also the phenomenon of individuals or even groups of people transgressing or crossing

10 Donahoe et al. (2009) have called such categories of groups of people "collective identity". They differentiate difference between "social identity" and "collective identity", arguing that the concept of "collective identity" takes a group of individuals as the point of reference, while "social identity" takes the individual with his/her multiple identities as a starting point of analysis (Donahoe et al. 2009: 4).

them, actions that do not necessarily affect the existence, durability or stability of the boundaries themselves (Barth 1969: 15).

The terms boundary, frontier and border are used inconsistently and by some authors interchangeably in the literature (Cohen 1994). Anthony Cohen (1994) stated that for the anthropological analysis of social relations, the term boundary was the most appropriate. Boundaries, he argued, are "essentially contestable", like social relations that are dynamic by nature, and have something in common with the "blurriness and elusiveness of symbols", while the terms border and frontier allude to a more static or physical separation (Cohen 1994: 70). However, when we speak of social boundaries in anthropological analysis, the terms border and boundary are used to indicate social, cultural and territorial dimensions of ethnic group relations. This implies that a single boundary between two groups can have all these three dimensions (Hastings & Wilson 1999: 19). Usually the concept of boundary is mentioned in connection with identity, and indeed these two concepts are linked and belong together. The term "identity" is understood as what people have in common i.e. the absence of difference, while the concept of boundary implies what separates one category from the other (Schlee 2002: 8).[11]

Alteration and making of boundaries

Many studies have revealed how social boundaries are defined and redefined according to the situation and the needs of the actors involved. Joan Vincent (1974 cf. Cohen 1978: 386) refers to this flexible nature of boundary the "mercurial character" of ethnic boundaries, Ronald Cohen (1978: 387) calls it "situational ethnicity" and Brian Donahoe et al. (2009: 30) "strategic alteration or manipulation of identity variables". According to Schlee (2002: 8), the number of possible recombinations of such features is endless.

Every group has a range of options of identification, and may choose to select one over the other to achieve greater inclusion or exclusion in group membership in specific situations (Donahoe et al. 2009: 30). Different authors (Elwert 2002: 37; Cohen 1978; Schlee 2004, 2009) have identified two main strategies that are used to redefine boundaries: the alternations between reference frames and the movement between different more-or-less inclusive conceptions of boundary.

Elwert (2002: 37) speaks of "switching frames of reference" when individuals or groups redefine the boundaries between themselves and others. The choice could be to prioritize one "frame of reference" over the other (for example to switch from religion as the most important identity marker to language), or to narrow or widen

[11] Fredrik Barth (2000: 20) noted that to an English native speaker the concept of boundary evokes different ideas, "ranging from an imagined line drawn on the ground through various abstract separations and distinctions in realms of political and social organization to a schema for conceptualizing the very idea of distinction." The concept of boundary, he explains, has originated in western culture, Barth suggest that other concepts might be useful in other cultural or linguistic contexts, and that it must be empirically demonstrated in each case whether the conceptual construct of boundary is really useful and salient to the people (*ibid.*).

the same "frame of reference" (for example to narrow down Christian identity by emphasizing that one is a protestant or a roman catholic; or to switch from emphasizing German or French citizenship to wider category of being European). Through this process of changing the frame of reference or narrowing or widening it, individuals or groups of people can be included in or excluded from the we-group (*ibid.* 2002: 37f).

Schlee (2004) stressed that actors may take cost and benefit calculations when identity change takes place. There may be situations when a narrow definition is advantageous and it is preferable to keep a group small, for example when it comes to sharing resources. In other contexts it might be better to widen the definition of the group and thereby include more people, for example when it comes to defense against enemies (Schlee 2009: 2f).[12]

Andreas Wimmer (2008: 987ff) identified five major types of strategic boundary making. The first one "Shifting Boundaries through Expansion" is about merging different categories into a new and wider one. Common examples are the grouping of smaller ethnic groups into larger entities, or the nation building in modern context when different people are subsumed under the label of one nation. The second type, "Shifting boundaries through contraction", refers to the promotion of narrow boundaries, for example in movements of ethnic localism when minorities or migrants insist on their originality. The third strategy, "Inversion", relates to depicting the rhetorical redefinition of hierarchical orders of groups. This is the case, for example, when despised or excluded minorities redefine themselves as morally physically or culturally superior to the originally dominant group. An example for this is the cultural nationalism among African-Americans. "Repositioning", the forth strategy, relates to the status change of individuals, or even a whole category of people within an existing system of hierarchical boundaries. Other than "inversion", this strategy is about shifting sides through the crossing of a boundary without changing the existing boundaries and their order. Religious conversion is a common example for this. "Blurring Boundaries" is the fifth strategy which refers to the efforts to abandon the concept of ethnicity as a principle of categorizing people. This is done through emphasizing other, crosscutting social cleavages, for example when individuals become followers of a world religion, followers of a certain lifestyle or stress the most universal category of "human being" in order to avoid classification as a specific minority. Though Wimmer speaks about ethnic identity, his ideas can be applied also to other demarcations of categories. While the first three types of strategic boundary making reveal how a specific category can be redefined, the latter two explain how a category can be abandoned.

12 Schlee (2004: 137) also emphasizes, that it is important to take into account that in bigger groups often few individuals decide for others on their common identity (e.g. priority of identity markers). In the analysis of a given situation one needs therefore needs identify those who are promoting the change of an identity (and may be benefitting from it) and those who are affected by the change.

Individual boundary crossing and status change

Already Fredrik Barth (1969) mentioned that boundaries could be crossed, individually or in a group, without changing or affecting the boundaries themselves. Doja (2003) even suggests that wherever there is a boundary, there also exists mobility across it, and he proposes that more attention must be given to "social change, transition and transformation", with a focus on mobility (spatial and temporal).

Studies on individual boundary crossing relate to individual change of membership in ethnic groups, such as the case of the Chinese Yao referred to by Barth (1969: 22) who regularly incorporate non-Yao people (Kandre 1967). Recent studies show how migrants or refugees crossed geo-political borders and are then forced to adapt to a new situation or culture (Buijs 1993; Alba 2005).

People also experience status change within their own group or society. Any kind of individual boundary crossing, whether it involves the crossing of geopolitical borders or the change of a status, demands a process of adjustment, even a reformulation of the self (Cohen 1994: 67) that means a fundamental change of identity going beyond the access to new knowledge, rights and obligations. Such transformations may be painful and hard to accept, and are often accompanied by rites of passage which serve different purposes. Catherine Bell (2009: 37) stressed that rituals are needed to clearly demarcate the boundaries of status groups and thereby contribute to the stability and continuity of social identities and roles. These could be religious or kin groups, professional classes or castes, age groups, the political and territorial community, the world of the living, the world before it, and the world of the deceased. Rituals ensure that the change or reconstitution of such groups is done smoothly without endangering the system as a whole (Bell 2009: 37). Secondly, as Anthony Cohen (1994: 67f) formulated, the painfulness of such rites is meant to deeply impress the individual and help him or her not only to change the social persona (e.g., status), but also the individual self.

Differential perceptions of social boundaries

Barth (2000: 31 cf. Tronvoll 2009: 13) considers the drawing of a boundary an "act of imposition (…), a cognitive act that lays down some premises; but (it) does not determine all forms that eventuate." Rather it is the social order of a given society, but also the individuals acting around that boundary which shape the outcome. This means that the people who are identified as belonging together by a social boundary do not respond uniformly to it, but rather "selectively and pragmatically". As every individual has his or her own history, the understanding and interpretation of boundaries of identity differ. Tronvoll (2009: 15) in that sense characterizes boundaries as "zones of reflection".

Besides, the construction of a boundary and assigning persons to groups involves not only those who are to be inside the boundary, but also those outside, i.e. for its definition the self-ascription matters as much as the ascription by others (Cohen 1978: 387). As a consequence, social boundaries often do not constitute clearly defined lines; one can expect differences between the endogenous and exogenous criteria used to establish them (Ross 1975: 54; Donahoe et al. 2009: 26). This implies that the way how boundaries are perceived and understood may vary. As Jennie-Keith Ross (1975: 54) put it: "Every border has two sides. It may not look the same to insiders as to outsiders, or to the anthropologist looking on."Social boundaries can also vary in their degree of definition ranging "from minimal acknowledgment of social similarity to (its) public and formal proclamation" (*ibid.*).

Organization of the book

The contributions in this volume discuss boundary issues in Ethiopia from different perspectives. Thematically, the papers have been organized into three sections. The first section on "Making, Alteration and Crossing of Boundaries" emphasizes how permeable and negotiable boundaries are, even in contexts or situations of power differences.

Yeraswork Admassie describes the recent changes of class relations in the Ethiopian capital, Addis Ababa and how they are expressed in architecture and city planning. In "When Physical Boundaries Express Social Differentiation: The gated communities of inner city Addis Ababa", he shows how the increasing separation of rich and poor in Addis Ababa has begun with the emergence of new economic elites. The class boundaries between rich and poor have become recently more emphasized and publicly articulated through the erection of fences that separate the rich from the poor. With the establishment of inner-city gated communities not only everyday interaction between rich and poor has been made nearly impossible, but it has also cut off previously existing social networks, mutual recognition, support and the feeling of belongingness.

Gebre Yntiso's paper titled "The Nyangatom Circle of Trust: Criteria for ethnic inclusion of exclusion" shows how the Nyangatom ethnic group consciously kept its physical and social boundaries completely open for some neighbours, blurred for others, and closed still for others. The Nyangatom people allied and intermingled with groups that posed a minimum risk and promised a maximum advantage. On the contrary, the boundary remained closed for neighbours outside of their circle of trust and those that posed a credible or perceived threat to their survival. The author argues that this rational and strategic decision-making behavior represents something more than cost-benefit analysis aimed at maximizing economic gain or attaining military superiority.

In "Reclaiming Lost Identity: Redemption of slave descendants among the Ganta", *Bosha Bombe* explores the contemporary differentiation between slave descendants and descendants of slave owners. He outlines in detail how the strong boundary based on perceived impurity of the former is continuously crossed in two directions: members of Ganta mainstream society get polluted and become members of the despised group through close interaction during rites of passage, while slave descendants can re-integrate into the mainstream society through undergoing a costly cleansing process.

The second section on "Status Change and Interdependencies across Intra-ethnic Divides" comprises four chapters. All contributions in this section speak of roles and statuses within the same ethnic group, looking at motivations and strategies for individual status change, communication as well as changing relationships between different status holders.

In her chapter "Adolescence, Bridehood and Marriage: Local perspectives on female status change in South Omo", *Susanne Epple* provides insights into the dynamics around status boundaries between different female roles. Focusing on girls' lives, she describes how they convince each other to identify with and adhere to cultural expectations, including the acceptance to undergo the difficult and often painful changes when girls cross the boundary between adolescence and adulthood and become wives and mothers. Besides providing comparative ethnographic data from seven ethnic groups, Epple analyses the dynamics that developed during a workshop when the participants described their lives in front of females from other groups—fully aware of the boundaries between them based on cultural difference.

Sophia Thubauville looks at how boundaries can be created through time and cultural change induced by modernity. In her chapter "'Time has brought it!' Narrating female identities and change in Maale" she shows the strong influence of religious conversion and formal education on the self-image of Maale females, which has led to a clash between the younger and the older generation. Thubauville specifically looks at how the cultural expressions of being "a good girl" and "a good woman" in Maale have changed through time, thereby demonstrating that time can be as important for identification of an individual as place may be, and that identity of a group is not only derived by dissociating from neighbors but also from different times the own group has experienced.

In "Daasanech Notions of Social Causation of Well-being and Misfortune" *Yvan Houtteman* looks at the diverse intra-ethnic boundaries, the complex interconnections between the different categories of people and how these influence the well-being of the individual. Using the examples of interdependencies (between different clans with different abilities), complementary relations (between male and female), and the exertion of control and support (among age-mates, between generations, and by ancestors spirits on their living descendants), he shows how the individual's wellbeing depends on his or her relationship with others.

Nicole Poissonnier describes how the clear boundary that usually separates the living from the dead becomes permeable at the time of death. In "Boundaries and Bridges between Life and Death among the Konso and their Neighbours" she outlines, that once the deceased has crossed the boundary in order to integrate into the world of the dead, the status he had during his lifetime can be manipulated and enhanced through great festivities and other demonstrations. This in turn has an impact on the social status of his descendants whose position is defined via the one of their ancestors.

In her contribution on "Convergence and Divergence through Objects: Material culture and identity in South Omo." *Tina Brüderlin* speaks about cultural artifacts as expressions of ethnic identity and values among ethnic different groups in Southern

Ethiopia. The objects were selected by the participants to a workshop in Jinka in 2001 who presented them as meaningful items representing key concepts and values of their respective groups. The discussions on the multilayered meanings of an object by the original owners vis-à-vis cultural others resulted in a shared understanding and also the discovery of converging meanings, ideas and functions of similar items among the different groups.

The third section on "Differential Perception of Boundaries" contains three papers that show how different and even opposed the views on the same boundary can be, depending on the background and interest of the people concerned.

Thomas Osmond's chapter on "Knowledge, Identity and Epistemological Choices: Competing theoretical trends in Oromo studies" looks critically at the historical development of anthropological and historical studies of Oromo culture. He outlines how the ethnic boundaries of the Oromo are being drawn and defined differently by different categories of people, how they have changed through time and also greatly depend on the researchers. He juxtaposes five ideal-types of views about Oromo studies: the official Ethiopian imperial historiography, the anthropological work of European Christian missionaries, the academic publications of Oromo social scientists, the cultural productions of the Ethiopian Federal State, and the studies conducted by contemporary Western social scientists.

In "The Way to Shashamane: The Rastafari return to a fictive Ethiopia" *Wolfgang Bender* explores the strong images that have developed in Jamaica on Ethiopia as an ancestral and holy land and finally brought Jamaican migrants to the country during Emperor Haile Selassie's times. The Rastafarians living in Shashamene speak of their migration to Ethiopia in terms of 'repatriation' to an ancestral homeland, implying that they are descendants of African slaves. Bender's text shows how a new identity has evolved in Jamaica and then exported to a different context. It also shows how differently their Ethiopian hosts interpret the situation. The Oromo people around Shashamane perceive the Rastafarian settlers rather as intruders and strangers than as relatives and therefore have been keeping the boundary between the Rastafarians and themselves alive and strong.

Susanne Epple and *Fabienne Braukmann* present the existing opposing views on the identities of two groups living on Gidiccho Island in the South of Ethiopia. Their paper "External Designation versus Self-identification: The case of the Bayso and the Haro people on Gidiccho Island, Lake Abbaya" shows how the culturally and linguistically very different Bayso and Haro people have always been observing a strict boundary between them. Externally, however, they have been perceived as belonging to one ethnic group called "Gidiccho", a label that has never been accepted by the two groups.

References

Abbink, Jon, 2003: *A Bibliography on Christianity in Ethiopia*. (Working Paper 52/2003). Leiden: African Studies Centre.

Alba, Richard, 2005: "Bright vs. blurred boundaries: Second-generation assimilation and exclusion in France, Germany, and the United States". *Ethnic and Racial Studies* 28, 1, 20-49.

Amborn, Herrmann, 1990: *Differenzierung und Integration: Vergleichende Untersuchungen zu Spezialisten und Handwerkern in südathiopischen Agrargesellschaften*. München: Trickster.

Ayalew Gebre, 1997: "Arbore Inter-Tribal Relations: An Historical Account". In: Richard Hogg (ed.): *Pastoralists, Ethnicity and the State in Ethiopia*. London: Haan, 143-167.

Barth, Fredrik (ed.), 1969: *Ethnic Groups and Boundaries: The Social Organization of Cultural Difference*. London: Allen and Unwin.

Barth, Fredrik, 2000: "Boundaries and Connections". In: Anthony P. Cohen (ed.): *Signifying Identities. Anthropological perspectives on boundaries and contested values*. London: Routledge, 17-36.

Belete Dawit, 2014: *The Commoditization of Culture: The effects of tourism on cultural heritages and the status of artisans in Fasha, Dokatu and Karat of Konso Woreda, Southern Ethiopia*. Department of Social Anthropology, Addis Ababa University. ((M.A. Thesis; unpublished manuscript).

Bell, Catherine, 2009: *Ritual: Perspectives and dimensions*. Oxford: Oxford University Press (revised edition).

Böll, Verena, Stephen Kaplan, Andreu Martinez d'Alos-Moner, Evelina Sokolinskaia (eds.), 2005: *Ethiopia and the Missions. Historical and Anthropological Insights*. Münster: Lit.

Braukämper, Ulrich, 2002: *Islamic History and Culture in Southern Ethiopia: Collected Essays*. Münster: Lit.

Buijs, Gina, 1993: *Migrant Women: Crossing boundaries and changing identities*. Oxford: Berg.

Clapham, Christopher, 2002: "Controlling Space in Ethiopia". In: Wendy James, Donald D. Donham, Eisei Kurimoto, and Alessandro Triulzi (eds.): *Remapping Ethiopia: Socialism & after*, Oxford: Currey, 9-32.

Cohen, Anthony, 1994: "Boundaries of Consciousness, Consciousness of Boundaries. Critical questions for anthropology". In: Han Vermeulen and Cora Govers (eds.): *The Anthropology of Ethnicity: Beyond Ethnic Groups and Boundaries*. Amsterdam: Het Spinhuis, 59-80.

Cohen, Anthony (ed.), 2000: *Signifying Identities: Anthropological perspectives on boundaries and contested values*. London: Routledge.

Cohen, Ronald, 1978: "Ethnicity: Problem and Focus in Anthropology". *Annual Review of Anthropology* 7, 379-403.

Doja, Albert, 2003: "The Boundary Condition in Social and Anthropological Theory." (Abstract) *Proceedings, Centre for Border Studies*. Wales: University of Glamorgan. (Accessed online at: http://discovery.ucl.ac.uk/77365/; last accessed

15.03.2014).

Donahoe, Brian et al., 2009: "The Formation and Mobilization of Collective Identities in Situations of Conflict and Integration". Working paper 116. Halle: Max Planck Institute for Social Anthropology.

Donnan, Hastings and Thomas M. Wilson, 1999: *Borders: Frontiers of identity, nation and the state.* Oxford, New York: Berg.

Elwert, Georg, 2002: "Switching identity Discourses: Primordial emotions and the social construction of we-groups". In: Günther Schlee (ed.): *Imagined Differences: Hatred and the construction of identity.* Hamburg: Lit, 33-56.

Epple, Susanne, 2005: "Missionary Work and Cultural Change among the Bashada and Banna of Southern Ethiopia. An emic perspective". In: Verena Böll, Stephen Kaplan, Andreu Martinez d'Alos-Moner, Evelina Sokolinskaia (eds.): *Ethiopia and the Missions. Historical and anthropological insights.* Münster: Lit, 153-170.

Epple, Susanne, 2010: "Culture, Contact and Identity. The multiethnic composition of the Bashada of Southern Ethiopia" In: Christina Gabbert and Sophia Thubauville (eds.): *To Live with Others. Essays on cultural neighborhood in southern Ethiopia.* Köln: Köppe, 47-67.

Epple, Susanne and Sophia Thubauville, 2012: "Cultural Diversity in Ethiopia between Appreciation and Suppression". *Paideuma* 58, 153-166. (Special Issue).

Federal Democratic Republic of Ethiopia, Population Census Commission, 2008: *Summary and Statistical Report of the 2007 Population and Housing Census. Population Size by Age and Sex.* CSA: Addis Ababa (Accessed online at http://www.csa.gov.et/ pdf/Cen2007_firstdraft.pdf, last accessed 1.1.2013).

Fekadu Adugna, 2011: "Overlapping Nationalist Projects and Contested Spaces: The Oromo—Somali borderlands in southern Ethiopia". In: Jon Abbink, Tobias Hagmann (eds.): *Ethiopia's Revolutionary Democracy, 1992-2011. Journal of Eastern African Studies 5, 4,* 773-787. (Special Issue).

Freeman, Dena and Alula Pankhurst (eds.) 2001: *Marginalized Minorities of Craft Workers and Hunters in Southern Ethiopia.* Addis Ababa: Addis Ababa University Press.

Fukui, Katsuyoshi, 1994. "Conflict and Ethnic Interaction. The Mela and their Neighbors". In: Katsuyoshi Fukui and John Markakis (eds.): *Ethnicity and Conflict in the Horn of Africa.* London: Currey, 33-61.

Gebre Yntiso, 1995: *The Ari of Southwest Ethiopia: An exploratory study of production practices.* Addis Ababa: Addis Ababa University, Department of Sociology, Social Anthropology and Social Work. (M.A. Thesis).

Gezaghn Petros, 1993: *The Karo of the Lower Omo Valley: Subsistence, social organisation and relations with neighboring groups.* Addis Ababa: Addis Ababa University. Department of Sociology, Social Anthropology and Social Work. (M.A. Thesis).

Girke, Felix, 2008: *The Aedamo of the Kara. Rhetoric in social relations on the Lower Omo.* Halle: Martin-Luther-Universität Halle-Wittenberg. FB Geschichte, Philosophie und Sozialwissenschaften. (PhD Dissertation).

Hobsbawm, Eric, and Terence Ranger (eds.), 1983: *The Invention of Tradition.* Cambridge: Cambridge University Press.

Isik, Ayse, 2011: "Boundaries and Ethnic Identities. The conception of boundary in a diverse area". *International Journal of Social Sciences and Humanity Studies* 3, 2, 41-48.

Ismagilova, Roza, 2004: "Ethnicity and Federalism: The case of Ethiopia". *Africa: Rivista trimestrale di studi e documentazione dell' Instituto italiano per l'Africa el'Oriente* 59, 2, 179-200.

James, Wendy, Donald L. Donham, Eisei Kurimoto, Alessandro Triulzi (eds.), 2002: *Remapping Ethiopia: Socialism and after.* Oxford: Currey.

Kandre, Peter, 1967: "Autonomy and Integration of Social Systems: The Iu Mien (Yao or Man) mountain populations and their neighbors". In: Peter Kunstadter (ed.): *Southeast Asian Tribes, Minorities and Nations* 2, 583-638.

Kaplan, Steven, 1995: *The Beta Israel: Falasha in Ethiopia. From earliest times to the twentieth century.* New York: New York University Press.

Kopytoff, Igor, 1987: *The African Frontier: The reproduction of African traditional society.* Bloomington: Indiana University Press.

Levine, Donald N., 1974: *Greater Ethiopia: The evolution of a multiethnic society.* Chicago: University of Chicago Press.

Lewis, M. Paul (ed.), 2009: *Ethnologue: Languages of the World (16th edition).* Dallas, Texas: SIL International. (Accessed online at http://www.ethnologue.com, last accessed 1.3.2014).

Lydall, Jean and Ivo Strecker, 1979: *The Hamar of Southern Ethiopia Vol II. Baldambe Explains.* Hohenschäftlarn: Renner.

Markakis, John, 2011: *Ethiopia. The last two frontiers.* Woodbridge: Currey.

Nishi Makoto, 2005: "Making and Unmaking of the National-State and Ethnicity in Modern Ethiopia. A study on the history of the Silte people". *African Study Monographs. Supplementary Issue* 29, 157-168.

Pellow, Deborah (ed.), 1996: *Setting Boundaries: The anthropology of spatial and social organization.* Westport, CT: Bergin and Garvey.

Ross, Jennie-Keith, 1975: "Social Borders: Definitions of diversity". *Current Anthropology* 16, 1, 53-61.

Schlee, Günther, 2002: "Introduction. Approaches to 'Identity' and 'Hatred': Some Somali and other perspectives". In: Günther Schlee (ed.): *Imagined Differences: Hatred and the Construction of Identity.* Hamburg: Lit, 3-32.

Schlee, Günther, 1989: *Identities on the Move: Clanship and Pastoralism in Northern Kenya.* Manchester: Manchester University Press.

Schlee, Günther (ed.), 2002: *Imagined Differences: Hatred and the Construction of Identity.* Hamburg: Lit.

Schlee, Günther, 2004: "Taking Sides and Constructing Identities: Reflections on conflict theory". *The Journal of the Royal Anthropological Institute* 10, 1, 135-156.

Schlee, Günther, 2008: *How Enemies are Made: Towards a theory of ethnic and religious conflict.* New York, Oxford: Berghahn.

Schlee, Günther and Elizabeth Watson (eds.), 2009: *Changing Identification and Alliances in North East Africa. Vol 1: Ethiopia and Kenya.* New York, Oxford: Berghahn.

Trimingham, John Spencer, 1965: *Islam in Ethiopia.* New York: Barnes & Noble.

Tronvoll, Kjetil, 2009: *War and the Politics of Identity in Ethiopia. The making of enemies and allies in the Horn of Africa.* Oxford: Currey.

Turton, David, 2006a: "Introduction". In: David Turton (ed.): Ethnic Federalism: The Ethiopian experience in comparative perspective. Oxford: Currey, 9-31.

Turton, David (ed.), 2006b: *Ethnic Federalism: The Ethiopian experience in comparative perspective.* Oxford: Currey.

Vermeulen, Hans and Cora Govers (eds.), 1996: *The Anthropology of Ethnicity: Beyond "Ethnic Groups and Boundaries".* Amsterdam: Het Spinhuis.

Wimmer, Andreas, 2008: "The Making and Unmaking of Ethnic Boundaries: A multilevel process theory". *AJS113, 4,* 970-1022.

Zerubavel, Eviatar, 1996: "Lumping and Splitting: Notes on social classification". *Sociological Forum* 11, 3, 421-433.

WEBSITES

http://www.snnprs.gov.et/about.html (last accessed on 10.09.2013).

Part I:

Alteration and Crossing of Boundaries

When Physical Boundaries Express Emerging Social Differentiation: The gated communities of inner Addis Ababa[1]

Yeraswork Admassie

Introduction

The significant demographic and economic changes taking place in Addis Ababa bring along new urban forms that are contributing to the transformation of the social and physical landscape of the city. City center high rise office buildings, multi-block condominium apartment sites, real-estate neighborhoods, luxury villa areas, ring-roads, multiple lane avenues, cobblestone side-streets, and urban light railway that is currently under construction are the most visible new urban forms that are changing the face of city. One transformation that is socially, if not materially, as significant as the aforementioned ones, is the development of gated communities that are creating excluded and segregated neighborhoods amidst the city. Guard-gated residential enclaves are spreading quickly both in inner city and in peripheral neighborhoods of Addis Ababa. Yet, in spite of their growing importance as a new urban phenomenon, gated communities have not attracted the attention of urban planners and municipal authorities.

Focusing on the inner city gated communities in Addis Ababa, this paper explores the case of older neighborhoods that were retrofitted with fences and/or gates, as well as the relatively recently planned government-sponsored condominium apartment building sites. It examines in detail their sub-types, emergence, main features, governance, internal integration and segregation from the broader society; major attributes of their residents; as well as their benefits and drawbacks. It also highlights trends in the development of gated communities and identifies policy recommendations directed at clarifying the legal ambiguity that is hanging over them.

The paper asserts that the emergence and spread of gated communities in inner Addis Ababa is causally linked to the absence of socially undifferentiated neighborhood that is, in its turn a result of the original settlement pattern of the city. Having followed a historical trajectory different from that of developed and some developing countries, Ethiopia's urban growth has acquired a number of peculiar characteristics (Garettson 2000). One of these characteristics is the distribution of its population, activities, and services. Contemporary urban development in Ethiopia, which began in earnest towards the end of the 19th century, was a process whereby the wandering "capitals" of the emperors and regional governors were gradually

1 By inner or inner city Addis Ababa we refer to the old core of the city excluding the neighborhoods at its periphery; as well as the suburbs outside of the city's boundary and those inside the territory of Oromia National Regional State that came into existence in the mid-1990s.

fixed at permanent sites. As a result, the layouts of most of these urban centers shave closely followed the "blueprints" according to which residents of the moving camps perched their tents in a predetermined order (Akalou 1973).

Addis Ababa, too, was settled following the hierarchical feudal organization of the state and the army. Following Emperor Menelik's decision on the present site of Addis Ababa for his capital, large tracts of land were allotted as sort of camping sites to high-ranking state officials including regional officials who paid periodic visits to the capital (Pankhurst 1961; Akalou 1973: 8, 15). After claiming the most favorable and dominant locations for their own residence, these high-officials distributed the remaining portion of the land among their vassals who, in turn, did the same with their respective allotments.

Addis Ababa's pattern of settlement also came to mirror the seemingly "disorderly" manner according to which army contingents and their dependents marched from place to place, with the rich and the mighty being surrounded by their vassals, retainers, servants and domestic slaves (Yeraswork 2007).

The pattern of settlement and land use that were established at the time of the establishment of Addis Ababa became entrenched because, given the realities of the time, social hierarchy could not, and need not, be marked with physical distance. Under the backward economy and underdeveloped division of labor, dominant at the time, members of the upper and lower classes were too interdependent to reside in separate quarters. The extremely low-levels of commodity production and exchange meant that most, if not all, of the benefits of the market that we take for granted today simply didn't exist. Hence, each and every household—from that of the Emperor's down to those of the ordinary town residents—had to undertake most of the processing of their food items and the making of their clothes and shelters by themselves. Thus, servants and serve—both the providers of services and those who received them—had to live side by side, if not exactly under the same roof, at least within the same compound or immediate neighborhood.

Likewise, social hierarchy did not need to be defined by physical boundaries, given the dominant reality of the time. It was enough for the elite that they were made distinct by the high office or social position they held, by the symbols of their high birth or office expressed in the minutely detailed courtly code dictating the ride, dress, processional umbrella, embroidered cloak, headdress, etc., which they were allowed to display in public. The most important indicator of high status and success was the size of one's entourage. Not only that the rich and mighty of those days could not do without their lowly subjects living close by them, but they also preferred to be surrounded at all times by as many of them as possible. Hence, the rich neither want nor need physical separation but rather proximity with the lowly in order to assert and enhance their social dominance and status, without for a moment compromising their distinctness.

Moreover, the critical need for mutual support and cooperation in undertaking social functions such as weddings and burials—under a situation in which neither *idirs*[2] nor funeral homes had evolved—made the cohabitation of persons endowed with different resources absolutely essential for their survival. As much as the poorer members of the interdependent neighborhood—usually the *sefer* or encampment of a certain lord or big man—needed the material contribution and participation of the lord in undertaking various essential social functions, the lord too could not do without the labor input of those below him on the social hierarchy. Thus, under the circumstances that were predominant during the establishment of Addis Ababa, residential segregation by social and economic status was not an option.

This early attribute of the settlement hindered the emergence of racially, ethnically, and socio-economically segregated neighborhoods. Even today, Addis Ababa is to a large extent a city of undifferentiated neighborhoods in which shacks and villas, rich and poor, foreigners and locals, and people of various religious and ethnic affiliations live side-by-side. It is still a city with a strikingly clear social proximity between various social groups. It maintains a high sense of neighborhood based community solidarity that cuts across class and ethnic divisions. Hence, even today, it is a place of considerably low levels of ethnic tension and violent forms of crime (Yeraswork 2007).

The contention that its original proto-urban pattern of settlement that was determined by the feudal hierarchy and domestic slavery has helped hinder the emergence of racially, ethnically and class-wise separated quarters in today's Addis Ababa does not appeal to simple reason. This is because, firstly, one of the hallmarks of the ecological organization of the preindustrial city is none other than "the rigid social segregation, which typically has led to the formation of quarters or wards"(Sjoberg 1955: 389). The existence of ethnic and occupational quarters such as the Latin, Jewish, Greek, and Armenian Quarters of Europe, the Mediterranean World and the Middle East testifies to this. Secondly, strictly speaking, traditional hierarchical societies are rarely, if ever, found to be leading to the emergence of an even distribution of resources such as urban land. But, as shown in the foregoing paragraphs, there is a valid causal link that ties together the main characteristics of both the original and the more recent pattern of settlement of Addis Ababa. The thesis and the arguments for it explains, in a counter-intuitive way, the more egalitarian and humane mix of contemporary Addis Ababa by appealing to the hierarchical and harsh features of its original settlement.

With the emergence of a totally different system of social differentiation and a class system based on income differences, a situation under which membership in the various social strata could no longer be signified easily as by the old marks of birth and symbols of office came into being. Members of the newly emerging classes could keep with those of the same group and status only by physically isolating themselves from those that are different from them and thus new patterns of resi-

2 *Idir* is the most ubiquitous neighborhood-based voluntary association in urban Ethiopia, whose main function is the provision of mutual support in the event of death, burial and mourning.

dential segregation emerged. In the 1990s and the first decade of the current century, during which the flight of the rich to the periphery and the suburbs was only beginning and not yet common, and with new kinds of anxieties about boundaries and borders arising on the footsteps of intensified income based class differentiation, a new pattern of residential segregation arose. Separation through physical fortification instead of physical distance became the only alternative for the inner city middle-class folks.[3] The incongruence, or contradiction, between the new social geography and the old physical layout had to be resolved somehow—and gating provided a practical solution.

As a consequence, the curious racial, ethnic and class mix that has been characteristic of the city for over a century, is currently changing and is likely to change even faster having come under the double pressures of external forces and internal dynamics. What exactly will come to replace the still persistent "salad-bowl" neighborhood structure remains to be seen. However, we can already tell from the direction of current developments that these changes are likely to proceed in ways that are distinctly Ethiopian in character.

The changes in the patterns of settlement are hinged on the basic socio-economic transformations taking place in Addis Ababa, as well as the reset of the country's large urban centers. Ever since the introduction elements of a free-market economy in the early 1990s, Ethiopia has been on a path of rapid social change and polarization. The number of the emerging socially distinct local elite, as well as that of the resident expatriate populace—including the burgeoning staff of the international and regional organizations, business community, and diplomatic corps—is growing by the day. The divide between the rich and the poor has widened over the past two decades. Nowhere is this polarity more visible than in the built-in environment of Addis Ababa, where the wide gulf separating the posh enclaves of the well-to-do from the shantytowns, slums, and hastily put up city-periphery squatter-settlements (*chereqa-bet*) of the poor is so stark as to literally jump to the eye. To paraphrase a statement made by the late Prime Minister Meles Zenawi (2007), there is no longer one Addis Ababa but two or more incomparable ones.

The main mechanism by which the "newly rich" are asserting their social distinctness is the establishment of separated and distant gated, or access-controlled, residential neighborhoods. This urban phenomenon has become commonplace in the cities of both developed and developing countries of the United States, Canada, Australia, the Middle East, Asia, and Africa. By the year 2001, some 13 million households were residing in more than 40,000 walled and access-controlled communities in the United States alone. This number is only going to continue to rise dramatically given that eight out of every ten new real-estate developments in the country are gated (Grant 2003). Most of Bangkok's estimated 12 million inhabitants live behind gates (Wissink et al. n. d.: 3).

3 For a better understanding of the respective roles of physical distance and borders/barriers in reinforcing social distinction, see Maher 2004.

Ethiopia, too, has entered the era of gated community in a significant way. However, this study shows that the gated communities of inner city Addis Ababa do not share many of the features with the gated communities in the developed countries or even of those in Sao Paulo, Johannesburg, Mexico City, or Ankara.

The empirical investigation informing this paper was designed as a comparative study and executed from November 2008 to April 2009. Four *kebeles*[4] were selected—three from the sub-city of Bole and one from that of Yeka—for the established existence of gated communities within them as well as their accessibility. The researcher conducted in-depth interviews with city and *kebele* officials, while a structured questionnaire (containing both close-ended and open-ended questions) was used to collect data on the gated communities in the four *kebeles* with the help of *kebele* officials and youth who are knowledgeable about the area. These were supplemented by field observations of the gated communities and in-depth interviews with their guards and residents. The researcher is a resident of one *kebele* covered in the study, namely, *Kebele* 11/12 of Yeka Sub-city; and has served since 1996 in the executive committee of the *Tematquate,* one of Addis Ababa University staff housing development cooperative, which is also covered in the study. As such, relevant information acquired in the capacity of a genuine participant observer has gone toward informing the study as retroactively reconstructed data.

Conceptualization and classification

The walling of cities, characteristic of medieval times, is coming back to redefine the "open city" of the industrial age, albeit with important modifications. Today, walls are the makings of groups of city residents that are put up primarily to protect neighborhoods.

The literature on gated communities is full of synonyms that essentially convey the same central concept. The terms *gated community, access-controlled community, gated enclave,* and *fortified enclave,* are interchangeably used—as they are in this paper. According to Blakely and Snyder:

> [Gated communities] are residential areas with restricted access that make normally public spaces private. Access is controlled by physical barriers, walled or fenced perimeters, and gated or guarded entrances. Gated communities include both new housing developments and older residential areas retrofitted with barricades and fences. They represent a phenomenon different from apartment or condominium buildings with security systems or doormen. There, a doorman precludes public access only to a lobby or hallways—the private space within a building. Gated communities preclude public

4 *Kebele* (ward) used to be the lowest tier of urban administration ever since the nationalization of all urban lands and extra houses in 1975. Right after the fieldwork informing this study was completed, however, all *kebele*in Addis Ababa were reorganized being merged to form larger units that came to be known as *woreda* (district). Yet, the former *kebele*are in some cases still maintained as "development posts" (የልማት ጣቢያ) for practical purposes.

access to roads, sidewalks, parks, open space, and playgrounds—all resources that in earlier eras would have been open and accessible to all citizens of a locality (1998. 53).

This definition is applicable to a variety of gated communities including those that: (a) employ different types of physical barriers to control access (walled or fenced perimeters, and gated or guarded entrances), (b) preclude public access from various types of spaces (roads, sidewalks, green-areas, open space, and playgrounds), and (c) are either pre-fitted or retrofitted with the physical barriers.

Notwithstanding the common features of the gating of communities, considerable regional variation exists in the emergence and the characteristic features of gated enclaves (Grant 2003: 1). The regional variation is partially captured by the three types of gated communities identified by Blakely and Snyder (1998), namely: *lifestyle communities, prestige communities*, and *security-zone communities*. One can also add the *purpose-designed community* as a fourth type.

In countries such as the Unites States, most gated communities are *lifestyle communities*, which are essentially country clubs and retirement enclaves built around a collection of exclusive recreational amenities, such as golf courses and parks (Blakely and Snyder 1998). In many developing countries such as China, for instance, most gated enclaves are *prestige communities* in which gates play the role of status symbols and objects of appeal. These gated enclaves cater to the growing affluent populations of expatriates and the local *nouveau riche* alike, both groups are held together by the common bond of belonging to the same socio-economic group (Blakely and Snyder 1998).

Security-zone communities are what Blakely and Snyder have labeled "enclaves of fear". In South America, Africa, and South and South-East Asian cities, where the gap between the poor and the rich is wide and insecurity is high, most gated enclaves are *security-zone communities*. For instance, in post-apartheid South Africa, gated communities that have mushroomed in response to the burgeoning violent crime are aptly classified as "security villages".

But *security-zone* communities are not necessarily the sole reserve of the affluent. In many developing countries, where crime does not discriminate, and fear of violence and feelings of insecurity are no longer restricted to the rich, gated communities also emerge in lower and middle-income neighborhoods and some public housing complexes (La Cour-Little and Malpezzi 2001). In Bangkok, for instance, the feeling of insecurity has permeated every section of society, to the extent that even low-income people are living in walled slums (Wissink et al. n. d: 3). This is precisely the case with some of the low-cost condominium housing sites in Addis Ababa—particularly the smaller ones—that get gated as soon as people start moving into them.

Blakely and Snyder (1998) capture the variation within the *security-zone* category by distinguishing three subtypes: the *city perch*, the *suburban perch* and the *barricade perch*. They are all referred to as "perches" because the gates are built by the residents themselves and not the real-estate developers. *City perches* are inner city neighborhoods that are retrofitted with gates by residents that can vary from the most affluent to the most desperately poor in order to protect themselves from the threat of crime and traffic that is surrounding them, and they correspond to the inner city gated communities of Addis Ababa. *Suburban perches* are located in both inner-suburbs and outer-suburbs that have more recently come to be walled and gated as inner city problems progressively started catching up with the middle-class that had taken flight to the suburbs. *Barricade perches* are secure suburban neighborhoods that are installed and secured with intentionally designed systems of barricade, without being fully enclosed. They exist in neighborhoods with public streets, making their complete walling and gating impossible. Interestingly, it appears that inner city developer-driven suburbs such as the Ayat village at the eastern periphery of the Addis Ababa are progressively taking this path of development.

The fourth type of gated community, the *purpose-designed community*, refers to those that are meant to exclusively house foreigners and have been in existence for quite some time. The worker compounds in the Gulf States and the closed cities of the Soviet era are examples of this type of gated communities. The CMC enclosure[5] in Addis Ababa was created to serve such a purpose, although its original objective was never realized and it is now a state-owned gated community of the security zone/prestige type run by a state rental agency.

Finally, it should be noted that variations in gated communities exist not only between regions and countries, but also within the same country and even the same city. Also it is noteworthy that the gated communities encountered in the real world do not completely correspond to any one of the four types, but include different aspects of the various "ideal types".

These regional variations on the nature of gated communities present urban sociologists with the challenge of investigating and identifying the commonalities as well as the peculiar characteristics of the sweeping global phenomenon of gated communities.

The advent of gated communities in Addis Ababa

Gated communities do not set off class segregation from naught—their widely recognized disadvantage. They are themselves the products of social differentiation and polarization, which they further enhance once they come into existence. In the case of Addis Ababa, gated communities have spread following the recent emergence of an affluent class that has attained a standard of living significantly higher than that of the majority of the city's population. In other words, gated communities have flourished as the culmination of a class distinction process that has come to physically and socially draw a boundary between, separate, and keep apart the already economically differentiated groups.

5 So named after *Cooperetiva Muratori and Cementisti* (CMC) of Ravenna, the firm that built it.

With the exception of the brief Italian attempt that has left us with *Casa INCIS* and *Casa Popolare*, the construction of multi-unit housing aspiring to exclusivity is of quite recent origin. Although the appearance of the first gated enclaves in Addis Ababa dates back to the twilight years of the imperial era, this was a matter of a few isolated cases. The so-called "Bole Homes" and "Old Airport Homes" that were realized in the early-1970s were the first multi-unit villa developments in the country. While the former consisted of small villas, the latter boasted larger and better-built villas with community services and a clubhouse with tennis courts. These housing developments were also the first to display features of controlled-access community such as communal guarding to keep out unwanted strangers.[6]

Incidentally, the emergence of Bole Homes and Old Airport Homes were contemporaneous with the construction of the SALCOST[7] residences, the first multi-block apartment-housing scheme close to the UN/ECA premises. Again, this housing scheme, which was properly gated and guarded, was quite small consisting of only five building blocks.[8]

The earlier development of controlled-access neighborhoods in Addis Ababa was nipped in the bud in 1974 with the outbreak of the Ethiopian Revolution that championed the principle and rhetoric of egalitarianism in nearly all aspects of social life. The 1975 nationalization of all urban land instead opened the way for the provision of free plots of land and low interest credit to those who owned no houses through a cooperative housing development program. The overall direction of the cooperative-based housing development of the *Derg* years (the military rule from 1974 to 1991) was characterized by strict economic rationalization and homogeneity of building typology. It was also marked by a sense of community that facilitated its implementation and which it, in turn, stimulated. None of the housing cooperative neighborhoods that were realized during those years were gated, with the single exception of BERTA's housing scheme in Wollo-Sefer.[9]

The CMC apartment enclave was the first large-scale, fortified housing development in Addis Ababa that was pre-fitted with fences and gates and policed by guards. It was created under the *Derg* as a *purpose-designed community*, the purpose being to keep members of the diplomatic community and other expatriates out of the inner city and in an enclave of their own. As its completion in the late-1980s coincided with the twilight of socialism in Ethiopia, the purpose-designed community opened its gates as a rental apartment estate owned and managed by the state's Rental Housing Agency and home to a disparate but well-heeled group of residents that could afford its relatively steep rent.[10]

6 Interview with Tefera Zenebe, Director of the Engineering Department of the Construction and Business Bank S.C, 2009; and interview with Architect Gebremeskel Tesfay who lived and worked in the Addis Ababa at the time, 2009.

7 Named after the acronym for the Saline Construction Company (SALCOST) that built it.

8 Interview with Tefera Zenebe 2009.

9 Interview with Zewde Teklu who was the Mayor of the city at the time.

10 Interviews with Zewde Teklu (see footnote 9) and Gebremeskel Tesfay, who also had

In the course of the last fifteen years, gated enclaves have sprung up in different parts of Addis Ababa. Small to medium sized access-controlled residential enclaves have spontaneously appeared in the older inner city part of town, retrofitting themselves with physical barriers to their inner streets. At the same time the large and trendy neighborhoods newly created by real-estate developers at the periphery of the city and the numerous condominium/tenement projects are following suit, albeit in a different manner. However, the rise and development of gated communities in the city has eluded the attention of urban researchers, planners, and practitioners, and has not become the subject of public discussion and debate.

Furthermore, in spite of their being on the scene for more than a decade and their going with strides, there is literally no documentation on gated enclaves of inner city Addis Ababa, and little on the access controlled real-estate development projects on its periphery. No one knows, for instance, the total number of gated communities at any level—city, sub-city, *woreda* or *kebele*; and there is only some scant information regarding their provenance and nature. As a result, the main body of the data informing this paper had to be generated by the study itself.

Subtypes and emergence of the inner city gated communities

The inner city gated communities of Addis Ababa fall under the category of *security zone gated community*. Yet, it is possible and useful to further categorize them into subtypes by stratifying them along the basis on which they arose: namely, cluster of individually obtained holdings, housing development cooperative site, and condominium development sites.

Clusters of individually obtained holdings account for 50 percent, housing development cooperatives for 33 percent and condominium sites for the remaining 17 percent of the gated neighborhoods. It also needs to be mentioned that the former two are generally the kinds to be retrofitted with gates, while the latter one represents a type that is government-sponsored, and hence usually pre-fitted with gates and fences.

As mentioned earlier, the spread of gated communities in Addis Ababa is mainly a post-1991 phenomenon. Only one of the 24 gated communities covered in the study predated the regime change of 1991. The city ushered in the era of gated communities and the subsequent economic liberalization and the temporary weakening of municipal administration and control. In particular, the heyday of retrofitting neighborhoods with physical barriers occurred during the first few years of the current regime during which government control and municipal administration were at their lowest point. On the other hand, those that came into being later on were pre-planned and government-sponsored gated condominiums.

close working relationship with the construction company, Cooperetiva Muratori and Cementisti, over the years.

As shown in Figure 1, out of the 24 gated communities, one dates back to 1981; half of the total (12) were gated in the 1990s, and 11 since 2000. Interestingly enough, whereas only five of the latter 11 neighborhoods were gated since the year 2004, four of these erections of gates refer to those of condominium sites.[11]

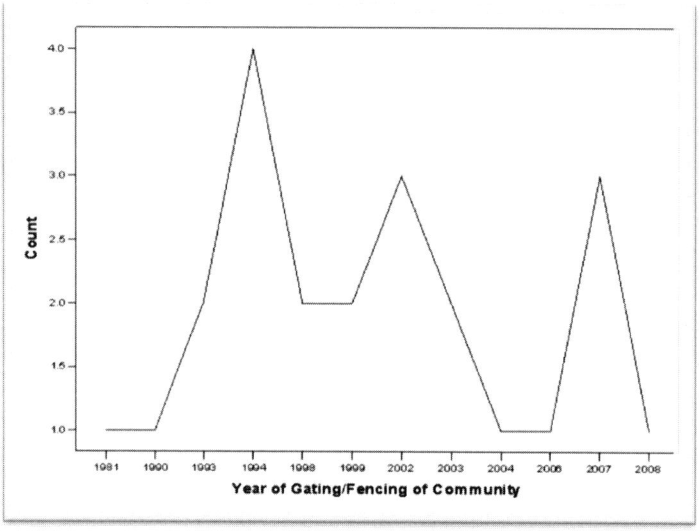

Figure 1: Number of communities gated between 1981 and 2008

Moreover, all of the gating of neighborhoods that took place prior to 1997 and most of what took place in the early-2000s relate to the retrofitting of neighborhoods based on either housing cooperatives or clusters of individually obtained holdings with gates and/or fences. All but one that took place after 2004 concerned the pre-fitting of government-sponsored condominium development sites with gates and fences.

Processes of gate retrofitting: Factors, challenges and strategies

Public spaces in inner city Addis Ababa were enclosed and gated differently than those in the US, Europe, the Middle East, and South Africa, where real-estate developers buy up land and fence the whole area as a homogenous private estate.

[11] A couple of years after this paper was published in its original form in JES Vol. XLI, No. 1-2, the difference between the small and moderate sized inner city condominiums and the very large ones on the city's periphery in terms of gating became very clear. The former that find themselves in the socially mixed inner city came to be gated more or less with no exception, while the latter that are located farther out on expanses of land that were rural and hence "empty" remained open as they house a more or less socially homogenous population and therefore need no fortification to ward off any unwanted group living in the vicinity.

Our study has revealed that a majority of the gated communities covered in the study (83.0 percent) were retrofitted with gates and fences through the spontaneous, yet calculated actions and omissions of their residents and the neighboring people. On the other hand, the government-sponsored condominium sites that make up the remaining 17 percent were enclosed as part of their pre-planned development scheme, with only one exception.

As already noted, the gated community phenomenon in Addis Ababa has materialized in response to a wider deeper socio-economic transformation that culminated in a clear social differentiation between rich and poor. However, a number of other factors also ought to be considered. These additional factors can be grouped into *direct causal factors* that drive communities to gate their neighborhoods, and *contextual factors* that merely facilitate such actions.

The literature on gated communities is awash with the reasons behind residents' preference for gating. Residents espouse them in order to avoid: (a) crime, fear of violence and feelings of insecurity, (b) increasing through-traffic and pedestrian passage, (c) free-riding of amenities that include using inner-streets as garbage dumps and places of relieving the calls of nature, (d) urban decay, and (e) decreasing property values due to unwanted land-use (Le Goix, 2005).

As regards the gated communities in inner-Addis Ababa, concern for personal security and protection of property from theft was the primary causal factor behind their gating, according to officials of all of the four *kebeles* under study. Officials of the *kebeles* added what they generally referred to as the 'shared concerns' of the community members: noise pollution, uncollected waste disposal, and straying beggars and peddlers. The vested interest of communities in protecting investments such as paved roads is a third causal factor. This is perceived by city officials as being a stratagem for gating public streets that starts with the placing of check-points beyond which heavy lorries would not be permitted, which are then gradually converted into proper gates.[12]

The first set of contextual factors that facilitated gating refers to the physical characteristics of the city. Numerous rivers, ravines, and very steep slopes that present natural barriers to surface movement at innumerable points traverse the rough terrain of Addis Ababa. A second physical factor is the irregular layout of the city's streets. Rough terrain and irregular layout of streets together created a situation where dead-end side-streets are the rule rather than the exception. Gating and/or fencing of public streets due to terrain or dead-end streets is less objectionnoble to those that are excluded, and *kebele* and city officials. The study has found that 18 out of the 24 gated communities (75 percent) in the four *kebeles* were gated due to the fact that the streets that enter them do not pass through but stop dead inside. Officials of three of the *kebeles* identified the existence of dead-end streets

12 Interview with Yonas Ayalew, Head, Infrastructural Development Coordination and Design Department, Addis Ababa City Administration, and Acting Manager, Infrastructure Development and Construction Authority, Addis Ababa City Administration. November 2008.

due to rivers and/or other compounds as a major factor behind the retrofitting of gates.

The second set of contextual factors that have played their part in the gating of inner city neighborhoods of Addis Ababa relate to institutional failure—namely, absence of adequate and enforceable rules and/or inability to implement them. It ranges from lack of clarity regarding the property rights of different stakeholders, absence of clear rules regarding construction permits and the enforcement of whatever exists, to the limited capacity of the various levels of the municipal administration to enforce existing regulations.

The third group of contextual factors refers to the basis on which the communities in question are founded. Firstly, government-sponsored condominium sites were mostly gated in the process of their establishment. Secondly, housing development cooperative sites emerged spontaneously and they account for a larger portion of the gated communities in the four *kebeles*. Although housing cooperative neighborhoods represent only a tiny minority among city neighborhoods, eight out of the 24 gated communities occurring in the four *kebeles* (33 percent) were found to be based on housing cooperative neighborhoods. This disparity is too large to be a matter of chance occurrence; and the success with gating must definitely be a function of the homogeneity of the membership, the organization, as well as the ability of housing cooperative neighborhoods to rise collectively in defense of their common interests.

Despite the factors that favor gating, conflict on account of gating was not unknown. Such conflict was reported by five of the 24 gated communities in the four *kebeles*. The clashes that four of the five gated communities experienced were between residents and external stakeholders, whereas the conflict that was experienced by the remaining one gated community (Wollega Sefer) was internal.

Surprisingly, only a few of the gated communities have reported any conflict arising from their being fenced and/or gated. A small number of the gated communities have had internal conflicts triggered almost always by failure/objection to abide by community regulations and norms, such as defaulting on payment of guarding fees or failure to contribute towards community development projects, blocking drainage channels, and objections to the night time closing hours of gates. These disagreements were internally resolved through the communities' own informal and formal mechanisms, with one exception. One resident of the Wollega Sefer gated-community was so defensive of her family's right to come and go as they pleased that she zealously pursued the case up to the *Kebele* 08/09 administration that reacted by temporarily removing the gate until tempers cooled and the conflicting parties found a mutually acceptable settlement.

On the other hand, three of the gated communities have experienced more serious conflicts involving external stakeholders on account of their fencing and/or gating. Two of these gated communities, namely *Tematquate* Addis Ababa University Teachers' Housing Development Cooperative and Signal-Site Condominium, both of *Kebele* 11/12 of Yeka Sub-city, had serious clashes with some of their neighbors. The third gated community, *Haile Ghibi* (popularly named so after its famous ex-resident, Haile Gebreselassie) of *Kebele* 02, Bole Sub-city, was gated in 1999 and has run into difficulty not with neighbors but with the *Kebele* administration.

Tematquate Addis Ababa University Staff Housing Development Cooperative had faced problems with two groups of neighboring communities, both of which have since been resolved. One of these occurred in 1992 when one of the owner-residents of the houses on one of the gravel access roads fenced a section of the road into her private compound. This was done in collusion with the other owner-residents on the same road who were in favor of barring the use of the road by the public and took advantage of the situation in rushing to place a gate at the other end of the street effectively gating their community. After a series of fruitless appeals to the *kebele* and higher-*kebele* administrations, *Tematquate* too came to terms with the situation that ironically facilitated its own gating process.

Tematquate's second conflict with external vested interests concerned its second and last northern alternative outlet to the main tarmac road. While interested in this road as an alternative exit route for emergency situations, the leadership of *Tematquate* wanted to fence and gate the compound to fill the gap at the junction between this gravel street and the cooperative's site, arguing that the stretch of open land in question was within the bounds of the housing cooperative's holdings, and on the pretext that the land was being used as a garbage dumping ground by people of the neighboring area. The latter opposed the project, pointing to their "established use rights" and threatening to turn to physical violence to make their point. This dispute continued with no apparent end until the Addis Ababa City Administration proposed to give the plot of land to a third party on which to build a house, a proposal to which the leadership of *Tematquate* readily agreed. As a result, the gap was completely sealed. Thus, in part by default and in part by design, the *Tematquate* housing cooperative site became a totally enclosed veritable gated community with a single gated and guarded entrance.

Signal-Site Apartment Condominium is the other community that has faced conflict related to gating in *Kebele* 11/12 of Yeka Sub-city. This condominium site was fenced and gated as a government-sponsored construction site, and had continued as such after it was conveyed to the new condominium apartment owners. However, an "investor" who wanted to obtain direct road access to the major double lane street between Megenagna and Adwa Bridge obtained an order from the Yeka Sub-city Administration for a section of the fence to be removed and for the gate to be open at all times to keep an inner passage across the site open to traffic and pedestrians—a decision which was duly implemented by *Kebele* 11/12. The site still operates as a partially fenced "open-gate" community watched over by a small detachment of guards paid for by the community. The dispute continues between the "investor" and the coordinating committee of the condominium apartment owners with the Sub-city and *Kebele* Administration caught in-between.

The third and last gated community that has experienced difficulties with its gating is *Haile Ghibi* of *Kebele* 02, Bole Sub-city. This community was gated in 1999 by taking advantage of the existence of only two entrances leading to few inner streets lined by a cluster of 24 villas. A gate was duly placed at one of the entrances while the second one was simply fenced and closed. The inner streets were asphalted and streetlights placed through the effort of the community members. Only a small section of one of the inner streets, one closest to the fenced entrance was left unpaved as it was made redundant and unused by the fencing. Then, after nearly a decade of existence, the *kebele* Administration removed the fence that was put up in order to close one of the entrances, when it discovered that the owners of the two villas closest to the small unused and now unpaved section of one of the inner streets had taken advantage of the situation by illegally fencing it into their respective private compounds on the pretext that it no longer served any purpose. The *kebele* Administration became adamant that this was not just a matter of gating, but an instance of illegal land grabbing that has become widespread in the city and which it is determined to fight by making no exceptions.

Main features of the inner city gated communities

A primary characteristic of gated communities, one that has implication for their other features, is the basis on which they were founded: namely, cluster of individually obtained holdings, housing development cooperative site, and condominium development sites as presented above.

In order not to repeat ourselves we shall directly proceed to consider the other features of inner city gated communities: namely, their size, barrier and surveillance status, and governance.

Size

Size is an important characteristic of a community—gated or otherwise—since size makes certain things possible and necessary as it makes other things impossible and unnecessary. For instance, large size of community being behind greater population heterogeneity and larger resource base, necessitate and permit the formal management of community business thereby enhancing a community's ability to undertake major cooperative projects. On the other hand, large size makes the existence of primary relations among community members difficult or impossible. The opposite of all of the above is true of small size of community.

The study has given due consideration to the size of the inner city gated communities of Addis Ababa, and its findings indicate that they are indeed small entities. Over one-third (37.5 percent) of the 24 gated communities in the four *kebeles* are very small enclosures with less than 25 housing units, 16.7 percent are small, holding 25 to 49 units, and still another 16.7 percent are medium seized having between 50 and 74 units, 8.3 percent are large with 75 to 99 units, and 20.8 percent of the gated communities are comparatively very large quarters accommodating more than 100 housing units.

Barrier and surveillance

Walls, gates, watch-guards, and electronic/video surveillance are the main means by which modern-day urban enclaves fortify themselves and exclude others. All of the gated communities covered in the study were found to be already fenced and/or gated, or in the process of becoming so. However, in the case of two of the already gated communities, their respective *kebele* administrations had temporarily removed their gates at the time of the fieldwork of this study.

Only four of the 24 gated communities—all condominium sites—were, or were being, enclosed as part and parcel of the overall development of the sites. These government-sponsored housing development schemes normally enjoy perimeters that are more-or-less homogenously fenced with stone, metal, wire mesh, barbed wire, or corrugated iron. Yet, there is one interesting variation that has emerged together with the gating of the condominium sites. While those sites with condominium buildings that are totally residential (Signal Site, Merte Zer Site, and Feres Bet Site) are enclosed in their entirety, the site with condominium buildings whose ground floors face main streets and are therefore dedicated for business establishments (Balderas Site), are not fully enclosed. The rooms on the ground floors of these buildings facing the outer streets being used as shops are made accessible to the general public. Yet, since even these buildings that face the outer streets and house business establishments serving the public including non-condominium residents are interconnected with grilles, mesh wire and gates, they serve as part of the barrier system that effectively enclose the gated community.

All of the remaining 20 (five-sixth) of the gated communities covered in the study were spontaneously retrofitted with fences and gates. Their retrofitting was mainly accomplished sometimes by default and at other times by design. As the retrofitting took place after the housing units were already in place, the walls of some of the constituent private compounds or houses were made to serve as parts of the barrier systems of the community enclosures that were then completely sealed by plugging the intermittent gaps and open stretches with fences and by placing controlled gates at their entrance points.

As far as the state of their barriers were concerned, at the time of the fieldwork informing the study, 19 of the 24 communities were properly enclosed and the fencing of three condominium sites was in progress, while the gates of two communities were temporarily removed by their respective *kebele* administrations for reasons that are discussed later in the paper. It should, however, be noted that even in the remaining communities and particularly those condominium schemes where residents had already moved in, guards were in place and the schemes showed the appearance of being access-controlled communities.

Guards play an important role in excluding outsiders in the gated communities of inner city Addis Ababa. All but one of the gated communities maintain guards;

the guards supported by the presence of communal guard-dogs. It is noteworthy that many foreign residents, westerners in particular, maintained their own private guards in addition to the community provided ones—obviously because they are willing to pay for the added security.

Unlike in more developed countries, there are no formal requirements to enter a gated community in Addis Ababa (with the exception of CMC Village), such as to be a registered resident with photo ID or for outsiders to be given specific entrance permission by someone who is a resident (via phone or internet). One can enter a gated community as long as one is known to the guard, has an apparent reason for entering the premises, or appears to be "respectable" enough as not to pose a threat. The guards have "their own ways" of sorting out and barring the intruding "types of strangers". Interestingly, man and beast are seen working in tandem in this regard as the guard-dogs in company of the guards often sniff out and bark at precisely those same "types of strangers".

Governance

All of the gated-communities in the four *kebeles*, except one, have some kind of governing bodies. Their governances, however, vary in terms of organizational structure as well as strength. Participation in all permanent and *ad hoc* committees is voluntary, and guards are the only paid staff that most of the gated communities maintain.[13]

The housing cooperative-based gated communities in particular, as well as some of the condominium-based ones, manage their businesses through formally constituted and legally recognized executive committees. Formed on the basis of official guidelines, the housing cooperative-based gated communities had at one time to satisfy requirements that include having constitutions, general assemblies, executive committees, audit and control officers, a bank account, and the perks of officialdom such as seals and logos. In this way, housing cooperative-based gated communities have residues of legal status, enforceable rules, and the organizational structure derived from their original status as government-sponsored housing development cooperatives.

To the contrary, those gated communities that have emerged on the basis of clusters of individually obtained landholdings run their communal affairs through semi-formal coordinating committees. Their management is based on agreed rules and regulations adopted by the membership and implemented by their governing bodies.

13 In 2011, the large Yeka Condominium Site No. 1 and No. 2 succeeded in setting up better organized management systems that are based on formal and enforceable regulations and procedures, that are manned by professional paid managers and secretaries, and that get all guarding and enforcement duties professionally undertaken by outsourcing them to commercial security companies.

The implication of size of community for the organizational structure and strength of the gated communities is borne by the data. The single gated community that has no governing body of any sort is also one of the smallest in size, with just 11 housing units. Moreover, six of the other eight very small gated communities (i.e., enclosing less than 25 housing units) were found to have very weak governing bodies of informal nature.

The management of most gated communities has become more lax and difficult in recent years, for two reasons. Firstly, in the case of the housing cooperative-based ones, members have started to ignore their communities' regulations and leadership with virtual impunity, since they have now obtained individual title deeds to their private plots and houses and are therefore legally free of the cooperatives in conducting their business vis-à-vis the municipal authorities, utilities or courts.

Secondly, the growing practice of renting out houses and the increase in the proportion of tenant-residents has made the management of gated communities difficult. The owners of the houses now turned absentee landlords are difficult to reach; and their tenants—some of whom are foreigners—are not so much aware of or do not recognize the communities' rules and norms. Hence, every piece of information and instruction needs to be passed to the nearby resident-tenants through the absentee-owners that live far away and are therefore difficult to communicate with. Also, as a result of the growing absentee-landlordism, it is becoming more and more difficult for the gated communities to hold general assemblies, effectively collect fees, and undertake communal development works.

On the other hand, a two-way relationship appears to exist between strong community management and communal development works. The data show that the gated communities that have strong and active management are the same ones as those that are undertaking infrastructural developments or those that have already made investments they must continue to protect.

The role of community norms in the smooth management of the gated communities cannot be overstated. These are real shared codes of behavior that hinge on the interdependence of people living in close proximity in a city of a developing country such as Addis Ababa as well as the sense of good neighborliness that is engendered by social cohesion indicated by the existence of neighborhood associations such as *idir* and formal and informal clubs for women and men. Often residents are made to abide by the rules and regulations of the gated communities by the application of informal pressures, making formal sanctions unnecessary. Nonetheless, while this can give an appearance of casualness to the management of the gated-communities' business, it ought to be noted that in most cases their executive committees can resort to the more formal measures.

Finally, municipal administrations, particularly the local *kebeles,* are as supportive of the managements of gated-communities as they are of most neighborhood associations. Pragmatically, working through associations that unite individual residents facilitates the work of *kebeles*. As shown further below, the leaders of the four *kebeles* recognize the usefulness of gated communities in this regard.

Major attributes of residents of the inner city gated communities

The data in Table 1 show that one-fifth of the gated communities to be the abode of the rich, with 75 percent occupied by the high and the medium income groups. Persons falling in the lower income bracket reside side-by-side with high and/or medium income group members in five of the gated communities, and exclusively low-income people occupy only one.

Income level	Frequency	Percent	Cumulative percent
High	5	20.8	20.8
High/Medium	8	33.3	54.2
Medium	5	20.8	70.0
High/Medium/Low	3	12.5	87.5
Medium/Low	2	8.3	95.8
Low	1	4.2	100.0
Total	24	100.0	

Table 1: Income level of current residents in gated communities

Contrary to the widely held belief that holds all gated communities are affluent enclaves, our empirical findings point to the existence of exceptional gated communities in which persons of low and medium income live side-by-side with those in the high-income bracket. Interestingly enough, these exceptional gated communities are among those that have emerged on the basis of clusters of individually obtained holdings, in which preexisting houses of diverse standards had to be enclosed, bringing together families belonging to different income brackets. One such instance is the gated communities of Bole Sub-city, *Kebele* 01 and 02.

In a poor country such as Ethiopia, gated communities appeal to foreign residents who are generally among the well-to-do that "are inclined to abandon the public sphere of the streets to the poor, the marginal, and the homeless retreating to the safety, order, and comfort of their fortified enclaves" (Caldeira 1996: 114). Yet, on the basis of what has been learned from the gated communities in the four *kebeles*, it is possible to affirm the absence of any gated community that is inhabited solely by foreign residents or refugees. Ethiopians reside in all of them, albeit in different proportions.

Citizenship of current residents	Frequency	Percent	Cumulative percent
Few Ethiopian, foreign residents &diplomats	2	8.3	8.3
Ethiopians & foreign residents	9	37.5	45.8
Ethiopians, foreign residents & Somali refugees	5	20.8	66.7
Ethiopians & Somali refugees	2	8.3	75.0
Ethiopians	6	25.0	100.0
Total	24	100.0	

Table 2: Citizenship of current residents of gated communities

The attraction that foreigners have for gated communities in Addis Ababa is borne by the data. Whereas foreigners (including non-Ethiopian Somalis) account for less than 1.0 percent of the city's population, many foreigners reside in 18 of the 24 gated communities in the four kebeles. Foreign residents and diplomats dominate two of the gated communities; share nine others with Ethiopians; and five more with Ethiopians and Somali refugees. Thus, 16 of the 24 gated communities (66.7 percent) house foreign residents living side-by-side with Ethiopians as well as with Somali refugees. Only a quarter of the gated communities are exclusively inhabited by Ethiopians, while Ethiopians and Somali refugees live side by side in two more.

		Citizenship of current residents					Total
		Foreign residents & diplomats/ few Ethiopians	Ethiopians/ foreign residents	Ethiopians/ foreign Residents/ Somali refugees	Ethiopians/ Somali refugees	Ethiopians only	
Income level of current residents in gated communities	High	2	3	0	0	0	5
	High/ Medium	0	6	2	0	0	8
	Medium	0	0	0	0	5	5
	High/ Med./Low	0	0	3	0	0	3
	Medium /Low	0	0	0	2	0	2
	Low	0	0	0	0	1	1
Total		**2**	**9**	**5**	**2**	**6**	**24**

Table 3: Income level of current residents of gated communities by citizenship

Table 3 shows that the gated communities where few Ethiopians and more foreign residents/diplomats reside, and some of those where only Ethiopians and foreign residents live, have higher income levels. Some of the gated communities that inhabited by only Ethiopians and foreign residents, and some of those where the two groups live side-by-side with few Somali refugees are enclaves of the 'high/medium' income groups. The gated communities where the overwhelming residents are Ethiopians are where the 'medium' income people reside. The three gated communities that have a mix of all three citizenship types have all three income groups represented in them. Finally, the gated communities that house the 'medium/low' and 'low' income groups happen to be those that have only Somali refugees and Ethiopians, or only Ethiopians, living in them.

It is not surprising that the variables of 'income level' and 'citizenship' of current residents are correlated in a city such as Addis Ababa where highly paid expatriates working for the various international of the non-refugee foreigner population. While this is borne out by the foregoing table that cross-tabulates the income level of current residents of gated communities by their citizenship, a word of caution is appropriate concerning the nature of the data. The determination of the income level of the residents of the various gated communities is directly derived from informants and not based on data on the actual income of residents.[14]

Integration and segregation

The study has used three dimensions as indicators of both the levels of social integration that potentially exist within the gated communities and their segregation from their neighboring communities: namely, 'existence and inclusiveness of *idir*', 'existence and inclusiveness of infrastructural development undertakings', and 'tenant to owner-resident ratio'.

Idir is the most ubiquitous neighborhood-based voluntary association in urban Ethiopia, one to which people generally strive to belong. The 'existence of *idir* in a gated community' is taken as an indicator of the emergence of a social community and the achievement of a level of social integration within a gated space. However, 'exclusivity of *idir* in a gated community' is employed as an indicator of the social separation or segregation of the gated community from its immediate surroundings. One-half of the 24 gated communities were found to have their proper *idirs*. In the case of the overwhelming majority of these (10 out of 12), the *idirs* were not only gated community-based but of a type the membership of which is also restricted to the members of the gated community excluding members from

[14] Informants were asked to estimate the composition of the residents of the respective gated documents on the basis of attributes of residents that are known to neighbors that are strong indicators of wealth status. The indicators included: the resident family members' profession and level of employment; car ownership, number and type of car owned; the qualification/salary level and specialization of domestic help the resident family employs, and such other visible indicators of level of consumption and standard of living as from where and in what amounts groceries are purchased, etc.

outside. This suggests that while slightly more than half of the gated communities have evolved to cohesive social communities, the overwhelming majority among them appear to do so separately and being segregated from their neighboring local societies.

On the other hand, another 12 of the gated communities occurring in the four *kebeles* have no *idir* based on them, which indicates an inability to form anything approaching a social community. Further analysis of the findings of the study indicates that the size of a gated community is a necessary if not a sufficient condition, for it to accede to a proper social community. A full two-thirds or eight of the 12 gated communities without any type of *idir* were from the 'very small' category of less than 25 housing units, and three of them were from the 'medium' sized ones with 50 to 74 housing units. Only one gated community belonging to the 'very large' category was without *idir,* which was due to its very recent establishment more than anything else.

The ability of a community to rise to the challenges of solving its problems and carry on with collective actions for collective benefit is an important indicator of its level of integration. With this in mind, we have used the variable, 'existence and inclusiveness of infrastructural development undertakings' among the gated communities. In the same way the variable 'type of existing *idir*' was used.

Fifteen of the 24 gated communities are, or have been, engaged with the development of either paved streets, street lighting and green-areas (12.5 percent), paved streets and street lighting (25.0 percent), or that of paved streets only (25.0 percent).Furthermore, all but one of the 15 gated communities that are or have been engaged in developing communal amenities are doing so, or have done so, without the involvement of their neighboring communities. This suggests an absence of coordinated action between gated communities on the one hand and their immediate neighbors on the other. In other words, gated communities appear to be guarding their exclusiveness even when it comes to undertaking infrastructural development.

The tenant to owner-resident ratio of a community has a lot to say about its level of integration. The higher the proportion of tenants in a community, the higher the turnover rate of residents, and the less likely people are to be acquainted with each other and to form durable relations. Informants spoke of some of the gated communities where tenants are the majority (such as Gulit Ghibi, Bole Sub-city, *Kebele* 02) as being bereft of a sense of community.

The study lacks data on 'resident's ownership status' in the gated communities since the question regarding the number of rented houses in the gated communities was considered too sensitive to ask since such a line of inquiry could have been construed as an investigation to determine the payment of rental income tax. Yet, it is possible to get a rough idea of the situation by using the variable of 'citizenship of residents of gated communities', the frequency distribution of which is given by the foregoing Table 3, as a proxy indicator of 'tenant/owner-resident status' that was not measured. Turning to the data in Table 3, we can observe that diplomats, foreign residents, and refugees reside in all but six of the 24 gated communities. Since Ethiopian nationals and "yellow card carrying" persons of Ethiopian descent are the only ones that are permitted by law to own buildings in this country, all the non-Ethiopians residing in the gated neighborhoods can only be tenants. With this in mind, it is not difficult to estimate the magnitude of tenancy and the turnover rate of residents in the 18 gated communities. Furthermore, one can more accurately comprehend the dominance of foreign tenants when one considers the fact that out of the six gated communities in which foreigners are not residing, four are condominium apartment sites, making the proportion of villa gated communities in which foreigners reside even higher (18 out of 20). All of these, taken together, suggest a serious level of absentee-landlordism that weakens the social integration, sense of community, and smooth management of the gated communities.

An interesting aspect of the gated community phenomenon is the balance between within-gate and cross-gate social relations. In this respect, an important feature of gated communities is that their residents are not isolated but only selectively insulated from their surrounding neighborhoods. Certain types of unwanted persons such as beggars, petty brokers and traders who pose potential security danger or breaches of the communities' codes of conduct and norms are kept at bay, but friends and relatives of residents that obviously belong to the same social stratum as their hosts are free to come and go across the physical barriers.

Although some of residents of gated communities—particularly of those that have emerged on the basis of housing development coops—identify with and exhibit a high degree of belongingness to their gated communities, this feeling appears to have strengthened following the gating process. The benefits accruing from gating, such as better security, order, cleanliness and beauty that lead to tangible financial benefits for house owners in the form of increased property value and higher rentals, continue to cement the solidarity of members through real and well perceived common interest. The emergence and strengthening of formal rules and norms governing the management as well as the utilization of the common spaces of most of the gated communities has led to further common identity among their members. Yet, it is also true that almost all of the residents of the gated communities maintain a certain level of social relations with people living immediately on the outside on a one-to-one basis and depending on their shared social standing and personal interests.

It is also noteworthy that the relationships between the communities behind the gates and those immediately outside them are characterized by both rivalry and cooperation. The relationship that we are concerned with here is not, as such, between individual members of the communities, but rather the rivalry related to conflicting interests between the inner-gate and outer-gate communities. This includes the grudge held by the outside communities against what they consider to be the unfair state of affairs in that the streets, sidewalks and open spaces in the non-gated surrounding areas are treated as public spaces open to all, while those within the perimeters of the gated communities are viewed and handled as if they were private goods to be enjoyed only by those behind the gates. Mutual over-arching common interests as well as the need for reciprocity—such as the paving of common streets and the joint construction of drainage ditches—arising from them, on the other hand, facilitate cooperation between the two types of communities.

Many residents of the gated communities covered in this study, as we have seen, are members of neighborhood voluntary organizations such as *idir* together with people living outside their gates. Interestingly enough *idir* associations—the function of which is limited to mutual support in the event of death, burial and mourning—serve in maintaining wider neighborhood-based community solidarity without much infringing on class differentiation. On the other hand, when it comes to informal groupings such as friendship circles that regularly meet at neighborhood bars and the like, class affiliation rather than territorial proximity is the vehicle of the cross-gate relations overcoming physical barrier.

Concerning the emergence of cohesive social relations and sense of solidarity among gated community members, it is worth mentioning forces that have come to work against them in recent years. In particular, the current citywide phenomenon of ever-rising house rentals that appear to know no limits is pushing fast the turn-over rate of tenants that are being constantly chased around by over-demanding landlords thereby undermining the stability of urban communities in general. This is rendered more severe in the case of gated communities because of the high demand for housing within them by expats in particular.

Two objective indicators show the extent to which residents appreciate life within gated communities. Firstly, being safer, cleaner, orderly and better managed, houses within gated communities tend to fetch higher monthly rentals. Secondly, when put on the market, houses within gated communities tend to be more quickly plucked by buyers and at a higher price as compared to similar house on the out-side. These two indicators substantiate the many laudatory remarks that are frequently heaped on life within gated communities by both of those living within and outside of the gates.

Benefits and drawbacks of gated communities

The literature on gated communities is almost universally negative, focusing entirely on their drawbacks. Even when their very obvious advantages, such as the ability to create safe and quiet private realms are raised, such qualifiers as their tendency to sustain and provoke more fear accompany them (Blakely and Snyder 1998; Low 2001; Grant 2007). Yet the advantages of gated communities of all types are variously given by the literature on the subject (Grant 2003; La Cour-Little and Malpezzi 2001; Le Goix 2005; Blakely and Snyder 1998; Low 2001) as follows: They provide residents with: (a) personal safety and security b) privacy (c) reduced traffic and pedestrian passage (d) separation from unwelcome strangers (e) tarmac roads and other infrastructure (f) neighborhood amenities (g) recreational facilities (h) parks or green-areas (i) beautiful landscaping, and (j) protection from decreasing property values. Furthermore, they are said to offer an important marketing niche for real-estate developers.

As regards the gated communities of inner city Addis Ababa, the study has identified a number of perceived benefits through interviews with their residents and city and *kebele* officials. Residents generally believe that gated communities have led to: (a) better security (b) privacy and the barring of unwanted strangers such as loiterers, peddlers, and beggars (c) fewer passers-by, pedestrians, and through traffic, and (d) higher house rent and property value. Both residents and officials generally point out that gated communities facilitate: (a) effective garbage collection and the maintenance of clean surroundings (b) development activities such as the paving of inner roads, provision of street lighting, drainage canals and passages (c) establishment of *idirs*, and (d) emergence of better understanding and sense of community among their residents. *Kebele* officials perceive the following additional advantages of gated communities. They maintain that gated communities help *kebele* administrations to better: (a) control crime and illegal activities, (b) acquire information through their guards, which is particularly important for *kebeles* with large resident refugee populations and strangers (ጠሡሬሌወፕሰወ) and (c) mobilize manpower and resources for *kebele*-level development schemes. Interestingly, the benefits of gated communities that were identified by the empirical investigation match the list of advantages garnered from the literature. The major difference between the two lists is the conspicuous absence of advantages relating to neighborhood amenities, recreational facilities, and aesthetic landscaping—all that are still luxury to inner city communities of Addis Ababa—from the former presented list.

Writers on gated communities have also identified a number of disadvantages (Grant 2003, 2004; Low 2001). Gated communities (a) limit access to formerly open landscapes and public spaces (b) fragment cities, by hindering connectivity and free circulation and forcing cars, cyclists, and pedestrians into roundabout routes, (c) lead to class and ethnic residential exclusion and segregation, exacerbating cleavages that already exist, and (d) raise housing costs, creating a problem of affordability, particularly when they are fitted with more amenities and recreational facilities.

Interviews with residents and city and *kebele* officials concerning the disadvantages of gated communities have turned up responses that are at great variance. From the perspectives of their residents (those of both owner/residents and tenants), gated communities have no drawbacks whatsoever. If anything, they want more of the gated enclave, and their displeasures are directed against the failures of particular gated communities in not acting as or being what they believe gated communities ought to be. They want fences to be higher and sturdier, gates and compounds to be well guarded, infrastructural development to be underway, and above all, the status of the community as a gated community to be preserved.

On the other hand, being concerned with broader issues and focusing on the larger picture, the interviewed city and *kebele* officials had a number of drawbacks of gated communities in mind. They maintained that gated communities have: (a) engendered an erroneous perception that confuses public/government property with private/community property, (b) facilitated illegal land-grabbing, (c) laid claim to the exclusive use of public sport fields and green-areas, (d) blocked short-cut routes for the residents of neighboring areas, (e) in some cases encouraged illegal constructions inside the gated communities hidden from the view of the *kebele* Administration, (f)in some cases, helped hide illegal undertakings such as illegal slaughter of animals and the movement of illegal persons, (g) blocked outsiders from coming to the rescue of persons in distress within the enclave, and (h) having no legal statuses and by-laws, remaining open to potential financial irregularities and fraud.

The first four drawbacks of gated communities identified by city and *kebele* officials are fundamental problems relating to legal/institutional failures. In the words of Yonas Ayalew:[15]

> The City operated without any official policy or directive concerning building/construction for a long time. In the absence of laws and regulations governing the issuance of construction permits, permits were nonetheless given on the basis of circulars that depended on the whims of officials of and in an irregular manner (ቀደም ሲል ለረዥም ጊዜ ሕግ ስለአልነበረ ግንባታ የሚፈቀደው በዘፈቀደ በጊዜው በነበሩ አዘጋጆች ፈቃድ በሚወጡ ሰርኩላሮች መሰረት ነበር።). Since five years ago, efforts have been made to have formal and legal procedures in place. Thus, in 1996 (E.C) the Rule for Building/Construction Permit (የግንባታ ፈቃድ ደንብ) was proclaimed, and in 1997 (E.C.) the Guideline for Issuance of Building/Construction Permit (የግንባታ ፈቃድ መመሪያ) was issued.
>
> As for gated communities, it is possible that some of them have obtained fencing and/or gating their neighborhood. However, this office has not found a written law or directive that gives them legal recognition and/or allows them to undertake such construction. Whichever way you look at it (ያም አለ ይህ) the City Administration has never given fencing and gating permit in whatever form.

Thus, surprisingly, the retrofitting of inner-neighborhoods with gates and/or walls has proceeded over the last two decades without any legal basis and in a manner that is not clear even to the city's officials.

The special case of emerging city periphery and suburban real-estate developer driven residential villages

This study has focused on inner city gated communities, rather than on what is happening in the emerging city-periphery and suburban real-estate developer-driven residential villages in this regard. However, a general description of the

15 Interview with Yonas Ayalew, Head, Infrastructural Development, Coordination and Design Department, and A/Manager, Infrastructure Development and Construction Authority, A.A. City Administration. November 2008.

latter is necessary for the purpose of indicating areas of future expansion of the gating phenomenon and potential research concerns.

A handful of real-estate enterprises are engaged in the development of residential villages at the periphery of Addis Ababa and within the territory of the Oromia Regional State that encircles the city. These new residential villages emerging at the city's periphery and suburbs—such as Ayat's, Sunshine's, Ambassador's, Ropack's, and Country Club villages—are different from the older inner city gated communities with which this paper is primarily concerned. They are planned and relatively vast settlements. In spite of internal differences in housing typologies, sizes, and standards, they are physically and socially homogenous posh environs that are the harbingers of genuinely exclusive residential quarters in the city of Addis Ababa. They are mainly inhabited by affluent elderly returnees of the Ethiopian Diaspora as well as local yuppies and retirees who have moved there not only to enjoy the appeal of "suburban" peace and quiet, but also to be amongst "their own" by keeping a safe distance from the diverse neighborhoods of the inner city.

Constructions still being in progress even in the most advanced of these city-periphery exclusive "villages", most of the real-estate developers continue to manage the neighborhoods as their construction sites. Thus they maintain road-blocks and guards ostensibly to secure their property. What the future holds, in terms of the custodianship and management of the new communities, is not exactly known. But it is not possible to overlook the likelihood of these real-estate developer driven residential villages or their constituent parts (as in the case of the zones and blocks at the Ayat village) becoming access-controlled neighborhoods of one type or another—such as Blakely and Snider's *barricade perch* type.

The central difference between the inner city and the city-periphery/suburban gated communities is significant: whereas the former are products of *in-situ/in-place* attempts at reinforcing emerging social separation with physical segregation, the latter are one of maintaining an already delineated social differentiation through the creation of totally new spaces that are made inaccessible to others, among other things, by their physical distance from the center. It is a case of the already evolved class of the well-to-do moving from abroad or from the inner city into newly established residential niches that are beyond the reach of persons of lower classes from the very outset. Thus, as opposed to the inner city gated communities, with which this paper is primarily concerned, the emerging city-periphery real-estate developer-driven "villages" share, to varying degrees, the characteristic features of "gated communities" of the more developed regions of the world.

Conclusion

Being products of the emerging social differentiation that is itself the outcome of external forces and internal social dynamics, as well as factors such as the real needs of the people residing in them for security and orderly life, and contextual factors such as the topography of the city that is favoring them, gated communities are already well entrenched in today's Addis Ababa. They are also likely to continue to spread, particularly following on the footsteps of the ongoing government-sponsored and subsidized condominium housing development program[16] as well as the real-estate developer-driven housing schemes in its peripheral and suburban areas. Whatever their merits and demerits, gated communities are here to stay and probably become the wave of the future.

As shown in this paper, the legal ambiguity concerning the gating of communities has already led to clashes between the various stakeholders in and around government-sponsored condominium neighborhoods. Lack of clear regulations is also impacting some of the emerging inner- and outer-city suburban "villages" that are supposedly planned and realized by real-estate developers. For instance, at Ayat Village, which is the most advanced of them all, residents of some of the quarters have taken matters into their hands following the collapse of the attempt to form the Ayat Tenants' Association in cooperation with the real-estate developer enterprise. Acting through neighborhood residents' committees and *idirs* they have placed barriers and gates at their respective street entrances and hired guards to man the gates and watch over the streets, thereby turning their strips of neighborhood into the special type of *security zone* gated community that Blakely and Snider (1998) have classified as *Barricade perches*. Such innovative adjustments notwithstanding, the legal and institutional lacunas under which gated communities come into being and operate are likely to become sources of pervasive conflict as this new form of community spreads to the different parts of the city.

It is necessary to fix the legal and institutional deficit hanging over gated communities, primarily by legalizing and regulating them. It would spare all concerned parties from unnecessary conflicts, wastage of resources, and the uneasiness of living and operating under uncertain circumstances. Such a step would remove a major urban entanglement facing an emerging urban physical and social phenomenon that cannot be stopped but controlled and given direction.

The official sanctioning and regulating of gated communities by the municipal administration would contribute towards enhancing their official stature and facilitating their internal management. On the other hand, this could also serve to reduce the potential for conflict between gated communities and the wider public

[16] This government subsidized housing program is of enormous magnitude and likely to transform not just the skyline, but also the life styles and social fabrics of the city. According to the City Administration 109,000 condominium apartments have been constructed and handed over by September 2013, while that of an additional 95,000 apartments is going to be completed within the following 12 months. On 25 October 2013 the National Service of Radio Ethiopia reported the Minister of Urban Development and Construction, Mr. Mekuria Haile, as saying that over one million apartments will be constructed and handed over in Addis Ababa in the course of the following 10 years—in order to benefit from the second round construction of condominium houses of three types that are earmarked for low-income, middle-income, and upper-middle-income groups respectively.

by removing a major stumbling block through the clear determination and specification of the rights and obligations of both sides.

Furthermore, we ought to point out the existence of several aspects of the gated communities of Addis Ababa—including class and age composition and dynamics—that require further investigation. Further empirical investigation would have to provide answers to research questions such as: What sort of relation exists between rising class awareness, on the one hand, and the class composition of gated communities on the other? What roles do economic factors such as house prices and rentals play in this? What are the actual situations and the trends regarding the proportion of the elderly/retiree in general and returnees/retirees from the Ethiopian Diaspora in particular among residents of the city-periphery and sub-urban gated communities? These and other similar research questions could be both academically interesting and useful to pursue.

In sum, the inner city condominium sites that are developing rapidly are likely to be gated in one form or another. As to those extremely large condominiums at the city's periphery and suburban areas, they tend to remain open access neighborhoods, as things stand now. However, considering the dynamics and the speed at which urban space is evolving in today's Addis Ababa, only the future will tell regarding the final culmination of the process even here. Hence, it is essential to continue to gauge this development, and propose appropriate policy measures that will spare a large number of city dwellers and secondary stakeholders wastages that can and should be prevented.

Addis Ababa is a city that emerged as a military camp and administrative seat of a feudal empire only 126 years ago. Moreover, not unlike many of the cities doting the developing world, it remained for quite a long time a center of population concentration mainly housing poor people of recent rural origin. For these reasons, the city demonstrated most the characteristics of the pre-industrial city of bygone days, chief among which was its very underdeveloped economy, division of labor, and their concomitant lack of social differentiation and marked interdependence cooperation as well as co-residence and solidarity between the few well-to-do, their dependants and the masses of destitute. Admittedly, these aspects of social and physical proximity and connectedness were all outcomes of the force of the circumstances of their existence rather than that of any preference of goodwill on the part of the participants. Yet, they were real and sociologically significant features.

Today's Addis Ababa is a vibrant city that is undergoing tremendous physical and social transformations. All urban development indicators suggest that the city's skyline as well as its social geography have changed beyond recognition during the past 39 years (since the 1974 Revolution) and more so in the course of the past decade. The current direction and the speed of these changes, suggest a fundamental break with the past. The future augurs well for the further expansion of a new urban order dominated by a built-in environment of multistory building and villa neighborhoods as well as the commodification of traditional productive and service activities. Commodity exchange and monetary relation are necessarily bringing about the widening of the gap between the rich, the well-to-do and the poor in their wake; and this in its turn is leading to the emphasizing of the emerging social distinction with physical separation—among others, through the fencing and gating of exclusive communities.

The spread of gated communities in Addis Ababa is a perfect case of physical boundaries expressing social differentiation by which they are caused and which they further crystallize. They are markers of a two-pronged process leading at the macro or city-level to what Durkheim (1997 (1893)) referred to as *organic solidarity* arising from division of labor, differentiation and interdependence, and at the neighborhood-level to a reversal of this to what he called *mechanical solidarity* that is characterized by the group members' commonality of social station, similarity and distinctiveness.

References

Blakely, Edward J., and Mary Gail Snyder, 1998: "Separate Places: Crime and security in gated communities." In: Marcus Felson and Richard B. Peiser (eds.): *Reducing Crime through Real Estate Development and Management.* Washington D.C.: Urban Land Institute, 53-70.

Caldeira, Teresa P. R. 1996: "Fortified Enclaves: The new urban segregation". *Public Culture 8. 2,* 303-328.

Durkheim, Emile, (1893) 1997: *The Division of Labor in Society.* New York: Free Press.

Grant, Jill, 2007: "Two sides of a Coin? New urbanism and gated communities". *Housing Policy Debate. Volume 18, Issue 3.* Metropolitan Institute at Virginia Tech.

Grant, Jill, 2003: *Planning Responses to Gated Communities in Canada.* Paper presented at the Conference: "Gated Communities: Building social division or safer communities? Glasgow, September 18-19, 2003.

Grant, Jill, 2004: "Why Planners are Ambivalent about Gated Communities". Paper presented at the session: Community Apart: Gated developments in Canada. 30 May 2004. School of Planning, Dalhousie University. (Accessible at: http://www.google.com.et/url?sa=t&rct=j&q=&esrc=s&source=web&cd=1&ved=0CCgQFjAA&url=http%3A%2F%2Fmall.lampnet.org%2Ffilemanager%2Fdownload%2F247%2Fgated_communities.pdf&ei=k0YtU828Lsua0AWCh4H4BQ&usg=AFQjCNFnZnsp5p3saiH1b42s2eMIF9XLJg&bvm=bv.62922401,d.bGE)

LaCour-Little, Michael and Stephen Malpezzi, 2001: Versions of the paper presented to the American Real Estate and Urban Economics Association's meetings in Washington, D.C. and Gävle, Sweden, and to Economics Workshops at Washington University-in-St.-Louis and the University of British Columbia.

Le Goix, Renaud, 2005: "Gated Communities as Predators of Public Resources: The outcomes of fading boundaries between private management and public authorities in southern California". In: Glasze G., C. J. Webster and K. Frantz (eds.): *Private Cities: Global and local perspectives.* Routledge, Taylor and Francis, 73-88.

Low, Setha M., 2001: "The Edge and the Center: Gated communities and the discourse of urban fear". *American Anthropologist* 103(1), 45-58.

Maher, Kristen Hill, 2004: "Borders and Social Distinction in the Global Suburb". *American Quarterly 56, 3,* 781-806.

Meles Zenawi, 2007: Speech Made to a meeting with the Forum of Addis Ababa Residents held at the Millennium Hall.

Sjoberg, Gideon, 1955: "The Preindustrial City". *American Journal of Sociology* 60, 5, 438-448.

Wissink, Bart, Dijkwel Renske, and Ronald Meijer, n.d.: "Bangkok Living: Social networks in a gated urban field". Paper presented at the international conference "Doing, thinking, feeling home: the mental geography of residential environments". October 14-15th OTB, Delft, the Netherlands. (Accessed online at: http://www.otb.tudelft.nl/pagina.jsp?id=4dc436be-acb543c2-88ff-b64e61af887d&lang=en).

Yeraswork Admassie, 2007: "The Origins, Development, and Special Features of the Distribution of People, Activities, and Services in Addis Ababa"(in Amharic). In: Millennium Office of the Addis Ababa City Administration, Addis Ababa (ed.):*The Looks of Addis Ababa in* the *Foregoing and the Coming Millennia*, 114-17. (Accessed online at: www.addismillennium.org)

The Nyangatom Circle of Trust

Criteria for ethnic inclusion and exclusion

Gebre Yntiso

Introduction

Ethnic boundaries are neither given attributes nor arbitrary constructs—rather they represent consented or contested cognitive lines of group inclusion and exclusion. Depending on self and mutual interests of the groups involved, social boundaries are defined and redefined; negotiated and renegotiated; and emphasized or downplayed by actors representing or claiming to represent their groups. At any given time and place, therefore, an ethnic group may employ different principles for defining and maintaining relationships with different groups. Hence, as Katherine Verdery (1994) noted, people use ethnic boundaries to dichotomize insiders from outsiders through collective efforts of construction and maintenance.

> The roots of this organizational form [viewing ethnicity as a form of social organization] are not in the *cultural content* associated with ethnic identities but rather in the fact of their *dichotomization*—the presence of boundaries separating groups. This shifts the emphasis from seemingly 'objective' cultural traits to behavior (including 'cultural' behavior) that is socially effective in maintaining group boundaries (Verdery 1994:35).

Ethnic groups claim to have identity markers that differentiate them from others. The common markers include mythical relation, common ancestors, shared a cultural heritage, a shared history, a common language, a common belief system, shared territory, and/or other shared experiences. It has long been recognized that ethnicity is a social construct (rather than a cultural given or basic human condition) and that ethnic groups do not represent cultural isolates or bounded entities. This is made apparent by the fluidity, permeability, overlaps, and the phenomenon of boundary shift that allows the inclusion or exclusion of ethnic membership. Social scientists have developed theoretical frameworks to explain the making and unmaking of ethnic boundaries. Andreas Wimmer (2008: 986), for example, summarized his five strategies of ethnic boundary making as follows:

> I distinguish between five types of such strategies: those that seek to establish a new boundary by expanding the range of people included; those that aim at reducing the range of the included by contracting boundaries; those that seek to change the meaning of an existing boundary by challenging the hierarchical ordering of ethnic categories; those that attempt crossing a boundary by changing one's own categorical membership; and those that aim to overcome ethnic boundaries by emphasizing other, cross-cutting social cleavage through what I call boundary blurring.

While some groups try to stay guarded by sealing their boundaries against potential crossing, others expand their frontiers by keeping permeable and blurred boundaries (Wimmer 2008), and still others maintain a mixture of strategies executed differently, depending on situations, which is the focus of this paper. In the literature, the widening or narrowing of group membership or inter-group alliance is explained in terms of, among others, political situation (Cohen 1978; Vincent 1974) and cost-benefit analysis (Schlee 2004: 137). Günther Schlee (2004) also called for caution that costs and benefits may be unintended consequences of group identifications, and that the freedom of rational decision-making should not be overemphasized.

With the above conceptual background in mind, this paper examines how the Nyangatom people of Ethiopia, who are surrounded by eight ethnic groups, have been maintaining various strategies of inclusion and exclusion.[1] Two of the eight neighbors, namely, the Toposa and the Turkana live across the international border in South Sudan and Kenya respectively. Three ethnic groups, the Nyangatom, Toposa and Turkana, are reported to have migrated to their present locations from a common original place called "Karamoja" in present day Uganda. They, thus, belong to the Karamojong Cluster (also referred to as the Ateker group), an ethno-geographic designation of numerous ethnic groups residing in northeastern Uganda, northwestern Kenya, southeastern South Sudan, and southwestern Ethiopia.[2] Moreover, they speak the same language, share a common belief system, common cultural values, and common practices. The Nyangatom have no common origin, long historical bonds, nor ethno-linguistic relationships with the other six neighbors (namely, Surma, Mursi, Koegu, Kara, Murle, and Daasanech) residing in Ethiopia.

Based on the existing historical, religious, cultural, and linguistic backgrounds, one might predict that the Nyangatom would maintain similar forms of relationships with their fellow Ateker neighbors in Kenya and South Sudan and yet a different one with the non-Ateker groups in Ethiopia. To the contrary, the Nyangatom's relationships with the Turkana and the Toposa are characterized by hostility and solidarity, respectively. Regarding the non-Ateker groups, the Nyangatom

1 A number of individuals deserve recognition for their contributions to the study. I would like to thank all the Nyangatom informants for sharing their experiences and insights without any reservation. Acknowledgements are due to government officials and experts at the district, zonal, and regional levels for providing information. I want to express my indebtedness to Ekal Nettir, the then Administrator of Nyangatom *Woreda*, for his support in providing information and facilitating my trip. Lobuwa Kakuata, William Achuka, and Markos Lokali deserve appreciation for serving as very reliable field assistants and informants. My special gratitude goes to Phillemon Nakali for sending from abroad useful insights about the history and culture of the Nyangatom, Samuel Batu and Fikru Nyakal for providing information, and Admasu Lokaley for commenting on the draft paper.

2 In the literature, there seems to be no clear consensus on which ethnic groups belong or do not belong to the Karamojong Cluster. Michael Quam (1999: 2) identified the Dodoth, Jie, Karamojong (which is further divided into Bokora, Matheniko, and Pian sub-groups), Teso, Turkana (Kenya), and one or two groups in Sudan, as the core groups of the Karamojong Cluster. Today, the Nyangatom, the Toposa, and Jiye (in South Sudan) are recognized as members of the Ateker group. The Chekwi, Kumam, Labwor, and Tepes are also reported to belong to the Cluster.

perceive the Murle and the Koegu as close affiliates, while the Daasanech, the Kara, the Mursi, and the Surma are regarded as archenemies. The Hamar, who reside further east (east of Murle), are considered enemies, while the Bashada, officially considered as part of the ethnic Hamar, are treated as friends of Nyangatom. This paper seeks to uncover the Nyangatom circle of trust and the criteria for ethnic inclusion and exclusion.

In order to understand the social proximity and distance, as well as the boundaries between the Nyangatom and their neighbors, it will be helpful to first understand the cultural principles that characterize intra-Nyangatom relationships and their identification with neighbors. People tend to behave towards members of ethnic groups that they consider to be allies, friends, or relatives in a way similar to the way that they behave towards members of their own group. Correspondingly, sets of other codes of conduct are employed to deal with members of ethnic groups considered as enemies. With this in mind, certain codes of responsibilities, cultural prohibitions, and permissible acts have been identified (see 'important cultural principles' below) to understand the internal relationships. These codes also provide clues to the nature of the external relations.

This paper is based on information obtained from the descriptions of 24 Nyangatom informants. The sample of informants, though small, consisted of both sexes and people from different age-groups, generation-sets, and territorial sections. Hence, their views are assumed to reflect common perceptions. Data were collected in 2010 and 2011 through interviews, focus group discussions, and observation. Data obtained from the local people have been validated through further inquiry with knowledgeable and educated Nyangatom living in urban area and overseas. Additional written sources have also been used to compare and contrast the emic perspectives with etic analysis and some related ethnographic accounts.

Apart from this introduction and the summary at the end, the paper is divided into five sections. The introductory section is followed by a brief ethnographic account on the Nyangatom. Section three focuses on boundary crossing in the context of Nyangatom-Murle and Nyangatom-Koegu relations. What may be described as a loosely defined blurry boundary between the Nyangatom and the Toposa is discussed under section four. The fifth and sixth sections are devoted to Nyangatom-Turkana relations that have detoriated from being close relatives to enemies and thus to an alteration of the boundary between them.

The Nyangatom people and culture

General background

The Nyangatom (also Gnangatom) people belong to the Nilo-Saharan language family and live in Southwestern Ethiopia in the border region between Ethiopia, Kenya, and South Sudan. The area is currently inhabited by the Nyangatom people and two smaller ethnic groups (namely, the Murle[3] and the Koegu) and comprises one administrative *woreda* (district), which is named after the dominant group—Nyangatom. The *woreda* is divided into 20 *kebeles*. *Kebeles* are the lowest-level, and most local, administrative tier. Kangaten, the capital of Nyangatom *woreda*, is located some 848 km southwest of Addis Ababa, the capital of Ethiopia. According to the latest national census, the population of the Nyangatom ethnic group is 25,252 (CSA 2007:85), and the land area of the *woreda* was estimated at 2,183.6 sq km.[4]

According to oral history, the Nyangatom and the Toposa left the Karamoja area, in northeastern Uganda, some 200 years ago due to severe drought that caused the death of both humans and livestock and after a volcanic eruption that dispersed the population of the Karamajong (NyaMuKo 2010: 25). One elderly informant in Kangaten noted that the eastward migration of the Nyangatom and the Toposa was not haphazard, but rather informed and planned:

> Some people first arrived in Nakuwa [Kibish] area tracking a missing ox. In Nakuwa, they not only found the missing ox but also saw a place rich in water and grass. Upon their return, they informed the elders about the rich area. The elders then decided to move to the new land to avoid drought in Karamajong.... Upon arrival, our people met the Mursi people living in Nakuwa. Since the Mursi were hostile, the Nysaqol [the first Nyangatom territorial section to arrive in Kibish] had to fight with them.... They kicked some Mursi out of the area and intermarried with others.

Gulliver 1968 (in Tornay 1979: 98) considered the Nyangatom as a splinter group of the Toposa, who, in turn originated from the Jie of Uganda. However, Tornay (1979: 98) noted that the separation of the Nyangatom from what he referred to as 'the related Paranilotes' might have occurred around 1800, at least concomitant with that of the Toposa. Upon arrival, some of the Nyangatom settled west of the Kibish River. Later others moved further east and settled at Lere, near the Omo River. During their journey eastwards from Kibish, in the direction of Mount Kuraz, they are reported to have met the Arbore[5] and the Daasanech people, other original inhabitants of the area. Traveler's accounts suggest that the Nyangatom were already in lower Omo valley by the time Count Samuel Teleki and Ludwig von Höhnel visited the area in 1888 (Tornay 1979: 98).

Today, the territory of the Nyangatom stretches from the Omo River in the east to the Kibish River in the west. The local people claim that the Kibish area (both sides of the Kibish River) was their traditional homeland with its western border further west from the river.

3 In this paper, the name Murle is used to refer to those people residing in lower Omo valley in Ethiopia rather than their non-contiguous kinfolks living in South Sudan.

4 The figure for land area was obtained from the South Omo Zone Administration.

5 It appears that there was some kind of Nyangatom-Arbore relationship/interaction. Some members of one of the territorial sections of the Nyangatom called *Ngilingaqo* claim to be related to the Arbore, who later migrated east and currently reside in the Boito valley near Lake Stephanie (today a dry lake bed).

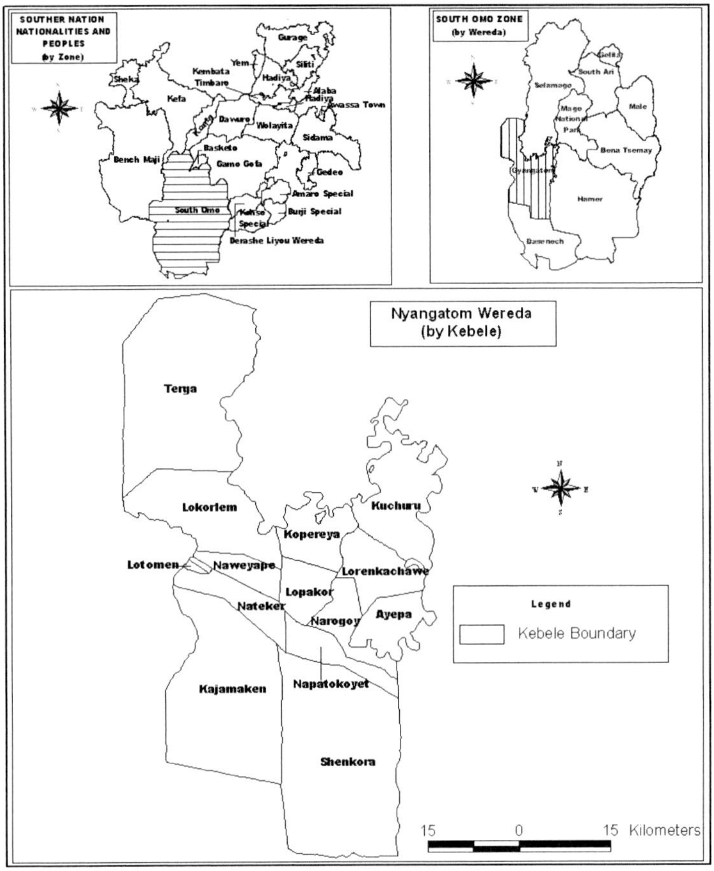

Figure 1: Map of Nyangatom *Woreda* (Source: Central Statistical Authority, 2011)

Those who live in the west and in central parts of the territory rely heavily on livestock production, while those in the east largely depend on flood retreat cultivation of sorghum, some maize, cowpeas, and tobacco along the Omo River. Some of those who reside along the river practice fishing as well. The Nyangatom send their livestock, especially cattle, to cattle camps located far away from permanent residential areas, where milking cows and small stocks are kept. Those taking care of animals in the cattle camp rely heavily on blood and milk for their subsistence, while those who live in permanent villages depend more on cereals. During the dry seasons, when animal products are in short supply, the herders in the cattle camp are provided with cereals produced along the Kibish and Omo Rivers.

Nyangatom is one of the remote districts in Ethiopia with bare minimum development activities, social services, and infrastructural facilities. Hence, modernity is still far from reality, as people continue to lead traditional lives relying mainly on their rich knowledge to exploit their natural environment. The introduction of the Protestant Christianity in 1972 by the Swedish Philadelphia Church

Mission (SPCM) represents the first Nyangatom contact with the western world. The Mission made contributions in terms of providing modern education in two primary schools (in Kibish and Kangaten), healthcare in two clinics (again located in Kibish and Kangaten), and irrigated agriculture using engine-pumps in Kangaten. Most of the educated Nyangatom currently serving or representing their people in various capacities have attended the SPCM schools. Although the Church existed for a long time, it was only from the second half of the 1980s that the teaching of the Bible spread among the population. During the research period in 2010/11, the followers of Christianity still remained a small minority. However, most of those Nyangatom serving their *woreda* belong to the Hiwot-Birhan (Life Light) or its splinter off-shoot and the newly formed Alem-Birhan (World Light) Churches—both Protestant sects.

The 2006 administrative restructuring in some parts of Ethiopia led to the division of the former Kuraz *Woreda* into Daasanech *Woreda* and Nyangatom *Woreda*. Since then, the newly established Nyangatom *Woreda* has taken steps in the area of office organization, health provision, school enrollment, agricultural extension, gender participation, transportation and communication, and investment attraction. The number of primary schools (including alternative schools), health posts, and agricultural extensions services are reported to cover most of the villages. During the dry season, there is a bus transport, twice weekly, from Jinka (the capital of South Omo Zone) to Kangaten, and there are both landline and mobile phone connections. According to the first issue of the Amharic annual magazine called NyaMuKo (2010: 11-12), which was published by Nyangatom *Woreda* Culture, Tourism and Government Communication Affairs Office, three agricultural investors have been given 10,000 hectares of land to grow cereals, sesame, cotton, and vegetables.

Social organizations

The Nyangatom have different types of social organizations that play important roles in their lives. There are seven[6] named territorial sections (sing. *ekitala*, pl. *ngiteala*), namely, *Ngilingaqol, Ngkapung, Ngsaqol, Ngutokoraman, Ngukumama, Nubune,* and *Ngarich*. An individual is born into a given territorial section through his or her father. Section names are not place names, but rather the collective names of people occupying a given place. Hence, sections can best be described as political units where important decisions are made. In other words, a territorial section serves as a social identity and fundamental political and organizing principle. Individuals and communities participate in public life through their territorial sections. As Tornay (1981:160) noted, "Members of the sections have rights to settlement, grazing and watering, cultivation, and transhumance within their territory."

6 NyaMuKo (2010: 25) reported the existence of eight territorial sections in Nyangatom, Ngiribo being the eighth. Further study is needed to confirm this claim.

The generation-sets (*ekas*) constitute another very important social organization in Nyangatom. They operate side-by-side and in conjunction with the territorial section. The men of one generation-set are considered as fathers of the men of the next generation-set. Hence, each male individual belongs to the generation junior to his father's. At any given time, two generation-sets with living members are recognized as dominant, and they are called the 'Fathers of the Country' and the 'Sons of the Country.' During the research period, the Ngitome (Elephants) and the Ngorukopi (Ostriches) represented the Fathers of the Country and the Sons of the Country respectively. Junior to the Ostriches are three generation-sets: Ngugoleteng (Antelopes), Ngkosowa (Buffaloes), and the youngest generation (not yet formally named, but temporarily called the Ngikinyaga (Crocodiles) ranked in order of seniority. Women belong to the generation-set of their husbands and they do not occupy public decision-making positions.[7]

Traditionally, secular (administrative, judicial, etc.) and ritual powers are vested in the hands of the Fathers of the Country. Serious matters of public concern are brought to their attention for deliberation. Since the entire Nyangatom society is organized according to the principle of generation-sets, every territorial section has the same generation-sets. Hence, in all territorial sections of Nyangatom, during the time of research it was the Elephants who were responsible for the management of public affairs. Theoretically, the Elephants are the sole decision-makers. Practically, however, they involve a certain number of members of the junior generation-sets (namely, Ostriches, Antelopes, and sometimes Buffalos) to attend crucial meetings. The Elephants can delegate power to the Ostriches to handle certain issues on their behalf. The Sons of the Country are responsible for ensuring the implementation of the decisions of the Elephants and for giving orders to the junior sets, who are in turn responsible for the actual implementation of decisions.[8]

The generation-sets of the Nyangatom are again divided into age-sets, which are formed in different localities and with different names. Age-mates willing to be initiated into a new age-set have to demonstrate their readiness by participating in some offensive or defensive actions. Moreover, they are expected to offer animals (e.g., goats) to the members of the senior age-sets within the same generation. As Tornay (1981:162) noted, the senior age-sets "in return allow the initiands to wear the adult mauve plastered head-dress and to adopt the new age-set name". The name could be chosen by the new initiates or imposed on them by the elder age-sets. More youth continue to join the newly initiated age-set until the group becomes numerous and strong enough to declare its autonomy. Although the dates of age-set formation and the names given to individual sets vary from one place to another, people know the ranks of the sets and their structural equivalence.

7 Although social change resulting from the expansion of modern education, the gender sensitization work of the government, and conversion to Protestant Christianity seem to have paved the way for some women to air their voices in public meetings, men continue to make ultimate decisions.

8 Despite the introduction of modern administrative and justice systems, the Nyangatom prefer to resolve intra- and inter-ethnic conflicts through traditional mechanisms.

The Nyangatom are divided into over 14 named patrilineal exogamous clans (*ngatekerea*, sing. *ateker*). These include Ngimuyoko, Ngıtoroy, Ngukuko, Ngıkakurecha, Ngidhocha, Ngikor, Nginyangia, Ngipucho, Ngiribo, Ngithiger, Ngiraputa, Ngilobol, Ngimeturuana, and Ngikuren.[9] An individual becomes a member of his or her father's clan at birth. Clans do not serve as organizing principles to form a political entity. They are also not territorial and thus do not claim resources (such as grazing land) in their names, and they do not have publicly recognized roles in major decision-making processes. However, certain clans are believed to have special powers, such as the power to make or stop rain, to deceive and trick enemies, to cure snake or scorpion bites, and to control disease. For instance, the Ngikuren are reported to be responsible for fire and war rituals. Apart from the differential ritual roles, clans are differentiated based on their marriage ceremonies, dressing (e.g., beads and leather) styles, body decoration, and physical marks placed on cattle.

Important cultural principles

In this sub-section, attempts are made to identify and elaborate certain important codes of conduct in Nyangatom. These cultural principles are helpful for understanding both internal and external relationships.

Sharing and caring. There are two major ritualized sharing and caring festivities: *apeyo* and *ekumamar*. *Apeyo* is an initiation ceremony during which young men slaughter animals for their immediate senior age-sets to be allowed to form and join a new age-set. After the *apeyo* ceremony, the initiates are recognized as men and a fighting force, who can assume responsibilities such as defending the Nyangatom territory and livestock. *Ekumamar* is a festival sponsored by generation-sets and territorial sections in rotation to care for their fathers (seniors) and secure their blessing in return. In 2009, the territorial section called Ngukumama coordinated an *ekumamar*, and the ceremony was sponsored by the generation-set called Buffalos, who organized the festivity for their fathers, who are called the Antelopes. Tornay (1998: 102) also reported that 'feed your fathers' and 'feed your peers' are two basic rules in Nyangatom.

Apart from *apeyo* and *ekumamar*, which take place only once in a while, non-ritualized gift-giving represents part of the sharing culture of the Nyangatom society. Sharing of food and other resources with peers, relatives, neighbors, and fellow Nyangatom who are in need due to natural or man-made adversities, is widely practiced. Grown-up children are expected to take care of their parents, grandparents, and other needy relatives. The herders share cereal foods sent to cattle camps and animal products from the cattle camps are shared among those living in permanent villages. The needy can expect to be helped by the resource-rich

9 Serge Tornay (1981: 153-4) counted 20 clans in Nyangatom and noted that some of the clan identities were carried by women who came to Nyangatom as wives from Dodoth, Lotuko, and Turkana ethnic groups. The reduction in the list of Nyangatom clans today may partly be explained in terms of the death of these women.

in the community. As discussed later in the paper, similar codes of behavior seem to govern the relationships between the Nyangatom and the Toposa.

Mutual assistance. In Nyangatom, social solidarity in offensive and defensive actions against enemies (*ngimoi*, sing. *emoit*) is expected. Enemy attack on a particular person is perceived as a perpetration of violence against the group (e.g., age-set, generation-set, and/or territorial section) to which the victim belongs. Since livestock belonging to different households are grazed together, loss of some animals belonging to one or few households due to raid would agitate the entire community for revenge. Traditionally, unprovoked raiding and killing by enemies are not tolerated. Revenge actions on enemy may be delayed for strategic reasons, but when the time comes or when the need arises, the fighting forces in a given territorial section are expected to cooperate with each other and, if necessary, with forces of other sections. Government officials, NGOs, and the local religious organizations have been discouraging revenge raiding and killing. However, the culture of retribution in kind, which showed significant decline in recent years due to these measures and shortage of firearms, is far from over. The principle of mutual assistance characterizes the relationship between the Nyangatom and their friendly neighbors.

Prohibition to kill and raid each other. Rhetorically, all Nyangatom people are considered as belonging to one family. Hence, the different social groups within the society (e.g., households, age-sets, generation-sets, and territorial sections) are not allowed to raid each other. Intra-Nyangatom raiding is unknown and unthinkable. However, there are cases when individuals or families may be motivated to confiscate all or some livestock of other individuals or families due to some acknowledged grievances such as adultery, bride-capture, theft of property, and failure to settle debts. Some Nyangatom people may consider such acts as justified or understandable. However, the customary law does not allow individuals to take the law into their own hands. Hence, the Ngukumama (the 'peace-makers' in the community) and senior members of the Elephant generation-set would interfere to resolve disputes through the customary mechanisms, which involve the returning of confiscated animals to the rightful owners and the punishment of the original wrongdoers.

Killing fellow Nyangatom is called *akiar itoon niyawi* (killing members of the household) and it is believed to cause ritual impurity and the bloating of the stomach of the killer. Despite the cultural prohibition of killing, however, the life of a fellow Nyangatom may be lost accidentally, in self-defense, or in a pre-meditated act of violence. If the act was a premeditated offense, the relatives of the deceased may opt to take the life of the actual killer. Therefore, the killer is expected to hide in the bush or take refuge with the Ngukumama until the conflict is resolved and the cleansing ceremony performed. The pollution caused by the *akiar itoon niyawi* may be cleansed through elaborate reconciliation and purification processes called *akikis akoit*. Apart from the cleansing rituals, homicide reconciliation involves the payment of blood indemnity to the relatives of the deceased. Acceptance of compensation is believed to represent public renouncement of retribution and reestablishment of broken ties. The prohibition to kill and raid is extended to groups affiliated to the Nyangatom (i.e. Toposa, Murle and Koegu).

Identification with the Ateker group. The Nyangatom people recognize the Karamojong of people in Uganda as the earliest ethnic group from which all Ateker members originated. According to one informant, the word "Karamojong" is made up of two terms: *ngikaru* (year) and *mojong* (old). Thus, the Nyangatom define the Karamojong as their ancestors who had lived in the original homeland, Karamoja (in Uganda), for many years before their migration to their current location. All ethnic groups that originated from the earliest group (Karamojong), are collectively called Ateker. In this context, the meaning of the term Ateker means 'related people' or 'relatives' (the term also refers to clan). The Ateker members commonly known to the Nyangatom include the Matheniko, Ngipian, Bokora, Dodoth, Jie, Kumam, Tepeth, Toposa, Jiye, Turkana, and Teso. When asked what the Ateker groups have in common, many informants listed the following: common ethnic origin, common geographic location in Uganda, mutually intelligible language, common religion (belief in *Akuj* and *ngakujo nachik* (or *ngamuroto*), God and ancestor spirits respectively), similar social organizations (e.g., territorial sections and age-system[10]), similar dances, and similar songs.

Boundary making and unmaking

Permeable boundary with Murle and Koegu

The Murle and the Koegu are non-Ateker people, who have been integrated into the Nyangatom society later in time. Of the six neighbors on the Ethiopian side of the border, the Nyangatom allowed only these two groups to cross their ethnic boundaries. Before their inclusion, the two groups were too small and powerless to defend themselves against their enemies. Why did the Nyangatom forge an alliance with powerless minorities and maintain enmity with their powerful neighbors? Attempts are made to briefly discuss historical factors and recent developments that led to the process of boundary crossing before answering this question.

The Murle (also the Omo Murle, Ngarich, Narich) people in Ethiopia represent a splinter group of the Murle ethnic group in South Sudan. The oral history about the splinter group goes on to state that during a regular dance party, a small group of

10 The Nyangatom perceive themselves as the only Ateker group that keeps the original generation-set system intact. The Nyangatom, the Toposa, and the Turkana seem to have comparable generation-sets. The Nyangatom informants believe that their generation-sets are structurally similar to that of the Toposa than Turkana, and markedly original compared to the generation-sets of the other two groups. According to Harald Müller-Dempf (2008), the Toposa and the Turkana changed their generation-set system later in time due to environmental stress and social unrest that resulted from demographic crisis. The Nyangatom managed to maintain the original generation-set layout because their population in the past did not experience major upsurges to complicate the operation of the age-system.

young Murle men decided to run away from their homeland (today's South Sudan), together with their sisters, to avoid whipping that youngsters were expected to endure. When they arrived near the Tepes Mountain in the Kibish area, the young migrants were warmly received by the Nyangatom, specifically the Ngikapung territorial section. The Murle then moved to a place called Lere, near the Omo River, looking for a missing donkey. The Ngilingaqol territorial section of the Nyangatom already inhabiting the area helped the newcomers settle amongst them at Lere. With the intention to live on their own and maintain their identity, the group later moved further north along the eastern course of the Omo River to what is now called Murleland. After many years in their new homeland, the Murle crossed the Omo River and rejoined the Nyangatom due to conflict with the Kara and the Hamar, and because of human death caused by sleeping sickness. Until recently, the Murle represented a powerless minority within the Nyangatom society.

According to oral history, the Murle took refuge with the Nyangatom before their assimilation into the host community to become the seventh territorial section. In concrete terms, this means that the Murle completely lost their mother tongue and adopted the language and identity of their hosts. Following the introduction of an ethnic-based federal system in Ethiopia, some educated Murle demanded ethnic recognition of their community. In the 2007 population and housing census of Ethiopia (CSA 2008:85), Murle is listed for the first time as an independent ethnic group with a population of 1,469.[11] The zonal and regional governments also recognize Murle as an independent ethnic group. The rebirth of Murle identity through official endorsements marked the reconfiguration of their ethnic boundary.

The Koegu ethnic group (also Kwegu, Koyego, Muguji), with a population of 1974 in 2007 (CSA 2008: 85), was constituted by three major clans (Garshma, Woreba, and Baada) that migrated to the area from different directions and different ethnic groups (NyaMuKo 2010: 23-24). NyaMuKo presented the movement details as follows. The Garshma clan originated from the Aari (to the north) living in Baytsimal area. The Garshma first settled at a place called Marsha on the eastern side of the Omo River and later relocated to Kuchuru, a village across the river. The Woreba clan, believed to have originated from the Arbore people located further east, is reported to have lived in Mugugna, Nakure, and Woreba areas before the Kara joined them to settle in Dus village. In the late 1980s, the Woreba clan left Dus and started to live with the Nyangatom at Galgida due to conflict with the Kara.[12] The Baada clan migrated from the Bodi and Bacha groups further north and first settled at Makule, and then joined the Garshma clan at Qalo and finally moved together to their present location—Kuchuru.

[11] This official recognition of the Murle as an ethnic group displeased people who consider them as part of the Nyangatom. Some informants dismissed the new development as a wrong move instigated by the educated youth.

[12] According to Eisei Kurimoto (1998), the Koegu, who occupied a subordinate social position in Kara, switched alliance from the Kara to the Nyangatom following the rise in the military dominance of the later.

According to Hiroshi Matsuda (2008), the Koegu ethnic group was constituted by five local groups: the Duuyu (or Duyi), Adara, Baada, Dukule, and Waruba. The Duuyu and the Adara are believed to have come from the Mursi, the Baada (also Naada) from the Bodi, the Dukule (who are sub-divided into Worle and Tsodi groups) from the Aari, and the Waruba from the Arbore. Obviously, there are some differences between the NyaMuKo report and Matsuda's accounts regarding the names of the original migrants and whether they represent clans. NyaMuKo did not mention anything about the two groups (Duuyu and Adara) that came from the Mursi. However, the two sources of information are consistent in the presentation of the ethno-history of the Koegu people. Like the Murle, the Koegu group represents a minority in Nyangatom in terms of population size, political representation, economic resources, and military power.

Although the Koegu action to leave Dus (the village they shared with Kara) was viewed as a survival strategy, Matsuda (1994) cautioned that the relationship of the Koegu may be shifting from annexation by the Kara to assimilation by the Nyangatom. Matsuda (1994: 48-49) narrated the late 1980s event as follows:

> Dus... had a mixed population of Koegu and Kara. The two groups were closely integrated in a relationship I call annexation.... While I was there [in 1988], this relationship broke down amidst conflict. As the distance between the Kara and the Koegu widened through violence, the latter moved closer to the powerful Nyangatom, a former enemy of both Kara and Koegu.

The Nyangatom ethnic boundary has been open for small non-Ateker groups desperately seeking refuge as a survival strategy. The Nyangatom take pride in shielding powerless groups against powerful enemies. The newly integrated groups are entitled to protection and resources available to ordinary Nyangatom. However, it has not been all about helping the weak on humanitarian grounds. The Nyangatom informants openly admitted that the incorporated ethnic groups brought several economic and security advantages. First, the Murle and the Koegu joined the Nyangatom with valuable resources: pasture and arable land along the Omo River. During the dry seasons, some Nyangatom move their livestock to Murle and Koaegu territories, while others grow crops along the river on permanent basis. Second, the two groups are viewed as dependable allies and buffer zones against strong Nyangatom enemies such as the Daasanech from the south and the Hamar and the Kara from the east. Third, the Murle and the Koegu are too small in number to put pressure on Nyangatom resources and militarily too weak to cause security concerns. In short, the incorporation of the new groups contributed to the Nyangatom's resource base and military strength, which in turn ensured the safety of the people and continuity of the group.[13]

13 In 2007, the population of the Nyangatom was 25,252 (CSA 2008: 84-85). According to the same census report, their neighbors considered as enemies were quite numerous: Dassanech (48,067), Hamar (46,532), and Surma (27,886). The Mursi (7,500) and the Kara (1,464) always allied with their respective kinfolks, the Surma and the Hamar respectively. Therefore, as a survival strategy, the Nyangatom had to refrain from inter-

Blurred boundary with the Toposa

The ethnic boundary between the Nyangatom and the Toposa is blurred due to heavy emphasis on brotherhood and group solidarity. Based on mythical narratives and oral history, the Nyangatom believe that they share a common ancestry with the Toposa. The oral history goes on to state that they out-migrated together, due to an environmental crisis. When they reached the Mount Tepes area, however, they split into two and moved in different directions to exploit the available resources. This is when they believe to have started an independent existence. Other informants explained the separation into two groups resulted from a disagreement over how to eat elephant meat. While one group proposed to eat the meat fresh and to keep on traveling, the other group suggested the need to take time to slice and dry the meat before eating it. Those who ate the fresh elephant meat and left the scene immediately came to be known as the Nyam-etom ('elephant eaters', later the name was transformed into Nyang-atom or 'yellow guns'), and those who camped for a while and ate the *tosa* ('dry meat') became the Toposa. After many years, the descendants of the original migrants accidentally met in the forest while hunting wild animals, and found out (through genealogical counting) that they were not only both members of the Ateker, but also close relatives. Hence, they consider one another as *amuro-katta* (grandmother's thigh), an expression that emphasizes common ancestry and the notion of brotherhood.

There are cultural prohibitions that the Nyangatom and the Toposa people should not raid and kill each other. In Nyangatom, the concept of *emoit* is used contextually to describe a 'stranger' or an 'enemy.' This term is never used to refer to the Toposa people. As explained above, for Nyangatom, killing a fellow Nyangatom causes ritual impurity and is called "killing a person from the household". Killing Toposa, although not designated by the same expression, is also believed to cause ritual impurity, as the two groups are believed to be closely related. Thus, inter-ethnic killing between the two groups involves special ritual cleansing and blood compensation to the family of the deceased in a similar manner as homicide is resolved within Nyangatom. On the contrary, the Nyangatom neither pay nor receive blood compensation following reconciliation with groups considered as enemies.

The Nyangatom view the Toposa as belonging to their circle of trust. Trustworthiness is partly measured in terms of observing cultural prescriptions that stress the sharing of food and other resources and solidarity at times of crisis. For instance, at the individual household level, when a Nyangatom slaughters an animal, any Toposa (old or young) who happens to be around is entitled to the hindquarter as a matter of cultural right. One elder Nyangatom remarked,

> The *amuro-katta* sharing is not based on age. Blood relationship does not matter. Marital affiliation is not necessary. Any male Toposa is my *amuro-katta*. Hence, it is my responsi-

mingling with their powerful neighbors to avoid subordination and recruit trustworthy allies to keep the power balance in the area.

bility to give the rear leg to my *amuro-katta*. As I carry the meat to him, I am supposed to walk slowly and limp,[14] as if my legs are injured or the load is heavy. This is how we share meat and express our respect for each other.

Any Nyangatom would expect the same when his Toposa neighbor has slaughtered an animal. Failure to live up to this expectation is considered culturally unacceptable and may provoke annoyance and cursing. Informants indicated that the Nyangatom curses are considered effective and highly feared by the Toposa. As friends, relatives, and neighbors, the Nyangatom and the Toposa also engage in non-ritualized sharing of other foods such as grain. At times of scarcity, the Nyangatom travel to Toposa to get or buy sorghum from bond friends, relatives, or sellers.

At a community level, the Nyangatom and the Toposa share pasture, water, and residential areas peacefully. Seasonally, some Nyangatom households are reported to be migrating to the Nyangatom-Toposa border with their livestock. The decision of moving livestock in the direction of the Toposa border is based on strategic factors and trust, not to mention the ecological dimension. Keeping Nyangatom livestock in the common border and in Toposa territory also provides maximum security against risks of raiding. In other words, when it comes to livestock security, the Toposa are fully trusted by the Nyangatom.

Some Nyangatom people have established permanent residence in the Toposa villages called "Lotimor" and "Matarba". Some seasonal Nyangatom transmigrants temporarily leave their wives and children behind under the protection of their Toposa friends. Although on small scale, there exists Nyangatom-Toposa intermarriage. In most cases, the Nyangatom men take Toposa women as wives because they travel more often to Toposa than the Toposa men travel to Nyangatom.

The depth of the relationship between the two goes beyond sharing of food, pasture, water, and residential areas. They often form alliances to fight against their common enemies such as the Surma, the Turkana, or each other's unshared enemies (e.g., the Daasanech are considered as Nyangatom's enemy and the Jiye as Toposa's). Cooperation involves not only fighting enemies together but also supplying or providing access to firearms. In the 1980s, it was through the Toposa that the Nyangatom acquired modern automatic rifles (AK 47) that gave them military superiority, at least temporarily, over their neighbors. Some offenders (e.g., criminals) from both communities are reported to be escaping to the other side to avoid capture and evade justice.

On the whole, the relationship between the Nyangatom and the Toposa is based on a deep cultural connection and a strong sense of cooperation in a manner that respects their respective identities and ensures their continuity as independent groups. At the same time, the depth of the historical and cultural affiliations, the

14 The limping and the slow walk represent respect and express that the giver is at the service of the receiver.

strength of the strategic alliances, and the level of mutual trust between the two groups are so enormous and enduring that their ethnic differences have been downplayed in favor of narratives that focus on communalities and cooperation. From the perspective of the Nyangatom, their relationship with the Toposa provides a maximum advantage and poses a minimum risk in terms of resource sharing, security, and continuity.

Alteration of boundary with Turkana

The Turkana are viewed as fellow Ateker with whom the Nyangatom lived in peace in the past, a time many people are nostalgic about. According to the elderly informants, the Turkana people have migrated from Lodwar area and peacefully joined the Nyangatom in Kibish area. The local narrative about the northward expansion of the Turkana is consistent with the reports of Alex De Waal (1991) and Nene Mburu (2003) that the boundary of Turkana grazing and the limits of Kenyan administration moved north over the years. Terrence McCabe (1996) also discusses Turkana early migration as well as later expansion during which they pushed to the north and east to Lake Turkana.

During their early contact in Kibish, the Nyangatom welcomed the Turkana migrants from Lodwar (giving them access to settlement, pasture and water points); they cherished their common identity as Ateker; experienced intermarriage; and sometimes allied against the Jie of Uganda. The Ngilingaqol and Ngikapung territorial sections in the border area are reported to have experienced extensive marital and economic interactions with their Turkana neighbors. In those days, due to their intimacy and intense interaction, the physical and social boundaries between the two groups were rather blurred. The occurrence of intermarriage has gradually decreased as conflict intensified and the Nyangatom moved further east from the western side of the Kibish River due to security concern. At times of peace, there existed movement of people back-and-forth across the border for business and family visitation. In recent decades, conflicts occurred more frequently and peace deals lasted briefly rendering the area to be perpetually insecure.[15]

Nyangatom informants were asked whether they grew up in Kibish area experiencing serenity and love or fear and hatred. The answers were mixed. The elderly informants recounted many positive stories that shaped their dreams to visit Turkana and to establish relationships through marriage or bond-friendship. They also remarked that in the past, stick-fighting with the Turkana was seen as a sibling rivalry aimed at demonstrating competence. In recent decades, the introduction of modern firearms turned the traditional competitive display of agility into deadly clashes of mutual destruction. Many informants recounted having lost their

15 Some writers noted that the Nyangatom people might originally have migrated from Uganda due to Turkana pressure (Tornay 1979: 98; Mburu 2001: 150), and this suggests that they may have been rivals from early on. However, the informants of the present research did not establish any association between the Nyangatom exodus from the Karamoja and a conflict with the Turkana.

relatives, livestock, and land to the Turkana, and that they could not regain control over the lost land in Kibish, their traditional homeland. Neither could they launch counter-offensives that matched the massive and frequent Turkana attacks. Thus, those who grew up witnessing death, destruction, displacement, and loss of livestock especially since the 1988 infamous Kibish massacre locally called the *dio* incident[16] have been deeply traumatized.

Nowadays, therefore, the Turkana are viewed as*emoit-loakora*, which literally means 'fighting enemies'—the same label given to the non-Ateker enemies such as the Surma and the Daasanech. The Nyangatom informants argued that their very existence as a dignified group has been shaken by their eviction from the western side of the Kibish river in 1988 and the continued displacement ever since. Hence, it was necessary to redefine their relationship. As mentioned above, killing other Nyangatom, Turkana, Toposa, and the newly incorporated members (Murle and Koegu) is traditionally associated with impurity that needs ritual cleansing and blood compensation. Since the level of enmity has grown so deep that killing the Turkana is no longer associated with ritual impurity, no purification is required, and no indemnity is paid (blood compensations is not paid to or received from enemies). The escalation of conflict, the brutality of the fights, the restriction of cross-border movement, the eviction of the Nyangatom from western side of the Kibish river, and the significant decline of intermarriage altered the physical and social boundaries between the Nyangatom and the Turkana from blurred to closed. Resisting Turkana advances is now considered as a survival strategy.

Despite the rise in the cycle of violence, the Nyangatom initiated repeated peace agreements, which were violated one after the other. For example, in 1998, ten years after the Kibish massacre of 700 people, the Nyangatom elders reached out to the Turkana elders and performed reconciliation rituals at Lokiriyama, Kenya. To the embarrassment of the Nyangatom, the Turkana launched an organized attack on the very day the Lokiriyama meeting was held. In 2004, elders from the two ethnic groups met at Kibish, Kenya, and swore not to attack and raid each other. Once again, according to Nyangatom informants, the Turkana violated the deal by launching an attack shortly after the meeting. In 2006, the Nyangatom *Woreda* administration sent a delegation to Lokitang, Kenya, to initiate peace talks. This initiative led to the January 2007 initial meeting at Kangaten, Ethiopia, and the March 2007 peace conference at Kibish. During this conference, elders of the Nyangatom and the Turkana signed a comprehensive peace agreement, which was violated in January 2008 allegedly by the Turkana. The 2008 Turmi Accord and the later peace agreements were similarly violated shortly after.

Although data are lacking from the Turkana side to counter the Nyangatom claims, it would be naïve to assume that the later have always been passive victims

[16] During this incident, according to Alexander De Waal (1991: 345-6), some 700 Nyangatom were killed by the Kenyan forces, and in the attack, at least five villages in Ethiopia were partly destroyed. Dio is taken from the abbreviation 'DO', which stands for District Office in Kenya from which the Kenyan forces came.

and were not to blame for any attacks on Turkana soil.[17] Also, given the portrayal of the Nyangatom, in the literature as expansionists, aggressors, fierce fighters, and/or dominant (Girke 2008; Turton 1994; Abbink 1993; Alvarsson 1989; Tornay 1979), one needs to understand the context for the new image that depicts them as tolerant and peace-seekers. It appears that a combination of factors, namely, the shortage of firearms, the military superiority of fighters on the Turkana side, modern education that provided an alternative life style for some youth, government programs that raised hope for social change, and religious teaching about sin/forgiveness may have discouraged the motivation towards offensive actions.

One might wonder why such intimately related and culturally connected people became enemies. The Nyangatom informants associated the problem with several recent changes/developments, including the growing tendency of the younger generation and the educated Turkana not to honor the decisions of their elders; commercial raiding and the participation of non-pastoral raiders; and the involvement of elements of the General Service Unit (military) of Kenya in assisting the Kenyan perpetrators. The downward spiral in the Nyangatom-Turkana relationship was actually set in motion by the British colonial administration during the first half of the 20th Century, and the conflict continued to escalate ever since. The following section sheds light on how pressure on scarce resources and military power imbalance altered the physical and social boundaries between the Nyangatom and the Turkana.

Some factors responsible for Nyangatom-Turkana discord

Land alienation and movement restriction

The northward expansion of the Turkana became evident during the colonial period. In the early 20th Century, certain Turkana sections are reported to have migrated to Ethiopia to avoid surrender to the British colonial army. According to Mburu (2001: 154), "Resistance to British military conquest was weak as some Turkana sections collaborated with the colonizers whereas those defiant evaded confrontation by simply relocating north to sanctuaries in Ethiopia." At this stage, the Turkana did not pose a real threat to Nyangatom interest. Probably the most serious blow to the pastoral economy in the Nyangatom area was the movement restrictions that followed the colonial demarcation of boundaries. The British colonial administration in Kenya took several measures that restricted free movement and denied access to traditional pastures and water points. In the 1920s and 1930s, the Ilemi Triangle was created and patrolled by the army called the King's African Rifles in the name of protecting the Turkana against the Nyangatom

[17] Informants admitted to have engaged in counter-raids and counter-attacks but only after repeated enemy offenses. This claim sounds credible from the incident narrations of researchers (Girke 2008; Tornay 1979) and the 2009 IGAD-CEWARN report that the Nyangatom exhibited tolerance against repetitive Turkana attacks.

and the Daasanech.[18] In July 1939, according to Mburu (2003), "Britain conducted a punitive raid with the King's African Rifles (KAR) supported by the Royal Air Force who dropped 250 pound bombs north of Ilemi."

The British troops of the KAR occupied Ilemi in 1941 and consolidated control over the area when the British entered Ethiopia to fight the Italians during World War II. In the 1940s, the British colonial administration in Kenya established "a series of police posts along the Ethiopian border at Kokuru, Liwan, Lokomarinyang, Kaiemothia and Kibish" (Almagor 1986: 98), thereby curtailing the movement of the Nyangatom and the Daasanech to their traditional grazing lands. This was a time when Ethiopia was deeply indebted to Britain for the help in expelling the Italian forces after five years of occupation. The Turkana were perceived as enemies of the British and had to be brutally pacified.[19] At the same time, they profited from the colonial policy in that the boundary demarcation expanded their grazing territory further north deep into the Daasanech and Nyangatom territories. The Nyangatom-Turkana relationship worsened after the enclosure of the so-called Ilemi Triangle.[20]

The Ilemi Triangle has been a disputed territory claimed by Ethiopia, Kenya, and the former Republic of Sudan for more than a century now. From the turn of the 20th Century to the 1970s, numerous meetings were held to determine the status of the area. Since the meetings were held without involving all disputants, the agreements failed to have binding effects. Temporary maps drawn during the colonial period place the triangle under Sudan's control. Sudan and Kenya made arrangements for the latter to administer the area. Hence, Kenya has *de facto* control over the triangle today.

The lack of demarcation meant underdevelopment of the area due to state neglect, prolonged Nyangatom hope to reclaim land, and protracted conflict to realize this hope. After 100 years, unfortunately, there seems to be no solution in sight. In the past, the three countries seemed to have chosen to avoid conflict over this remote and inaccessible location perceived to have marginal economic importance. With the Ilemi Triangle now described as potentially rich in unexplored oil reserves, the prospect for peace in the area remains bleak.

[18] Paradoxically, during the same period the Turkana needed protection, the British military was responsible for the protection of the Karamoja of Uganda from Turkana aggressors (USAID 2002: 23).

[19] The establishment of the colonial rule involved brutal military expeditions against the Turkana and the consequent disarmament, which made them vulnerable to attacks and raids by their northern neighbors (Mburu 2001).

[20] Nyangatom and Turkana were not the only to experience hostility partly due to the colonial legacy. More than half of what became Turkana District was transferred from Uganda to Kenya in 1926 (USAID 2002: 24) thereby exacerbating conflict between the Turkana and those who lost their land. The report further noted that during the punitive military expeditions in Turkana, the British seized large number of livestock, which were passed on to members of the Pokot ethnic group for taking part in the campaign on the side of the colonial power, and this increased the animosity of Turkana towards Pokot.

Nyangatom eviction from Kibish

The ordeals of the Nyangatom did not stop with the end of British colonial rule in Africa. Reports and informants revealed that they have continued to lose more land and more lives ever since. Tornay (1979: 103) reported his observation in 1970 as follows:

> The Nyangatom feared the Kenyan police who were stationed 2 km from the Kibish... They said that if they crossed the river, the police would shoot at them. Since they had settlements on both sides of the river, they did in fact cross it daily to pasture their herds...They showed me the remains of a settlement, which they said the Kenyan police had destroyed a few years ago, killing the occupants in the process. For their part, the Kenyan police told me that they had orders to make a no man's land of the Ilemi Triangle.

In July 1988, the Kenyan government, which was planning to annex the Ilemi Triangle earlier in the year, massacred many Nyangatom and displaced the rest from the Kibish river valley (de Waal 1991; Matsuda 1994). Alexander de Waal (1991: 345-6) wrote:

> [In] July 1988, the Kenyan police clashed with a group of Toposa or Nyangatom raiders who had previously attacked the Daasanech, and came of worst. Fifteen [Kenyan] policemen were killed, and some taken hostage. The Kenyan government responded the following day with an attack using helicopter gunships and paramilitary forces on the Nyangatom area of Kibish, which straddles Ethiopia, Kenya and Sudan. About 200 Nyangatom raiders and a minimum of 500 civilians were killed by the Kenyan forces over the following 18 days. In the attack, at least five villages in Ethiopia were partly destroyed, the Swedish Philadelphia Mission at Kibish was burned.

The 1988 Kibish massacre is locally known as the Dio incident, after the District Office of Kenya at Kibish from which the attack was launched. The Dio incident led to the forced relocation of some Nyangatom eastward as far as the Omo River, while others fled further north to Mount Naita. On the very day the Kenyans bombed the Nyangatom positions, the survivors fled the area in disarray, abandoning their chief called Loguti Lobotol, who died shortly after. The local people believe that the disappointed and humiliated chief cursed his people and the land, and that the curse is being manifested through natural disasters and man-made adversities.

Soon after the Kibish massacre, the Kenyan government is reported to have strengthened its presence by increasing the police force, establishing a military camp, and reinforcing the district administrative post. Since the 1988 incident, the grazing area that stretches from the Kibish River to the Tepes Mountain has been under Turkana control. The Turkana continued to attack and raid the Nyangatom by crossing the Kibish River, deep into Ethiopian territory. A large-scale attack in December 2008 on Lebere, Kajamakin and Natikar villages caused property destruction and a massive displacement of the Nyangatom people eastwards. In June 2011, the Turkana occupied Lebere for weeks and then withdrew reportedly after high-level government officials of the two countries were alerted.

Livestock raids

Among most pastoral groups, raiding is widely practiced to replenish lost stock or build new one. A USAID (2002: 5) report stated, "In some respects, this raiding can be seen as a quasi-legitimate sharing of resources, permitting groups on the verge of economic ruin and even starvation to reestablish their systems of food production and natural resource management." Traditionally, in Nyangatom, loss of animals to pastoral raiders was downplayed by comparing it against loss of animals to drought or animal disease. An informant remarked, "If your cattle are taken by your neighbors, you could get them back later. It is better that they are in the hands of people. If they perish due to drought, you lose them forever." Today, this perception has changed because raiding involves killing of people, raiders are not necessarily Turkana pastorals, and raided animals are sometimes sold out to butchers. As the frequency and intensity of raiding increased, the cycle of retribution and violent conflict in the Ilemi Triangle intensified. A high-profile raid took place in August 2009 when the Turkana allegedly raided more than 13,316 livestock from the Nyangatom.

The practice of raiding is reported to have transformed because of the alleged involvement of some elements of the Kenyan security force, livestock traders, arms dealers, and armed gangsters (Omolo 2011; Teshome 2010). The alleged non-pastoral actors behind cattle rustling are reported to be employing sophisticated strategies to ensure success in raiding. These include meticulous planning and execution of raids, the use of advanced automatic weapons, the use of trucks to load and drive the animals away, and the selling of animals immediately. This makes the defense and retrieval of raided animals almost impossible.

On the whole, despite their historical connection and close cooperation, the Nyangatom and the Turkana have become archenemies locked in protracted bloody fighting and livestock raiding. The Turkana are portrayed as deceitful, untrustworthy, aggressors, merciless killers, and averse to reconciliation. Since defending the people and livestock of the Nyangatom is considered as a duty, and since revenge against strong enemies brings prestige, the Nyangatom people revere killing and raiding the Turkana and other enemies.

Conclusion

Ethnic boundaries are characterized by fluidity, permeability, or shifts and these features serve as mechanisms for ethnic inclusion and exclusion. While the typical tendency of most ethnic groups seems to be upholding the principle of either expansion, contraction or keeping blurred boundary, the Nyangatom people appear to have developed a unique cultural adaptation that combines all elements at the same time. To be specific, the Nyangatom expanded their boundaries through the incorporation of the powerless Murle and Koegu; maintained strong alliance with the Toposa to the extent of blurring the boundary between them; severed alliance with the powerful Turkana that led to boundary alteration; and refrained from intermingling with the powerful Dassanech and Surma to avoid subordination. The differential adaptation of boundary mechanisms can be explained in terms of strategic reasons: control over resources and maintaining power balance. The Nyangatom chose to cooperate with groups (whether Ateker or non-Ateker) that posed a minimum risk and promised a maximum advantage both economically and militarily. The physical and social boundaries are kept open for those who earned their trust and closed for those outside of their circle of trust. This conscious and rational decision-making behavior should not be reduced to a cost-benefit analysis aimed at maximizing economic gain or attaining military superiority. In Nyangatom, the boundary management mechanism is dictated by the need to maintain social identity and ensure continuity with integrity and dignity.

References

Abbink, John, 1993: "Famine, Gold, and Guns: The Suri of South-West Ethiopia, 1985-1991". *Journal of Disaster, 17 (3)*, 219-225.

Almagor, Uri, 1986: "Institutionalizing a Fringe Periphery: Dassanetch-Amhara relations". In: Donald Donham and Wendy James (eds.): *The Southern Marches of Imperial Ethiopia*. Cambridge: Cambridge University Press, 96-115.

Alvarsson, Jan-Åke, 1989: *Starvation and Peace, or Food and War? Aspects of armed conflict in Lower Omo Valley, Ethiopia.* Uppsala: Department of Cultural Anthropology, University of Uppsala (Uppsala Research Reports in Cultural Anthropology, 8).

Barrett, Joseph Anthony, 1998: *Turkana Iconography: Desert nomads and their symbols.* Lodwar, Kenya: self-published.

Cohen, Ronald, 1978: "Ethnicity: Problem and focus in anthropology". *Annual Review of Anthropology* 7, 379-404.

CSA (Central Statistical Authority), 2008: *Summary and Statistical Report of the 2007 Population and Housing Census: Population size by age and sex*. Addis Ababa: CSA.

CSA (Central Statistical Authority), 1984: *The 1984 Population and Housing Census of Ethiopia: Analytical report at national level*. Addis Ababa: CSA.

de Waal, Alex, 1991: *Evil Days: Thirty years of war and famine in Ethiopia.* New York: Human Rights Watch.

Dyson-Hudson, Neville, 1963: "The Karimojong Age System". *Ethnology* 2, 353-401.

Gebre Yntiso, 2011: *Understanding the Dynamics of Pastoral Conflict in Lower Omo Valley: The case of the Dassanech and the Gnangatom groups in Ethiopia.* Unpublished research report submitted to Inter Africa Group. Addis Ababa.

Girke, Felix, 2008: "The Kara-Nyangatom War of 2006-2007: Dynamics of escalating violence in the tribal zone". In: Eva Maria Bruchhaus and Monika Sommer (eds.): *Hot Spot Horn of Africa Revisited: Approaches to make sense of conflict*. Münster: Lit, 192-207.

Gulliver, Philip, 1951: *A Preliminary Survey of the Turkana*. Cape Town: Commonwealth School of African Studies.

Kurimoto, Eisei, 1998: "Resonance of Age Systems in Southern Sudan." In: Eisei Kurimoto and Simon Simonse (eds.): *Conflict, Age and Power in North East Africa,*

Oxford: Currey, 29-50.

Matsuda, Hiroshi, 2008: "The Muguji: Historical perspectives on the peripheral minority." In: Katsuyoshi Fukui, Shoichiro Takezawa and Yukiyo Miyawaki (eds.): *The First Peoples of Sub-Sahara Africa* (First Peoples Vol.5), Tokyo: Akashi Shoten Bookseller, 47-62. (in Japanese).

Matsuda, Hiroshi, 1994: "Annexation and Assimilation: Koegu and their neighbors." In: Katsuyoshi Fukui and John Markakis (eds): *Ethnicity and Conflict in the Horn of Africa*, London: Currey, 48-62.

McCabe, J. Terrence, 1996: "Turkana." *Encyclopedia of World Cultures*. Encyclopedia.com. (Accessible online at: http://www.encyclopedia.com/doc/1G2-3458001584.html, last accessed 28.10.2011).

Mburu, Nene, 2003: "Delimitation of the Ilemi Triangle: A history of abrogation of responsibility". *African Studies Quarterly* 6 (4) (Accessible online at http://web.africa.ufl.edu/asq/v7/v7i1a2.htm).

Mburu, Nene 2001: "Firearms and Political Power: The military decline of the Turkana of Kenya 1900-2000".*Nordic Journal of African Studies* 10(2), 148-162.

NyaMuKo, 2010: *A Magazine of Nyangatom Woreda Culture, Tourism, and Government Communication Office*1, January (in Amharic).

Omolo, N., 2011: *Gender and Climate-Change Induced Conflict in Pastoral Communities: Case study of the Turkana in northwestern Kenya*. (Accessible online at: http://www.foresightfordevelopment.org/sobi2/Resources/ Gender-and-climate-change-induced-conflict-in-pastoral-communities-Case-study-of-Turkana-in-northwestern-Kenya).

Quam, Michael, 1999: "A Bibliography of Karamoja, Uganda: Books and articles published in English". *Electric Journal of Africana Bibliography* 5, 1-8.

Teshome Mekonnen, 2010: "Cross-Border Pastoral Conflict: The case of Dassanetch and Nyangatom in Southern Ethiopia". *Anthology of Peace and Security Research*. Addis Ababa: Institute of Peace and Security Studies and Friedrich Ebert Stiftung, 173-217.

Tornay, Serge, 1998: "Generational Systems in the Threshold of the Third Millennium: An anthropological perspective." In: Eisei Kurimoto and Simon Simonse (eds.): *Conflict, Age and Power in North East Africa*, Oxford: Currey, 98-120.

Tornay, Serge, 1981: "The Nyangatom: An outline of their ecology and social organization". In: M. L. Bender (ed.): *People and Cultures of the Ethio-Sudan Borderlands*. East Lansing: African Studies Center, 137-177.

Tornay, Serge, 1979: "Armed Conflicts in the Lower Omo Valley, 1970-1976: An analysis from within Nyangatom society." In: Katsuyoshi Fukui and David Turton (eds.): *Warfare among East African Herders*, Osaka: The National Museum of Ethnology, 97-117.

Turton, David, 1994: "Mursi Political Identity and Warfare: The survival of an idea". In: Katsuyoshi Fukui and John Markakis (eds.): *Ethnicity and Conflict in the Horn of Africa*. London: Currey,15-32.

Vincent, Joan, 1974: "The Structure of Ethnicity". *Human Organization, 33(4)*, 375-379.

Wimmer, Andreas, 2008: "The Making and Unmaking of Ethnic Boundaries: A multilevel process theory". *American Journal of Sociology, 113 (4)*, 970-1022.

USAID, 2002: *Greater Horn of Africa Peace-Building Project: Assessment and Programmatic Recommendations: Addressing pastoralist conflict in the Karamoja Cluster of Kenya, Uganda and Sudan*. Washington DC. (Unpublished research report).

Reclaiming Lost Identity

Redemption of Slave Descendants Among the Ganta

Bosha Bombe

Introduction

Slavery was officially banned in Ethiopia in 1942 by Emperor Haile Selassie but in some parts of the country people's lives are still influenced by the social boundaries that existed between slaves and non-slaves before the abolishment of this practice. In the Gamo highlands, descendants of slaves continue to be excluded from mainstream society and, though nowadays they are free and economically independent, they are still considered as ritually impure and as linked to the descendants of their former slave owners. This paper looks at the history of slavery in Ganta, the contemporary forms of social differentiation between slave descendants, descendants of slave owners and other members of the society and ways of overcoming the social boundaries between them through ritual redemption and re-inclusion of slave descendants into the society.

Descent and occupation based exclusion in Ethiopia has existed for a long time and is still a common phenomenon today (Freeman and Pankhurst 2001). Also, in the Gamo highlands of south western Ethiopia, descent and occupation based exclusion has been a persistent condition in the past and continues into the present. Farmers constitute the mainstream of Gamo society. They belong to the highest stratum called *mala*. Craftworkers (potters, blacksmiths and leatherworkers/ tanners) who are collectively called *mana/degela* and considered inferior to them (Freeman 2001). At the very bottom of Gamo society are the so-called *ayle*, the 'slaves' or, in contemporary context the 'descendents of slaves'. Especially in Ganta, Bonke and Kamba, three Gamo *dere* (communities/subdivisions of Gamo), the occupational groups and the *ayle* are still excluded from mainstream society, though the exclusion of the latter is more extreme. The *mala* avoid eating and drinking with both the *mana/degela*[1] and the *ayle*, as both are considered as polluted or impure people. However, the pollution of the *ayle* is more severe, because not only does it render others impure, but it actually turns them into an *ayle* as well. Dangerous situations in which one can be 'infected' by *ayle* (and, thereby, become infectious as well) are marriages, funerals, and childbirth rituals. To avoid becoming impure and being excluded themselves, the *mala*, and also the *mana*, stay away from these events whenever they take place in an *ayle's* home.

[1] The situation of *mana/degela* has changed recently. In the past, they were not allowed to enter a *mala* home and eat and drink with them because that was believed to pollute the *mala*. The polluted *mala* then had to be ritually cleansed by the ritual leader of his clan (*uma angus*). Today, the majority of *mala* eats and drinks with the *mana*, though some continue to avoid very close contact with them.

To escape social exclusion, many *ayle* have been integrating into mainstream 1ommunity through the so-called *wozzo* ritual. This indigenous mechanism demands high payments of the slave descendents to the descendents of their masters as well as to the ritual leaders and the community who then accept them back as full members of society. Once integrated, due to the high cost of the ritual, the redeemed *ayle* are mostly economically ruined. Recently the Synod of the Mekane Yesus Church of South Western Ethiopia based at Arbaminch started a project work in Ganta to eliminate the discrimination of slave descendants. They persuaded the ritual leaders of Ganta to end slavery. With the help of these local leaders slavery was locally officially condemned and abolished in October 2012. Nevertheless, as this researcher could observe, members of the Ganta community members still hesitate to closely associate with slave descendants today.

Caste groups, slavery and slave redemption in Africa and Ethiopia

In many parts of the world, millions of people are excluded from mainstream society because of their ethnic identity, history, or occupation. Literature indicates that there are an estimated 260 million people throughout the world suffering from descent and occupation based exclusion (Pinto 2001: 2817, 2002: 3988). Also, in parts of Africa there exist several different kinds of social exclusion based on occupational specialization or descent from slaves. Membership in occupational groups is determined by birth, and relationships between their members and other individuals or groups are usually regulated by the dogma of pollutedness and unpollutedness.[2] In several West African countries and in the sub-Saharan region, descendants of slaves are ostracized and denied access to employment and political power even today (Dilley 2000; Pinto 2001, 2002; Todd 1977). Members of lineages who are believed to be descendents of slaves are detested and denied access to employment and political power. In Eastern Africa, descendents of hunter-gatherer groups are subjected to similar discrimination. Hahonou & Pelckmans (2011) indicate that, in addition to contemporary forms of slavery such as sexual servitude, human trafficking, child labor and forced labor; various kinds of slavery such as 'benign slavery' and 'chattel slavery' are still practiced in sub-Saharan Africa, especially in the West African countries of Senegal, Mauritania, Benin, Niger, Mali, Nigeria, Serra Leone, and Burkina Faso. In these countries, the exclusion of slave descendents was neither been banished during colonialism nor with post colonial policies. Slave descendants are still being marginalized and impeded from upward social mobility (Hahonou & Pelckmans 2011: 141-142). In Madagascar, discrimination of slave descendents is also persistent and based on belief in ancestral wrath and social sanction. Intermarriage between slave descendants and freeborn has been banned in Betsileo over the last four or five generations (Regnier 2012: 149-151). Sudan is

2 Discrimination based on descent in Africa. The International Dalit Solidarity Network ("Working globally against discrimination by work and descent"). (Accessible online at www.dalitfreedom.org., last accessed on 02.09.2012).

known for its long history of human bondage. Ancient Kush, medieval Nubia, and numerous periods of foreign rule bear witness to widespread slavery and slave trading in Sudan. After independence, the practice of slavery continued, particularly in the southern Sudan in the area of Abyei. In this area, the Humr Misseriya have regularly been raiding and enslaving the Ngok Dinka, who have been almost constantly in transit between capture, sale, release, redemption, escape, dumping, and capture again (Fegley 2008; Jok 2011).

Arrowsmith and Miniter present contrasting ideas about slave redemption and the integration of slaves into mainstream society in Sudan. Arrowsmith argues that in many communities with ineffective antislavery legislation and ineffective law enforcement to emancipate slaves, redemption is the only way to help victims escape bondage. He describes a Western charity, in southern Sudan which is paying $50 per person to free Dinka people who were enslaved after their villages had been invaded by militia of northern Sudan. In other parts of the world, paying a debt bondage to free slaves is also practiced (Arrowsmith 2004: 45). Miniter describes the negative effect of such interventions. He argues that purchasing the freedom of slaves increases the market value of slaves and, thus, encourages slave raiders to abduct even more people to sell to slave redeemers. Eliminating the economic incentive for trading slaves, rather than increasing it, would be a more effective way to reduce slavery in Sudan (Miniter 2004: 49).

Slavery in Ethiopia has very long history. According to Smidt (2010), slavery was accepted as an institution in the *fetha nagast*.[3] Slaves were captured during war, sold in the markets, and inherited from generation to generation. The growing demand of labor in Arabia, Persia, Egypt and Eastern Mediterranean was the fundamental cause for the slave trade. The major slave supplying regions by then were Oromo, Sidama, Kaffa, Magi, Gamo, Gimira, Gofa, Wolayta, Kullo and Konta (Smidt 2010: 673-75). An attempt to eliminate slavery started in 1923 when Emperor Haile Selassie was asked to abolish slavery as precondition for admittance into the League of the Nations. Following the Italian occupation in 1942, a new proclamation was issued by the emperor abolishing any form of slave trade and the legal institution of slave itself. However, despite such efforts slaves and their descendants have continually been marginalized in the country, especially in the peripheral parts of southwestern Ethiopia until today (*ibid.*: 675ff).

Slavery in Ganta, Gamo highlands

Origin and history

The Gamo highlands are located in Southern Ethiopia, 505 km from Addis Ababa, in Gamo Gofa Zone, which is one of the administrative Zones of Southern Nations,

[3] In the 12th and 13th century the *fetha nagast* was the civil and religious code which served as constitution before the advent of the modern written constitution.

Nationalities and Peoples Regional State (SNNPRS). The Gamo people are an Omotic speaking group and their language is closely related to that of the Gofa, Wolayta and Dawro people. During the 19th century, the Gamo highlands were politically autonomous and divided into small territorially discrete political units locally called *dere*, each of which had its own hereditary king (*kawo*). Today, Gamo is still divided into nearly forty *dere*, which occupy areas ranging in size from five to fifty square miles (Olmstead 1975: 223ff). Ganta has been one of about forty Gamo *dere* ruled by a local king (*kati*)[4] since roughly the beginning of 16th and 17th century. The Ganta (Gamo) highlands were brought under the Ethiopian Empire in 1894. The traditional government structure was preserved and their kings became the *balabat*[5] through whom the different units were governed. When the *gabbar*[6] system was introduced, the local *balabats* played a significant role in organizing land tax payment to the Ethiopian Empire.

Currently, Ganta is under the administrative structure of Arbaminch Zuria *woreda* (district) and it is divided into four *kebele* (here: villages): Meyche, Bonke, Kanchama-Ochole, and Afeze. According to the 2007 population and housing census, the total population of Ganta was 13,392 in the year 2007 (CSA 2007) with a total of 2934 households. During my field stay in 2013, I was able to identify 71 *ayle* households in Ganta (about 300 individuals). The research was mainly done in Kanchama-Ochole, Meyche and Bonk because in these places the problem was severe. The upper town of Arbaminch was also part of the study, as many slave descendants came to the town to escape severe exclusion.

The emergence of slavery in Ganta (and also other parts of the Gamo highlands) is locally associated with recurrent droughts and periods of hunger in the area at the beginning of the 19th century. During that time, many people were impoverished and had to subjugate themselves to those few who still had resources to share. Most people were unable to pay back what they had received and, as a result, became the property of those who had given them food. Some informants even mentioned that some families had 'bartered' their children for food in order to survive.[7] Descendants of slaveholders who were interviewed confirmed that their ancestors had bought slaves with small amounts of grain and flour. These slaves came from all of the various lineages of the Gamo, even to the point that even impoverished *mala* became slaves of their own relatives and neighbors.

4 The language of Ganta (locally referred to as *ganta* or *gantigna*) is a dialect of the Gamo language. The Ganta refer to their kings as *kati*, while in other Gamo areas the king is called *kawo*.

5 *Balabat* was an administrative position during the imperial reign; the *balabat* were intermediaries between the state and the local communities. In Gamo, this position was usually given to the *kawos* (Freeman 2004).

6 During this time, tenant farmers had to provide food and labor to the Amhara settlers (Freeman 2004).

7 Some redeemed slave descendants whose ancestors had experienced this indicated, that the main the intention of parents to give away their children away was to have them be adopted by new parents and thus survive the drought. However, these children were later claimed as property (i.e. slaves) rather than adopted children by the "new parents".

Besides the local situation, the 19th century slave trade in Ethiopia had a strong impact on the rise and intensification of slavery in the Gamo highlands. Oral tradition says that the Gamo highlands in general, and Ganta in particular had been connected to the long distance caravan trade routes of 19thcentury in south-western Ethiopia. The Shoshane market in Kanchama-Ochole was a known slave market at the time. Informants from Ochole asserted that a part of the marketplace was dedicated to the selling of slaves (*ayle do'o*). Peple say they were traded like animals, bargaining was common and the price of an individual slave depended on his or her age, sex and health status. The Shoshane market was connected to another market, the market of Wortsiso (today: Amaro-Kelle) which was another leading slave market in the south west of the Gamo highlands. Some informants stated that the Shoshane market was also linked to other Omotic states, such as Wolayta, Dawro, Kaffa and Konta. The existence of slavery and slave trade in Gamo in the 19th century was also reported by other researchers. Smidt (2010: 675) indicated that the Gamo highlands were one of the major slave supplying regions in the 19th century long-distance slave trade. Freeman (2004: 29) emphasized the significant role slavery played in the Gamo economy and that the desire to capture slaves was generally high and often a cause for conflict (*ibid.*: 29-30). In the 19th century, conflicts among the different subgroups of Gamo were common. Their causes ranged from stolen livestock, to a runaway wife, to competition over pasture between two *dere*. These inter-Gamo conflicts are said to have aggravated the slavery situation, because war captives were often an additional source of slaves (Olmstead 1975: 226).

Categories of slaves in Ganta

As mentioned above, Ganta society is stratified into three main groups: the *mala*, the *mana*, and the *ayle*. The *mala* constitute the mainstream of society. They are conceived of as pure, and provide the ritual experts (*maga*) and kings (*kati*). The *mana* are craftworkers, including potters, tanners, and blacksmiths. They are considered to be impure due to their occupations, which are generally associated with uncleanliness. The term *ayle* stands for slaves, and, nowadays, for descendants of slaves. They are considered different from *mala* and *mana* because their ancestors are said to have lost their humanity the moment they turned into slaves. The *ayle* are subdivided into three major subcategories: *bacha ayle, laati ayle* and *chancha ayle.* While the first two refer to *ayle* who inherited their status, the latter refers to a self-acquired status through close contact with *ayle* during certain ceremonies. The term *bacha* literally means 'sickle', i.e. a tool used for cutting grass and weeds. The category of *bacha ayle* refers to those *ayle* whose ancestors were bought on a market and had to serve their master by cutting grass for his mules and cattle, by farming, tending the cattle, washing the feet of their master, collecting firewood, and guiding and accompanying their master wherever he went. Though Ganta society is otherwise patrilineal, the status of *bacha ayle* is inherited and is passed on through both lineages, the mother's and the father's. This category of slaves has the lowest position of all slave descendants and the redemption of *bacha ayle* is the most complex and costly of all *ayle*. The so-called *laata ayle*[8] (literally 'slaves by descent') are descendants of those who became slave through other mechanisms like during times of famine, during inter-Gamo wars (as war captives), and through marriage with an *ayle*).

A third slave category is called *chancha ayle*. The term *chancha* stands for the food and drink offered to relatives or neighbors in the house of a deceased slave descendant or during a marriage ceremony or childbirth. Non-*ayle* consider the *chancha* as polluted food and it is believed that eating it would to automatically turn a *mala* into a slave. Touching items used during such ceremonies has the same effect. In this sense, slavery is transferable through close social contact with slave descendants as if it was a kind of communicable disease. Therefore, non-*ayle* stay away from the above mentioned ceremonies to avoid turning into slaves themselves.

Slaves (or slave descendants) are considered as inferior creatures. In the context of the *bacha ayle* and the *laata ayle*, slavery is perceived as an innate debt, i.e. the money or goods that were given in exchange for slave ancestors. Their inferiority is thus not materialized in any physical, mental or economical difference, but associated with their ancestors' dehumanization in the moment they became slaves, as from that moment on they had been treated no better than any other commodity or animal traded in the market. Only through redemption, when slave descendents repay what had been given for their ancestors, can they retrieve their humanity.

During the redemption process the difference between the three categories becomes obvious. The *bacha ayle* have to give up any property they have accumulated (including their houses and farms) and hand it over to their *lathi* ('master' or better: 'descendants of their master'), as when they arrived they were also without any property. The *laata ayle* do not have to give up their land and property, as they are descendants of war captives. They process the *wozzo* ritual with a limited amount of money which is determined according to their economic power. The same is true for the *chancha ayle*, who received their status through close interaction.

All members of Ganta I talked to seemed to accept the hierarchical order between *mala*, *mana* and *ayle*. However, some *ayle* argued that they were actually superior to the *mana*, as an *ayle* has the chance to be redeemed and become member of the *mala* stratum, while the *mana* have no way of improving their status.

Slave-descendants, craft workers and mainstream society

Everyday life and ritual contexts

The social boundaries between mainstream society, the craftworkers and the slave descendants were more visible in the past than today, especially in regard to

8 Some informants (descendants of slave holders) argued that the *lataa ayle* can also be called *bacha ayle* if they have been *ayle* in the fourth or fifth generations, arguing that one of the essential attributes of the *bacha ayle* is that their status is inheritable and the *lataa ayle* share this at tribute.

interaction between the craftworkers and the other two groups. In everyday life the *ayle* were eating and drinking and interacting with the *mala*, while the *mana* were neither allowed to eat with the *mala*, nor even to enter their houses. Especially milk and milk products were not given or even shown to the *mana*, as it was believed that this would cause cattle diseases. The *mana* were also excluded from churches and community based organizations.

This has changed in the last few decades, and daily life in Ganta at first glance seems to be a peaceful coexistence of slave descendants, members of *mala* and craftworkers, as informants from all three strata confirmed. Today, the *mana* live in the same neighborhood, eat and drink with the *mala* and slave descendants freely and go to the same churches.[9]*Mala, mana* and *ayle* eat, drink and work together, help each other out and visit each other. In the church they worship and serve together. As informants from Protestant churches explained, today there are *ayle* church leaders, deacons, evangelists, singers, Sunday school teachers and worship-leaders. In community based organizations, such as *idir*[10] and *iqub*[11], the *ayle* share equal rights with the other *mana* and *mala*, some *ayle* even serve in leadership positions. Some *mana* and *ayle* inhabit important positions in government institutions (in courts, schools or in the police). Both *mana* and *mala* informants asserted that they had equal rights in using local infrastructure: their children go to school with the other children of community, they equally use the piped water set-up in each *kebele*, and at local level government structure they equally participate with the rest of the community.

All informants emphasized that in everyday life no one talks about the social difference between the *ayle, mana* and other members of the society. They said that they were living in unity, cooperating with each other, and the social barrier between the *ayle* and the rest of the community was mostly invisible. It is only intermarriage between the *mana* and *mala* and *ayle* that is still avoided.

It is only in ritual contexts (such as marriage, funeral and child birth, see below) that the boundaries are strictly observed. Daily life is mostly rather peaceful in Ganta. However, there are instances of conflict when the differences between *mala* and *ayle* can be observed. When, for example a *mala* gets drunk, he might publicly use the derogative term *ayle* as an insult towards a slave descendant. Some informants also stated that a drunken *mala* will ridicule an *ayle* publically, for example by saying "I smell bad odor" when they sit together in a drinking house.

Only the *chancha ayle* are continuously discriminated against, i.e. those *ayle* who originally were *mala* and turned into *ayle* through participation in marriage, funeral/mourning, or child delivery. The *chancha ayle* are insulted and ridiculed especially by their own relatives, because, as my *mala* informants explained, turning into a slave through close association with slave descendants is considered more shameful than being a slave by descent. While being a slave by descent is consi-

9 In the upper town of Arbaminch the *ayle* were segregated from the church

10 Burial association.

11 Savings association.

dered as a part of a person's identity, i.e. an inborn inferior attribute, turning into a slave at a later stage (whether on purpose or accidentally) in life is like having choosing disgrace i.e. having wasted one's honored identity. Relatives of a *chancha ayle* feel that the change from *mala* into *ayle* is not only a shame for the person himself but also for the whole family. Especially those *mala* who turned into *ayle* through marriage with a slave descendant are severely discriminated by their own kin. Those I met during my field stay had been evicted from their land, banished from co-residence with their relatives, and completely cut off from any kin ties. They were practically forced to move to another area.

Exclusion of slaves during rites of passage

The social differentiation of *ayle* (slave descendants) is most clearly manifested during rites of passage when their status can be transmitted to others.

Marriage, Arranged marriage was common in Ganta in the past. Parents selected the spouse for their children, sent elders and a go-between (*lazantha*) to the family of a potential spouse, decided on the schedule, organized the ceremony, and provided all necessary resources needed for the marriage. Nowadays, children are allowed to select their spouses, but their selection still has to be approved by the parents. What has remained to be of utmost importance is to make sure that the background of a potential spouse is 'clean'. The main criterion is the cleanness of the *uma* (clan), which means that the potential spouse should be a descendant of a freeborn and not of an *ayle*. To make sure that the future spouse of their child is not a slave descendant, parents usually engage in intensive genealogical counting and checking. Discussions with informants indicated that parents may go as far back as the 7th generation. In cases where any link to slave origin is detected, on either the father's or the mother's side, the marriage is avoided. Because of the strict parental involvement in investigating the origin of a potential spouse, informants asserted that marriages between slave descendants and non-slaves have been very uncommon since the introduction of slavery in the study community.[12]

Despite the ban on intermarriage there are few cases of mixed marriage. During my field stay I identified four such cases, two in Kanchama-Ochole and two in the upper town of Arbaminch. In Kanchama-Ochole a rich slave descendant and his son both married *mala* women. The women had volunteered to marry the *ayle* because the *ayle* men were wealthy. Such women, I was told, say "*Uma ala othai, santemewa*!" (What is important about the clan? That what is important is money!) or "*Athi meyoda hedes ayleko gele*!" (If you want to have a luxurious life, marry a slave!). Having married *ayle,* these women were completely cut off from their parents and kin groups. They were now seen as ayle themselves and, thus, perceived as potential sources of contagious impurity. The families of these women

[12] The marriage genealogies collected during the research showed that actually many of the redeemed slave descendants had assumed their status through marrying another *ayle*.

argued that "*Tsagara durora alawa bu'asi!*" (Goats and sheep cannot mix!), meaning that slave descendants cannot mix with freeborn.

The other cases that I came across were two freeborn men from Kanchama-Ochole who married *ayle* women. They were facing severe discrimination by their parents, kin groups and other *mala*. Their parents and kinsmen wept and mourned after the marriage, saying that they had lost their sons who had now turned into slaves. The two men indicated to me that they felt as if they had lost their status as humans, because they were continuously insulted and scorned. Because of the serious discrimination from their kin and other community members, they finally decided to move to Arbaminch.

The *mana* (craftworkers) also avoid intermarriage with the *ayle*. They likewise say that marrying an *ayle* would turn the spouse into an *ayle* and would lead to the same kind of exclusion as for *mala*.

Funeral. Exclusion during funerals is the most serious slave descendants are facing as close interaction at the event of death. All interviewed *mala, mana* and *ayle* stated that from the beginning of slavery there existed a taboo in participating in an *ayle's* funeral. This included the avoidance of eating and drinking at the funeral and the prohibition of staying overnight in that house before the temporary impurity of the place had vanished after six days (*la'a*).[13] To ignore these prohibitions meant that one automatically turns into a slave oneself. The pollution or contamination then spreads to the family line unless one gets redeemed, i.e. until one gets cleaned through ritual purification of all close family members (spouse and children). Therefore, when death occurs at an *ayle's* home, people (including *mala* and *mana*) come to weep and mourn with the descendants, but never stay overnight. They carry food and drink to the deceased slave's family to support them, but they do not eat anything there, not even their own food which they brought to support the mourning family, because the food is believed to turn *chancha* (polluted and inedible) as soon as it has been handed over to the deceased slave's family.

The only exceptions are the descendants of the *lathi* (slave master) and his family. The *lathi* have to initiate all activities related to the postmortem care to the deceased whose ancestors were owned by his own ancestors. If anyone would initiate the activities before the *lathi* that person immediately turns into his slave.[14] The *lathi* also support the family of the deceased: they stay overnight, they comfort them,

13 *La'a* is complex concept with various meaning in different contexts. Here, the following two are of relevance: first, it denotes the complete and permanent cleanness of slave descendant. When a slave descendant is redeemed, it this is called *la'atis*. The term also refers the cleansing from temporary impurity: when an *ayle* dies or gives birth, the first six days are considered as the period of pollution. The seventh day is called *la'a* and indicates the end of the impure period. There is no ritual required of the slave descendant to get cleaned. According to the customary law the seventh day is considered pure. Some of my informants especially descendants of slave holders associated *la'a* with the Mosaic laws of the Old Testament.

14 Postmortem care is then finalized by the deceased person's family, but they also must wait until the master has initiated it.

and they eat and drink with them and even help burying the dead body. They can do that because, people say, the slaves are considered to be their masters' kinsmen, because at the moment that they became slaves they were cut off from their own kin group and established new ties with their masters.

Childbirth. Exclusion of the slave descendants during child delivery is the third major area of discrimination and it resembles the exclusion which occurs during funerals. Different informants described that non-*ayle* do not help when an *ayle* woman gives birth. Additionally, when the non-*ayle* visit the mother after she gave birth, they do not eat and drink at her home before the *la'a*. *Mala* informants explained that the blood the mother loses during child delivery is said to contaminate the *ayle* and their homes. Only after the *la'a* does the consumption of food and drink not contaminate them.

Recent reinforcement of boundaries and efforts to overcome

In the past few decades new avoidance rules between *mala* and *ayle* were introduced. *Mala, ayle* and *mana* informants asserted that the introduction of the new avoidance rules had to do with the "commercialization" of slave redemption. Since the 1990s many slave descendants started redeeming themselves and thereby got integrated into the mainstream society. As a reaction the ritual experts (*lathies, maga,* and *kati*) became concerned that all original slave descendants might be integrated into the mainstream society and there could be no more *ayle.* Thus they introduced new avoidance rules for generating new members of the slave class from the non-slave class.

The first newly introduced custom was that a freeborn should not be in the house of an *ayle* when someone dies there. As a consequence the *mala* do not go to see their sick *ayle* neighbors anymore, fearing that the *ayle* could die during the visit and turn them into a slave of the dying person's master. The second new rule is to avoid giving postmortem care to a deceased *ayle*. As mentioned above, it is the right and duty of a slave master to initiate it, and anyone else interfering would immediately turn into his slave. The third kind of newly introduced avoidance rules encompasses any contact with objects during a funeral, including washing hands, brushing teeth, sitting on wet grass, initiating the erecting of the tent for the funeral guests, and smoking cigarettes before six days have elapsed. Any exchange of household tools with the deceased slave descendant's family is also strictly prohibited before the time of impurity is over. This means also that when a *mala* brings food and drink to the deceased person's family, he/she will only get the plates and bowls back after the *la'a* period. The fourth prohibition relates to the burying of the corpse. When a slave descendant dies, the freeborn cannot initiate the digging of the tomb, and they should also not initiate the carrying of the corpse to the tomb. Carrying the corpse and participation in filling up the grave with soil is allowed, but to initiate it is believed to be dangerous and turn one into an *ayle*. Finally, it is prohibited to give any gifts (*mogo*) to the family that has assisted the family in bury the dead. The gifts usually consist of clothes, cattle, and money and they are given by the first born of a deceased's family and by the husbands of the daughters. If the oldest son or the daughters are married to slave descendants they are not allowed to present *mogo* at the event of their relatives. The practice of gift-giving to assistants of a funeral is an honored practice in Ganta. To be unable to do so is considered a shame and thus another example of the serious exclusion of *ayle* in Ganta.

The discrimination during funerals is also supported by the churches. Members of both, Protestant and Orthodox Churches hold the assumption that embracing Christianity cannot change the impure status of slave descendants and participation in funerals is contagious. However, there are few exceptions. Some individual Protestant Christians I talked to claimed that all humans were equal, referring to the bible, Galatians 3:26-28:

> For you are all children of God, through faith in Christ Jesus. For as many of you as were baptized into Christ have put on Christ. There is neither Jew nor Greek, there is neither slave nor free man, there is neither male nor female; for you are all one in Christ Jesus (World English Bible)

Having internalized this scripture, some *mala* Protestants went so far as consciously associating themselves with slave descendants during the death of their relatives. When in 2002 a devoted *ayle* Christian died in the upper town of Arba-minch, twelve *mala* Protestants went to the funeral and ate the *chancha* food given to them by the deceased man's family. Soon after they were condemned by their relatives and community who said that the twelve had now turned into slaves of the deceased *ayle's* master. This had dramatic consequences for all. The wives of many ran away and the husband and children were cut off from their kinsmen and the rest of the community. Instead of being a trigger for better acceptance of the *ayle*, as they had hoped, the situation turned out to be very different. All except one could not bear the isolation and finally renounced their decision and got redeemed and restored to their former status. The one who remained a *chancha ayle* continues to be discriminated and isolated from his family. None of his family members visited him even when his son died shortly the event.

Slave redemption: The *wozzo* ritual

Wozzo is a word in the Ganta language the meaning of which implies redeeming or ransoming, and refers to "the buying back" of the "sold" and lost identity of the *mala*. The *wozzo* ritual is the most trusted indigenous mechanism through which slave descendants have been able to integrate into the mainstream society since ancient times when slaves and their descendants began to accumulate wealth. The ritual consists of several complex steps and leaving out even one of them is said to lead to the complete failure of the process. In case where all of the required ritual steps are completed, guarantees that an *ayle* is fully integrated into mainstream society and assumes all rights and privileges of the *mala*. The intricate and exact procedure of the ritual performance depends on the category of the slave to be redeemed.

According to interviews I conducted with redeemed slave descendants, slave owners and local ritual experts (*maga* and *kati*) there are four basic levels or steps in the *wozzo* ritual that all have to undergo to complete the redemption process.

At level one, the slave descendants accomplish the redemption process with their master. When a slave descendant decides to undergo the ritual process, he selects several *lazantha* (knowledgeable, senior, respected and influential elders). They should also be familiar with all details of the *wozzo* ritual and know the master's family and lineage very well. The *lazantha* and the *ayle* go to the master's home together. There, the *lazantha* fall down at the master's feet on behalf of the *ayle*. Kissing the soil they plead, *"Tsela! Tsela! Tsela!"* ('Look! Look! Look!'), hereby asking the master to accept the request of his slave to be redeemed. At this level the pleading and continued negotiation and bargaining over redemption prices is tedious and complex. The *lathi* has the absolute power to either accept or reject the request of the slave descendant. He can handle the whole procedure fairly, but he can also make it difficult. Once the basic agreement has been achieved, the *lathi* initiates the redemption process by demanding the payment for the first ancestor of the slave descendant (*uma harafa*), usually about 300-400ETB. Paying the *uma harafa* is the first step to redeem everyone in the descent line.[15] When the *lathi* has collected the *uma harafa*, he directs the next steps by ordering the *lazantha* of slave descendants: *"Gaydi eshayto!"*(Drive my oxen/cows), referring to the *ayle* whom he considers to be his ox/cow. Then he tells the price of each of his ancestors up to the first in the descent line. The elders lead the *ayle* to the master, saying: *"Eshayto gaydi! Hiti! Hiti! Hiti!"* (Your ox/cow is this!). Now the *ayle* has to fall down on his knees and walk like an ox/cow before his master, roaring and mooing.

The cost of the redemption is not fixed. It depends on the category of the slave (*bacha* or *chancha*), sex and the economy power of the slave descendants. *Bacha ayle* must give up their residence and farm land, and anything they have produced and attained in their life time and hand it to their master. They also cut their nails, shave their heads and leave being completely naked after being redeemed, and start new life in new area. *Chancha ayle* have no impurity in their descent line and they, therefore, undergo only their own case. The cost for their redemption is therefore much less. The cost of female *ayle* is usually higher than that of male because female slaves can give birth to new slaves. The order of redemption is flexible, e.g. a married *ayle* can decide to either redeem first his own or his wife's descent line.[16] He

[15] During slave redemption slave descendants not only redeem themselves but all deceased ancestors starting from the apical ancestor. Without redeeming deceased ancestors redemption cannot be complete. In addition to redeeming the deceased ancestors individually they redeem the works their ancestors delivered to their masters. According to informants this is the most fraud and deceptive part of the redemption process.

[16] Redeemed slave descendants indicated to me that often husbands redeem their own descent line first and afterwards they redeem that of their wives.

can also either redeem his deceased ancestors first or he can redeem himself, his family and his living parents first and his deceased ancestors at last.

When the *ayle* has finished paying the required amount for his father, himself and his children, the *lathi* starts the ritual redemption. The *ayle* should be present. His children can be there in person or represented by ritual sticks, one for each child. The *lathi* relieves him from being an *ayle* and blesses him:

> *Hanzofe ede nena anjakotede, nena dere maqada la'akotede, kati shato maqe, dana shato maqe ne shatora ta shatora eputi geluti.*
>
> (From now on I have blessed you, so that you can be a citizen, live like a king and noble man, May your children and mine marry each other!)

Then he puts wet grass on the *ayle* which means that now he is redeemed. Now, the redeemed *ayle* starts singing (*gayro*):

> *Ntsa kesisade wozitisade, lathi kare halsutesadee, hanzope gede galape kastakotedemetope kesokotede.*
>
> (I am set free, I am redeemed, and I finished at master gate, from today on I am released from my debt. My problem is solved!)

After being blessed, the redeemed *ayle* runs away. He avoids looking behind the *lathi* because gazing at back the *lathi* during the ritual process is believed to disqualify the redemption.

The next step of the *wozzo* ritual is performed at the *maga's* gateway. The *maga* is a ritual expert positioned below the *kati* (king). At the *maga's* gate the *lazantha* once again fall down on behalf of the *ayle*. Laying at the *maga's* feet they kiss the soil and plead *"Tsela! Tsela! Tsela!"* (Look! Look! Look!). Again there is negotiation over the price for redemption which is now determined considering the economic capacity of the *ayle*. Other than at the master's house, many people come to the *maga's* home to attend. These may include the elders of the community, the family of the redeemed *ayle*, the *lazantha* and the family members of the *ayle*'s master. The main task of *maga* is to make sure that the *ayle* has completely finished his redemption with various *lathies*. He has to confirm that the redemption, i.e. the payment to all involved master's families has been completed before one can proceed. This is considered as crucial because an unfinished redemption process means that the *ayle* has not changed his status and, therefore, can still pass on his impurity to the *maga* and other community members. The *maga* and his wife also receive a payment for their service. After the payment has been given the *maga* purifies and blesses *ayle* by saying:

> *Hanzofe gede nena anjakotede, nena dere maqada la'akotede, kati shato maqe, dana shato maqe nu shatora ne shatora eputi geluti.*
>
> (Now that I have blessed you, be a citizen, live like a king and noble man may our children and your children marry each other).

Then he puts wet grass on the *ayle* head suggesting he has been purified and is free. Now, the *ayle* starts expressing his happiness by singing the following lines (*gayro*):

Ntsa kesisade wozitisade, maga kare halsutesadee, hanzope gede metope kesokotede.

('I am set free, I am redeemed, my freedom is assured by the maga, and my problem is solved')

Ritual purification of the slave descendant with the *kati* is the third and most important step. Again, the elders of the slave descendant accompany him and on his behalf fall down at the *kati's* feet. While kissing the soil he says *"Tsela! Tsela! Tsela!"*('Look! Look! Look!'). The difference between the *maga* and the *kati* redemption is that the *maga* recognizes the redemption of the slave descendant to his own locality only, while the *kati* acknowledges his redemption to the entire Ganta community. The *kati* and his wife are also paid for the ritual process. The *kati* ends the redemption by saying:

Hanzofe gede la'a maqe apute, gelute.

(From now on you are emancipated and integrated into the community, marry and be married with them).

The fourth, and final, step is the *soffe* celebration which involves the public announcement of the new status of the *ayle*. The *soffe* is performed at the Shoshane market which nowadays is the meeting point of the entire Ganta community, including Arbaminch and other Gamo communities. The basic objective of celebrating the redemption at this market is to announce to the entire community, i.e. the people from nearby and from far that the slave descendant is redeemed and integrated. Hereby, future confusion in marriage arrangements shall be avoided, and the full participation and interaction during funerals, marriage and childbirth be granted for the redeemed and all his family.

Regardless of its complex and economically destructive aspects, the community trusts in the *wozzo* ritual. Out of 71 households in three Ganta villages (Kanchama-Ochole, Meyche and Bonke) with a total population of 300 people, 51 households were integrated through the *wozzo* ritual, having completed the above mentioned noted levels and steps. There were five households who had interrupted the *wozzo* ritual after the first step when the Synod's project started. They are today locally still perceived as potential sources of impurity. The remaining fifteen households remained unredeemed.

Summary and conclusion

The community of the Ganta people differentiates between three kinds of people, i.e. the *mala* (mainstream society), the *mana* (craft workers) and the *ayle* (slave descendants). The three are separated by strict and clearly defined boundaries that regulate everyday and ritual life. While the differentiation between craftworkers and non-craftworkers is quite common in Ethiopia and has been the topic of numerous publications,[17] the exclusion of slave descendants has been neglected and not been the focus of any study on Southern Ethiopia.

The case of the Ganta community is especially interesting, as here most of the slaves (and their descendants) originally came from the same community and not from other groups. The introduction of slavery in Ganta, therefore, was meant to create distinctions between people who were originally the same: not only did they belong to the same ethnic, linguistic and religious group and came from the same locality, they were even members of the same lineages and clans. It was, thus, historical circumstance (i.e. drought and famine) that led to a strict boundary between people who actually until then had shared the same identity, and this boundary has continued to exist even when historical circumstance has changed, i.e. when slavery was abandoned.

The boundaries between the three different sections of Ganta are all based on the concepts of "purity" and "impurity", labeling the *mala* as "pure" and the *mana* and *ayle* as "impure". However, while the boundaries between the craftworkers and mainstream society are impermeable (though less strict in the last decades), those between slave descendants and the *mala* can be crossed. The costly redemption process (i.e. the *wozzo* ritual) enables slave descendants to join the mainstream society, as it actually eliminates the boundary between them, redefines their relationship and allows them to return to a common identity.

The ideas connected to slavery and the different qualities of being human associated with slaves (and descendents of slaves) and slave owners (and descendents of slave owners) are deeply entrenched in the customary politico-religious setting of the Ganta, and besides the former slave owners (*lathi*), is has been mainly the traditional religious and political leaders who contributed to maintaining the boundary (and thus the discrimination of slave descendants) until these days. The continuation of exclusion of slave descendants is obviously intentional, as the descendants of slave masters and the ritual leaders have been benefitting from it. It is an example of what Sen (2000) called "active exclusion", i.e. a kind of deliberate discrimination which could be on the basis of gender, caste, social origin or age. In Ganta, the ascriptions of purity and impurity are accepted by all three sections of the society, but obviously kept alive by the *mala*, who constitute the majority and most powerful section of Ganta community and hereby keep their superior status.

How deep-rooted the ideas related to slavery are in Ganta is shown by the fact that they have not only continued to exist after the banning of slavery, but also after the introduction of Christianity and also during several subsequent political regimes that have put pressure in different ways on local communities to abolish discriminatory aspects of their culture. The recent effort to eliminate the boundaries between *ayle* and non-*ayle* by involving the ritual and political leaders seems more promising, however, whether the behavior of the people will really change future has to show.

17 See for example the edited volume on Southern Ethiopia by Freeman and Pankhurst (eds.) 2001, also Amborn 1990, and Freeman on the Gamo highlands 2001, 2004

References

Amborn, Hermann, 1990: *Differenzierung und Integration: vergleichende Untersuchungen zu Spezialisten und Handwerkern in südäthiopischen Agrargesellschaften*. München: Trickster.

Arrowsmith, Martin, 2004: "Slave Redemption has a Role in combating Slavery in Sudan". In: Auriana Ojeda (ed.): *Slavery Today*. San Diego and New York: Green Heaven Press, 45-48.

Dilley, Roy M., 2000: "The Question of Caste in West Africa with Special Reference to Tukulor Craftsmen". *Anthropos 95*, 1, 149-165.

Fegley, Randall, 2008: "Comparative Perspectives on the Rehabilitation of Ex-Slaves and Former Child Soldiers with Special Reference to Sudan". *African Studies Quarterly 10*, 1, 35-69.

Freeman, Dena and Alula Pankhurst (eds.), 2001: *Marginalized Minorities of Craft Workers and Hunters in Southern Ethiopia*. Addis Ababa: Addis Ababa University Press.

Freeman, Dena, 2001: "Marginalized Minorities in Gamo". In: Freeman Dena and Aula Pankhurst (eds.), 2001: *Marginalized Minorities of Craft Workers and Hunters in Southern Ethiopia*. Addis Ababa: Addis Ababa University Press, 186-205.

Freeman, Dena, 2004: *Initiating Change in Highland Ethiopia: Causes and Consequences of Cultural Transformation*. Cambridge: Cambridge University Press.

Hahonou, Eric & Lotte Pelckmans, 2011: "West African Antislavery Movements: Citizenship". *Struggles and the Legacies of Slavery'. Stichproben. Wiener Zeitschrift für kritische Afrikastudien 20*, 141-162.

Jok, Jok Madut, 2011: *War and Slavery in Sudan*. Philadelphia: University of Pennsylvania Press.

Miniter, Richard, 2004: "Slave Redemption Increases Slavery in Sudan". In: Auriana Ojeda, (ed.). *Slavery Today*. San Diego and New York: Green Heaven Press, 49-59.

Olmstead, Judith, 1973: "Agricultural Land and Social Stratification in the Gamo Highlands of South-Western Ethiopia". In: Harold Marcus (ed.): *Proceedings of the First United States Conference on Ethiopian Studies*. East Lansing: African Studies Center Michigan State University, 223-234.

Pinto, Ambrose, 2001: "UN Conference against Racism: Is caste race?" *Economic and Political Weekly, 30 (36)*, 2817-2820.

Pinto, Ambrose, 2002: "Caste Discrimination and UN". *Economic and Political Weekly, 37(39)*, 3988-3990.

Regnier, Denis A. P., 2012: *Why Not Marry Them? History, essentialism and the condition of slave descendants among the Southern Betsileo (Madagascar)*. London: London School of Economics, Department of Anthropology. (PhD Thesis).

Sen, Amartya, 2000: "Social Exclusion: Concept, application and scrutiny". *Social Development Paper One, 1*. Manila: Asian Development Bank, 1-54

Smidt, Wolbert, 2010: "Slavery". In: Siegbert Uhlig (ed.): *Encyclopedia Aethiopica 4, O-X*. Wiesbaden: Harrassowitz, 673-681.

Todd, David, 1977: "Caste in Africa?". *Journal of the International African Institute 47, 4*, 398-412.

Part II:

Status Change and Interdependencies across Intra-ethnic Divides

ADOLESCENCE, BRIDEHOOD AND MARRIAGE

LOCAL PERSPECTIVES ON FEMALE STATUS CHANGE IN SOUTH OMO

Susanne Epple

Girlhood and coming of age among East African pastoralists

When compared to the literature on male pastoralists' worlds not much has been written on the lives of women in Eastern African pastoralist or agro-pastoralist groups.[1] Hardly any ethnographic material can be found on the lives of girls (i.e. unmarried females), on their self-image, their thoughts, fears, hopes and wishes and their expectations on their future lives as wives and mothers. This paper tries to fill this gap a little by giving insights into girlhood and the transitional phase of becoming a woman in different ethnic groups of South Omo. All groups discussed here are agro-pastoralists, some focusing more strongly on agriculture, others emphasizing pastoralism. All follow patrilineal descent, prefer patrilocal post-marital residence and can be considered as patriarchal, though great variations exist in how things are put into practice.

In the research area, girlhood, especially adolescence, is a time when females are enjoying relative freedom, but at the same time are expectant of major changes in their lives to come, most of them related to marriage. In South Omo, marriage for females usually means to leave the natal family, often also their localities and friends, in order to join and become a member of a new family often unknown to them beforehand. For females assuming the role of a wife and mother means to assume new duties, to carry responsibility for their own family, and to establish a relationship with a known or unknown husband as well as the new in-laws. What are females' views on these different life-stages, how do they deal with the changes, or their fear of such changes, and how do they convince themselves and each other to adhere to cultural expectations, even if they are difficult to bear? These and other questions will be elucidated from the perspectives of adolescent girls and married women from different ethnic background.

[1] Females are mainly mentioned in the context of marriage arrangements and gender relations (for example Spencer 1965;Talle 1998; Llewellyn-Davies 1978, 1981). Few researchers described daily lives of women in age-set societies (Kawai 1998; Von Mitzlaff 1987). Among the scholars working specifically on women's lives in South Omo, Jean Lydall deserves first mention. Especially in her ethnographic films (1990, 1991, 1994, 2001), but also in numerous articles, she has provided deep insights into the feelings of some Hamar girls and women before, during and after marriage. Among recent publications on females in South Omo are Peller (2002) who wrote on Arbore, Thubauville on Maale (2010), LaTosky (2006, 2011) on Mursi, Elfmann on Daasanech (2004), Epple on Bashada (2006, 2010), and Brüderlin (2004) on Hamar.

Female encounters in Jinka, southern Ethiopia

Most of the data presented here was collected during a workshop on "The Pride and Social Worthiness of Women in South Omo", held at the South Omo Research Centre (SORC) in 2002 in Jinka, the capital of the South Omo zone of the Southern Nations, Nationalities and Peoples' Region (SNNPR). 21 girls and women from eight different ethnic groups, three female anthropologists from Germany and England and eight German students of anthropology participated in the workshop. The main objective was to examine culture specific experiences and perspectives of females living in different environments and cultural contexts; to see whether differences in livelihood would lead to different worldviews, and, more specifically, to females' self-images and conceptions about their value within their respective groups. In short, one guiding question was to explore whether there existed different sources of cultural self-esteem.[2] Secondly, we wanted to observe how the workshop participants present themselves in the presence of women from neighboring or distant ethnic groups and also to foreign females. The assumption was that the workshop situation, i.e. the direct contact with females from different cultural background, and with females from the same cultural background, but who are in different life stages, would enhance the participants' awareness of their own cultural particularities and also of their individual statuses and roles.

The organizers hoped that this situation would enhance self-reflection more than is the case for example, during interviews held in the field, when women are in their own familiar setting. Besides, the absence of males was believed to enable the guests to speak freely about gender issues and personal experiences.[3]

Guiding questions during the workshop concerned the ideal concepts of a "good girl", "a proper bride", "a proud woman, wife and mother" and related sources of female self-esteem and pride. To address these questions the guests were asked

2 Ivo Strecker suggested having a women's workshop on this topic as a follow-up of the workshop held in 2001 (see Brüderlin, this volume). It was organized in connection with a field excursion of seven students of the Department of Anthropology and African Studies at Mainz University. The students spent several weeks in groups of two among the Maale, Ari, Dassanetch, Kara and Bashada observing and participating in girls' and women's lives. Each student group then invited three females to the workshop (a girl, a young married woman and an elderly woman). Additionally, guests were invited from Arbore, Hamar and Banna by Jean Lydall, and by Christina Gabbert and Susanne Epple, both of whom were at that time research fellows of the SFB 295, subproject C7 (later E2, see Strecker, preface to this volume). The workshop was held over a three-day period with morning and afternoon sessions. The participants were split up into small groups of six to ten people and new discussion rounds were set up daily so that each participant had the chance to meet and talk with all others. Though some women were bilingual, there were still four different languages to be translated (Hamar, Aari, Daasanech and Maale).

3 Some women were accompanied to Jinka by their husbands, but males were not allowed to attend the discussions.

about visible and invisible markers of female statuses, including questions on age and gender specific dress and adornment and their social and symbolical meaning; on expected behavior at different life stages; rites of passage and connected changes in social relationships. Besides comparing cultural concepts and practices related to girl- and womanhood in different ethnic groups, we also wanted to explore the participants' feelings towards their roles in their respective societies, for example by extending enquiry on cultural ideals towards individual experiences. The fact that from each group participants with different ages had come provided us with accounts based on remembered or immediate experience by senior representatives on their past and present life stages, as well as with immediate experience and wishes and worries about their future by younger participants on present and future phases of life.

The outcomes of the workshop resulted in a combination of a comparative analysis of the girls' and women's accounts and dialogues on their lived experiences as females in specific cultural context and also on their views on cultural difference among neighboring groups, as well as reflections on the dynamics of individual workshop sessions. Ethnographic literature, where available, has been used to supplement the recorded data where needed.

Convincing oneself and others

In all societies individuals pass through a series of life stages that are connected to cultural expectations, rights and duties, and specific role behavior. The status of an individual is usually made visible to others (for example through dress or behavior) to set the frame for interaction and avoid misunderstandings (Goffman 1974). Status changes are often even more emphasized than the somewhat stable status: they are usually marked by rites of passage meant to help the individual not only to endure and adapt to sometimes painful transformations, but also to inform the public on the new social person and implicit new relationships (Van Gennep 1960; Gluckman 1962). Initiation, or 'life-crisis rituals' (Turner 1969), such as the transition from childhood or adolescence into adulthood, are often the most dramatic rites of passage, but also smaller steps can be marked visibly and have great impact on an individual's life.

Rites of passage can involve painful procedures both physically or psychologically, and also a new social status can be connected to difficult tasks, unpleasant duties, or complicated relationships. Therefore, it is essential that individuals are culturally and socially motivated to undergo such status changes instead of avoiding them or simply running away. Motivations could be the prospect of achieving a higher social status than the previous one and to thereby enjoy additional social recognition and privileges; or becoming the member of a social group of individuals who share the same status including its privileges and duties. The identification with a certain new status or group of people also means to distance oneself and create boundaries to other statuses or groups.

Ideas on social inclusion and exclusion through the creation of boundaries have been elaborated mainly in the context of interethnic relations (Barth 1969; Schlee 2008, 2009). According to Schlee, identification with a certain group of people can be widened and also narrowed, depending on the situation and preference of the agents. There may be situations in which it is preferable to keep a group small, he explains, for example when it comes to sharing resources, and others when it is advantageous of identifying with a bigger group, for example when it comes to defense against enemies (2009: 2f). Generally, he explains, different categories of identification can be chosen to be used as identity markers. Common categories are language, religion, common descent or shared ancestry, skin-color, but also any other kind of "subsystems of culture or complexes of symbols" can serve the same purpose and be used as "identity markers at various levels of inclusivity" (Schlee 2009: 2). The criteria of one category can be broadened or narrowed in order to increase or decrease inclusiveness and thereby manipulate the number of people who are considered to share the same identity. Schlee gives the example of language, where one could stress the local dialect (a small entity), the linguistic community (medium level), or the language family (broadest category), which would include the greatest number of people (Schlee 2008: 45). Another way of in- or excluding others is to "switch" to a different category[4] of identification (Schlee 2009: 2), instead of for example stressing common language one can decide to give priority to common religion and thereby switch alliances. Such categories do not exclude each other, but rather coexist and are ordered hierarchically by importance. This order can change during specific interactions with people from different cultural background at a given moment when an individual, calculating the cost and benefit, determines which aspect or category of his/her identity should be prioritized (Schlee 2008: 43-49).

Gregory Bateson said that "cases of contact between differentiated groups of individuals, e.g., between the sexes, between old and young, between aristocracy and plebs, between clans, etc., groups which live together in approximate equilibrium" can also be considered as culture contact (1972: 64). Following this I suggest Schlee's idea can be applied to intra-ethnic contact between people of different statuses who may want to identify with people of a different status in a given situation and to draw a boundary between them in another situation. Hereby, they convince themselves and others of their 'public self-image' (Goffman 1967) and also protect their 'face' (Brown/Levinson 1978) in a situation of cultural contact.[5] To understand the different sides/aspects of an individual's Self that are enacted in different situations, yet kept together as a kind of unit through inner dialogue the concept of the 'dialogical Self' as described by Van Meijl (2008) is useful. Van Meijl uses the concept for individuals who live in multicultural situations, such as

4 Schlee uses the terms 'category' and 'dimension of identification' interchangeably in different publications (2008, 2009).

5 On "cultural contact" and "face" in Southern Ethiopia see Strecker and Lydall (eds.) 2006.

migrants, to describe the multiplicity of the inner Self which identifies at the same time with its original culture and the new society—depending on the situation. I suggest that the concept also helps to understand individuals who are confronted with various, possibly even conflicting roles they have to accept within their own society, such as when they are at the verge of changing their role, for example adolescent girls who are close to getting married. It can also help to understand people's memories or views of their own past, such as when an elderly woman remembers her own youth.

The workshop participants' background

South Omo is known for its cultural and linguistic diversity. The geography of the land varies from midland to lowland and people have adapted their livelihood accordingly, practicing pastoralism in combination with slash and burn or flood-retreat cultivation, fishing, hunting, gathering and apiculture. The girls and women who attended the workshop came from eight different ethnic groups. Some of these groups are culturally and linguistically very similar, others different. The Bashada, Hamar, Banna for example are nearly identical in language and customs, and the Kara speak a variation of the same South-Omotic language and also have close cultural ties. The Arbore and Daasanech belong to the Cushitic language family and have cultural and historical connections with each other, while the Omotic Maale and Aari also show similarities in language and livelihood. Besides such clusters of ethnic groups who share a similar language and culture, there also exist many intersections and historical links with others. These relations are too complex to be discussed here in detail, but it is important to mention that there are complex economic, ritual and social ties and frequent interaction between the various peoples living in South Omo. Knowledge about cultural neighbors is primarily achieved and sustained through intermarriage, bondfriendships, ritual cooperation, sharing common pastures, trade and exchange. However, as it is mostly males who travel, females' knowledge on the neighboring groups is limited.[6] The workshop was therefore an opportunity for the participants to meet women about whose lives they knew little or nothing or only by hearsay.

Elements of social recognition during adolescence

During the workshop, many of the discussions dealt with girlhood, i.e. the time before marriage and the changes expected when a girl gets married and moves to her husband. Most participants agreed that girlhood is the time of most freedom in a female's life. Although girls usually learn how to do the household chores at an

6 See for example Sobania 1991 and Ayalew 1995, 1997 on economic exchange; Girke 2010 on bondfriendship; Epple 2010b on historical and social links, and Thubauville 2010b on intermarriage in South Omo.

early age and contribute significantly to the work done in the household, they still take the liberty to enjoy themselves with peers and friends. In different sessions on the daily lives of girls various areas of social recognition were identified.

The social meanings of dress, jewellery and body-adornment

As statuses can be made visible through dress, hairstyle or decorations, the culture-specific dresses and adornments of girls and women were one of the first topics to be discussed. It quickly became apparent that these visual markers are not only visible indicators of social status but tell additional stories about their wearers (see WT: 8 on brides in Arbore, 22-25 dress of girls in Maale and Ari, 63, dress of girls in Daasanech, 120-124 dress of girls in Bashada and Kara)

In contrast to males, females are usually adorned already at very early age, having their gender emphasized from the time when they are young. Dress is changing with growing age, and the older a girl gets the more will she be adorned. Adolescent girls usually wear a lot of jewellery and are considered as most beautiful. Skirts and capes made of goat or antelope skin are still common in many parts of South Omo, such as in Hamar, Banna, Bashada, Kara, Daasanech and Arbore, and to some extent still in Maale, and size, shape, type of leather or decoration of dresses differ depending on whether they belong to a girl, a bride or a married woman. In Maale, for example, small girls until the age of twelve traditionally wore a special skirt called *shiro*, made out of cotton strings, which later, with the beginning of puberty, would be replaced by leather skirts made from goat-skin. At marriage this leather skirt was decorated with a black leather strip, which clearly showed that the female had become a bride. Today, many Maale women have traded their leather clothing for cotton skirts (WT: 26). In some areas where leather is still commonly used, such as Bashada, Banna and Hamar, girls usually adorn their leather skirts and aprons with colorful beads and cowry shells, and sometimes wear furry leather strings below their knees or above their elbows. But also among these groups, at the time of marriage, all dresses and decorations have to be removed and are replaced by new ones which indicate the individual's new status.

While leather skirts are rarely found in Maale today, beads and bracelets are still commonly worn, and the older a girl gets, the more jewellery she will wear. Jewellery was traditionally given to the girls by their fathers as a sign of their appreciation for the work the daughters do at home:

> Kalamo (girl from Maale): Like in Aari, we in Maale work in work parties for our father. After the harvest has been collected, our father exchanges a goat with the blacksmith for these bracelets and gives them to us. (…) As nowadays there are markets all over Maale, we (girls) can make beer or something else and sell it so that we can buy the bracelets ourselves. Only in Gongoda Maale (lowland area) where there is no market, the giving of gifts is still practiced. To know the right size the father measures his daughter's hand with grass, fixes it and takes it to the blacksmith. Before giving the bracelets to his

> daughter he will perform a ritual for the bracelets. Only then will he put them around her arm (WT: 23f).[7]

To express one's appreciation of the girls' work by rewarding them with jewellery is also in Hamar and Bashada, where girls receive iron rings or brass bracelets for their arms, legs and necks as a kind of payment for their work in their own or in their relative's houses (Lydall on Hamar 1993: 39; Epple 2007: 129 on Bashada). As the girls traditionally do not buy their own jewellery, wearing many beads or rings is besides decoration also an indicator that a girl is appreciated for the work she contributes to the family.

Decorations can also be applied directly on girls' bodies at different stages of their lives. The hairstyle, for example, tells in many groups about social age and marital status of a female, but also decorative scarring on arms, chests or backs as well as tattooing of faces, the removal of the lower incisors, the piercing or cutting of the lower lip are common practices in South Omo. Other than dress and jewellery, these applications on the body are permanent and thus become a permanent part of the self-image of a person. Among the Maale, girls have their faces beautified by permanent tattoos known as *konko*: one long line leads from forehead down to the nose, three half circles are cut next to each eye and three vertical lines on the chin (see Thubauville 2010a: 105f). The lines are first applied by a mixture of charcoal and the juice of a certain plant, and then inserted by a thorn or knife. The procedure is performed by female local specialists on adolescent girls who are preparing to get married. According to Thubauville, the Maale tattoos are considered as a sign of beauty and do not have any further symbolic meaning (2010a: 105f). During the workshop the Maale guests explained the meaning of the tattoos:

> Dasa (married woman/Maale): In Maale the girls get *konko*, 'permanent tattoos', after they have had their first menstruation.
>
> Sophia (student): Why do some women only have *konko* on their forehead and nose and others also on their chin and around their eyes?
>
> Zeleketch (elderly woman/Maale): A girl has to be very strong to get all three konko as it hurts a lot to have them made. The painted tattoos you saw in Maale on some girls' hands were non-permanent. These are just for decoration and can be worn at any age. Nowadays, girls prefer the non-permanent ones because there is no pain involved.[8]

As its application involves the endurance of physical pain, a facial tattoo in Maale not only shows that a girl has achieved fertility, but is also a sign of individual strength and courage. Among the ethnic groups who live further south differing concepts of beauty which involve changes of the body have continued to exist,

7 In the following I will refer to quotations from the workshop transcriptions as WT. The full transcriptions of the workshop (Epple/Brüderlin 2004) are available online (http://www.uni-mainz.de/Organisationen/SORC/ content/ view/58/41/). In some places I refer to an earlier unpublished version of the workshop transcripts (Epple/Brüderlin 2003), which contains some dialogues that have later been taken out as some sessions were incompletely recorded.

8 See Epple/Brüderlin (2003: 19).

some of which are also physically painful. The removal of the lower incisors among the Bashada, Hamar, Banna and Kara and to some extent also Daasanech and Arbore, is common among girls who are in their early teens (in some groups also among males).[9] In Bashada, the removal of the teeth leads to an increase of the girl's status and recognition within her local peer-group: girls who had their incisors removed become socially senior to their peers who still have them and they provoke and insult their now socially junior peers. "*Ukuli* (lit.: donkey), you may not dance with me anymore!" is a common swearword, and the perceived status difference is made public during the night dances where girls who had their teeth removed will stand and dance together, while those who still have them must stand with much younger and smaller ones. The public exclusion and insult motivates girls who have been afraid to undergo the same procedure in order to re-join her original peer-group (Epple 2010: 106).[10] During the workshop, Arti from Bashada explained the feelings the insult causes in a girl:

> Arti (girl/Bashada): If my friends have taken their teeth out without me knowing, then they will come up to me and tell me. "Who has taken them out for you?" I will ask. "So and so has taken them out."—"I will not have mine pulled out", I will say. "It is too painful."—"Well, then you are not allowed to walk around with me anymore!" she [my friend] will say and be mad at me. And I will say: "What am I afraid of? Will I die?" Then I go and get my teeth pulled out, too. Everything that hurts I can bear. (…) Then I will go and provoke the others and quarrel with them… (WT: 58f)

When asked why the teeth are pulled out, Arti said that she did not know the reason why.

> Arti (girl/Bashada): I do not know why. In former times people would not do it. You cannot bite meat any more. Some girls say they do not want to have the teeth pulled out. The girls who are very proud will not have them pulled out. If you don't want to you don't have to. It is not a *gilo* [here: ritual that must be performed]. (WT: 59). Kerri, a young married woman from Bashada and at the time of the workshop the mother of an about 8 years old daughter, added to Arti's explanations:
>
> But if you are very, very proud you have them pulled out. Those girls who are brave and proud have them pulled out. But there is nothing special to it. (…) It is only a matter of beauty. Now, at the moment, all the small girls in our village are having it done.
>
> My daughter Mirja has also been provoked by her peers. But we told her to have it done next year. I said to my daughter: "Do not do that! You won't be able to eat corn

9 Teeth are given special attention in Bashada, Hamar, Banna and Kara: for example white and straight teeth are often commented on as a sign of beauty when talking about people's looks; the coming out of the first teeth (lower incisors) is closely observed, as in case the upper incisors or other teeth grow before them this is seen as an indicator that a child is impure and has been conceived before the mother has performed the necessary rituals. Such children are believed to bring misfortune to their society and therefore abandoned in the bush or, in more recent times, given for adoption to towns' people.

10 Bashada boys use the same strategy of insulting each other when it comes to circumcision. Here, circumcised boys pretend that the uncircumcised ones stink, while they, the circumcised boys pretend that they are about to become sexually active (see more on this in Epple 2010a: 101-104).

> anymore!" I don't want her to have it done. If you pull out your front teeth, all the others will fall out too. All of them will be ruined. That is why I told her not to do it. Maybe she will do it secretly. If she does it secretly there is nothing I can do. The girls who want to be pretty do not listen to their mothers. They go ahead and have it done. But if my daughter has her teeth pulled out I will not be mad at her (WT: 59).

The discussion showed different perspectives of two females belonging to the same ethnic group on the same issue. While both identified with the practice and agreed that the removing of the incisors was a voluntary decision mainly done out of aesthetic reasons, Arti presented the perspective of an adolescent girl stressing that not only bearing the pain, but also withstanding the peer-group's pressure could be seen as the sign of pride and strength. She here alluded to the individuality and independence males and females enjoy and are expected to display in Bashada—while at the same time adhering to cultural norms and values. Kerri argued from the position of a young mother, who is proud of her growing daughter but at the same time concerned about her well-being. She was undecided whether she should approve of this practice: on the one hand she wanted to act as a responsible mother who would like to stop her daughter from having her teeth removed, and she even dramatized the effects of the teeth removal by saying that it would cause all other teeth to fall out. On the other hand, Kerri emphasized that only the very courageous and proud girls choose to bear the physical pain to become more beautiful, hereby appreciating the practice. By telling that her daughter had already been asked by her friends to have the teeth taken out and that she would accept if her daughter decided to have the teeth removed without her parents' knowledge, Kerri implied that this secret act would be a sign of her daughter's strength and courage. Next, the Kara females presented their views on the issue:

> Torgo (married woman/Kara): In Kara, all girls of one age meet secretly at night and say, "We want to have our teeth pulled out now!" and the next morning they will go and have it done.
>
> Galte (girl/Kara): Men do not do it anymore. They used to have it done in former times. In Kara, only girls will do that. You only start wearing the nail through your lower lip after you have taken out your teeth.[11](...) we all have it done. There is nobody who says "I am afraid" and who does not have it done. We do not provoke each other. We do not fight with each other. We meet secretly and then have it done the next morning. (WT: 59)

Both Galte and Torgo asserted that in Kara, provocation among age-peers was not needed to motivate girls to have their teeth taken out. By juxtaposing these two approaches, the Kara females drew a clear line between Bashada and Kara. Indirectly they expressed that in Kara, girls' peer groups are rather homogenous, while in Bashada they constitute rather heterogeneous groups of individuals some of which need the direct pressure of their peers to have enough courage to undergo

[11] Kara girls pierce their lower lips with nails for decorative purposes. This is not common in Bashada.

the painful procedure. This image was further confirmed when Torgo went on explaining how the decorative scarring on Kara females' bodies was done:

> Torgo (married woman/ Kara): (With scarring) it is the same. We say: "Tomorrow we all will have our scars cut together!" and all girls will go and have their scars cut. You have them done when you are already grown up though. All will have them done together.
>
> Pitta (elderly women/Bashada): We used to do that when we were younger. A lot of people have done that in former times.
>
> Kerri (married woman/Bashada): In Bashada some will start having scars cut, but then they become afraid and stop in the midst of it. My mother still has some on her back and shoulders. (...) About the ones who have themselves scarred one says that they are brave and strong. And of the ones who have it not done people will say that they were afraid and weak. (WT: 60f.)

Pitta and Kerri from Bashada here re-entered the discussion and confirmed that also in the context of scarring, Bashada females decide individually instead of acting as a group. Pitta remembered times when scarring was much more common in Bashada, hereby probably referring to the time of her youth, a time when the Bashada say they were culturally much closer to the Kara. Kerri, as a younger woman, stressed again that decorative scarring was seen as a sign of strength and that refraining from it may cause gossip. This, however, does not seem to be a real intimidation to individuals, as to my own observation in Bashada, only very few women have decorative scars, and only about half of the females have their incisors removed. It rather has to be understood as a cultural ideal that one can choose follow, but is not obliged to, comparable to beauty ideals in the western world that one can adhere to but can also choose to ignore.

Besides scars cut for decorative purpose, most Hamar, Banna Bashada and Kara females also have big scars on their backs from ritualized whipping. During male initiation, the classificatory sisters of an initiate (both girls and women) let themselves be whipped to publicly demonstrate their grief that their brother is becoming an adult now. The scars they receive during the whipping are not only a sign of their love for their brother, but also a testimony of their braveness and courage to endure physical pain.[12] These scars are very visible and shown with pride, and the initiates sing about those females who let themselves be beaten by them. Tina, a student from Germany, wanted to know what the scars mean in comparison to the decorative scars:

> Tina (student): What about the whipping scars? Do you consider them pretty? In Dambaiti (Hamar) I was told that they symbolize the strength of the woman.
>
> Kerri (married woman/Bashada) and Alga (elderly woman/Bashada)(both talking at the same time, complementing each other's sentences): You do not have the beating scars out of beauty, it is our gilo (here: meaningful ritual/practice that should be performed). If a girl does not have any scars from her brother's *ukuli* (initiation), people will say, 'Didn't she let herself be beaten for her brothers? What kind of a girl is that?' (WT: 61)

12 This practice has been widely discussed in Strecker 1993; Lydall 1994; Epple 2009, 2010.

Kerri and Alga here strongly emphasized the difference between scarring for decorative and aesthetic purposes and the scars obtained from ritual whipping, when they said that the whipping scars are worn due to 'tradition', and not for the 'beauty'. Hereby they made clear that they are much more meaningful.[13] I can confirm this from my own observation, as I have never seen any adult female without the whipping scars on her back though the whipping is in fact voluntary. But I have observed young girls who were actually crying out of disappointment because their fathers forbid them to be whipped as they were too small. When next, the Kara women were asked whether they are also beaten by the initiates, Kerri answered first:

> Kerri (married woman/Bashada) (laughing): No. They take their *gungulo* (calabashes) with them and beat the *maz* (initiates) on their heads with it!
>
> Torgo (married woman/Kara): In Kara, the *maz* (initiates) do not beat you. The *donza* (married men) are the ones who beat you. You (towards Bashada women) are beaten by the *maz*. In Kara, all men leap over the cattle together in one night. The *donza* (married men) are the ones who beat you (shows a new scar from the last leap over the cattle in Kara). My relative has been initiated recently. We were whipped there and the wounds are still fresh.
>
> Kerri (married woman/Bashada): If a girl or a woman only has a few scars people say, that she does not bear the pain for her brothers. She is considered a coward. (…)
>
> Galte (girl from Kara): When my brother Ariyo leaps, I am going to get myself severely whipped for him! (WT: 61)

Kerri here interrupted the conversation joking about the Kara practices that were slightly different from those in Bashada. Generally females are not allowed to beat males in Bashada, so that the very idea of smashing something on a man's head may not only seem funny, but also against cultural norms, and the idea had often caused laughter when I heard people in Bashada talk about it. Torgo from Kara reacted by explaining further differences between Kara and Bashada, mentioning that different to Bashada, where initiation is individual, while in Kara it is done in group. Despite the differences in the performance of the initiation ritual and the whipping, the females from Kara also clearly identified with the idea that the ritual whipping was a sign of a female's bravery: Torgo, by showing her most recent scars, and Galte by asserting she would let herself be whipped severely soon. Besides, other than in the context of decorative scarring, none of the participants expressed any doubt that females might refrain from participating in the whipping.

Such mutilations, it became very clear, are not part of the initiation from childhood to adulthood, but nevertheless mark a boundary between categories of adolescents, i.e. those who have undergone or those who have not undergone these procedure. As Van Gennep (1960: 72) explained, "the mutilated individual is

13 Generally whipping with a wand made of a tree called *baraza* is seen as a way of guiding and blessing someone and common in different domains of Bashada culture (see also Epple 2009; Brüderlin, in this volume).

removed from the common mass of humanity by rite of separation (this is the idea behind cutting, piercing etc.), which automatically incorporates him into a defined group; since the operation leaves ineradicable traces, the incorporation is permanent". Tattoos, scars and removed incisors can thus be seen as visible identity markers of adolescent peer groups, or of 'sub-categories' to the category of 'unmarried girl'.

Labor participation as source of pride

During the workshop, participants from different backgrounds expressed that another source of female social recognition was the participation in labor activities (in Bashada and Kara WT: 27-35; in Arbore; Aari Maale WT: 125-127). Children are usually involved in daily household chores from an early age on, and girls grow into their social roles as females by assisting their mothers. In many of the South Omo groups, the adolescent girl is expected to be able to perform all the tasks of an adult woman.[14]

In the various groups, different patterns exist in the division of labor, determining which chores should be done by whom. In a discussion among Ari, Maale, Arbore, Bashada and Kara females, the girls and women told each other about their duties at home. In this context, differences between the Arbore who rely more on livestock and the Aari who rely more on agriculture came up:

> Lago (married woman/Arbore) (*to the Aari girl*): Don't you go to fetch wood, don't you get water, and don't you herd the cattle?
>
> Galchi (girl/Aari): No, we do not herd the cattle. The boys do not let us herd cattle. If I have no brothers, my father will bring my cousin.
>
> Lago (married woman/Arbore): So why do you drink the milk if you do not herd the cattle? *(laughter)* As a girl it is good to herd the cattle for your father, you become proud. You drink the milk and you become proud. You drink the milk and herd the cattle together with all your age-mates and friends, that is good. What is good about having the boys herd the cattle and not the girls? *(laughter among participants)*
>
> Galchi (girl/Aari): But we do all the work in the house, everything for our mother and our father, that's our pride.
>
> Lago (married woman/Arbore): Our boys herd the cattle when they go to the cattle camps, but most of the cattle tended close to the house are herded by the girls. A girl who tends cattle, tends cattle, tends cattle a lot makes her father very proud. (...) He will say, "I have a girl who is as strong as a boy!"
>
> If a father does not have any grown up sons, the cattle will be sent to far places with other boys, but his daughters will herd the cattle that are close to the house. (...). All Arbore-girls can do this on their own.
>
> Galchi (girl/Aari): But if you have brothers, why do you need to herd the cattle?
>
> Lago (married woman/Arbore): It is our tradition. *(laughter)*. First of all, one work we girls do not do is to plough the fields. The men go to plough the fields and make the

[14] On growing up in Daasanech see Elfmann 2004, on Maale Thubauville 2010, on Hamar Lydall 1993 and on Bashada Epple 2010.

> fences of the cattle-enclosures. The men plough the fields with the digging-stick. We women plant the seeds and harvest. (...)
>
> Baro (married woman/Arbore): The girls tend the cattle and bring the cattle to the water-holes. But the water-hole itself and the digging of the fields is done by the men. The hard work is done by the boys and our brothers. And we tend the cattle. (...) (WT: 125-126)

As can be seen from the contributions of the participants and the occasional laughter, the tone in this session was playful and yet somewhat provocative. When Lago from Arbore expressed surprise that the Aari girls were not actively involved in cattle herding and milking, she did this by challenging the Aari girl. Claiming that by herding cattle a girl proves to be as strong as a boy, and only thereby deserves to drink milk and make her father proud she ridiculed the Aari division of labor. Galchi responded similarly provocative, explaining that Aari girls had an easier life, as they mainly work in the household and do not need to suffer herding cattle—a clear responsibility of males among the more agricultural Aari.

This session showed the variations in the economic activities of females in different ethnic groups and it appeared that where pastoralism is the primary mode of subsistence, there is a tendency that females are more integrated in the herding process than in primarily agricultural societies. In the discussions on this topic, differing areas of female identification were presented (work in the household, on the fields or with cattle), all of which were used to assert or measure pride, self-esteem, and individual relevance in the respective societies.

Painful passages and the identification with new roles

Leaving girlhood

The passage from girlhood to womanhood represents one of the greatest changes in a female's life. It is visibly marked among the groups the workshop guests came from by a change in clothing, jewellery and hairstyle and can involve other different ritual steps, such as circumcision among the Arbore, and/or by a period of seclusion among the Maale, Bashada, Hamar, Banna and Kara (WT: 9, 22, 39ff, 82, 119, 123ff). It also often involves that a girl moves far away from her family and thus begins a new life in an unknown environment with a husband, family and people she in many cases also has not known before.[15] Several workshop participants mentioned that married women have less freedom to move around spatially and to spend time with their friends, as they carry the responsibility for their own household and family. These drastic changes, it was expressed, are perceived as difficult and even painful by many women, and they scare many girls before marriage. The girls from Bashada and Kara asserted that they would like to continue living as girls as long as

[15] For more detailed descriptions on marriage and the bridal period see Lydall 1994, 1991F, 1992F, 1994F on the Hamar; Elfmann 2004 on the Daassanech, Epple 2010 on the Bashada; Peller 2002 on the Arbore; Thubauville 2010 on the Maale.

possible (WT: 38). However, as the discussions also showed, assuming a new role as a wife also contributes to gaining new pride and self-esteem:

> Kerri (married woman/Bashada): When you are a girl you think it is awful to marry. But when you have become a bride and you have your first child, you start thinking that being a girl is awful. Then you say, "I should have married earlier. If I had married earlier, I could have had two children by now! Maybe I could have three children like this other woman. I would have a grown-up daughter like her, and my daughter could grind the flour for me." That is how we think and talk then [as women]. (WT: 38)

Kerri being a young woman here remembers her own feelings from when she was a girl, and that it was only after becoming a young adult, that she could see things differently. Hereby she acknowledges that perspectives change when statuses change, and also that it is culturally appropriate and accepted for girls to be afraid to get married. In Bashada and Hamar girls are even culturally expected to express their reluctance to get married and that they dislike their future husbands lest they could be ridiculed (Epple 2010: 185; Lydall 1994).

The day of moving in with the husband constitutes the greatest step. In Bashada, Hamar and Banna, girls are sometimes betrothed at a very young age, but then continue living with their families until they have reached the appropriate age. To move in shortly after the sealing of the marriage is very uncommon.[16] In Kara and Arbore girls are not betrothed but directly married as adolescents or young adults and then move to their husbands immediately. These differences were emphasized in the discussions and again used for comparison between the different cultures:

> Arti (girl/Bashada): The good thing in Bashada is that when you get married, you do not start living with your husband immediately. You stay at your parents' house for some more years. And during these years you are still free to go dancing. You are free. You are still a real girl.
>
> When you have grown up, your husband might get hold of you [means: abduct you] in the bush and take you to his house. Maybe you run away again and then he gets hold of you again. Then you run away again. If you do not want to become a woman yet, you run away.
>
> If your father does not give you to your husband for a long time you can also decide, "Ah, I do not want to be a girl anymore!" You go by yourself to live with your husband. Or maybe your father decides and says, "She is big now, she will go with her husband!" Then you will have a big feast. All your friends come, it is called *gaido*. After this you leave and go to live with your husband.
>
> So the good thing is that we do not go to live with our husbands after we have been married. In Arbore, as far as I understood, you get married and then you immediately go and live with your husband. Your girlhood is finished from that day on. (…) (WT: 124).

[16] Sometimes, when a man is in urgent need of a wife (for example a widower who needs a female to care and cook for him and his children) the process is speeded up, so that only a few months after the sealing of the marriage the wife is brought in.

Arti here stressed that in the time before a girl moves to her husband she girl can still enjoy freedom, but also prepare herself and get used to the idea of being someone's wife. The rather common practice of abduction of adolescent girls by their husbands was presented as very undramatic. Arti did not mention the force with which girls are kidnapped on their way to the market or to the waterhole and taken to the husband's home to be made into a bride. She rather decided to emphasize the girls' agency saying that a girl who is not ready to become a wife yet can decide to run away, return to their father's house and continue living as girl for another one or two years. In fact, as common as the abduction of girls is in Bashada, it is also very common that girls escape. It often happens several consecutive years until a girl finally stays with her husband. She also mentions the cultural ideal that a girl is given by her parents who organize a farewell celebration for her, and the rare cases in which a girl leaves her parents and moves to her husband by her own initiative. Arti's final provocative comment on Arbore practices: "Your girlhood is finished from that day [the day of marriage] on!" was immediately answered in a similar tone:

> Baro (married woman/Arbore): So in Bashada you go to live with your husband's when you are very old. We in Arbore go when we are still young! (*laughter*) For us it is good to go when we are still young.
>
> Arti (girl/Bashada): But we are the same age! Maybe I will go to my husband next year, you already have gone there! I will be a girl for one more year! It is much better! (WT: 125f)

Though earlier in the discussion all females had agreed that it was best to enjoy freedom as a girl long as possible, here again differences were emphasized and own cultural practices presented as being better than those of the others, though Arti's last comment, i.e. that the actual age when a girl leaves home may not really differ much in Arbore and Bashada, is probably close to reality. It was not clear why the tone of this session was rather provocative and even aggressive in the wording used by the participants. The reason may lie in the fact that departure from home is generally perceived as painful and thus constitutes an emotionally sensitive issue. The girls and young women in the workshop may have been trying to convince themselves and others that in their own cultural context at least the time for freedom given to girls was longer than in other places.

Bridehood

In many groups moving in with the husband means to enter a time of seclusion as a bride. Torgo from Kara and Kerri from Bashada gave a description of what it means to be a bride:

> Torgo (married woman/Kara): While you are a bride you do not talk much. You are shy. You talk once, twice and then you do not say anything anymore. But after you have given birth to one, two or three children, you talk a lot.
>
> Kerri (married woman/Bashada): It is the same in Bashada. (...). When I was a bride my husband did not talk to me. He just looked at me. He would step out of the door and

> I would follow him and bring him his rifle and his bullet belt. (…) I had to know what to do by myself. I handed him his sandals. He took everything and left. Then I sat inside the house. When he came back I was sitting there. I had been sitting there the whole time, waiting for him. When he came I went outside to take his things. I took his rifle. I took off his sandals, but he would step hard on the ground so that I could not pull them off. I had to try hard to take them off. I brought the rifle into the house. I took some cool water and placed it outside so that he could wash himself with it. Meanwhile I had laid out the cowhide for him. He sat down on it. I put on my cape to pour some coffee and I served him some. First, I placed it next to me so that it cooled off. I first checked if it was cool enough before I handed it to him. But he would not take it. He simply sat there and looked around. My arm had nearly fallen off until he finally accepted the coffee. As a bride you suffer a lot![17]
>
> Once my bridal time has ended and after I have given birth to a child, I won't take his things anymore when he comes home. I won't give him any tooth stick anymore. Only slowly, and with a lot of effort, do we get used to each other. (WT: 55 ff)

As Torgo indicated and Kerri described at length, the rather distanced behavior between husband and wife goes on for months and sometimes years. Typically, it is said to change after the first child is born and becomes even more relaxed when a woman has given birth to several children. Like Kerri, many women in Bashada I talked to seemed to be delighted in talking about their bridehood as a time of distress and suffering. To my observation, however, many brides are treated friendly by their husbands, especially if the husband is young. I did observe though, that husbands generally do not talk much to their wives, especially in front of others. It seems that Kerri's account partly represents a more conservative notion from the past, which is still considered as the culturally appropriate way of interaction between husband and wife. Part of the cultural ideal or norm is that husband and wife do not like each other, and especially females are expected to display resentment and antipathy. Only after years are the spouses expected to like each other. Females are even expected to resist the dominance of their husbands by deliberately performing household tasks badly and, thereby, provoking them (see more on this in Epple 2010, and on Hamar in Lydall 1994). Kerri did not mention this, but after having vividly described a bride's suffering, she made clear that women should bear this difficult time:

> Kerri (married woman/Bashada): That's why the stupid girls run away from their husbands. They are scared. The ones who say they do not want to suffer like this run away. Those who say that their father has given them do not run away, they stay with their husbands. They will say that they will get used to it, no matter how hard it is. (WT: 55 ff)

[17] Kerri went on describing how he finally took the coffee, she handed other things to him, and how she had to read from his eyes what he expected her to do. See transcription of the workshop for the full account.

With this comment on the expected behavior of females at the time of marriage, Kerri explained that enduring the difficulties of being a young wife can serve as a source of pride for females, as it is an opportunity to prove their strength.

Female genital cutting

In South Omo, only the Daasanech and Arbore practice female genital cutting and in both groups it is a prerequisite for marriage. While in Arbore the operation is done individually as part of the marriage ritual at late adolescence, Daasanech girls are cut in groups before puberty (Elfmann: 2005: 67ff). The various meanings and complex interpretations of this practice cannot be discussed here, and they were also not discussed during the workshop. However, the way the women from Arbore and Daasanech explained this practice to women from groups where this practice is unknown deserves some further mention. Elelle, a married woman from Daasanech, elaborated that this practice was meant to clearly identify a girl as a female and as a human being. She also indicated that group pressure plays a role in motivating girls to be circumcised:

> Elelle (Daasanech): If you are not cut the other people will insult you and say that you are like a wild animal. They say that the clitoris must be removed because it is something male. To become a woman you have to cut off the clitoris. If you want to insult someone you say "You are a clitoris!" They will say you are a wild animal if you have this thing which is male. A girl will be teased until she gets circumcised.[18]

The cutting is a rite of passage after which a Daasanech girl is considered a full female and allowed to wear the women's cotton dresses and to get married.[19] Similar to girls who undergo the scarring and removal of teeth in Bashada, Hamar, Banna and Kara, the girls are provoked or insulted in order to embarrass and thereby motivate them to have this painful procedure done and then be accepted into the group of 'real females'.

During a workshop session on bridehood and marriage, Lago explained how the circumcision was done in Arbore. When Kerri from Bashada showed herself irritated, Lago emphasized that girls strive to be cut because they want to be like the other Arbore women:

> Kerri (married woman/Bashada): Bride! Is the cutting bad? Wouldn't it be good to leave that custom?
>
> Lago (married woman/Arbore): No. You have to do it. When you are a girl you want to have it done because it is your tradition. Your grandmother, your mother, everybody has had it done. If you were told, "You will not be circumcised!" you would be very unhappy and think "Why? What have I done wrong? Am I a Hamar woman? Why don't they do it for me?" Then you would run away. (WT: 119)

18 Epple/Brüderlin 2003: 92.

19 Exceptions can be made when a girl is 'forgotten' during the circumcision of her age-mates, i.e. when she is absent, in the fields or so. In such a case, Allele explained during the workshop, the girl gets married and circumcised later, when she has given birth to her first child and is under pain anyways (Elfmann 2005: 79).

In an informal conversation before this workshop session, the young woman from Arbore had described to me how painful this procedure had been for her. She talked about how she had suffered, not only from the physical pain, but also from the fact that she was married to someone else than the boyfriend of her girlhood.[20] During the encounter with women from other ethnic groups, Lago defended her own cultural background in a way that not only emphasized the differences between Arbore and Hamar practices, but even represented the Hamar as people an Arbore girl would not like to be identified with. This situation clearly showed that practices which are painful and difficult to undergo for the individual can be presented as important and desirable in a public situation when confronted with women from other ethnic groups. She here presents the female circumcision as an identity marker to draw a clear line between the Arbore and other ethnic groups, and also between girls and married women in Arbore. Female genital cutting is unknown, considered strange or even harmful among the other groups in South Omo. In Hamar, Banna and Bashada the removal or the injury of genital organs is believed to turn a human into a *mingi*, i.e., someone who is ritually unclean and thereby a danger to the community. A *mingi* person must be killed to avoid droughts, diseases or other disasters, and a *mingi* also loses all ties to his or her relatives, including not even being considered an ancestor after death.[21] Therefore, the reaction of Kerri from Bashada was probably not only based on the idea that the procedure is very painful, but also on the emic understanding that the practice would make a woman ritually unclean. Though she did not mention this in the discussion, Lago may have been aware of the Hamar view and therefore felt the need to defend the practice even more strongly.

Bridewealth as a source of pride

In all groups that participated in the workshop, bridewealth is common, even though the time when it is given (all at once before marriage or over several years in smaller installments), and also the kind and amount of gifts (cattle, small stock, honey, money, other items) varies. In a discussion round on the last day of the workshop, the participants turned to this topic, and instead of explaining their own practices, they started asking the anthropologists, the *ferenji* (foreigners) about their practices. Many had obviously heard that *ferenji* usually do not own cattle and when Arti from Bashada began asking questions about marriage and bridewealth customs in the '*ferenji*-land', the other girls and women began giggling and laughing:

[20] In Arbore it is not uncommon that premarital partners get married (personal communication, Christina Gabber 2004). In this case, however, this was not possible.

[21] The fact that some groups do cut the genitals of their females and others do not creates marriage prohibitions between the respective groups. However, there exist accounts of Hamar girls who had fallen in love with Arbore men. In order to get married the girls had to be circumcised according to Arbore customs. Having done so, their ties to their Hamar families were considered as being cut off, because they had turned *mingi* in the eyes of their relatives. Instead, these girls had fully assumed Arbore identity.

> Arti (girl/Bashada): When you marry and go to live with your husband, will anything be given to your father? Will there be honey and goats and cows? What is given to him? *(laughter among guests)*
>
> Lago (married woman/Arbore): They do not have goats! What shall they give? Or do they give money? They do not have goats! *(loud laughter)*
>
> Kristin (student/Germany): When you marry it is your own decision to get married and nobody will pay for it. But the father of the bride usually pays for the wedding. (...) And everybody brings presents for the couple. *(laughter)*
>
> Lago (married woman/Arbore): So, your father does not get anything when his daughter goes to marry (means: to live with her husband)? *(loud laughter)* Your mother has suffered a lot to give birth to you! But as the mother has suffered a lot, why should she just...
>
> Arti (girl/Bashada): She carried you around. What is that? She carried you around and she suffered and gave birth to you and she cannot eat (means here: does not receive) anything when you leave?
>
> Tina (student/Germany): But she is happy that you found somebody who will take care of you. And she will be proud and happy that you found somebody good.
>
> Arti (girl/Bashada): What is that? You are like wild creatures in the bush! You are animals! *(loud laughter)*
>
> Lago (married woman/Arbore): You are like animals because you just marry without any reason and you go away and you do not leave anything behind. Just like animals! (WT: 117)

Obviously, in the question of bridewealth, the girls and women from all the different groups were united in their feelings. The idea that that *ferenji* parents, especially mothers, do not get anything for all the pain they endured to bring up their daughters, caused laughter and was presented as unthinkable to them. The atmosphere during this session was increasingly excited, and when all participants were giggling and laughing, Arti from Bashada and Lago from Arbore felt free enough to compare the *ferenji* and their customs with animals in the bush, in short, they presented the *ferenji* to be closer to nature than to culture.[22]

Bridewealth, as presented here by the participants, is seen as a compensation for the pain a mother has endured during birth and the upbringing of her daughter. As girls leave their homes and lineages, the effort of their natal families must be recognized and valued. The girls also stressed the wealth of their families who are able to give bridewealth as opposed to the *ferenji* who do not own any cattle, a common indicator that someone is poor. Questions of the nature and amount of bridewealth were not discussed in detail, and the whole direction of the discussion in the end was to draw a boundary between the local people and the foreigners. Having been the subjects of discussion for several days, this session also appeared to have been used to release some of the stress that these dialogues may have put on some of the

[22] The only exceptions were the guests from Maale who were generally very shy to talk during the workshop. One reason why they kept quiet during this discussion may have been that, as we found out later, the Maale traditionally did not pay any bridewealth for their girls, so that the laughter the *ferenji* practice aroused may have intimidated them even more.

participants. By switching the roles of interviewers and interviewees, the rather powerful and also intrusive position of the organizers, the foreigners, was questioned and challenged. By ridiculing the foreigners' marriage practices, which do not involve any bridewealth, the workshop participants attacked the 'face' of the foreigners and hereby defended their own, which was in this situation 'the united or common face of South Omo women'.

Conclusion

Throughout the workshop, it was revealed how deeply rooted the participants felt in their respective cultural backgrounds, and how strongly they were able to identify with their roles especially in this situation of contact with 'Others'. During breaks between workshops sessions individual experiences were described more personally, but during the discussion rounds all participants strove to keep their face in front of the others. The strategies used ranged from keeping quiet on very personal issues (such as secret or premarital lovers, painful experience during circumcision, etc.), representing only the cultural ideal, defending one's own cultural background by admitting that certain practices are difficult to bear but in the next instant stressing that these were an opportunity to show one's strength and courage, to challenging or even ridiculing practices of the other guests. Whether these 'Others' were members of the same ethnic or a similar cultural background, or from a very different one, whether from the same age-group or senior or junior to oneself, depended on the context and content of the ongoing discussion. There were only very few instances when voices became critical of their own cultural practices, and in some of these moments, such as when girls expressed their fears or discomfort when thinking about getting married in Bashada, these feelings are actually considered to be culturally expected. A common pattern seemed to be that females are well aware of difficult situations and changes in their lives, and that they are well able to identify them and express them verbally. There is a cultural and linguistic repertoire for the expression of suffering and some women were very articulate in vividly describing what they had gone through when for example they got married. At the same time undergoing physically painful and psychologically difficult phases in life is expected and seemed fully accepted by all workshop participants as part of becoming adult. These practices are always connected with social recognition and public appreciation, and the prospect of belonging to "those who have done it", be it removing teeth, being whipped or circumcised, or assuming the role of a wife, and also the public provocations and to some extent social pressure to prove one's strength and courage appear to be strong enough to motivate the females to endure and undergo what may have scared them before.

In their dialogues, the females used different categories identification for inclusion and exclusion. The widest category of identification could have been the category of the female gender itself, as opposed to 'male', but this category was hardly referred to at all, probably because no men were attending the discussions. The participants rather chose to play around with the gender subcategories related to social age which had been suggested by the workshop organizers, i.e. 'unmarried girl', 'bride', 'married woman' or 'senior woman beyond menopause'. In the discussion on beauty and decorations for example, it became apparent that besides the more general category of "unmarried girl" there exist also subcategories which draw fine lines between girls who have performed a certain ritual and those who have not. The tattoos, scars and removed incisors are thus visible identity markers of different adolescent peer groups. To belong to one of those who have endured a practice means to have come closer to the cultural ideal and thus clearly contributes to a female's cultural image of Self. In the conversation on marriage all (unmarried) girls, disregarding ethnic background, agreed that staying a girl as long as possible was better than being a married woman. They also agreed on the importance of bridewealth as a compensation for the loss their leaving causes to their families. Differing livelihood strategies were used as categories of identification in the discussion among Arbore and Aari on labor participation, and ethnic background and ritual practice were combined to draw a boundary between the Arbore and Hamar to defend the practice of female genital cutting. It could thus be clearly observed that the group of people with whom individual workshop participants associated with varied from session to session, topic to topic, choosing individually which identification would contribute to a positive public self-image in a specific situation brought about by the workshop.

References

Ayalew Gebre, 1995: *The Arbore of Southern Ethiopia: A study of inter-ethnic relations, social organisation and production practices*. Addis Ababa: Addis Ababa University, Department of Sociology, Anthropology and Social Administration. (MA Thesis).

Ayalew Gebre, 1997: "Arbore Inter-Tribal Relations: A historical account". In: Richard Hogg (ed.): *Pastoralists, Ethnicity and the State in Ethiopia*. London: Haan, 143-167.

Barth, Frederic (ed.), 1969: *Ethnic Groups and Boundaries: The social organization of cultural difference*. Bergen: Universitets Forlaget.

Bateson, Gregory 1972. *Culture Contact and Schismogenesis. Steps to an ecology of mind.* New York: Ballantine Books.

Brown, Penelope and Stephen C. Levinson, 1987. *Politeness: Some universals in language usage*. Cambridge: Cambridge University Press.

Elfmann, Peggy, 2005: *Women's Worlds in Daasanech, Southern Ethiopia*. Mainz: Johannes-Gutenberg-Universität, Institut für Ethnologie und Afrikastudien, Working Papers Nr. 53 (Online publication at www.ifeas.uni-mainz.de/workingpapers/AP53.pdf). (M.A. Thesis).

Epple, Susanne & Tina Brüderlin, 2004: *The Pride and Social Worthiness of Women in South Omo*, Working papers of the SORC, Nr 3. Online publication at http://www.uni-mainz.de/Organisationen/SORC/content/view/58/41/.

Epple, Susanne & Tina Brüderlin, 2003: *The Pride and Social Worthiness of Women in South Omo*. (Unpublished manuscript).

Epple, Susanne, 2009: "Whipping as Guidance and Blessing. Childhood and Socialization among the Bashada, Southern Ethiopia". In: Gebre Yntiso (ed.): *Understanding Children and Childhood in Ethiopia: Children at risk, child protection and socialization.* Addis Ababa: ESSSWA.

Epple, Susanne, 2010: *The Bashada of Southern Ethiopia. A study of age, gender and social discourse.* Köln: Köppe.

Epple, Susanne, 2010: "Culture Contact and Identity: The multiethnic composition of the Bashada of Southern Ethiopia" In: Christina Gabbert & Sophia Thubauville (eds.): *To Live with Others. Essays on cultural neighborhood in southern Ethiopia.* Köln: Köppe, 47-67.

Gabbert, Christina & Sophia Thubauville (eds.), 2010: *To Live with Others. Essays on cultural neighborhood in southern Ethiopia.* Köln: Köppe.

Girke, Felix, 2010: "Bondfriendship in the Cultural Neighborhood: Dyadic ties and their public appreciation in South Omo". In: Christina Gabbert & Sophia Thubauville (eds.): *To Live with Others. Essays on cultural neighborhood in southern Ethiopia.* Köln: Köppe, 68-98.

Gluckman, Max, 1962: *Essays on the Ritual of Social Relations.* Manchester: Manchester University Press.

Goffman, Erving, 1967. *Interaction Ritual: Essays in face-to-face behavior.* New York: Random House.

Goffman, Erving, 1974. *Frame analysis: An essay on the organization of experience.* Cambridge, MA, US: Harvard University Press.

Kawai, Kaori, 1998: "Women's Age Categories in a Male-Dominated Society: The case of the Chamus in Kenya". In: Eisei Kurimoto and Simon Simonse (eds.): *Conflict, Age and Power in North East Africa. Age systems in transition.* Oxford: Currey.

LaTosky, Shauna, 2006. Mursi Women's Lip-plates as a Source of Stigma and Self-Esteem. In: Ivo Strecker and Jean Lydall: *The Perils of Face: Essays on cultural contact, respect and self-esteem in southern Ethiopia.* Berlin: Lit, 371-386.

LaTosky, Shauna, 2013. *Predicaments of Mursi (Mun) Women in a Changing World.* Köln: Köppe.

Llewellyn-Davies, Melissa, 1978: "Two Contexts of Solidarity among Pastoral Maasai Women". In: Pat Caplan (ed.): *Women United Women Divided: Cross-cultural perspectives on female solidarity.* London: Tavistock, 206-237.

Llewellyn-Davies, Melissa, 1981: "Women, Warriors and Patriarchs". In: Sherry Ortner and Harriet Whitehead (eds.): *Sexual Meanings.* Cambridge: Cambridge University Press, 330-358.

Lydall, Jean, 1993: "Versöhnte Kontraste: Mit meinen Kindern bei den Hamar Äthiopiens". In: Marie-José van der Loo and Margarete Reinhart (eds.): *Kinder: Ethnologische Forschung in fünf Kontinenten.*München: Trickster, 18-44.

Lydall, Jean, 1994: "Beating around the Bush". In: Bahru Zewde, Richard Pankhurst and Tadesse Beyene (eds.): *Proceedings of the XIth International Conference of Ethiopian Studies, Vol. II.* Addis Ababa: Institute of Ethiopian Studies, 205-225.

Lydall, Jean and Johanna Head, 1990: *The women who smile* [ethn. film]. Bristol: BBC.

Lydall, Jean and Johanna Head, 1991: *Two girls go hunting* [ethn. film]. Bristol: BBC.

Lydall, Jean and Johanna Head, 1994: *Our way of loving,* [ethn. film]. Bristol: BBC.

Lydall Jean and Kaira Strecker, 2001: *Duka's Dilemma,* [ethn. film]. Köln: WDR,

Göttingen: IWF.

Mitzlaff, Ulrike von, 1994: *Maasai Women. Life in a patriarchal society. Fieldwork among the Parakuyo, Tanzania.* München: Trickster.

Peller, Annette, 2002: *Chiffrierte Körper—Disziplinierte Körper. Female genital cutting. Rituelle Verwundung als Statussymbol*. Berlin: Weißensee.

Schlee, Günther, 2008: *How Enemies are Made: Towards a Theory of ethnic and religious conflict*. New York, Oxford: Berghahn.

Schlee, Günther & Elizabeth Watson, 2009: *Changing Identification and Alliances in North East Africa. Vol 1: Ethiopia and Kenya*. New York, Oxford: Berghahn.

Sobania, Neal, 1991: "Feasts, Famines and Friends: Nineteenth century exchange and ethnicity in the eastern Lake Turkana Region". In: John Galaty and Pierre Bonte: *Herders, Warriors and Traders: Pastoralism in Africa*. Boulder, San Francisco, Oxford: Westview, 118-144.

Spencer, Paul, 1965: *Samburu: A study of gerontocracy in a nomadic tribe.* London: Routledge and Kegan Paul.

Strecker, Ivo and Jean Lydall, 2006: *The Perils of Face. Essays on cultural contact, respect and self-esteem in southern Ethiopia*. Münster: Lit.

Talle, Aud, 1998: "Female and Male in Maasai Life: Aging and fertility". In: Mario Aguilar (ed.): *The Politics of Age and Gerontocracy in Africa*. Asmara: Africa World, 125-150.

Thubauville, Sophia, 2010: "Amity through Intermarriage. Some outcomes of a workshop on intermarriage between the Maale, Aari and Banna people of Southern Ethiopia." In: Christina Gabbert and Sophia Thubauville (eds.): *To Live with Others. Essays on cultural neighborhood in southern Ethiopia.*Köln: Köppe, 252-267.

Thubauville, Sophia, 2010: *Die Wandernde ist ein Kuh. Lebenswege von Frauen in Maale, Südäthiopien,* Köln: Köppe.

Turner, Victor, 1969: *The Ritual Process: Structure and antistructure*. Chicago: Aldine

Van Gennep, Arnold, 1960: *The Rites of Passage*. Chicago: University of Chicago Press.

Van Meijl, Toon, 2008. "Culture and Identity in Anthropology: Reflections on 'unity' and 'uncertainty' in the dialogical self". *International Journal for Dialogical Science 3 (1)*, 165-190.

"Time has brought it!"

Narrating female identities and change in Maale

Sophia Thubauville

Na'i erranda'o eyanne; garchi eyanda'o errane.

Children being lazy will have knowledge in future; elders having knowledge will be lazy in future. (Maale saying).

It seems to be a universal that the past is idealized while the present—and especially young generations of people—are criticized. While conducting field research among the Maale people of southern Ethiopia on the life cycle and life histories of women, the idealization of the past and especially of the behavior of past people was a continuously recurring phenomenon. Old and middle-aged women often made derogatory remarks about today's girls and women—not only indirectly by using proverbs like the one above, but also directly. I listened to them interestedly, cautiously and with an inner smile, realizing that talking about present and past seems to bring forth the same reactions everywhere in the world.

Unlike most other contributions to this volume, the boundaries between different categories of people in my paper are not determined by place, but by time. Listening to women's narratives about the past, one might not only feel taken to another time, but the past often seems so different that one feels taken to another place. The described past, its people and practices differ so much from the present that one can get the impression that the past is a 'foreign country', another place instead of another time (Lowenthal 1985). The narratives show that time is as important as place for the identification of an individual.

I would like to share with the reader three rejoinders of my Maale informants that reveal much about the transformation of different life stages of Maale women. The women, whose remarks I will quote in the following are from different villages, of different age, religion, and marital status. KolteInda and Deginesh are both above 60 years, widowed and live in the lowland village Gudo. Danjite, a middle-aged married woman of a former polygynous household, converted with her husband to Protestant belief and lives today monogamously with her husband, their children and step-children. Zeleketch and Bako live in the highland village Baneta. While Zeleketch is around 55 years old, divorced and protestant, Bako is about five years her senior, widowed and practices the traditional belief. None of my informants referred to in this chapter was below 35 years of age during the time of the research.

I chose examples from conversations with them that show that different women share very similar feelings about certain changes in their lives. The changes they experienced concern very different aspects: the ways in which they got married, the presents they received from their fiancés and the hairstyles of women (and girls). Using these three examples I will show that old women (*minna lali*), who grew up under circumstances and followed customs that have disappeared or changed today, distance themselves from the women of today (*hatsa lali*) and their changing way of life. They identify with the past and with their lost customs and criticize contemporary transformations.

Recording Maale women's lives

Durmippa tammi ekenne, garchipa hayse ekanne.

Fire comes out of wood; stories come out of old people. (Maale saying).

The Maale of southern Ethiopia count 74.517 people according to Ethiopia`s 2005 census.[1]They are agro-pastoralists who raise cattle and goats and cultivate sorghum and maize. Since the 1960s the Maale have been facing serious transformations in their lives, above all through the increasing influence of Protestant Christianity and the conversion of many Maale, as well as through the integration into the Ethiopian nation (see Donham 1990 and 1999; Thubauville 2009).

I began research in southern Ethiopia in 2002, and conducted extensive field studies on Maale women's lives for my PhD between June 2006 and October 2009 (see Thubauville 2009). During that time I had the chance to gain insight into women's lives in the lowlands as well as the highlands of Maale, as I lived with three different Maale families in the villages of Gudo (lowland), Baneta (highland) and Bunka (highland). The economy and accordingly the tasks and live circumstances of women differed a lot due to the geographic differences within the Maale territory. I accompanied and observed the women while they were carrying out their daily tasks and relaxing and chatting while drinking tea prepared from coffee leaves. I joined their celebrations, listened to them relating episodes of their past lives during idle hours or interviews, as well as to their gossip on other women and daily worries. I documented their stories in my field diary, and also recorded interviews to be able to reproduce and quote their statements in their own words. Especially while I was transcribing interviews of elderly and middle-aged women I frequently came across passages where they romanticized and idealized the past and accused the present generation of women of being idle and dependent on their husbands.

When I compared my experience from Maale with other research on life histories, I found that the idealization of the past is a topic much discussed in anthropological research on life histories (Cruikshank 1990; Rosenwald and Ochberg 1992). It is also an issue of anthropological discussions about memory (Bal et al. 1999; Lowenthal 1985; Tonkin 1992). From those discussions we can learn that the past is often idealized for mainly two reasons: first, it is a completed period and therefore remembered as safe and stable compared to the chaotic and seemingly disordered present (Lowenthal 1985: 4). Second, the past and its people might seem brighter in the memories. When people recall earlier days, they remember themselves as more

1 Statistical source from the South Omo Zone Administration.

vivacious than today, as now they are older and in often in a poorer health condition (Lowenthal 1985: 8).[2]

From grinding grain to having fun at markets

Boka eroatsi, tutti workenne.

One who doesn't know the market, spends his night dressing up. (Maale saying).

A first example of elderly women's critical attitude towards today's women's behavior is about the tasks of girls and their ways of marrying. According to old and middle-aged women, the main job of girls a few decades ago was to grind sorghum with grinding stones. Sorghum is the main foodstuff in Maale. It is processed into hard bread, crumble and beer, and as grinding is a hard task, it took up the better part of the day. Bako, a widow of about 60 years, explains the task of grinding when she was young as follows:

> When I was young I had to go to the river to fetch water. We girls had to grind a lot. Sometimes we were falling asleep over the grinding stones. We slept a little bit and then started grinding again. We always had *ala* [local beer]. When visitors came we could offer them some. It was a good time, not like today. (Bako, February 2005)

Bako describes the disadvantages of her youth—the ceaseless task of grinding—but also recalls its advantage—the ability to have always some beer to offer spontaneously to guests. About forty years ago, when Bako was about 20 years old, markets began to be organized in Maale and grinding mills were built in the market villages (Thubauville 2010). As a consequence women started to have their grain ground in grinding mills. The money needed to pay for mechanical grinding was raised by selling surplus of grain or butter at markets. As a result of the introduction of mechanical grinding mills, girls have more leisure time today and some of this time they spend visiting markets. There they not only meet girlfriends, look at the newest goods that traders bring in and compare prices, but also look out for possible boyfriends. Before the introduction of mills girls only had the chance to meet boys during work on the fields, and during celebrations such as funerals and dances. These celebrations took place irregularly—other than the weekly markets. The weekly occasion for young people to meet seems to have contributed to a lowering of marriage age of females from around twenty to around sixteen.

In a conversation I had during a group discussion with women from different Maale villages, two of the participants explained the recent decrease of the marriage age and its connection with the introduction of markets and increasing leisure time of girls in the highlands as well as in the lowlands. Note the stress on 'time' by Danjite at the end of the conversation:

> Sophia: Why did girls marry at later age in former times?

[2] Compare Lowenthal's (1985:8) statement "...nostalgia is memory with the pain removed".

Zeleketch: In former times they didn't meet anybody. There was no place to meet. A boy met a girl when she was sent to the field. Then he asked her where she lived and [in which house she] lay at night and said: „I will go to her for *gochitsi*!"[3] This is what he said. Then he went and found her. Today they go to the market with their flashlights. They [the girls] fill sugar into their flashlights [into the metal cover of the flashlights] and buy sugar cane [and give it to their boyfriends].

Sophia: What do you think, Danjite?

Danjite: Time has brought it that girls marry early. Today there are grinding mills and the girls don't have much work anymore. They can visit markets. (Workshop, 28.03.08)[4]

Besides making it easier for boys and girls to meet, the markets have brought another transformation that older women criticize. In former times, the ideal way of dating, as Zeleketch mentioned above, was *gochitsi* (Thubauville 2010). This meant that a boy and a girl, having met for the first time at a celebration or work party, continued to meet regularly in the evenings at the house of the girl. The boy would wake her up by calling her out and then the two would go to a place nearby the homestead and spend several hours sitting next to each other on two stones to chat and flirt.

When one asks in Maale how someone has met his or her spouse, and especially about their time of *gochitsi*, one will be told how one visited or was visited by his sweetheart over a long period of time (sometimes for several years), how they spent the nights together chatting and then were tired throughout the following day. As virginity at marriage is highly valued among the Maale, the couples were expected not to have any sexual relationship during that time (see Thubauville 2009: 175f). Today the number of people who engage in *gochitsi* before marriage has decreased. Old people disapprove of this and accuse young people of being impatient and choosing a fast way to marry by meeting just once at the market or in another place:

If the girls of today go to the market and a man says: "Let us go to so-and-so's house and drink!" they enter, drink together and go [marry]. She [the girl] doesn't take clothes out of her father's house. She doesn't change the clothes that she wears on her body. She marries[5] on the way to the market. When she goes to the river, she leaves her jerry can back at the river and marries on the way to the river. When she collects firewood, she leaves her wood in the forest and marries on the way to the firewood. If you look at the children of today, you become afraid. (Danjite, August 2006)

3 Ideal way of dating, for more explanation see below and Donham (1990: 108f). *Gochitsi* literally means 'pulling', i.e. pulling out a girl by her hand.

4 The workshop "Power and Resistance—Stories from Maale women's lives" was held in March 2008 at the South Omo Research Center in Jinka. Eight Maale women from four different villages and of different ages participated.

5 Marriages are no elaborated celebrations in Maale. Even in former times girls often didn't tell their parents in advance when they married and just went together with a small marriage party of female friends and relatives to the husband's homestead. There the bride would enter like a bondfriend through the cattle entrance, would be seated on a cowhide with her groom, offered some coffee and would put a feather from her hair into the roof of the house of the groom's family as a sign of affiliation (see Thubauville 2010).

This way of marrying that is made possible above all by the weekly opportunity of visiting markets and meeting marriage partners, as well as the reduced workload of today's girls, as I have already pointed out, is disapproved by older women. Interestingly even women, whose past was not only bright but rather unpleasant, make it today look desirable and condemn the present as well as present practices. Danjite, for example, who disapproves of young people who marry in a rush out of love (see above), was herself abducted by her husband as a very young girl.[6]

Considering her own experiences, one might think that she would approve the current situation, in which women have some say on whom they want to marry. Instead she idealizes the past and disassociates from the young generation and their practices. Even though she went through hard times because of practices like abduction that were still common in her youth, she appreciates and identifies with the former customs.[7]

From activity to passivity

Boza atinke lali woitsanne.

A lazy man is led by a woman. (Maale saying)

Another change related to marriage concerns the exchange of presents between young couples. In former times a girl gave parts of her own jewelry as presents to her boyfriend when he visited her at nighttime for *gochitsi* (Thubauville 2010). Giving bracelets or necklaces to one's boyfriend was seen as a positive reply to his advances, and a kind of promise to get married to him in the future. A boyfriend did not offer any gift in return to his girlfriend, but he proudly wore her gifts that marked him as engaged in a love relationship. The period of *gochitsi* could continue for months or even years. At one point the couple decided on a date to marry, and the boy handed the girl a rope with a knot for every week[8] left until the day of their marriage.

When preparing for marriage, a girl had to get her own marriage outfit and local cotton blankets prepared, which she took with her later on to her husband's house. She also had to prove her maturity by helping her parents during a last harvest and by collecting several piles of firewood for her mother. Altogether preparing for marriage was a hard, responsible and lengthy work for girls. But according to old women, mastering those preparations by themselves had made them proud and at the same time well-prepared for their marriage life and future tasks, i.e. carrying and threshing sorghum or collecting firewood.

6 See Danjite's portrait in Thubauville 2010.

7 In former times abductions took place frequently in Maale. Marriages were only seldom arranged by family members, but clan-exogamy and the possibility of women to reject a marriage proposal made many man to choose this way of marrying (see Thubauville 2010). Today abduction is restricted by the Ethiopian constitution and happens only rarely in remote areas of Maale, where police is not present.

8 Weeks again were counted according to market days.

Today the preparations for marriage and exchange of gifts look quite different. Many girls do not give presents anymore to their boyfriends. Instead girls receive money from their boyfriends, which they use to pay for their wedding clothes. They do not have to make cotton blankets anymore by themselves and often marry in such a rush that they do not even prove their maturity in demonstratively assisting their parents a last time with the harvest.

This new situation was criticized by two old women during interviews. One of them, Deginesh, a widow of about sixty years, who converted to Protestantism some years ago:

> Girls of today neither work for their fathers, nor for their mothers. They rather earn money by selling items at markets. They use the money that they earn for themselves and then go to the house of their husbands. They marry in the clothes that he has bought for them. Today the wedding clothes are bought by the groom and given to her [the bride]. (Deginesh, August 2006)

Another old woman, KolteInda, my host-grandmother, made the following statement about the generation of her grandchildren:

> In former times we [lovers] gave each other brass bracelets. Today he [the boy] gives 100 up to 145 Birr [to the girl]. At our time we did not give 100 Birr. We went to the house of the blacksmith and ordered something. We took rings [from the blacksmith's house]; we took bracelets and gave them [to the boyfriends]. In the past, women gave [presents], today the men give. Men already buy clothes when she [the girlfriend] is still in the house of her father. When she leaves from there, she has everything. (KolteInda, Gudo, 23.08.06)

Talking about these changes, old women were proud that they have been active and independent from their boyfriends in former times. KolteInda recalls "Before women gave!" and opposes it to "Today men give!" Saying this, she proudly identifies with the self-determined women of the past while distancing herself from present women. She criticizes the girls of today to be passive and depending on their future husbands already before marriage. This reality also emphasizes the rush and impatience that is characteristic of current marriage arrangements. The girls hurry into marriage without being prepared, without having proven their maturity and ability as adult women. Compared to former times they are young, immature and dependent when they marry and in this way even jeopardize the former gender complementarity.

Being immature and passive, brides and their families nowadays receive the wedding clothes as well as a bride price from the husband and his family. Some old women criticize this fact and say the wedding clothes and the additional bride price are too much to be given for the young, pathetic brides of today. Deginesh explained:

> Well, in our times, when I was a girl, girls spun cotton, ground grain, joined work groups and prepared the fields. When they wanted to marry, they had to fill the grain store of their fathers; otherwise they were insulted and called useless. If a girl wanted to marry she had to put money aside for her mother and fill up two stores with firewood.

> Then she ordered a huge cotton blanket, a medium one and a marriage dress [from a local weaver]. After that she married. The girls of today [...] go to their husband's house in the clothes that he paid for. [...] Which bride price should he pay for them after all? In earlier times we [the Maale] gave neither a bride price, nor did we take anything else from the groom.(Deginesh, Gudo, 24.08.06)

But even though today's brides are called embarrassing by older generations of women, bride prices have indeed increased during the last decades and were possibly even an innovation altogether in Maale. The information about the bride wealth differs. Some Maale say in former times no bride price had been given at all, others say little money has always been paid. Donham recognized an increase in the bride price during his field research in Maale in the 1970s, but was not sure whether or not bride wealth had existed at all in Maale in former times (1979: 67). What can be said for sure is that today the amount given as bride wealth varies according to the clan of the bride, the wealth of the groom's family, and the circumstances of the marriage, e.g. for example whether the bride's family had been informed about the wedding beforehand or whether the bride is married as first or second wife (Thubauville 2010). Generally, bridewealth is rather low today among the Maale compared to neighboring ethnic groups. The family of the groom transfers between a few hundred to two thousand Ethiopian Birr[9] to the family of the girl.

The low price of payments for brides of the Maale is an exception in South Omo, where large amounts of livestock are usually transferred from the groom's to the bride's family (Thubauville 2010). Bossen (1988: 133) argues that a low bridewealth goes along with wives being low at their husbands' command. Listening to the narratives of older generations of women, one gets the impression that the small amount of bridewealth is not an indicator that women in Maale are more independent than women among other ethnic groups as proposed in the narratives, but rather that the slow increase or even new invention of the bride wealth is a sign for a decrease of their self-determination.

From meaning to beauty

Tokko majintanne ada'o, gulinti ye'enne.

The one who goes to get the hair made, returns with his hair shaved.

While I conducted my Ph.D. research among the Maale, I looked for another host family in the highlands to compare the data that I had already collected in the lowlands. Gattifo, whom I chose as a third host-mother in the mountain village Bunka had a *muddo*[10] and *konko*[11], a hairstyle and face tattoo that have become rare

[9] Birr is the Ethiopian currency (ETB). In September 2010, 100 ETB were equivalent to approximately € 4,50.

[10] The hairstyle *muddo* identified a woman as mother in former times and today is only worn by some middle-aged women anymore. It consists of a thin braid that encircles the head.

nowadays.[12] While staying with her I learned about the former beauty ideals of the Maale and why women of her age wore that same hairstyle, a thin braid that is laid around the otherwise shaven head.

Gattifo was an elderly woman of about 65 years. She and other old Maale women, who are still wearing the *muddo*-hairstyle, explained to me that in former times women started wearing this hairstyle seven days after the birth of their first child. After the head of the child was shaved the mother had the *muddo* made (see Thubauville 2009: 129f). After having given birth for the first time, a woman was addressed as *lali*, woman, while before most people would call her *Utah*, bride. Wearing a *muddo* a woman was immediately recognized as being a mother, one reason for women to wear this hairstyle. Another reason was, according to Gattifo, to spiritually take care of the well-being of her child. By leaving the ring made by the braid open to one side, women wanted to make sure that the child can digest food properly and will never become hungry. A third reason for wearing this hairstyle is that women, who have given birth at least once, a second burial is celebrated some years after their death. Such a second burial is of high ritual importance and also adds to the fame of an individual and his/her descendants (see Thubauville 2010).

Today, because many Maale have converted to Protestantism and are not allowed celebrating second burials anymore. Additionally, the Ethiopian government considers second burials as 'traditional harmful practice'. The increasing presence of police even in small villages therefore also contributes to the rareness of second burials. Thus women have yet again less reason to wear the *muddo*.

Most young women of today let their hair grow and then get it braided. Those braided hairstyles are common all over Ethiopia. Such popular hairstyles do not have a culturally rooted meaning or purpose as the *muddo* did. I often heard old women making derogatory remarks or fun about young women, who spent a lot of time on their sophisticated hairstyles, which seem to be meaningless to older generations of women:

> While drinking *tukko* [tea made from coffee leaves] in the house, Gimcha and Agatto [two young women] made plans for whom they would make which kind of hairstyle today. Gimcha started to make Mungatsi [a little girl] small braids. KolteInda commented this by saying that women in former times had spun cotton in their leisure time, while today they are busy in making each other new hairstyles. (11.11.07, field diary, Gudo)

KolteInda was one of many elderly women who I heard making comments like this on young women who spent much of their time doing their hair. With her comment she did not allude so much to the lack of cultural significance of the new hairstyles, but rather to the increasing vanity of women, who spend more time on

11 The typical face tattoos in Maale consist of a long black line from the top of the forehead to the tip of the nose, three parallel vertical lines on the chin and three half circles around each eye.

12 See portrait of Gattifo in my PhD thesis (Thubauville 2009: 92ff).

their looks than on purposeful activities, such as spinning cotton. Moreover, the women she addressed in the above mentioned conversation knew that KolteInda herself is not vain about her appearance at all. Instead of spending time on making hairstyles, she spends her leisure time spinning together with other elderly women. KolteInda distinguished with her comment young women, who sit together and make hairstyles and the women, with whom she identifies, who jointly spin cotton.

As we can learn for example from anthropological life history studies meaning is often added in retrospective, while in the beginning many things seem to be meaningless. This fact is true not only for life histories, but for history in general. Thinking about a life or a cultural practice at some point one can give meaning to certain actions and achievements that seemed to be meaningless without the historic perspective (Röttger-Rössler 2003: 34). If one applies that idea to the example of hairstyles, one could hypothesize that the *muddo* which is worn today only by few old women, was once also a new and fashionable hairstyle. With time and from retrospective people added different meanings to it, like the one that the opening of the braid to one end would keep the child of the woman satisfied and healthy. The new hairstyles of women in Maale are today considered meaningless, but maybe with time and increasing age of the women who wear them, some meaning will be added to them, too.

Identifying by dissociating

Inda na'o sorri, baka'o pero gobadenne.

A mother advises her children, but becomes pregnant herself. (Maale saying).

Listening to the critique of old women (*minna lali*), gives the impression that the women of today (*hatsa lali*) are subject to rapid change and that they happily accept it. They are said to ignore those cultural practices that contributed to female self-determination and strength of former generations, but instead are choosing an idle way of life that does not need much effort, but leads to greater dependence on husbands. Cultural practices that were meaningful to the old generation are said to be abandoned by the young and replaced by practices that appear to be meaningless.

In the cultural mosaic of South Omo, where many groups with differing cultural traits live in close neighborhood, much of the identity of a group is derived negatively by dissociating from neighbors (see Schlee 1989 and 2002). The same can be said for certain generations within one ethnic group, especially for generations before and after being affected by far-reaching transformations. This is true also for my example from Maale, where women use explicitly markers of time—*minna wodde* (former times) and *hatsa* (today)—to distinguish themselves and draw a line between the younger and the older generations. Using those markers is a mechanism of identification and disassociation at the same time. Time is not marked itself, but made by humans (see James 2003: 73) as in this case as a sign of disassociation from another generation.

Women who are today thirty or more years old and got married more than fifteen years ago, have passed through the life stages of marrying and being young mothers differently than the women of today. In their youth the Maale were less integrated into the Ethiopian state, Protestants were much fewer in number and the hardly existing infrastructure cut them off from trade and other foreign influences. Looking back these women recounted to me mostly only the positive sides of their past and distanced themselves from today's 'modern' women and their new cultural practices. In all of their accounts the difference between "former times (*minna wodde*)" and "today (*hatsa*)" were stressed. They described the women of today as not hard working (as they do not have to grind anymore), irresponsible (as they marry young and in a rush), dependent (as they make themselves financially dependent on their husbands already before marriage), idle (as they prefer making hairstyles and visiting markets to valuable work), replacing meaningful practices by meaningless ones (see the example of current hair fashion) and finally giving up valuable traditions, such as the long period of dating. In their continual comparisons of past and present they stressed that though life was harder in their youth, the clever women of their generation did the best out of it, while today's life has become undemanding. Nevertheless, today's girls and women constantly look for relief from responsibility and work load instead of bearing former female duties and at the same time being independent and strong.

What did the women want to tell me through their numerous narratives about the past? Did they really want to let me know that the past was better than the present, that they were cleverer than young women today? Understanding their narratives as social action (Tonkin 1992: 97) deliberately directed to a specific audience—myself—they must have had a reason. I do not believe any of those women would like to be taken back into the past. Instead most of them would agree to KolteInda's statement, which clearly states that she would have approved of an earlier arrival of mechanical grinding mills and accordingly less hard work in her youth:

> Imagine we would have had a grinding mill in our time! Ooh! Now we have become old because of that work. (KolteInda, Gudo, 23.08.06)

However, living in a rapidly changing present that is, of course, chaotic compared to the past which is over and therefore complete, they long for the past because of its stability and safety. Being sick, disillusioned, married to drunkards or good-for-nothings, middle-aged and old women remember the past as a time when they themselves and their generation of women were as vivid, strong and full of hope as today's young generation that they criticize (see Lowenthal 1985: 8). In the end their differences to the women of today might be imagined (see Schlee 2002). The elderly women of today were once also young and being young also might have transformed some of the traditions of their mothers and grandmothers. Their innovations may have seemed as meaningless at that time as the practices introduced by today's young women do. Only with time those practices might have been culturally embedded and value and meaning added to them. Because, as

James (2003) has so truthfully put it: "'Modern' time is certainly asymmetrical, in measurable stages, leaving things behind and inventing new things."

References

Bal, Mieke et al., 1999: *Acts of Memory: Cultural recall in the present*. Hanover and London: University Press of England.

Bossen, Laurel, 1988: "Toward a Theory of Marriage. The economic anthropology of marriage transactions."*Ethnology* 27, 2, 127-144.

Cruikshank, Julie, 1990: *Life lived like a story*. Nebraska, Vancouver: University of Nebraska Press.

Donham, Donald, 1979: *Work and Power in Maale, Ethiopia*. New York: Cambridge University Press

Donham, Donald, 1990: *History, Power, Ideology. Central issues in Marxism and anthropology*. Berkeley, Los Angeles, London: University of California Press.

Donham, Donald, 1999: *Marxist Modern. An ethnographic history of the Ethiopian Revolution*. Berkeley, Los Angeles: University of California Press.

James, Wendy, 2003: *The Ceremonial Animal. A new portrait of anthropology*. New York: Oxford University Press.

Lowenthal, David, 1985: *The Past is a Foreign Country*. Cambridge: Cambridge University Press.

Rosenwald, George and Richard Ochberg, 1992: *Storied Lives. The cultural politics of self understanding*. New Haven: Yale University Press.

Röttger-Rössler, Birgit, 2003: "Gegenwärtige Vergangenheit: Rekonstruktionen eines interethnischen Ehekonfliktes in biographischen Gesprächen". In: Birgit Röttger-Rössler and Elfriede Hermann (eds.), *Lebenswege im Spannungsfeld lokaler und globaler Prozesse. Person, Selbst und Emotion in der ethnologischen Biographieforschung*. Münster: Lit.

Röttger-Rössler, Birgit and Elfriede Hermann (eds.), 2003: *Lebenswege im Spannungsfeld lokaler und globaler Prozesse. Person, Selbst und Emotion in der ethnologischen Biographieforschung*. Münster: Lit.

Schlee, Günther, 1989: *Identities on the Move. Clanship and pastoralism in northern Kenya*. Manchester/Nairobi: Manchester University Press/Gideon S. Were Press.

Schlee, Günther, 2002: *Imagined Differences. Hatred and the construction of identity*. Münster: Lit.

Thubauville, Sophia, 2005: *Maale Material Objects in Their Cultural and Ritual Context*. Arbeitspapiere des Instituts für Ethnologie und Afrikastudien der Johannes-Gutenberg Universität Mainz. No. 61 (http://www.ifeas.uni-mainz.de/working papers/AP56.pdf). (M.A. Thesis).

Thubauville, Sophia, 2009: *Ritual und Lebensweg. Eine Untersuchung zum Wandel weiblicher Machtnischen in Maale, Südäthiopien*. Mainz: Johannes-Gutenberg Universität Mainz, Institut fuer Ethnologie und Afrikastudien.

Tonkin, Elizabeth, 1992: *Narrating our Pasts. The Social Construction of Oral History*. Cambridge: Cambridge University Press.

Daasanech Notions on Social Causation of Well-being and Misfortune

Yvan Houtteman

Anthropological research among pastoralists and agropastoralists in South-West Ethiopia has mainly focused on history, ethnicity and conflict and often deals with the explanation of the complex social organization and age-systems of the groups under study. Far less has been written on the knowledge systems of these peoples. This paper is a close examination of different social relationships within Daasanech society and how disturbances of the latter are believed to cause disease and misfortune within the community.

When I did research among the Daasanech in 1995 and 1997 on the relationship between human body and social identity, I learned how features of identity and life history of a person are expressed on the body of a person and how bodies are being modified during different rites of passage. In the course of my research, two other correlations between the human body and the social environment became apparent: the importance of blessing to obtain personal well-being and the negative effects of social tensions and antisocial behavior. Disease, death and infertility were often explained as results of curses, witchcraft or the impure status of an individual, in short by disturbed social relationships between relatives, seniors and juniors or other members of society believed to have evil powers.

The Daasanech: Origin and social organisation

The Daasanech are an east Cushitic speaking group of about 50.000 people who mainly live in villages along the Omo-river in South-West Ethiopia. They actually form a cluster of eight different named sections or subgroups. These groups became one in the course of the 18th and 19th century, when groups of proto-Daasanech arrived in their present territories from a place to the South West called Ger, where they met with other groups.

Daasanech subsistence consists of a unique combination of flood-retreat cultivation along the banks of the Omo River and extensive pastoralism. They keep cattle, goats and sheep in an oscillating pattern in the river delta during the dry season, and in cattle camps further away during the rainy season. Boys and young married men are in charge of the herds, under the supervision of elder men, while the cultivation of the sorghum fields largely the task of women.

The Daasanech live in small igloo-shaped huts that are traditionally covered with cattle skins. These are relatively easy to deconstruct and to transport on the back of a donkey. A hut is called *bil*, a term that is also used for a single household, i.e. the married wife and her unmarried children who live in the hut. The word *bil* however, can also denote the larger social units, all wives of a polygamous husband and their respective children, an extended family under supervision of the elder father and even to a sub-clan, a group of families which share the same name and similar cattle brands.

Every named sub-clan belongs to one of the many exogamous clans. Each clan is associated with specific talents or skills which are played out during ritual occasions, when the members of specific clans are involved to take certain ritual steps, like the cutting of a ritual tree, the making of fire, calling the rain and others. The clans do not form cooperative units. Social cohesion and cooperation is rather achieved through the generation system, which operates in a similar way than the one of the Karimojong. This means that society is divided into two main generations, the generation of the Fathers and the generation of the Sons. Similar to the organisation of a single household where the father has the authority, the Fathers of the country are in charge of the whole section. They serve as ritual leaders and possess the spiritual and political power. Children are born into the generation alternating the one of their parents. When they grow into adulthood, men are initiated into a specific age-set through the spearing of an ox or a goat for the elders. This act allows them to wear a clay-cap and a headrest and brings at the same time specific responsibilities and tasks related to herding and defense. Regularly, new sets are formed until the generation is complete and may be closed.

The way the age-system functions cannot be explained in detail here, but it must be mentioned that the eldest living generation provides the group of *jeleba*. The *jeleba* serve as judges for the community in matters related to marriage and bridewealth.

Concepts of body and disease

For the Daasanech, the living body (*gon*) is not considered a mechanical interaction between different organs, as in the western bio-medical model. Daasanech rather conceptualize their body in terms of a continuous transformation of fluids and food, generated and sustained by a pulsating principle called *sidha*. This life force, which "holds" all living organisms, originates from *Waag*. The concept of *Waag* has different meanings. Literally, it means "Sky" or "the Above", and refers to the source of rain. Besides, the notion is associated with well-being and prosperity. Upon conception, *Waag* "places" the *sidha* in the womb when the white (male) and red[1](female) blood stick together[2] and form the child. In a healthy person, the pulse is fine and flow of fluids and food faces no obstructions. Disease however may be caused by an obstruction in the bodily flow. The body then becomes hot and feverish (*kulla,* also means sick). The Daasanech word for disease or illness is *baash* (pl.

1 The female blood will form the flesh and the semen forms the bones of the child.

2 The *sidha* of a newborn baby is very well observable at the fontanel (*daadich*) and remains tangible at vital places like the throat area and the plexus solaris (*kidicho*). When young males are excited, they sometimes hit their *kidicho* hard to express their emotions. The *kidicho* is also the place where the *nyebolli*, a typical decoration, 'beats' while men jump during ox-dances.

baasham).[3] *Baash* refers to the state of fever or pain. Other words used are *kulla* (heat), *ali* (being sick in a certain part) or *nyedeke* (derived from the Turkana word *edeke*). Different images are used to model disease: one is the tangling of the veins due to clotting of blood. Massaging the painful parts is believed to bring 'the veins back in line' by removing the obstruction and reactivating the bodily flow. Cupping is practiced in order to remove the 'bad' or 'dark' blood. When the food-flow is obstructed, food clots and remains stuck and 'becomes a stone'. 'Stoned food' can be removed through induced vomiting or through special techniques, like sucking it out through the skin. Some diseases are labeled as *daafo*. This word literally refers to a physical 'swelling' or an 'injury' caused by an accident or by being beaten. The word is also used for internal pain caused by a curse. Internal swellings occur when an area inside the body is believed to have become too wet and thereby weakened.[4] In order to remove a swelling, patients are not allowed to drink any (cold) beverages except a very small amount of hot water (just one spoonful) in the morning, as the intake of fluids is believed to make the sick area even more spongy and weak. Abstaining from water is said to have the opposite effect in that the swelling dries out and shrinks, just like grass shrinks without rain.

Another term used in the context of disease is *hirich*. This term literally refers to a needle, but is also used to refer to a sharp pain in one part of the body and sometimes as synonymous for a curse. Chest, liver and heart are the most principal organs affected by *hirich*. When a person does not recover, his *sidha* ultimately stops pulsating and the person dies. At the moment of death, the *sidha* leaves the body and returns up to its place of origin.[5] What is left is a dead body (*riif*)[6] which soon will fall apart and turn into bones. When the body dies, the spirit or *gaaram* remains.[7] *Gaaram* are ancestor spirits. They exist in a shadowlike state and may appear in dreams. They may dwell around the grave, but usually remain at specific places, like places where there are holes in the earth and dark forests. They are associated with the West and with the below. *Gaaram* are ambivalent beings. As will be explained in more detail below, the *gaaram* may be asked for help in times of need, but they are also feared because they may afflict their living descendents in various ways.

3 Another word used is *furso* which refers more to pests and epidemics.

4 Just like among the Turkana (Broch-Due 1990), wetness is associated with weakness and strength with dryness.

5 Some say the *sidha* leaves the body through the fontanel at the top of the head, others say it leaves through the space between the lower front-teeth—they imply that the two middle ones are extracted for this reason. The death of a person is often mirrored through a shooting star. Daasanech say that each human being is connected with a star and at the moment of death, the star fades out.

6 Note that *riif* (dead body; skeleton) is different from *gon* (body with *sidha*).

7 Only people who have performed their *'dimi* are believed to turn into *gaaram*, but children and young men and women do not.

Blessing and cursing and the causation of misfortune and disease

When I lived among the Daasanech, the prominence of blessings was very obvious. Blessing is called *Waag hiviny* in Daasanech, which means "to bring forth *Waag*", and thereby well-being of the people, the land and the cattle.

"Let there be plenty" (les he heyyiyo)
"let there be peace"*(les naana rayyo)*
"wipe out epidemics from the land" *(furs man, les gaabadisia)*
"let there be plenty of (black) people" *(muu kamur gaal nyirecha shiia)*
"let the circumcised men increase" *(muu herle 'darmeye)*
"give more marriage cows" *(dongol muu dongol shiia)*
"let the calves multiply" *('guo modo fadhe)*
"fill the kraal" *(muu deeyle kochoyo)*

Blessing is consistent with the gerontocratic principle which is visible in other domains of Daasanech social organisation: the elder bless the young, the men bless the women. On the individual level, the father of a household blesses his offspring, his cattle and the lands each morning before the sons will guide the stock to the grazing areas or when coffee is prepared when guests visit. On the level of the community, blessings are involved during all ritual occasions. Within the generation system, the elder generation blesses the younger one and the elder age-sets bless their "younger brothers". Such blessings usually involve the killing and communal eating of oxen or smallstock (and sometimes even camels). Blessings are also part of the different rites of passage a person goes through in life. Two of those are very specific for the Daasanech, at least when compared with their immediate neighbours. One is the male circumcision or *bilte*, which is—besides the initiation into an age-set—a second type of initiation into manhood. After the operation, which happens collectively, the circumcised men remain in a seclusion hut for several months. During that time, they are considered to be in a state of bliss and people may visit them in order to obtain their blessings. The second special ritual is the *'dimi*, which is only performed by six of the eight sections. During that ritual, the parents of all girls who are coming of age move to a certain place where they construct their huts in a large circle in the centre of a yard. In that centre, the hut of the ritual leader is build and all other *jeleba* are invited every day to enjoy food and beverage. This goes on for several months until sorghum beer is brewed and the *jeleba* bless the girls and wish them a fertile future.

Besides the category of the *jeleba*, members of specific clans called *nyerim* are renowned for their strong capacity to bless (*nyerich*). These clans are said to be able to communicate with *Waag*. This ability makes them responsible to call forth rain. They bless the land each time the new moon appears and they are also involved in the blessing of warriors when they prepare for war. Clans which do not possess this *nyerim* are called *mesatich*. They also have specific innate abilities associated with specific domains in the world, like fire, the river, the wind and certain animals.

Daasanech bless in different ways. The most common way is to spray saliva, water or coffee on the one to be blessed, while uttering an incantation of positive wants. Circumcised men use the aromatic root of the *gunite* plant when they spray saliva. Another substance often used is *erer*, a mixture of milk and water, which is sprinkled on the body of guests. Also butter (*shiebite*) or oil (*salap*) is used as a substance to induce wellbeing and prosperity. The same is true for the use of *muor*, the fatty wall of the stomach which is cut into stripes and then draped around the neck of the one being blessed. A very specific blessing substance is called *shuom*, a mixture of milk, butter and the clay of a termite hill. This mixture is used during the initiation of men into ritual leaders (*ara)* and to clean away social pollution in families who have committed homicide. During meat-feasts for men where animals are sacrificed and the meat is roasted, the chyme from the rumen of the sacrificed ox is used to smear the body of the young guests, emphasizing to their unity. A detailed explication of all these different substances would lead too far here. The most important thing for our argument is that blessings are an integral part of different ritual practices and they constitute an important aspect of behavior and a means to gain, to maintain or to restore wellbeing. Blessings are most often derived from elders who are offered food in return.

Without blessings and without *Waag*, a man is vulnerable to misfortune and the flow of life is obstructed. Drought and hunger, war, pests and diseases all are indications of this obstruction. While the experience of wellbeing is considered as a state close to *Waag* where everything is fine, the experience of misfortune is perceived as rather the opposite. When misfortune strikes, Daasanech say that *Waag* has abandoned his people[8] or that *Waag* refused (*Waag' hidiito*). At that point, people start to realize that something severely bad (*he deenadhe*) is going on which might lead to permanent infertility or death. Home remedies and medicines do not seem to work and the situation of patients worsen: a woman remains barren, a sick person loses weight, has growing fever, starts to hallucinate or loses consciousness. At that point questions like: "Why do or did things turn out the bad way?" arise and causes are now sought in the social sphere, usually in the social environment of the victim, i.e. among relatives, age mates or ancestor spirits. Now, causes for disease shift from "naturalistic" to "spiritual."

Natural diseases are called *baasham aada* or *baasham Waagiet*, spiritual diseases are called *baasham 'doriet*. It may be surprising that the word *waagiet* is used for natural diseases. This adjective does not refer to the fact that such diseases are caused by *Waag*, but rather that these diseases are not life threatening. The term *waagiet* here refers to the "innocent" aspect of *Waag*.

This equation of *Waag* with wellbeing and good fortune shares a similar fragrance with the way the neighboring Hamar conceptualize *barjo*. Indeed,

8 *Waag* is feminine in Daasanech language, although informants stress that *Waag* cannot be seen as a person or a mother. I would like to refer in this sense to the different myths of origin found among the Daasanech and other neighbouring people in which Heaven and Earth were once very close, until some deeds separated Heaven from Earth and man had to suffer.

according to Lydall and Strecker (1979), who analyzed this concept elaborately, *barjo* denotes a quality and refers to a state of good fortune (rain, fertility, wellbeing, health), a feature which that concept clearly shares with the adjective *waagiet* among the Daasanech. Besides, just like *barjo, Waag* is finished when a person dies.

Hence the difference between natural and spiritual diseases is a matter of severity. Daasanech usually keep to a naturalistic explanation as long as the disease is not life threatening. Naturalistic causes for discomforts such as flu (*ufute*), pneumonia (*veerente*) or malaria (*baash baricho*) may be found in a sudden exposure of the body from heat to cold, excess or lack of food or beverages (too much or too little of it),or the drinking of 'bad' water or milk and the eating of spoiled meat.[9]The bad part of that meat or beverage is often contagious.

Divination and curing diseases

In the course of affliction, when it becomes apparent that something wrong is going on, when the family starts to fear for the life of a patient or when somebody remains barren after the house and garden methods failed, a healer is called. Daasanech know different healers, depending on the methods they use to make a diagnosis.[10] The first type of healers investigates directly on the body. They are called *gaal gil onyi*, those who 'know by hands'. A *maa gil onyi* is usually a women who is also specialized in midwifery. By kneading and touching the body and feeling the *sidha* and the bodily flows, she investigates in which areas of the body obstructions are hindering. Doing so, she uses the body as a map for the social relations. Pain or obstructions at the right side of the body for instance refer to agnatic ties while the left side is related to the affinal ties.[11] Problems at the legs and the area around the neck are an indication that age mates might be involved, while pain in the head and problems at the back seem to point out that ancestors are involved. In the meantime or after her investigation, she narrates what her hands tell her. Doing so, she insinuates possible causes for the disease. Through the dialogue which follows, she seems to guide the patient into introspection in order to reveal a narrative which makes sense.

The second type of diviners does not work directly on the body, but divines through an oracle. The most prominent of these diviners make use of entrails. Such a specialist is always male, called the 'man of the animal stomach' (*maa aɲ gere*). The client brings a goat or a sheep of his own kraal and puts forward the question or problem he has. Then, the animal is slaughtered and the entrails are spread out at

9 These smaller complaints will usually be treated with plants or other substances such as milk or soup.

10 Here I mention the three main ones. Actually, I heard also about a fourth type, which is only found among the Randal section. These so-called *maa any dhagasaane* ("the one looking at the cattle") use the skin colours of animals to investigate problems.

11 It is tempting to draw a 'map' to denote all places with the different social relationships a person has, but I still don't know if discriminations made are more detailed than the ones quoted here. Nobody of the interviewed women told me more than this left-right dichotomy.

the back of a calabash. Slowly, the diviner 'reads' and interprets the different black and white spots and vessels of the entrails. The entrails hereby figure as a kind of 'map' of the relationships of the client.[12] Like the *maa gil onyi*, the reader of the entrails also suggests some possibilities while dialoguing with those around him, until a diagnosis is found which makes sense and is acceptable by all. After that, the diviner advises some steps to heal.

A similar but shorter way to divine is through throwing of sandals or necklaces. I was told that sandal-throwing is learned from the Nyangatom while the throwing of necklaces came from Arbore. Most of these diviners are male, though I met one woman who used the art of the necklaces.

The last type of diviner is the dream-interpreter who literally is referred to as 'the one with the sleeping head' (*maa mee rafit* or *maa mee rafanana*). This man uses his own dreams to diagnose the problems of his clients. Therefore, he abstains from food[13] for several days until he receives eloquent dreams (*amadh*) which offer him the needed insights. These insights are channeled by spirits which are messengers from *Waag*. They are said to be different from ancestor spirits. A dream interpreter is especially consulted for the more heavy cases, like diseases caused by ancestors and inherited *adaab*. Because of his dreams, he is able to return several generations until he reaches the root of the problem.

Treatment of these diseases may be performed by women who know about medicines (*'guor*)[14] or by men from the *nyerim* clans who are believed to possess special healing powers to treat such "natural diseases". Besides these *nyerim*, also people from other clans may intervene to treat specific diseases. The Murle for instance have power to cure pneumonia (*veerente*) and sleeping disease, the *Edhe* cure eye diseases and the *Tiemle* have the power to cure malaria (*baash baricho* or the disease of the spleen).In addition, some men of different clans may know how to set bones (*maa laf mamarwa*) in case of fractures or how to make incisions (*maa ched agalokha*) to remove swellings (*daafo*) or let out the bad blood.

When the intensity of a disease exceeds the "normal" and when simple methods do not resort the expected result, the body is no longer "with *Waag*" (*gonle waagiet man*) and people start to fear for the life of the patient.[15] This is the point where a shift occurs between the normal/ natural and the more dangerous human inflicted diseases. We may discriminate between four main categories or human inflicted diseases, although I am aware that some of these categories overtly overlap:

(1) Baasham 'doriet, diseases caused by curse (*'dor*):

[12] An interesting film on this topic is "The Father of the Goats: sacrifice and divination among the Hamar of Southern Ethiopia" (Strecker 1984).Jon Abbink (1996) also offers a valuable contribution.

[13] One of these people I interviewed admitted he also used alcohol in order to facilitate the process of dreaming.

[14] These people are called *gaal 'guorshioga* (those giving medicines), the word *'guor* is being used for both tree and medicine.

[15] The same holds for infertility. When a woman remains barren after massaging and other methods, the causes are sought in the social and spiritual realm.

The vast majority of curses are provoked by close relatives or agemates, often without their conscious intention to harm. Other curses are made intentionally by people with powerful psychic capacities, such as the ritual leaders, people of the *nyerim* clans and witches.

(2) Gaaram, spirits of the ancestors:

The spirits of the ancestors are said to "sit on top" of their victim or to afflict him because they are disturbed or angry for a certain reason.

(3) Evil eye and evil tongue:

A third category is caused by jealousy, envy and gossip of non-kin. Daasanech discriminate here between. Both leave a substratum behind in the body. Certain families are more suspected for this capacity than others.

(4) Adaab and nyogich, moral pollution:

The fourth category is related to the moral state of the victim. When a person is morally polluted, he or she is said to be morally polluted. This concept refers both to the crime(s) committed by somebody as to the impure state that person is into. Also the concept of *nyogich* refers to a state of impurity caused by intrusions against customary laws or taboos. The strongest *nyogich* is caused by homicide.
Below, these categories will be discussed in detail.

Baasham 'doriet, diseases caused by curse (*'dor*)

Curses (*'dor*) are the opposite of blessings.[16] They counter the flow of life and induce misfortune, infertility and disease. Most curses are associated with anger (*idho*). Daasanech say: "like a stick (*ul*) can cause an injury (*daafo*), anger can do as well".[17] Besides anger, also sadness (*wodhin deen*)[18] and any other kind of negative emotions between related people may turn into a curse. Contrarily to what is usually understood as curse, these kinds of curses are usually not deliberate. The one who cursed is often not aware that he or she provoked misfortune towards someone else. In fact, Daasanech highly disapprove deliberate curses among kinsmen. Actively putting a spell on somebody should be reserved for enemies and, in rare cases, to punish wrongdoers and antisocial individuals.

Daasanech curses also differ in another way from what we usually understand as curse. As a matter of fact, a curse usually does not inflict the one who provoked the anger or conflict, but rather inflicts one of his or her junior close kin, such as a child or grandchild. We may say that all those who are 'held' by an individual in the sense that they are blessed and taken care of, are those who can become the victim of somebody else's curse, as if the shield of blessing which should protect them fails to do so.

16 The result of a curse is also called *'dor.*

17 Evidence for this hypothesis that thoughts have manifesting power are found in the many narratives that tell about ancient diviners who manifested the world, in the daily prayers and blessings household heads perform while spitting coffee or other substances and in the conscious curses made by different men or groups towards enemies.

18 *Wozindeen* literally means 'a bad heart'.

Curses among relatives

Disputes about cattle transfers are a main source of conflict among relatives and as they involve strong emotions, i.e. easily cause anger that can develop into a curse. Examples are the neglect to transfer bridewealth payment and matters of heritage and levirate. The next fictive case may serve as an archetypical example of what I mean:

> Aarbabesh was upset by the fact that he didn't receive bridewealth for his brother's daughter Nakinech, although she gave birth twice already. Together with his two brothers, he went to ask for his animals, but Loya, the husband of Nakinech, sent them away with the message that his herds were not around and that they should come back later after the big rains. Few months later, Loya's eldest daughter, Nyerube, became very sick. Investigating the disease of Nyerube, a diviner may find that the cause for her sickness was a dispute between Loya and Aarbanesh about the delay in bridewealth transactions. It is likely that Aarbanesh was not aware that he had cursed someone, let alone that he had cursed Nyerube, a girl whom he may not even have known about. Curses among relatives may also be triggered when family members disapprove somebody's behavior. Greed, dishonesty, overbearing, gossip, lack of sexual interest of the husband or lack of hospitality, were reasons for cursing among relatives that I encountered during fieldwork.

Interesting to note here is that the place where the effects of a curse are felt reveals something about the identity of the one who cursed. Generally, curses of cognates manifest themselves on the right side of the body, while curses from the side of the mother (affines) occur at the left side. More specific insights are then figured out by the reader or healer who touches the body of the sick person or reads the intestines of a slaughtered animal.

Curses among age-mates (*'dor kaabana*)

A second source of curses are age mates, both those of the same age set as well as members of senior age-sets within the same generations. Curses from within the same generation are a common cause of affliction among young men. Other than curses of relatives, they usually hit the man himself and not his wife or offspring. *'Dor kaabana* are mostly related to disputes over cattle, or with bad behavior of individual men. Especially greed (*maarga*) and not sharing what one got, but also abuse of power (*maɲan*), a lack of hospitality (*gilmesich man*) and in a broader sense a lack of respect (*kiaan man*) all may trigger the curse of the age-mates. In this way, age mates act as guardians of customs and traditions, and the senior sets control the junior ones. Inside each age-set, members are very keen to keep a good name and thus may punish anyone in their group who spoils their name by misbehavior. The reasons why age-mates may curse reveal a lot about the values and norms that govern their relationship. In fact, they correspond pretty much to what Almagor (1978b) called "the ethos of equality" between age-peers. A dramatic example of this happened by the end of the rainy season in 1997. At that time, several youngsters were selected to fight in the war against Eritrea. When these cut their hair as future soldiers of the Ethiopian army, this caused a lot of anger among the senior generation, as according to Daasanech custom cutting hair without the permission of the elders is prohibited. When later only few returned from the war and many were seriously wounded, this was explained as the outcome anger they had caused among the members of the elder age sets. Although deliberate curses among kinsmen are disapproved, curses among age-mates are often intentional, especially when age-mates feel that other measures taken, such as advice, scolding or even physical punishment by whipping did not help improve a wrong-doer's behavior.[19]

Generally incantations with specific words to put a spell on somebody are preserved for cursing enemies during public meetings of the generation and especially in times of war, often in addition with symbolic acts and materials. Such spells are often made during meetings of age sets and are a must when going to war.

Above, I already introduced the *jeleba* as judges and the spiritual leaders blessing the girls during *'dimi*. The power of these elders to bless is equal to their power to curse, which is the reason why people accept their decisions easily. The Daasanech especially fear the *jeleba's* stick (*gasser'ara*), because deliberately pointing the end of this stick at somebody is believed to be enough to cause that person's death. *Jeleba* may also kill in a more formal way after having judged on someone's case. If decided so, the senior most *jeleba* who belongs to the clan of the accused should break a termite hill while mentioning the wrong-doer's name, hereby he puts a spell on him and his family. A common reason for a *jeleba* curse is when a young girl menstruates before her father has performed the *'dimi*. This curse may affect the girl herself or anybody of the family. Such a curse is not only a punishment because the customs are not followed, but it also serves as an act of self-defense because it is believed that a girl menstruating before her *'dimi* causes misfortune for the whole community.[20] The *jeleba* may also curse during a *'dimi ritual*, if they are not satisfied with the hospitality offered to them by the parents of the girls and complain about shortage of food or beverages, this may inhibit the girl's fertility or lead to misfortune for her family.

When a diviner reveals that the cause for a disease is a curse, the curse can be removed by a reconciliation ritual. This process is called *makan 'himi*. During *makan* all parties involved gather and the one who is cursed or the person whose child or grandchild has been cursed through confesses to have done something wrong. Hereby, the causes for anger, sadness or other forms of ill temperedness are removed from the one who caused the curse. As explained above, curses are spontaneous results of unresolved social tensions. Therefore, the one afflicted is not

[19] Especially when drunk, Daasanech often swear using expressions such as *'baashga'* (become sick), *'kuf'* (die), *'nyungutiyega'* (go into your mother's vagina). This way of speaking is called *chaarim* (to abuse somebody with words) and is considered very bad because it may develop into a curse.

[20] In case a girl has her first menstruation before she has been circumcised it is believed to endanger the *jeleba* and thus the whole community.

upset but rather embarrassed, because he was the trigger of his own misfortune or the cause that one of his children turned sick. After *makan*, the provoker of the curse must remove his curse by blessing the victim. This is done often by simply spitting saliva (*abaraaɲ*) or "hot water" (*biye kulla*)[21] over the head of the cursed one. Besides, this act is often followed by an exchange of the bark of a ritual *miede* tree.[22] Both parties make strings of that bark and bind them around the wrests of the other party. These pieces of bark remain there until they fall of.

According to Daasanech logic, the investigation into the cause of a curse is aimed at finding somebody guilty for someone else's disease (as it is the case when witches are involved), but rather a way to restore social tensions. This means that the victim of a curse usually is relieved because the causes of his affliction became clear and that things may change for the better.

Severe cases of cursing may involve the giving of compensation, for example slaughtering an animal to appease the one who has cursed. This is especially the case among age-mates where the afflicted first has to walk under the spilled blood of a slaughtered goat (*aaɲ fasiet*), together with his family. This blood takes the 'bad' away with it into the soil, where it belongs.[23] Afterwards, the skin of the sacrificed animal is cut into strips and all people involved receive a part to wear around their arms or neck.

When deliberate curses are involved and curses were meant as a punishment, reconciliation might not be accepted. This is especially the case when *nyerim* and *jeleba* are involved. In case somebody is affected by the *maa muor'guo.*

Gaaram, spirits of the ancestors

Not only the living may influence the health of others, also the ancestors can. Indeed, the Daasanech believe that the influence of a person onto his relatives does not stop after he has died.[24] When a person is buried and his *soda* has left, the *gaaram* or (ancestor) spirit remains.[25] These spirits are believed to be similar to a shadow, and to continue existing in a land beneath the earth as *gaal lesiet* (people of the

21 *Biyekulla* is another word for *shoboro* or *buun*, all referring to the "coffee" made out of coffee husks;

22 The *miede* or 'grey leaved saucer berry' (*cordia sinensis*) is a ritually very important tree among the Daasanech. Unlike other trees, it stays green all year around. The small orange berries are associated with fertility. During rituals, the bark is often used to clean the polluted.

23 Another explanation is that the blood is an offer for the ancestors, just as milk and tobacco.

24 When asking a Daasanech about what happens with a person after his death, a common answer is "We don't know" or "When we go, we go. We don't come back anymore", as if pure agnostics or as if the matter of dead is not of their concern.

25 In Daasanech language, the word *gaach* (plural: *gaasam*) means 'shadow', while ancestor spirits are called *gaaram* (sing. and plural). At first, I confused both terms. Daasanech however don't make an etymologic link between both concepts. *Gaaram* is related to the Turkana word *ngikameran* (Broch-Due 1990: 196) and also means ancestral spirits.

earth).[26] Their so-called 'land of the *gaaram'* is associated with specific places, especially in the neighborhood of big Acacia trees[27] or special stone formations, and also the lands to the West where the sun goes down. *Gaaram* are said to have white eyes (*gaal in edha*) and to feed themselves with flowers. In a poetic way, Daasanech describe the stars as the fires of the people out there and shooting stars indicate the death of somebody, implying that every human being is linked with a star.

In the private sphere as well as during public ceremonies, the dead are often acknowledged by pouring milk, tobacco and salt on the ground. During major rituals such as the *'dimi* ancestors are respectfully addressed by offering them tobacco and salt. "*Waag* is above and the *gaaram* are below and we are living in between", Daasanech say and *Waag* may communicate to the living by making use of ancestors spirits who appear in their dreams. During incantations in the morning, a household head often addresses the ancestors and asks them to bring prosperity and leave misfortune behind. This is done by pouring coffee or tobacco near the fire stones and asking the ancestors to give the good (*adabaana shish).* Since ancestors only act in the private sphere, this is not done during public meetings, except at times of great misfortune. Then, Daasanech pledge offers of milk, tobacco and even sheep to the *gaaram* (and *Waag*) in return for protection of the *gaaram*. This ritual is called *suoriyo*.[28] The same term is used for all rituals where a junior group of men sacrifices animals to their seniors in return for their blessings which indicates that the ancestors are addressed like living elders; they are in fact hierarchically ranked above the living elders.

Gaaram serve as guards for the traditions and they are therefore upset when descendants do not perform rituals in the right way or even worse, when they do not perform them at all. As far as I understood, mistakes during the death rituals are a major cause why ancestors remain restless and disturb their descendants. Even the slightest mistakes may trouble them and make him disturb his kinsmen, even after many years.[29] This is explained as a kind of "revenge"(*hala*) of an ancestor: "A man who disturbed his father, who beat his mother, who touched the leg of his father, they remember when they are dead."

Ancestors may be disturbed by the actual behavior of their living family members, just like an elder may be angry at his sons or age-mates toward their peers. In such cases, the deceased acts as if he was alive and curses his quarrelsome or greedy sons.

Another reason for *gaaram* to intervene with the living is that the latter have difficulties to renounce and let go of the deceased. It is said that when memory of a

26 Not only the dead, but also the living have a shadow. The evidence for their existence is that one can see an image of somebody when imagining or dreaming about him.

27 "The acacia is connected with our ancestors. There is the Acacia. These trees you cannot cut. They are there because of them (the ancestors). Also the *miede* (grey leaved cordia). The big tree is the cordia."

28 *Suoriyo* is also the annual ritual performed by the Randal, who do not perform a *'dimi*as the 'real' Daasanech do.

29 The *shurte* is the front part of the hair. This should be shaved when the father dies.

deceased member of family turns into sadness, the ancestor spirit will not be able to find rest and takes possession of the mourner. Therefore, it is only allowed to cry over the dead until the grave is filled with sand. After that, all crying should stop, while mourning still goes for a while. During this period, ornaments are discarded and no butter is smeared on the body and people should not speak about the deceased. If they do, they should never use the proper name because "this would call him up". Then people reply: "Hush, let him sleep, don't use his name"[30] or "be careful, when you keep crying, his shadow will come".

One specific case which occurred in a neighboring village caught my attention. A young boy was lost for several weeks. People already give up their search until he was suddenly found lying in the bush near to the riverside. When people found him, he was confused and did not remember anything anymore. The boy had become very skinny. A diviner was called and he found out that the boy was taken to the land of the ancestors by his diseased grandfather. The grandfather was upset because his sons were quarrelling. During the reconciliation ritual, a black sheep was killed along the riverside and left behind as food for the grandfather. The boy fully recovered. This kind of disappearance happens quite often, especially among boys and young men.

Different metaphors are used to express the fact that a spirit has afflicted someone: *gaaram* "sit on top of" somebody, they "cover the victim with their shadow" or they "take somebody to their land".[31]*Gaaram*-possession leads inevitably to loss of health and ultimately to death. Typical symptoms are high fever, confusion and hallucinations and pain associated with it is usually situated at the upper side of the body or at the back.

In order to remove or calm down the ancestor spirits, all family members should take part in a reconciliation ritual. Such ritual takes place by preference on a growing moon and on an even day, by preference the 4th or 8th day of the new moon.[32] The ritual starts by pouring tobacco and salt next to the fire in the hut, which is a way to contact the spirit. Then the leader of the ritual talks to the spirit and asks him or her to assist. He may say: "Father, grandfather, grandmother, show me the good way." When spirit possession is caused by neglect of rituals or by ritual mistakes, reconciliation implies that the rituals should be repeated but now in the proper way. Also here, all family members should be present and everything should be done a prescribed. Rituals of reconciliation for *gaaram* usually involve the

30 Speaking about a deceased, one should use metaphors, neither mentioning his name nor the fact that he died.

31 To be taken to the land of the gaaram can be understood metaphorically and literally. One case I encountered, people really seemed to believe that a boy was taken away for some time by his deceased grandfather. The boy from his village in Akudungule disappeared for a couple of weeks. People thought he was taken by the river, until he suddenly returned home, bewildered and skinny. Rituals were performed in which a black goat was killed. The boy had to walk under the blood and afterwards washed himself in the river. When he was better again, he admitted he survived because he fed on flowers.

32 Four and eight are perfect numbers and the waxing moon expresses the positive.

sacrifice of an animal, mostly a red colored goat. During the bleeding ritual, the throat of the animal is cut and the diseased and his family members have to walk four times under the dripping blood, similar to the removal of a curse described above. In this bleeding ritual, the blood takes away the bad to the earth. Often, a second black goat is also killed and left as food for the *gaaram*. Nobody is allowed to touch that meat. This practice seems to obey to a tit for that principle where the goat replaces a victim. This principle became clear to me when I heard about a pregnant woman, who became sick because of *gaaram*. A goat was slaughtered and she *walked under the blood*. The next day, she aborted. It was said that the bad left her body together with the fetus. The blood which washed her made her well again and the fetus "took her death". The same principle was performed long time ago when somebody was about to die. Then, a donkey was taken, a grave dug and the donkey was put in the grave to deceive the ancestor.

When the sacrifice is an ox or a cow, the blood is poured in a hole next to the fire stones.[33] Part of the meat of the slaughtered animals is bailed and eaten, but at least a part is left untouched to be thrown at the west, "as food for the ancestors". Usually, the skin of the sacrificed animal is cut into tiny long strips and each participant gets a string, but contrary to the bleeding ritual performed to remove a curse, the knot of the string is worn at the back and not at the front.

Other reconciliation rituals make use of a substance called *kuch*, which is the substance the termite hills are made of. This substance is used in a special ritual called *chaddo* (mud).[34] The *kuch* is heated up in the fire until it becomes red. Then, the hot clay is thrown in a calabash filled with water and aromatic plants like *'gor lugul* and the *bierkerech*.[35] Then, the victim sniffs the steam while facing east. After that, the victim is washed with mud of the river and smeared with butter. Finally, a bleeding ritual is performed. *Aalaɲ* plants[36] growing on a grave are an indication that the *gaaram* of the person buried has been disturbed. Then a purification ritual called *salla* is performed. In this ritual, all family members are invited and gather around the grave. A (female) sheep is killed and its blood is spilled on the grave. Coffee, tobacco and oil are then poured on the grave to satisfy the disturbed spirit and finally all family members raise and move to the east without looking back (to the west).

Evil eye (*il*) and the Evil tongue (*erbo*)

A third cause of human-induced sickness is the evil eye, which Daasanech simply call *il* (eye). *Il* is the result of jealousy or envy. Unlike curses, provokers of the evil

[33] At that place, the father usually pours tobacco, tobacco salt and milk to please the ancestors.

[34] Termite hills are associated with the ancestors, just like dung beetles and black crows.

[35] No identification made for these plants.

[36] *Aalany* (*Cadabarotundi folia*) is a very common scrubby plant in the savannah. The leaves of this plant are used to cover the grass huts. They also serve to put on the meat during communal meat feasts. The wood is used to smoke out the calabashes and milk containers.

eye are often strangers who pass by. The most common victims of *il* are young children and pregnant women. Among weaning babies and small children, evil eye may cause serious gastro-dermal disorders. It leads to abortions among pregnant women or to death during delivery. Prevention against *il* is taken very seriously. Pregnant women protect themselves by covering their belly with a dark colored coat (*sara*) and weaning babies and kids are always hidden and covered when the mother leaves the village so nobody could glimpse them. Small kids wear special amulets around their neck and arms and people will often add some *'gor nyerimo* (magical wood) to a nicely made hairstyle in order to prevent the evil eye. Somebody who is eating well may also attract the evil eye.

Besides the evil eye, there is something called evil tongue (*erbo*). The evil tongue operates in a similar way as the evil eye and is linked with jealousy. It occurs especially when somebody compares himself with somebody who is better or prettier or in cases of gossip (*hem*). Speaking badly about somebody else then makes a creature—also called *erbo*—to enter the body of the person spoken about. This *erbo* moves around, itching and driving him to madness. Unlike curses, evil eye and evil tongue are beyond a victim's impact. The only thing one can do against the evil eye is to protect oneself from foreign gazes.

In the case of the evil eye and the evil tongue reconciliation between a victim and the source is seldom possible, because the source is often unknown or very difficult to trace.[37] Besides, they are not purely mental, but materialized as creatures which live inside the body of the victim. The effect of the evil eye is sucked out by a female specialist. During fieldwork, I underwent this practice twice. The female healer touched my belly. When she located the 'thing', she started to suck my skin right above the navel and then showed me a black smelling piece (of rotten meat?) from her mouth, which she referred to as *il*.[38]

Removing the evil tongue is different. In such a case, the specialist called the *maa erb shugunua* uses a calabash filled with water which he places on different parts of the body while he knocks on it with his knuckles. When the calabash is placed on the right spot, the *erbo* creature leaves the body and falls into the water. There it makes a high sound. This is the sign for the healer to spit on it. Then, he throws out the water and beats the crawling creature to death with a stick.

Witchcraft (*muor*) and occult powers (*nyerim*)

Besides the above-mentioned curses, there are also forms of affliction which are caused by specific psychic powers. At least two concepts are used to label these psychic abilities, *muor(o)* and *nyerim(o)*. In mentioned already the power of the *nyerim* clans above. This clan related ability to bless, curse and call forth rain are inherited from father to son and are activated after circumcision. This *nyerim* is

37 I noted a case in which a woman was asked to bless someone because she was believed to have 'infected' a young mother with the Eye.

38 Some people claim that the healer puts rotten meat inside his mouth before and just plays a trick, others clearly believe the ritual act to be genuine.

considered as a gift (*ewi*) from *Waag* and a power (*fargoginte*). A man who has this *nyerim* can bless everybody, not only people of his own proper clan. Every section has some clans who possess *nyerim*. Among Shir and Oro, they are called Turnyerim and Fargaro, the *nyerim* of the Kuoro are called Lukumoi of the Kuoro and those of the Randal are called Saanle and Dabalbien.[39]

Besides blessing and calling forth rain, some of these people with *nyerim* are renowned for other magic abilities, like healing, fortune telling/divination and cursing the enemies. These people are consulted to curse the enemies in times of war and to bless the proper warriors before they go out to fight.[40] Their power is embodied in a special kind of whimsical sticks called *gurre* which are kept inside their huts.[41] Sometimes people who have *nyerim* are asked to use their power to curse a thief or somebody who committed adultery, by collecting the sand of a footprint or by taking the neck rest of a suspect. I was told that such a spell only works in case the accusation is based on truth.

The concept *muor* has different meanings in different contexts. In the first sense, *muor* refers to the fat around the stomach of a slaughtered animal, both small stock and cattle. Strings made out of this white fat tissue are put around the neck during rites of passage (such as *'dimi* or male circumcision). In this context, *muor* has a strong association with strength and prosperity and as such applies to another meaning of *muor*, namely leopard of cheetah. In a third sense, *muor* refers to the ability to divine and a diviner is called a *maa muoro*. As explained above, the Daasanech know different types of diviners, those who consult oracles by throwing sandals or necklaces on the ground and interpreting the way they fall, those who interpret dreams, and those who can read the intestines of the slaughtered goat. The latter are the most trusted diviners in Daasanech. In the fourth sense, the word *muor* refers to a very specific form of witchcraft which is used by members of certain lineages.[42] They are called *maa muor'guo*, "people with *muoro*", a concept which only slightly differs from *maa muoro* or diviner. Their *muoro* is their psychic ability to gain personal wellbeing through the use of a powder (*nyakeek)*. That powder is prepared by crunching the bones of people who have recently died.[43] This powder is added to the dung fire for the cattle or to the stove inside his hut for their kids to inhale the smoke. The smoke brings them prosperity, fertility and wealth.[44] Besides, people say that if somebody is touched by that powder or grabbed by a *maa*

39 The Rendille call their *nyerim 'iipire'*, the Samburu call them *lais*.

40 In addition, a member of these nyerim-clans should always participate in any fighting group to hold the ritual fire sticks.

41 These are often the eldest brothers of a lineage.

42 Typical subclans who have *muoro* are Edhe Khamgayo and Gaalbur Nekulo.

43 *Nyakeek* is a substance, which only is effective if the user sacrifices something else for it. The profit of it is at the cost of something else, pointing at the idea that in the long run, everything is in balance.

44 The story also goes that such witches can go on 'hunts' for other Daasanech whom they attack with their long fingernails filled with this poison. The victims might become paralysed and die. It is said that their dead brings life and prosperity to the family of the killer.

muor'guo, that person will get paralyzed and die. There is a strong belief that the death of the victim causes new life for the *maa muor'guo*. Therefore, people with *muor* are feared very much, as I could witness, even among elder people,[45] although these people are not very common within the community.

Adaab and vulnerability for accidents

So far, I described several causes of human affliction which originate in the other, be it a relative, an age mate, an ancestor, an elder or somebody with special powers. Alongside this intrusion from the outside, affliction may also originate from the internal moral state of a person. The Daasanech have two different terms describing this state of pollution or moral contamination: *adaab* and *nyogich*.

The notion of *adaab* refers to crimes, but in a wider sense to any form of misbehavior, to all kinds of *deen* (bad) a person committed the Daasanech say. The notion of *nyogich* refers in the first place to murder of a fellow tribesman,[46] but may in a broader sense be applied to every heavy intrusion of Daasanech customary laws. *Nyogich* can be removed through ritual cleansing, but *adaab* remains as a state of contamination which is the result of bad actions. Hence *adaab* is not only something which one commits, but also something which one carries, in the same way that the term *'dor* is used for a curse but also for the result of it. When I asked to clarify the difference between *'dor* and *adaab*, I was told: "*'Dor* happens to you. *Adaab* are the bad things you committed. You strike a man. You carry blood on your hands. You have *adaab*." The reference to blood on the hands clearly illustrates that *adaab* is a state of impurity which may sooner or later result in misfortune. The specific term for this type of misfortune is called *feen*: "*Feen* happens when you have *adaab*. Then, the horns of the bulls come closer and closer until they reach. Then you are finished *(kuun bye)*."

The image employed here is that somebody may behave badly until this misbehavior reaches a final point and bursts out into *feen*. *Feen* may be translated as accident, but clearly not an accident that happens "by accident". Examples of *feen* are death by lightning and death due to a snake bite, because lightning and snakes are closely associated with *Waag* and hence seen as straight punishments from *Waag*, but also other accidents like death in a battle, death by a lost bullet, death by stroke or suicide are labeled as *feen*. This seems to indicate that *Waag* is the ultimate source of justice and at the same time that there is a strong sense of inner justice which reigns the world. Daasanech believe that misbehavior sooner or later leads to death. When I asked if there were utterly bad people who nevertheless lived a long and prosperous life and died at old age in the midst of their family, the response was positive. Informants however responded that even if that person goes free, his offspring would suffer for three generations to come.

45 During my last visit in 2009, I got the chance to interview a *maamuor 'guo*. He didn't confirm this zero sum principle I mention here. He claimed that he used the powder only in the fires and never went out to kill others.

46 I went deeper into the concept of *nyogich* in Houtteman (2010).

Conclusion

In this essay, I tried to explain the images that exist for different members and segments within Daasanech society and how they are used for indigenous explanations of wellbeing and misfortune or disease, and, indirectly to enforce Daasanech morality, control individuals' behavior and maintain or restore social relationships.

I started by introducing the concept of *Waag* as the source of wellbeing and life, and argued that a harmonious relationship with *Waag* goes along with to a harmonious relation with the social environment and the ancestors. The qualities of *Waag*, i.e. good fortune and fertility, are induced by the blessings of the males, both at the individual household level, where the father blesses the family members, as well as in the realm of the community, where initiated males bless together during different rites of passage and meetings. Through these blessing, the Daasanech say, the flow of life is sustained.

By contrast, social conflicts, immoral behavior and neglect of certain rituals distort these qualities and obstruct the flow of life. Health and wellbeing are very much dependent on the moral other, the father, the mother, and the harmony between close kin and between a family and their affines. Ancestors may inflict the body and cause obstructions, leading to disease, infertility and ultimately to death. There is a strong awareness among the Daasanech that every form of misbehavior has its negative consequences, as misbehavior and antisocial attitude are believed to somehow "pollute" a person and can harm him, and also those close to him and even generations to come. The harmful influence of strangers is limited to evil eye and tongue, to conscious cursing of people with *nyerim* and of a kind of witch, called *maa muor'guo*.

In such a contextualized universe, misfortune is never seen as accidental. Disease and accidents call for meaning and serve as triggers for the moral agents to become aware of their past and their mistakes committed. In this process, the role of diviners cannot be underestimated. They offer an explanation for the affliction out of a repertoire of possible causes and the methods they suggest to regain wellbeing are in the first place aimed to restore the broken social ties and restore social harmony, be it with the living or with the ancestors. Ultimately, people aim to sustain the flow of life which is conceived as "to be with *Waag*".

One would expect that an individual who lives and behaves in a moral way towards others, i.e. who cares for his kin and age mates and who respects customs and norms, would be well off and live a long and prosperous life, until he finally dies of old age on the lap of his first born son. When I confronted some elders with this conclusion, most of them agreed, although some insisted that nobody is free from *adaab* and that ultimately *Waag* is the one who decides to take life back.

References

Almagor, Uri, 1978a: *Pastoral Partners. Affinity and bond-partnership among the Daasanech of South-West Ethiopia.* Manchester: Manchester University Press.

Almagor, Uri, 1978b: "The Ethos of Equality among Daasanech Age Peers". In: Paul Trevor William Baxter and Uri Almagor (eds.): *Age, Generation and Time. Some features of East African age organisations.* London: C. Hurst and Company, 69-94.

Broch-Due, Vigdis, 1990: *The Bodies within the Body. Journeys in Turkana thought and practice.* Bergen: University of Bergen. (PhD thesis).

Evans-Pritchard, Edward, 1956: *Nuer Religion.* Oxford: Clarendon.

Evans-Pritchard, Edward, 1976. *Witchcraft, Oracles and Magic among the Azande.* Oxford: Oxford University Press. (Abridged edition 1937).

Hallpike, Christopher R, 1972: *The Konso of Ethiopia. A study of the values of a Cushitic people.* Oxford: Clarendon.

Geertz, Clifford, 1973: "Religion as a Cultural System". In: Clifford Geertz: *The Interpretation of Cultures.* New York: Basic Books, 87-125.

Gulliver, Phillip H, 1955: *The Family Herds: A study of two pastoral tribes in East Africa, the Jie and Turkana.* London: Routledge and Kegan Paul.

Houtteman, Yvan 2010: "Murder as a Marker of Ethnicity. Ideas and practices concerning homicide among the Daasanech" In: Christina Gabbert and Sophia Thubauville (eds.): *To Live with Others. Essays on cultural neighbourhood in Southern Ethiopia.* Köln: Köppe, 128-156.

Lamphear, John, 1993: "Aspects of 'Becoming Turkana'. Interaction and assimilation between Maa and Ateker speakers". In: Thomas Spear and Richard Waller (eds.): *Being Maasai. Ethnicity and identity in East Africa.* Oxford: Currey, 87 -110.

Messing, Simon, 1968: "Interdigitation of Mystical and Physical Healing". In: *Ethiopia: Towards a theory of medical anthropology.* Behavioral Science Notes 2(3): 87-104.

Lienhardt, Godfrey, 1961: *Divinity and Experience. The religion of the Dinka.* Oxford: Clarendon.

Lydall, Jean and Ivo Strecker, 1979: *The Hamar of Southern Ethiopia. Vol. II: Baldambe explains.* Hohenschäftlarn: Renner.(Arbeiten aus dem Institut für Völkerkunde Göttingen,13).

Sagawa, Toru, 2006: "Domestic and Political Activities at Home. The space of coffee drinking among the Daasanetch of southwestern Ethiopia". *African Study Monographs.* Kyoto, 63-82.

Spencer, Paul, 1973: *Nomads in Alliance: Symbiosis and growth among the Rendille and Samburu of Kenya.* London: Oxford University Press.

Tosco, Mauro, 2001: *The Dhaasanac Language.* Köln: Köppe.

Giving Birth to An Ancestor

Boundaries and bridges between life and death among the Konso

Nicole Poissonnier

Introduction

Depending on the status a person has had during his lifetime, his death means a lesser or greater crisis for his society. This crisis is founded in the fact that roles and relations among all those who were in a given relation with the deceased have to be redefined (Loo 1991: 210). The two main functions of rituals and ceremonies for the dead are then firstly to detach them from society and then to integrate them into the community of the dead; and secondly to reorganize the society of the living (Van Gennep (1986: 142-159). There is a clear boundary that separates the living from the dead and death generally arouses fear among the living. This "crisis" of an occurred death is a time when the boundary necessarily becomes permeable so that the dead can leave the world of the living; on the other hand it is also a time of great danger for the descendants as among many ethnic groups there is a belief that death is contagious (see Hertz 1960: 78). This belief exists also among different groups in southern Ethiopia (for example among the Arsi, see Haberland 1963b: 103f), including the Konso.

As I will show in this paper, among the Konso the moment of death means also a time of creativity. This is especially the case with old people, clan chiefs and other people who have reached each possible status in life. When such people of high status die, their identity is retrospectively newly defined in order to enhance the position and role of their living relatives. Deceased and descendants enter interdependency in order to secure social roles and status and in order to do this bridges are established between the two worlds.[1]

The Konso live in south western Ethiopia, near to the Kenyan border. The administrative district of Konso is divided into *kebele* (smallest administrative unit, here: villages): Karat, Kolme, Fasha and Tuuro. My research in Konso (from 1998-2003) has revealed that belief system, burial rites and ceremonies for deceased are basically very similar all over Konso, though there are a number of variations in the different villages of Konso when it comes to the erection of the *waakaa* stele. The practices and rules in Kolme are very similar to those of the neighboring ethnic group, the Gewwada. In the following I will therefore treat examples from both Konso and Gewwada to describe how life and death are seen as connected.

The Konso inhabit a very densely populated mountainous area, where they grow maize, sorghum and some vegetables on steep terraced hills. Animals are kept in stables or herded in lowlands, but an accent is clearly made on agriculture. The

[1] Research on which this article is based was carried out among the Konso and Gewwada during the period of 1998-2003 in preparation of a dissertation.

Konso have become well known for their carved wooden anthropomorphic sculptures, *waakaa*, that are erected on pathways or on the entrance of villages to commemorate outstanding members of their society such as clan chiefs and killers of enemies or of big game (see Poissonnier 2009). The erection of the *waakaa* is strongly related to the post-mortem increase in status of the deceased person. As I will explain more amply below, the *waakaa* sculptures depict deceased clan chiefs or people who have been able to rise in status by killing a wild beast or an enemy. In order to understand how and why this rise in status of single persons is in the interest of society and celebrated at time of their death, some notions concerning death and funerals shall be put forward here.

Funeral and time in-between

When a person has died, he or she is taken to the grave on the same day, if possible. The grave is dug by the men of the neighborhood. In the regions of Tuuro and Pa'ayte, people use plots of forest as a common cemetery. In all the other regions, a lineage head designs a field to be used as cemetery by the lineage. The prescribed period of mourning for adult people in the villages of Karat is six days for a woman and nine for a man (see also Jensen (1936: 419); six days for both genders in Debana (some people spoke of only three days). During these days, people from the lineage and the neighborhood are hosted. At the end of this period, the house is ritually cleansed from the presence of the dead.

In traditional Konso perception, the spirit of a dead person lives on after death in a similar way as during lifetime. This is why family members should be buried together. Eventually however, the spirit of the deceased should reach a sort of continuum of ancestor spirits in which it is not perceived as an individual spirit anymore. Offerings of food and drink are then not done individually in a given homestead anymore but collectively for all dead ancestors at the main entrance of a village before harvest time.

In order for the spirit to get to this continuum, the descendents organize several rituals that have to be performed after the death of a person. Generally, the first step is the funeral of the dead body, which is the ceremony that helps the family and community to detach themselves emotionally from the dead person. For children and young unmarried people, the ceremonies end after this. My interlocutors in Konso held the opinion that one should finish all post-mortem duties for this group of persons as soon as possible and in one single ceremony. It is believed that people who were not able to leave offspring cannot be integrated into the continuum of ancestor-spirits, them not being an ancestor of anyone. As they cannot live forth in their descendants they are jealous spirits who remain aggressive after their death (see also Hallpike 1972: 156).

Those who die as adults with offspring enter a liminal status after death in which they neither belong to the living nor to the dead. Because of the belief that death is contagious for the descendants of a person who has just died, close relatives also are isolated from society and in a way share the liminal status.

In most existing societies, many of the social roles and relations that are connected in one way or the other during the lifetime of a person become unclear after his death and thus need to be confirmed or newly defined, in some places, the relatives of a deceased symbolically die as well (Thiel 1978: 45). Commonly, descendants leave their former role in society in order to integrate into a new one: the eldest son of a deceased man for example would probably become the head of the family, the wife of the deceased becomes a widow, the children are orphans etc. These new definitions also mean that responsibilities among the remaining descendants are redefined, and their behavior is adapted to their new role just as the behavior of other people towards them changes.

During this time, the descendants have a very complex relationship to the spirit of the dead. On the one hand, the spirit is venerated and people try to fulfill all its desires; on the other hand, everybody tries to keep it distant by fear that it could take others with it into death (Hertz 1960: 36-37). This ambivalent relationship is expressed in the way that relatives try to please it but also protect themselves by giving things into the grave for example and thereby appeasing it. Baudry (1999: 151-60) interprets this giving of things into the grave as a effort to destroy memories related to things too much identified with the deceased. This seems to apply also to the Gewwada, as one informant told me that clothing and jewellery are buried with the dead because otherwise "one would always look at those things and never stop crying". On the other hand, items left on the grave and acts performed during the mourning period reflect the role and position the dead had in society during lifetime. They are usually done by certain people who had a close/special relationship to the dead. Among the Konso the widow spills a little food or drink for her deceased husband at the entrance of her compound before she eats herself every day. In Gewwada, one puts a small amount of food into the bowl of a deceased clan chief (*bogoloho*) until the mourning period is over.

For those who have accomplished at least marriage in their lifetime, a second ceremony is organized. It is this second ceremony which integrates the deceased into the continuum of the ancestors. In Konso, the main fear people have during the time "in between", e.g. before the second ceremony has been performed, is that the spirits of the dead might pressurize them to organize their second obsequies by causing sickness, death or sterility of people or fields. A man from Konso explained to me:

> We say that someone for whom the obsequies are not organized and no animals are slaughtered remains a guest over there among the dead. Therefore he feels obliged to trouble his living relatives. They need to spill the blood of an animal so that he can integrate himself in the world of the dead instead of remaining a guest for eternity. This spirit can even bring sickness or kill someone from his family so that they understand it is high time to slaughter an animal for him (Interview with Koora from Debana/Konso in 2003).

The social roles of people of high offices (for example the clan heads in Konso) and the relationships they have with others are more complex than those of ordinary people as they go beyond family-ties and thus are more broadly distributed than to less prominent people, the death of such a person concerns many more people directly. The separation from a person of high ranking is therefore more difficult for a whole society than from a child. Bloch (1982) argues that this is because their offices are thought of being everlasting (e.g. people come and go, but institutions last).

Second obsequies (*sahaita*)

The second obsequies, *sahaita*, should ideally be organized one year later for all deceased adults who had had children. But in reality, it often takes up to several years. These ceremonies resemble the funeral: again mainly lineage members and neighbours attend and need to be hosted, a ceremony is held some parts of which are performed at the grave which now obtains its definite form, and the house of the deceased is ritually cleansed a second time. The deeds and relations of the dead are lined out in songs which stir emotions among the guests and make many people cry. Only if the deceased had reached grandparenthood, people should refrain from crying, as people of grandparenthood are said to have reached all necessary steps in life that a person should reach. The spirits of such people are also the less feared as having fulfilled the main goals in life—produce offspring—the spirits are said to be less aggressive. One elderly informant from Konso described the special songs (*shileta*) that are exhibited at such grandparent's obsequies:

> During the *shileta*, the singers name all the relatives and ancestors; they remember the highlights in the life of the deceased and get money for this. Later on, this money is used to buy drinks for the guests (Interview with Kotana from Patinkalto/Konso in March 2003)

This venerating of exploits, great deeds and successes of the dead during lifetime is a way to define the status of the deceased. As mentioned above, the money given to the singers is used to buy drinks for the guests. Guests will usually remember the amount of drink served to them and use this as an indicator for the greatness of the deceased. In that way, the singing for the deceased can be seen as a way to increase his reputation.

Generally, second obsequies are much more of a festivity and much more costly than a funeral concerning the number of guests and the amount food and drink. Depending on the status and wealth of the deceased, a certain number of animals should be slaughtered. Kotana said:

> In our forefather's time, one ox was slaughtered if the person who died had borne children. Today, the family adds two times nine bowls of *kurkufa*[2] if it was a man and two

[2] Konso dish made from maize and leaves of the *moringa* tree.

times six bowls of *kurkufa* if it was a woman (Interview with Kotana from Patinkalto/Konso in March 2003).

If the person was a local clan chief, nine goats and one ox should be slaughtered and if it was a regional clan chief, the family should host the guests with nine oxen and ten further animals [goats, sheep]. Also, the ceremonies take more time which raises also the amount of drink that is to be served (Watson 1998: 167-168). It should be noted, that clan chiefs are also regarded as "fathers" of the whole clan so that his descendants are considerably numerous. Wealth and thus economic and social position of power of the deceased as well as his family or clan are demonstrated through the number of days, invitees, number of slaughtered animals and exposition of goods belonging to the dead person.[3]

As descendants do not always have enough resources to organize a ceremony worthy of the status of the deceased shortly after his death, there is a tendency to wait and hope for better crops. This often leads to a longer period of continued postponing of the ceremony during which the descendants feel threatened by bad luck, bad crops and sickness that could be caused by their impatient ancestor.

Hero-killers

Among the Konso, as among other ethnic groups in Ethiopia, men can improve their status by killing a big game animal (lion or leopard among the Konso) or a male enemy. For successful hunters and killers of enemies, just as for clan chiefs, *waakaa* are erected during second obsequies as a representation of the dead to venerate their deeds. These monuments depicting the dead with symbols of his status in life are brought to their erection-place (details see below) by family-members or neighbours (depending on the different rules in the different regions).[4]

The obsequies for such hunters and hero-killers are occasions on which other hero-killers arrive with all of their insignia. Also relatives will carry special jewellery on this occasion which identifies them as relatives of a hero-killer. Very often, the widow of such a man will wear all the insignia of her deceased husband.[5]

Most of the male participants of the ceremony will bring their arms. In Konso, spears are still most prominent besides guns at these occasions, because, as I was told, it is seen as more heroic to kill with a spear than with a gun. Even animals

3 Such practices are documented in Ethiopia from among the Sheko (Straube 1963b: 68), Sala (Straube 1963b: 371), Oromo (Wassmann 1935: 46-47), but also from European middle ages (Mischke 1996: 44, 50).

4 In many societies of Ethiopia, a representation of the dead is brought to the grave a second time. Straube(1963b: 136) for example writes of a bamboo-construction (*kombotse*) among the Koorete that represents the dead and is decorated with signs of his status in society.

5 Apart from Konso, this is also done among the Arsi (Haberland 1963a: 494; Haberland 1963b: 104), the Sidama (Lonfernini 1971: 143), the Koorete (Straube 1963b: 128) and Sheko (Straube 1963b: 70).

killed with a gun are often stabbed again with a spear after its death. The killers present at such a ceremony in Konso (the same is true for Gewwada), and especially those who are 'witnesses' for the killer act out a pantomime of the scene of killing during this ceremony.[6] The other killers demonstrate their status by holding their guns up high or by making their spears tremble over their heads.[7] The songs sung at the ceremony for a killer tell about his qualities as a war leader and hunter.

The serving of huge amounts of food and drink and especially the slaughtering of big and fat animals is central in order to demonstrate the wealth of the deceased person's family which is a sign for its industriousness, a strong bonding, and productivity (economic and reproductive). The expenses for such a ceremony can never be met by a single household, rather, all the members of the extended family have to contribute (see also Haberland 1957b: 327). The relations evoked during the feast are also those that have been entered into through the killing (such as witness, generation sets,[8] member of the group of killers of the same game...) and thus are extended beyond those of biological kinship and neighborhood.

These ceremonies with huge numbers of invitees and a generous hospitality are all clearly made to demonstrate and enhance the celebrity of the deceased. At the same time, however, this celebrity constitutes the pride and identity of the ones capable of organizing such a feast.

Besides the grandeur of the feast, also the size of the grave-marker (*waakaa*) erected by the descendants is seen as indicator of the personal success of the dead and depends on the quantity of his descendants. A big monument is extremely costly (as I will describe further below), therefore it indicates a large number of descendants who serve as proof of his fertility and ability to produce powerful and industrious offspring (able to organize and pay the erection of a monument) and thus increases his prestige. Vice-versa, the descendants prove themselves worthy of a prestigious man, and worthy to aspire to as much prestige as him.

The grave-markers are made by only few wood carvers in Konso who are authorized to make *waakaa*. They are ordered and paid by the family of the deceased and usually extremely costly. While they work on the *waakaa*, the wood carvers live in the compound of the families. During that time they demand food, drink and pay daily on behalf of the deceased, saying that they are in connection with him. Prices are negotiated on the base of the assumed wealth of the family, and the more it is paid, the more prestigious later the monument. Usually, the amount spent is communicated orally and speculations about the cost amount will

6 Gewwada (Kap. 3.3), Sheko (Straube 1963b: 70), Sidama (Hamer 1987: 535, 543; Lonfernini 1971: 145), Gedeo (FOK 70, S. 65: 38/21); Shangama (FOK, 60, S. 118: Wd 62/3-6 und Wd 62/10-12), Dorze (Samson Giorgis/Guillaume Terver: ‚Polyphonies éthiopiennes', 55 min. colour); Arsi (FOK 63: S. 86; P 21/31 + 32; Je 5/16a).

7 A missionary of the Catholic Church told me that among the Gamo, all killers hold a stick during these festivities which they throw up as many times as they have killed an enemy.

8 In Konso, a new generation-set to be formed needs to hunt one lion or leopard in order to get its name. The hunter kills the animal in behalf of the whole generation.

spread based on the observation of time the carver spends in the homestead and on the amount of coats or sheep slaughtered there. One family had even decided to write the final price in Ethiopian *birr* on the statues themselves. This way again, the prestige of the deceased depends on the wealth of his descendants.[9]

Whether the sculpture is erected on the grave or in another place depends on the social standing of the deceased. Only outstanding people are allowed to erect a monument on a communal village ground. Whether a person is accredited such a status allowing a monument on a communal village ground again is discussed in village meetings beforehand and depends among others on the wealth of the descendants (Poissonnier 2009: 232-239). The monuments for hunters and killers should always be placed in a place where as many people as possible can see them. This may be on a public meeting place or the main entrance of the village or on private ground along a pathway used by the public. People depicted on public places will be remembered as "more heroic" than people being represented on their private field. Here the negotiation of the deceased person's status becomes very clear and verbally outspoken.

But also the statues themselves are full of symbolism. The more simple monuments consist of a sculpture of the hero and his wife. The hero-figure may be depicted with killer's insignia such as a special necklace. If this is missing, he probably is venerated for other reasons. Beside the hero, other figures reveal facts about his status—or the status that descendants like to accord him. The hairstyle of his wife can tell the instructed spectator whether they had had children or even grandchildren. The number of wives depicted indicates wealth as this demands capacity to nourish two or more households. But also again it indicates offspring because only wives who have born children are represented in the monument. The greater monuments consist in sculptures of the hero-killer, often two or even three wives, enemies and animals slain, and several other signs of success and wealth such as little stones symbolizing plots of land owned, monkeys which are held (simply for distraction) only by rich families etc. These symbols were always attributable to the deceased during his lifetime but may be exaggerated or re-interpreted after his death. About one sculpture that was carved with a gun for example, I was explained that the deceased had "bought a gun" and so the sculpture was ordered with this gun though he had never used it to hunt big game.

The wood used for *waakaa* among the Konso must be of the holy juniper tree which grows in the forests of the clan chiefs and which need cutting permission. A sculpture monument can thus not be carved without the approval of the clan chief, who decides in the name of the whole clan. Therefore, these monuments are not only to demonstrate the greatness of the deceased ancestor but also to demonstrate the acknowledgement of the deceased and his family's power and influence by the

[9] See Poissonnier 2009; Poissonnier 2010a, 2010b for a more detailed description of the *waakaa* production.

clan and the clan head. Therefore the *waakaa* of one deceased person should actually be considered as a monument for the whole lineage.

In Gewwada, where only stele from stone are erected, but no wooden sculptures, all stele of one family are placed together on one ground. During my research I visited one of these places that belonged to the family of a clan chief (*bogoloho*). The steles were fit into clusters of up to five, each cluster belonging to one deceased man of the lineage who had hunted big game. The smaller stones of the cluster represented each the first born son of one of his four wives. Here, the monument grows as the family grows and augments its fame until one member breaks off to initiate his own ground.

One can conclude then, that the importance of a kill is not put restricted to an individual man, but also of importance in a broader social context for his clan and lineage. Descendants can identify and take pride in their relationship with a hero-killer which will mark them even after his death.

Ceremonies and monuments for clan chiefs

In Konso, there are three regional or big clan chiefs and a number of local ones. Through their ritual work, they guarantee that the relation between god, people and the ancestors but also the people among each other is well balanced and harmonious. While the local clan chiefs may hunt, the regional ones stand for fertility and well-being of the whole country and should not kill the smallest animal with their own hands. During my research in the year 2003, I witnessed the erection of one stone stele (as mentioned above, in Gewwada only stone and not wood is used) for a deceased clan chief (*bogoloho*) and lion hunter in Gollango/Gewwada:[10]

> When I arrived with my informant Chabo at the homestead where the ceremony was to be held, two women were already singing and evoking the deeds of the deceased, their relationships with family members, people who had be given land etc. and the circumstances of their deaths. At around noon, a diviner came to touch all those of the guests that were "of no fault" (as my informant explained) with a particular plant (*ako*; lat. probably *sansivieria*) and the forehead of all the relatives with the leaves of another plant (*maske*). Since the diviner acts as a medium in contact with the spirit of the dead, this gesture is probably done to demonstrate that the spirit approves of the presence of these people and that they have no unaccomplished duties left towards it. After some time, an ivory horn was blown, which is another item used only at obsequies for high officials. This is only done, so my informant, when a very important person has died.
>
> Through time, more guests arrived grouped as families or groups of killers and witnesses to exhibit their song and dance, and then again left the compound to come back later or settle to sit. The different groups who represented different families were clearly separated so that the different sets of relationships to the dead became apparent.

[10] As my observations were quite similar to how my interlocutors described the erection ceremonies of *waakaa* in Konso, I will use this case for illustration.

Around fifteen killers were present and dancing in front of the compound in a way that expressed their anger and fury about the loss of one of their members. Their heads and weapons were decorated with a creeper plant that identified them as killers and they frequently forced their way through into the compound. Some of them pierced their spears into the thatched roof of the house of the deceased, and others pantomimed a fight. A Gewwada informant explained to me that only those who had killed the same animal may look into each other's faces while dancing; others have to dance beside each other. In the late afternoon, the killers played a pantomime showing the lion-hunt of the deceased. Also the next day, the killers and witnesses clearly dominated the ceremonial exhibition with their dances and throwing spears.

After the dancing, the invitees ran to the place to which the killers and witnesses had carried the stele some days prior to the ceremony. "Are there any strong men around"? It was said, "If there are, let them now carry the stone". The stele was carried about 1 km to the place where it was to be erected by 8 men. But in fact a whole lot of people were involved and it looked as if it needed at least 20 men to carry (Poissonnier 2009: 247-254).

Photo 1: The stele is carried to its erection place. (Photo: Poissonnier 2003)

The involvement of many people clearly is an exaggeration of the weight and size of the stele. The groups of killers and hunters and their exhibitions are very important as they confirm the status of the deceased as a hunter of big game. At the same time, they demonstrate their social relationship with the deceased and that they all belonged to the same group of hunters or killers. This became very clear shortly after erection, when the killers and hunters had their weapons smeared with a mixture of ochre and butter. Here, the status of the living killers and hunters is confirmed publicly. Those who have not really killed or who have done so in an inappropriate manner[11] may not present their weapon to be smeared with ochre at this occasion.

[11] I was told that some people claim to be killers having stabbed with their spear into an animal that they have found already dead. Others have well hunted down a big game but failed to fulfill the prescribed slaughtering of goats afterwards.

My interlocutor during this ceremony pointed out to me that shortly before people went to fetch the stele, the diviner present at the ceremony went to pay a visit to "the sick" clan chief (who had actually died and been buried years ago). Once he came out of the house, he officially announced the death of the clan leader.

This hiding or denying of death and declaring it as disease is a particularity of some high-status people that we can find throughout Ethiopia.[12] In Konso, the regional clan chiefs should not even be buried as in the Gewwada case mentioned above, but be declared as "sick" or "suffering" for a period of nine years and nine months. This means, that the funeral—which usually is the first step of detaching a dead from society—does not take place; but at official "discovery" of death, preparations are made directly for the second obsequies. Kotana explained:

> If the person was a *poqalla*, the corpse is kept for a year. The corpse is cleaned well and stays in his compound. During this time, people will say that he has caught a cold. Everybody would say: 'Oh Kala... 'Or '... Shirtu has caught a cold 'even though this is not true and in fact he has already died long ago. Only, when the second mourning is organized after one year, one will also talk about his death (Interview with Kotana from Patinkalto/Konso in March 2003).

Until the death of a *poqalla* is officially announced, visitors will come to the compound saying they want to see the 'sick' one in his hut and how he's doing. They bring food and drink for the 'sick' which will be eaten by the people charged with watching and cleaning the corpse.

Tadesse (1992: 12-21) describes in detail how the Kayote Kala—*poqalla* of the Kala lineage, one of the three regional clan chief families in Konso—was kept and mummified when he died in 1990. This procedure should have last nine years and nine months, but in reality, this time was shortened to less than seven months.[13] During the ceremony, Tadesse depicts, the sculpture of Kayote was first erected and then rubbed with a mixture of ochre and goat's blood. Then, a cord of grass was fixed on the tail of the ox' skin in which the dead was wrapped. The other end of the cord was fixed on the sculpture. Finally, the copse was put into the grave in a sitting position together with the stool he was sitting on. After filling the grave, the *waakaa* as well as the wooden poles were put on without ever interrupting the connection of the *poqalla* and the sculpture by the grass cord.

[12] Brøgger (1986: 100) states that the length of time one hesitates to publish the death of a person in Sidama is directly connected with his social status. The time prescribed for the period between the death and the second obesity was said to be several days among the Guji (Haberland 1963: 335), a length of time according to the wealth of a person among the Ari (*ibid.*). Other groups who deny the death of a ritual leader for some time are the Bashada (own observation.); the Yem (Kronenberg 1963: 514, 517f; Straube 1963b: 349); and the Sheko (Straube 1964: 51). Among the Burji, the death will not be kept secret as such, but the whole population denies it hereafter, although they know better (Haberland 1963a: 308).

[13] The journalist Collomb (2003: 41f) was able to witness the funeral of a mummified wife of a *poqalla* (*poqalteeta*). He was also told that the deceased had stayed in her hut for nine years before.

Collomb (2003: 38) mentions also such a cord of grass, which, according to him, was arranged by the children of the village. His informants told him that it symbolized the umbilical cord that exists between the living and the dead. On his pictures, this cord can be seen on the sculpture as well as on the mummy.

It is in these ceremonies for clan chiefs and, to a lesser extent, hero-killers that symbols for a connection between the worlds of the living and the dead become most apparent.

While none of the other authors on Konso mention this cord as symbol of an umbilical cord, my own observations in Konso and in Gewwada show similarities: the relatives may bring some grass or leaves to the statues or stele of a deceased ancestor 'to greet him'. This grass, as I was told, symbolizes the living—"those who are still there"—by being a symbol of fertility and well-being.

Similarly, the corpse of a deceased clan chief of the Gewwada should be accompanied by a small green calabash (insignia of clan chief in Gewwada) and an ostrich egg; (insignia of the office of the clan chief in Konso and Gewwada). On the grave, a peeled and decorated juniper tree is thrust into the earth. "The stele is put up for the deceased, but the wooden poles represent the descendants, the ones who are still living", my Gewwada informant explained (see Poissonnier 2009: 247-254). The juniper trees are considered as holy in both Konso and Gewwada. In Konso, their wood is used for *waakaa*, but also to put up a pole to symbolize the creation of a new generation. The trees grow in the holy forest of the clan chiefs of the Konso. Demeulenaere (pers. comm.) interprets them as a sort of "antenna" that clan chiefs use in order to communicate with god and the ancestors.

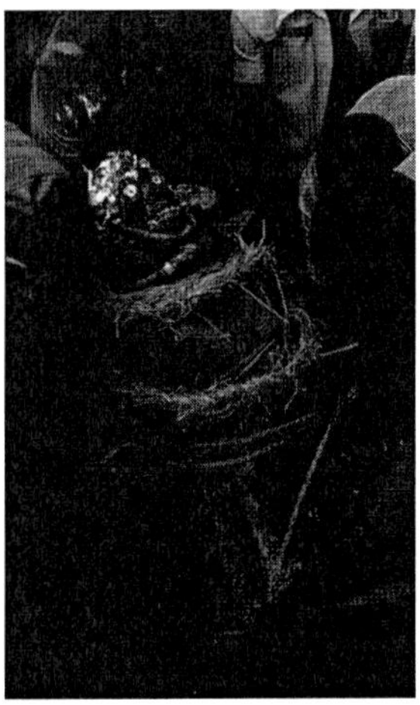

Photos 2 and 3: Mummy of the deceased wife of a *poqalla*; *Waakaa* representing the same woman (Photos: Marc Deville in Machelo 2003)

On the day of the erection of the stele in the region of Kolme, the witness of the killer decorates it with three red circles on the top made from ochre and butter. Butter is also a symbol of fertility as it can be produced only when cows have calves and give a lot of milk. He then not only decorates the stele with the hero's creepers plant *xalala* (*cissum rotundifolia*), but also plants it on the foot of the stele. After some time, this plant will completely cover the grave and the stele which can be hard to discover. In the long run not the monument for the dead prevails, but rather new life in form of a plant taking its roots in the grave (see Poissonnier 2009: 262). The grass cord attached to the *poqalla* in this sense should be interpreted as a symbol for the connection between the living and the dead represented in their sculptures.[14] Juniper trees and cord are both strong symbols of the connection between the world of the living and the dead and of continuity of the society.

As pointed out above, the regional *poqalla* and *bogoloho* stand for well-being and fertility of their country and are responsible fora harmonious relationship between the people in it, including the ancestors, and people and god. They may not leave their country, because the destiny of the whole country and its people it is intertwined with their own. Therefore, the death of such an office-holder is experienced as quite a danger in society. In the examples of Konso and Gewwada, one tries to trick out this danger by simply denying the death and this way, he can be integrated into the world of the ancestors directly and without socially dying through a funeral. On the other hand, the regional chief is already seen as the representative of the world beyond human life and as the guardian of life and fertility during his lifetime. The *poqalla* being in this in-between-status means that he is not a member of society like other "normal" people and therefore he does not need to be disembodied after his death.

Eligibility to ancestorhood

As mentioned earlier, in Konso, it is considered important to reunite family members after their death in a common burial field. As Korra from Konso explained, it seems that the ones becoming ancestors after the ceremonies integrate a sort of continuum of family-spirit. The ideal would be to integrate all deceased members of the lineage into this sort of 'lineage spirit' to make it grow big and strong.[15] As we have seen, Konso put an importance on burying people together in family-clusters in one of their fields. A great number of complete graves on the family burial ground with a considerable number of monuments for killers thus become a symbol of a strong lineage-spirit.

But not all members can be buried together. Newborn babies for example are buried behind the house Children (usually a baby would start being a child when it

[14] This symbolic of connection between the world of the dead and of the living is also found among other groups: Hamer (1987: 543ff) interprets a long wooden pole (*dore*) that the Sidama put up on a mourning feast for a man in a similar way. Unlike the grass cord of the *poqalla* however, this stake is taken down when the ceremony is over to make sure that the connection between the two worlds expires.

[15] Among many groups (e.g. Arbore (Tadesse 1999: 115); Macha-Oromo (Bartels 1983: 221; Knutsson 1963)), people cited greater devotion to their clan or lineage than to their broader ethnic group.

starts walking and / or stops breast feeding) are buried in the family field, but not together with the others. Instead they are given a place at the far edge of the field. But also, a person from whose body a trophy was cut is denied a funeral and thus has no place in the family burial ground, which is tantamount to being denied a among the ancestors.[16] In case a mutilated body was found after battle, one would just "dig him up in a hole" but not in a grave. This way, a lineage or even a whole society can be weakened in a much more sustainable manner if trophies are taken. Bloch (1982: 229) has called this technique of deliberately cutting short on the ancestor-line of enemies "negative predation"

Those who remain without ceremony cannot integrate the world of the ancestors but remain individual and lonely (often angry) spirits without belonging. Instead of caring for the well-being of their descendants, they seek revenge and cause sickness and infertility of fields and people. If a lineage only manages to integrate very few people into their circle of ancestors because too many of them die before being married or are mutilated in battle, this will weaken the lineage which cannot identify with a long range of prestigious ancestors.

Giving birth to an ancestor: constructing a new identity

In Konso, there is a saying that people will triumph over death through their children (Amborn 2002: 91). Following this logic, a person may only be integrated into the community of ancestors if he or she has borne children, because the further existence of people after their death depends on the memory of them. The memory can be promoted and sustained by the living descendants through more or less regular offerings to the dead, feasting and the erection of monuments.

The interdependence between ancestors and descendants is shown by the fact that memorials are generally erected for people by their children. Katamo from Gera in Konso told me that the only reason to erect a monument for an ancestor was the pride of his descendants. The descendants are also the ones who negotiate permission, payment and modalities for the cutting of the wood from the holy forest of the *poqalla*. My informant Chabo told me about the Gewwada who use only stone stele:

> When the deceased had had many relatives, then they can go very far, endure thirst, heat, hunger and look for a really good and tall stone to erect on his grave. If he has had but very few descendants, they will only bring a small stone. The relatives carry that stone near to the house and everybody comes to admire it and says 'Ah, this one has had many relatives!' (Poissonnier 2009: 184).

16 Among many of the societies in southern Ethiopia, men cannot become ancestors, when trophies are cut from their bodies, especially the prominent symbol of fertility: their penis. In a legend related by Sahlu (2002: 150), a Borana begs his enemy who is about to kill him for mercy and to leave his body intact, because "the castrated one is eaten by the vultures". Not death itself, but the mutilation of the body is seen as unbearable because the mutilated is refused the crucial ceremony that brings him into ancestorhood.

Having many descendants is important not only for reasons of prestige, but is connected with the power ascribed to an ancestor of influencing fertility and well-being of a group. Among the Konso and many of their neighbours, the well-being of the land and people, the fertility of fields, animals and people depends largely on the correct observation of given ritual and social rules.[17] To grant and see to these rules and the social order being observed is the main role of the ancestors who become the guardian of rules and their mood more or less depends on the behavior of the descendants. In order to exercise this role however, these ancestors need contact people among the living. These are generally very old people and diviners who can interpret the wishes and opinions of the dead. At the erection ceremony I could witness in Gewwada, the diviner played this role of being in connection with both the world of the living and the dead. His presence guaranteed that the deceased appreciated the way the ceremony was held because people presumed that disapproval would be communicated through this diviner. Hamer (1987: 94) stated that generally rites of second obsequies are supposed to ensure this connection of the authority of the ancestors with the authority of the elders and direct descendants. This way, the existence of death conditions life and thereby death is undeniably connected with fertility.

The power and influence a person has had during his life are demonstrated during the ceremonies in order to assure him the highest possible status among the ancestors or the highest possible value added to this group. The ceremony of mourning is not only an occasion to venerate the greatness of an ancestor, but also to determine the power and influence, that he will have in his new position as an ancestor because of the remembered status of a deceased, the meaning and power attributed to him depends on the way his second obsequies were organized by his descendants.

The status of the living in society again depends in some way on whether and how they may relate to their ancestors, as shown through a series of symbols of continuity during the obsequies. The jewellery and insignia worn on these occasions not only identify the own (new) status of the people and consolidate it, a very important role of this jewellery is that they show off the relation the bearer has with the deceased.

The status of the deceased is defined (confirmed, enhanced or played down) by this last ceremony. Because of the interrelatedness of the status of the descendants and the ancestor, the former are interested in according the highest prestige possible since it is the verdict on their own future status as a group within society. The main interest of the descendants in organizing the second obsequies would then be to redefine their own status and to legitimize this through their relation with an ancestor as prestigious as possible. If the status of the deceased and thus the power of the deceased fall back on his descendants, then the latter are very interested in remembering and reminding the status of the dead even after the

[17] See also Amborn (1998: 356ff) on the Burji; Freeman (2002: 134f) on the Gamo; Hamer (1987: 82f) and Schulz (1941/43: 535) on the Sidama.

ceremony. Because the descendants continue to refer to him in order to secure their own newly negotiated status, the ancestor remains influential.

This strong identification of the descendants with their ancestors explains why society refuses the totality of rituals to some of their members. People who have not yet proven their belonging to the community or else whose belonging has expired by own fault or by mutilation, are excluded from the community of ancestors because they are not apt to live up to the ideal that the living could identify with and improve their proper position. It is thus a clear decision to restrict the number of those who may become ancestors to a small portion of society who have accomplished all main goals set for them (see Amborn 2002: 86).

As we have seen, the greatness of the ceremonies of the second obsequies depends on the status the deceased had achieved during life. The status of a person in life depends on his age, the number of his descendants, and his economic power. The circumstances of his death can be used to negotiate a better status such as that of a hero if the person has died in battle or while killing a big game animal. Once the deceased is integrated into the community of the ancestors, new social exploits are not possible. The mourning feast is the last opportunity to re-negotiate his status among the ancestors. The ancestors are the ground on which a society is built and social fertility of a group depends on their amount and ranking of the ancestors. The felt strength and power of a society lies in the amount of people it has managed to make reach the status of an ancestor after having reached all goals in life set out for them. Because then, the social order is intact, people continue influence after their death through their descendants and those can identify with their dead forefathers. As Jamin (1979: 290-292) said, with the second obsequies, society can "give birth" to an ancestor.[18]

References

Amborn, Hermann, 1988: "History of Events and Internal Development: The example of the 'Burji-Konso cluster'". In: Tadesse Beyene (ed.), *Proceedings of the Eighth International Conference of Ethiopian Studies, Addis Ababa 1984*. Huntingdon: Elm Publications, 751-767.

Amborn, Hermann, 2002: "Concepts in Wood and Stone. Socio-religious monuments of the Konso of southern Ethiopia." *Zeitschrift für Ethnologie* 127, 77-101.

Bartels, Lambert, 1983: *Oromo Religion*. Berlin: Reimer.

Baudry, Patrick, 1999: *La Place Des Morts: Enjeux et rites*. Paris: Armand Colin.

Bloch, Maurice and Jonathan Parry (eds.), 1982: *Death and the Regeneration of Life*. Cambridge: Cambridge University Press.

Collomb, Etienne, 2003: Le Peuple Konso Honore Ses Héros. *GEO* 291, 34-42.

FOK. Fotoarchiv (FOK) des Frobenius-Instituts Frankfurt/ Main.

Gennep, Arnold van, 1986 (1981): *Übergangsriten*. Frankfurt/ New York: Campus. (Édition de la Maison des Sciences de l'Homme).

[18] "La société peut alors accoucher d'un ancêtre".

Haberland, Eike, 1957: "Verdienstfeste in Süd-Äthiopien".*Paideuma* VI, 326-341.

Haberland, Eike, 1963a. *Galla Süd-Äthiopiens*. Stuttgart: Kohlhammer.

Haberland, Eike, 1963b: "Grabsteine der Arussi und ihre Beziehung zu megalithischen Denkmälern und Totenmalen anderer äthiopischer Völker". *Acta Ethnographica* XII, 100-138.

Hallpike, Christopher R., 1972: *The Konso of Ethiopia*. Oxford: Oxford University Press.

Hamer, John H., 1987: *Humane Development: Participation and Change among the Sidama of Ethiopia*. Tuscaloosa: The University of Alabama Press.

Hertz, Robert, 1960: *Death and the Right Hand*. Aberdeen: Aberdeen University Press.

Jamin, Jean and Nabé Vincent Coulibaly, 1979: "A bout de souffle. La dette de vie chez les Sénoufo". In: Jean Guiart (ed.), *Les hommes et la mort—Rituels funéraires a travers le monde*. Paris: Abexpress. (Le Sycomore—Objets et Mondes), 281-292.

Jensen, Adolf E., 1936: *Im Lande des Gada*. Stuttgart: Strecker und Schröder.

Poissonnier, Nicole, 2010a: "Favourite Enemies. The Case of the Konso". In: Sophia Thubauville and Christina Gabbert (eds.): *To Live with Others. Essays on cultural neighbourhood in Southern Ethiopia*. Köln: Köppe, 236-251.

Poissonnier, Nicole, 2010b: "Killing—a Rite of Passage?" In: Alke Dohrmann, Dirk Bustorf, Nicole Poissonnier (eds.): *Schweifgebiete. Festschrift für Ulrich Braukämper*. Hamburg: Lit, 42-51.

Poissonnier, Nicole, 2009: *Das Erbe der "Helden". Grabkultur der Konso und kulturverwandter Ethnien Süd-Äthiopiens*. Universitätsverlag Göttingen (Göttinger Beiträge zur Ethnologie Band 3).

Tadesse, Wolde, 1992: "The Death and Burial of Kalla Qänazmach Kayoté, a Ritual Leader of the Konso People of Southern Ethiopia". *Sociology Ethnology Bulletin 1*, 12-21.

Thiel, Josef Franz, 1978: "Tod- und Jenseitsglaube im Bantuafrika". In: Hans-Joachim Klimkeit(ed.): *Tod und Jenseits im Glauben der Völker*. Wiesbaden: Harrassowitz, 40-47.

Thiel, Josef Franz. 1984:*Religionsethnologie*. Berlin: Reimer. (Collectanea Instituti Anthropos).

Wassmann, Dietrich, 1935: *Das Oromovolk auf unserem abessinischen Missionsfelde.* Hermannsburg: Verlag der Missionshandlung.

MATERIAL CULTURE AND IDENTITY IN SOUTH OMO

CONVERGENCE AND DIVERGENCE

Tina Brüderlin

Looking behind the scene into the storage spaces of major anthropological museums, the visitor is generally struck with awe when confronted with countless shelves filled with thousands and thousands of objects—objects from all over the world, neatly stored, numbered, catalogued, grouped and labeled, sitting on paper cushions, conserved to be protected from time and decay. Some might immediately stand out due to their beauty, some due to the craftsmanship, artistic expression or precious materials processed, but some might also be inconspicuous and silent owing to their minimalist reticence.

Once physically and contextually detached from their originating context, ethnographic artifacts become "stranded" (Schildkrout 1988: 159) and a blank canvas for the projections of their beholder. Consequently, ethnographic collections have been utilized and manipulated for multiple museological, scientific and economical agendas, changing through time, depending on the *Zeitgeist* and paradigms in which the objects were acquired and exhibitions were curated. These agendas served many purposes, ranging from emphasizing power relations, demonstrating national authority, satisfying curiosity, proving scientific theories or following particular educational means, to name just a few. Due to the history of the major western museum collections, not rarely rooted in a colonial past, the perspectives of the original owner or user of the object often remained peripheral or altogether silent within this context. If recorded, they stayed confined to notes in the accession files or archives, leaving the task to explain, interpret and position the object's history, meaning and emic value to the curators. Over decades this dilemma of heteronomy has significantly affected and complicated the relationship between museums and originating communities[1] and most contemporary anthropological museums now assign themselves to the continuous endeavor of building up relationships of trust and cooperation with originating communities and to thereby complement their resources with emic contextualization (Simpson 2001). Consequently, museums are faced with the intensive research task to elicit documentations to enable historic and ethnographic embedding of their holdings and to include emic content into collections and exhibits.[2] This involves manifold processes of learning, rethinking and reevaluating museum collections and exhibition

1 The term "originating community", often also referred to as "source community", is in this context applied to the groups among which artifacts were collected in the past, as well as their descendants today. This term may apply to indigenous groups from which objects were collected, but also includes all other groups from which objects were obtained, such as diaspora, immigrant, minority communities etc. (Brown/Peer 2003: 2).

2 Various such museum projects and the results achieved through this cooperative approach are described in Brown/Peers 2003.

methods in cultural institutions, which are—and will continue to be so—under constant revision themselves, as can be observed in current discussions on the most recent European museum projects such as the Musée de Quai Branly, Paris or the future Humboldt Forum, Berlin (Brown/Peer 2003; Flier/Parzinger 2009; Jolly 2011; Krieger/Koch 1973; Phillips 1999; Schildkrout/Keim 1990; Steiner 1994; Stanley 1989; Stelzig 2004; Vogel 1988).

The efforts to include emic perspectives and voices into collections and exhibits taken by the museum's side[3] is a process paralleled and accelerated by the demand for a change in perspectives by the originating communities themselves from which the objects once were obtained. Political, as well as social decolonization, cultural sovereignty and indigenous self-representation and empowerment processes have triggered the urge to "speak up", to alter hierarchical relations and to reconstitute one's own tangible (and intangible) cultural heritage from "western" interpretations. It long has become clear, that "…museums are no longer the sole voice of authority in displaying and interpreting those objects, but acknowledge a moral and ethical (and sometimes political) obligation to involve source communities in decisions affecting their material heritage" (Brown/Peer 2003: 2). Globalization, accessibility via Internet[4] and other technical developments, such as searchable databases,[5] accelerate the process of reclaiming, even if only virtually, what has been physically removed from its original context. Within this process of reconstituting one's own cultural heritage and identity, museums are very well utilized as archival resource by the representatives of indigenous communities, as it is in these institutions that objects, cultural and historic knowledge and legacies have been preserved, which might in some cases even be lost to the originating communities today (Phillips 2002, Simpson 2009, Stanley 2007). Ethnographic collections therefore "are no longer images of the past, but they relate to the present and, more importantly, to the future" (Stanley 1989: 120) of the indigenous communities and their cultural prosperity.

The importance for originating communities to repatriate their material culture ideologically, and sometimes even physically, from foreign appropriation and

3 Two examples for such museum approaches from the Ethnologische Museum Berlin are the exhibition "Afrika in Berlin" (2009) in which the curators cooperated with Berlin Diaspora communities from Benin in developing the exhibition concept and the ongoing research project "One-History—Two Perspectives" on the Berlin Northwest Coast collection by the Ethnologische Museum Berlin and the Free University. For more information on the latter project, see http://www.jfki.fu-berlin.de/v/uebersetzungs funktionen/en/index.html (accessed 11.10.2011).

4 Access to their museum collection is provided, for example, by the American Museum of Natural History NYC/USA via their website http://research.amnh.org/anthropology/database/collections, or by the Smithsonian, Washington/USA, website: http://www.si.edu/ Collections and also by the Musée de Quai Branly in Paris/France, website: http://www.quaibranly.fr/cc/pod/recherche.aspx?b=1&t=1 (accessed 10.10.2011).

5 See the *Reciprocal Research Network (RRN)* at http://www.rrnpilot.org/ or the *Plateau Peoples' Web Portal* at http://plateauportal.wsulibs.wsu.edu/html/ppp/index.php (accessed 10.10.2011) as examples for cooperative database projects.

outsider's perspectives on their cultural expressions, also materializes itself in the growing number of community and local museums or cultural centers arising worldwide. Especially in regions in which tourism has become part of the local economy, more and more indigenous communities seek to establish their own cultural centers and museum spaces.[6] These exhibition spaces are—aside from being an economic resource—understood as forums in which indigenous groups can narrate their own history and heritage, as well as preserve and foster their living traditions and cultural identity (Bunten 2010; Simpson 2009; Stanley 2004). Local museums hereby offer an opportunity for the communities to engage with their cultural expressions and to present their own perspectives, as well as for visitors to experience these within what could be interpreted as "authentic" setting (Comaroff/Comaroff 2009).[7]

And even though the event that I want to introduce in this chapter—the workshop "Convergence and Divergence", held at the South Omo Research Center and Museum (SORC)[8] in 2001—was not deliberately conceptualized with regard to the previously mentioned debates of representation of "the other", but rather was born out of the given situational circumstances, it nonetheless deserves to be re-evaluated within this context. The methodological approach taken in the workshop well exemplifies the potential of such above-mentioned cooperative research projects when seeking new perspectives onto material culture and its contribution to cultural representation and understanding. A review of the transcripts of the workshop unravels the depth and quality of ethnographic data that was collected during this project. The results of the three-day dialogue in which the participants discussed amongst themselves and with the anthropologists about the particularities of their material culture, provide insights on a variety of topics. These include

6 Another regional example is the Konso Museum in Ethiopia, which was inaugurated on Dec. 18th 2009 in the town of Kyriat in the Konso region, which was also inscribed as an UNESCO Cultural Landscape in 2011 (French Embassy, News: http://www.ambafrance-et.org/Konso-museum, http://whc.unesco.org/en/list/1333, accessed 10.10.2011).

7 Some exemplary mission statements taken from the websites of local cultural centers, from the Haida Heritage Center, Canada: "The Haida Heritage Centre is a place where elders can share their wisdom, a place that showcases Haida history and continues to develop Haida art, language and culture." (http://www.haidaheritagecentre.com/about.html, accessed 11.10.2011) and from the Maasai Cultural Heritage Center, Kenya: "It is critical, now more than ever before, to preserve the last remaining and most important aspects of Maasai culture. After completion, the Maasai Cultural Heritage Center will provide the Maasai and foreign visitors the opportunity to see, learn, and celebrate Maasai cultural heritage through colorful and vibrant collections (…) of work and artifacts of the past, present, and the future" (http://www.maasai-association.org/mcc/mission.html, accessed 11.10.2011).

8 The South Omo Research Center and Museum is located in the Southern Nations, Nationalities, and Peoples Region in the town of Jinka, the administrative capital of South Omo region. The SORC was founded as a research center and forum for transcultural understanding and is "meant to enhance mutual understanding and cooperation between the various peoples of Ethiopia (...) to discuss their similarities and the possibility of working jointly together in the future". (see http://www.uni-mainz.de/Organisationen /SORC/, accessed 10.10.2011).

continuity and change, inter-ethnic relationships and dependencies, perceptions and images of the Self and the own cultural background and the Other, i.e. cultural practices and particularities of neighboring ethnic groups, and most prominently, variations in cultural identity within the South Omo region. By leaving the choice of the artifacts to be presented exclusively to the guests of the workshop, the anthropologists also left the choice of topics to be discussed in the hands of the participants. The selection made consequently indicate the cultural particularity of the associated group that the contributors of the objects felt important to emphasize within this museological and dialogical context. The discussions and conversations triggered through the artifacts, by talking about their usage, their manufacture, their ritual and social significance, enabled a dialogue on cultural particularities, commonalities and interdependencies that otherwise would not have been articulated. By engaging with material culture and with the stories "behind" the artifacts, new perspectives were opened up—not only for the museological context, but also for empirical anthropology and most importantly, for the participants themselves. Although the data was collected in 2001, it remained unused for the past ten years and its revision shows that the power of its contribution to the anthropological study of the people of South Omo stays undiminished. This is specifically true as the "Convergence and Divergence" workshop and the resulting exhibition[9] remain the only documented interethnic dialogue dedicated solely to the topic of material culture from this culturally highly diverse region.[10] It therefore feels appropriate to finally take the opportunity and re-examine the transcripts and their contributions to the ethnography and study of material expressions of the various ethnic groups of South Omo.

A workshop on convergence and divergence

Before turning to the dialogue excerpts from the workshop, I want to provide some background information to the circumstances of its coming about, as it was a unique situation out of which the anthropologists Susanne Epple and Christina Gabbert, as well as my fellow student Judith Melzer and I, decided to invite repre-

[9] Results from this workshop and the objects donated were incorporated into the exhibition "Convergence and Divergence—The Diversity of Material Culture in South Omo", which opened in 2002 at the SORC. For an online version of the exhibition, see the website http://www.uni-mainz.de/Organisationen/SORC/content/view/31/51/ (last accessed 10.10.2011).

[10] There have been two exhibits which included or focused on material culture of South Omo, one in 2008 at the Museu de Prehistòria de Valéncia, Spain called "Mundos Tribales. Una Visión Ethnoarqueológica", shown from Nov. 5th 2008 to March 22nd 2009, and most recently one called "Omo. People and Design" shown at the Royal Museum for Central Africa Tervuren, Belgium, shown from Nov. 7th 2008 to Jan. 3rd 2010. The curatorial concept, however, did not include any inter-ethnic perspectives into the exhibitions. Please see the exhibition catalogues Salazar/Domingo 2008 and Verswijver/Silvester 2008 for more information on the contents.

sentatives of various groups from the area to come to join us for a workshop on local material culture at the SORC in 2001.[11] The SORC had been a research center for several years, but it was in that year that the construction of the main building was completed and finally its grand hall was equipped to host its first exhibition. The challenge to be faced was that the SORC did not own any ethnographic collection at the time. While thinking about possible exhibitions and displays, it became obvious to the anthropologists involved that it was not just on them to make the decision on what should be exhibited in this new museum space. From the beginning the SORC was conceptualized to be a meeting point, a dialogical space for international researchers working in the area and importantly, also for the people from the various groups in South Omo to engage with each other and the scientists. Consequently, the museum exhibit had to provide a space for the local people to represent their way of life from their own perspective while at the same time providing educational information to non-local visitors coming to Jinka.[12]

So rather than have the anthropologists curate the collection and exhibition by themselves, the situation was accepted as a windfall opportunity to take a new approach. It was decided that it would be best if representatives from various groups from South Omo could take an active part in the creation and formation of the exhibition space. Consequently, the idea was formulated to invite various representatives from the main ethnic groups living in South Omo to come to the SORC and to ask each one of them to bring an object, which they considered essential for the cultural identity of their group and which they wanted to contribute to the permanent collection and share in the exhibition display of the SORC. As mentioned before, it was important to the organizers not to give any restrictions or parameters on the kind of objects to be chosen and donated: the object selection lay purely in the hands of the participants.

Finally, on the Sept. 15th twenty-four guests from eight different ethnic groups in South Omo arrived in Jinka.[13] Among them were men (and one woman) from

[11] The workshop was organizedandsupportedbythe Sonderforschungsbereich 295, "Kulturelle und sprachliche Kontakte: Prozesse des Wandels in historischen Spannungsfeldern Nordostafrika/Westasien" of the Johannes-Gutenberg University, Mainz.

[12] Tourism has become an increasing economic and social factor for the people living in the South Omo region. On tourism and some of its consequences, see for example Abbink 2000; Getachew 2010; Turton 2004.

[13] The organizers of the workshop decided to invite male representatives, mainly due to logistical issues, as it is problematic for women to stay away from their domestic responsibilities for a longer period of time. An exception was Duka Aike who accompanied her husband Sago Bargar. The choice of guests was primarily based on previous contacts of the anthropologists and the availability of the informants. The final guests were: Nakwa Dal'o, Belaini Nakwa, Bashiri Arbala and Gude Dalko from Bashada, Maldo Lito, Sago Bargar and his wife Duka Aike from Banne, Choke Bajje, Tsasi Aike and Shada Alma from Hamar, Joseph Loteng from Nyangatom, Kutsha Bulle and Horra Surra from Arbore, Ateme Sonko from Maale, Ariyo Dore from Kara and Natia Berea from Daasanech. In the following text I will refer to the participants by their first name.

Bashada, Banna, Hamar, Nyangatom, Arbore, Kara, Maale and Daasanech. Some of these groups have close inter-ethnical ties; some however, continue to have hostile relationships that are tainted by conflict and dispute. To come together in this constellation for a joined project was a very new experience for all participants.

During the three days the donors first presented each object and then each presentation was followed by open discussions among the participants. Due to the scope of the material, I will not be able to introduce each of the nineteen artifacts donated to the SORC in this article. Rather, will I focus on some key examples that are of particular interest to the study of material culture in South Omo and which are of great expressiveness and significance for the understanding of cultural particularities, cultural self-conception, inter-ethnic relationships or interdependence among the groups of South Omo. If not otherwise noted, the material and quotes referred to in the following are citations taken from the transcripts of the workshop discussions, and the bracketed references indicate the page number of the transcribed manuscript.[14]

Objects and dialogues

Clay pots, trade and inter-ethnic relations

The first object was presented by the senior most donor, Bashiri from Bashada.[15] He brought a clay pot, locally called *daa*,[16] which he introduced with the words

> "...in former times the Hamar used to get the pots from the Bashada. The Galeba [Daasanech] got the pots from Bashada. The Bume [Nyangatom] get them from Bashada. (...) I brought this, because only we, the Bashada, used to make these pots before" (p. 9).

And even though men prefer not to be seen carrying or handling pots, Bashiri decided on bringing this particular object to the SORC, due to its great value "for us Bashada. Otherwise I would have never brought a pot here. Only the really weak and stupid men will carry pots." (p.18) By saying this, Bashiri emphasized that pots usually are considered to belong to the domain of the women, as women are the ones who manufacture and handle them in domestic situations. It is women's knowledge where to go to gather the clay and how to shape and process it to make

[14] The full transcript (Epple/Brüderlin 2003) can be accessed online as an electronic document: www.uni-mainz.de/Organisationen/SORC/content/view/58/41 (last accessed 10.10.2011).

[15] The senior most guest at the workshop was Nakwa Da'lo from Bashada. Due to his health conditions, Nakwa chose not to present an object during the discussion sessions, but his son and heir Belaini donated a ritual staff, the *parko*, to the collection of the SORC.

[16] If not otherwise noted, the indigenous names of the objects are here cited in Hamar, because Hamar was the common language used by most guests during the workshop. However, parts of the discussions were translated, either into Hamar or Amharic and Hamar, this was especially the case for the contributions from Daasanech, Nyangatom and Arbore.

it last and become "stronger" (Sago, p. 19) with each use. Women have to follow various restrictions accompanying the manufacture of pots, such as the taboos on digging clay when having their period or being illegitimately pregnant.[17] If these restrictions are disregarded, the clay will spoil, as Gude and Bashiri illustrated,

> These [impure] women may not go and dig clay. If they go, the clay becomes bad and all the pots made by it will die. So when many pots die, people say: 'Oh, who has been digging the clay? Maybe someone who was not pure has been digging the clay.' And then a cold person, that means someone from the Binnas[18] moiety, goes there and drops some *gali* [kind of soft creeper plant] leaves. He takes the *gali* leaves, spits on them and places them there, saying: 'Don't die out!'(p. 19)

The importance of the clay pots for the Bashada derives primarily from the fact that pots used to and continue to be an economic resource. Pots are one of the few imperishable trade items, which the Bashada can rely upon for access to butter, sorghum, stock and cash in times of scarcity. As Bashiri emphasized, "...there was a lot of walking. In times of hunger, we carried the pots on our backs and we exchanged them for sorghum" (p. 9). Bashiri talked about how the Bashada exchanged pots with their neighbors, the Ts'amakko and the Banna and even used to go as far as Daasanech and Arbore for trade, extending their trade network through most of the southern areas of South Omo. Nowadays though, the pots are sold at local markets to traders who then bring them to more distant places. Though pots still remain an economic resource, the long trading expeditions have become rare.

On this note, Joseph from Nyangatom shared a story from his father's generation, which demonstrates how trade is not only of economic value, but how it may even have stabilizing effects on interethnic relations. The incident described by Joseph would have ended with a massive bloodshed between the Kara and the Nyangatom (whose relationship has been—and still is—marked by continuous intertribal conflicts) if not for the pots.[19] He recounted that it was the Nyangatom's desire for clay pots traded to them by the Kara which prevented the Nyangatom from engaging in a more severe attack on their neighbors at the Omo River:

> ...the Nyangatom and Kara had started a conflict. (...) The Kara captured one of my father's sisters. (...) So the Nyangatom people organized themselves to fight against the Kara. (...) They started to encircle all the Kara. They fought and killed. (...) The Kara were hiding in the reeds, in the high grass. Then the Nyangatom people came there: 'Let us kill all those who are inside the grass!' (...) 'But it is not good to kill all the people. We should let some live, so we can keep getting pots from them'. Finally the Nyangatom agreed to the idea of sparing some of the Kara. 'All right, we will not extinguish them, because of the pots.' So the Nyangatom left. And peace was set. (pp. 10-11)

17 On female taboos and aspects concerning pregnancies among the Hamar and other groups of South Omo see Epple/Brüderlin 2004 and Brüderlin 2005.

18 On clans and moieties in Bashada and Hamar see Strecker/Lydall 1979 and Epple 2010.

19 On a more recent examination of the Nyangatom-Kara relations, see Girke 2008.

The historical interethnic trade network in South Omo is very complex and often accompanied by taboos for specific groups to produce certain items, even though the resource and skill might be available to them.[20] Why this is so, and the reason why the value of specific items cannot merely be assessed as commodity, is further explained by Tsasi's account. Tsasi from Hamar shed light on the question why the provenience of certain pots is of such importance within specific contexts.

> One reason why the Hamar did not make pots[21] is that there are special rituals for which pots are needed; they are used, for example, for the *gali* ritual, when a newborn baby receives its name.[22] So in Hamar we say that the Bashada are our *gilo edi*, which means that they are the people who make the rituals for us. They are the ones who make the pots for us, which we use in rituals. (p. 12)

For the Hamar, the Bashada *daa* is not just a domestic utensil; its full essence derives from its metonymical[23] association with the close ritual relations between the Hamar and the Bashada. The following example demonstrates how a similar metonymical association applies to the relationship between the Hamar and the Aari and how this is also manifested through pots. Tsasi continued,

> The Aari are our ritual people (…). Originally we all came from Aari. Our people came from Aari, our rituals came from Aari; the coffee is from Aari, the sorghum comes from Aari. Our *bittas* [spiritual leaders], they all came from Aari. We all came from there and we moved down to the lowlands to herd the cattle. (Sago, Gude and Tsasi, p. 14)[24]

This ancestral relatedness between the Aari and the Hamar documented in the Hamar oral history is acknowledged through the Hamar's high valuation of certain items made by or traded from Aari. The Hamar, Banna and Bashada consider these items to be *barjo* [blessed][25] and to be "*ch'arangi*, they are ritually pure" (p. 14). This positive connotation is, for example, reflected in ceremonial offerings in Hamar in which whole coffee beans from Aari are given to the ancestors, or in the ritual usage of a specific Aari clay pot, which is—in addition to the Bashada pot—needed for the

20 While focusing on bond friendship, Girke also provides specifics on the significance of trade relations in South Omo (Girke 2010). Further insights on historic aspects and the complexity of trade networks in this region are also provided by Sobania 1991 and Ayalew 1995.

21 Clay pots are nowadays also produced in Hamar, but the ritual significance of certain pots from other areas is still acknowledged and remains relevant in certain ritual contexts.

22 On children's rites see Brüderlin 2005.

23 Hahn emphasizes that in the context of material cultures studies the concept of metonymy should be applied when objects stand for something else without applying any of their own properties onto the other. This concept is of specific interest when comparing it with the notion of metaphor, in which the metaphorical object is said to actually apply one or all of its characteristics onto the other matter (Hahn 2005: 157ff).

24 For a detailed narration on the mythological descent of the Hamar from the Aari people see Epple 2010:58ff and Strecker/Lydall 1979: ch. 1.

25 In Hamar, Bashada and Banna, *barjo* is a concept of wellbeing and blessing. See Strecker 1988 for a detailed description of various notions and implications of *barjo*.

child's naming ceremony.[26] Shada from Hamar referred to this specific pot as "the elder brother of the Bashada pot" (p. 13). And Sago from Banna pointed out, that this Aari pot is also needed for the *duki*, the second funeral ritual, held for the deceased after some years of his/her death. Sago recounted,

> "After the man has been already buried you have a ritual called *duki* or *sala*. You perform this ritual and then you say, 'The dead man has crossed the big water.' Or you also say: 'We have finished the Aari pot ritual.'" His account is further supplemented by Tsasi, Gude from Bashada and Shada who said, "Without an Aari pot you cannot finish the funeral ritual. (...) Then your whole family might get sick or die" (pp. 13-14).

We learn from this narrative that for two of the main rites of passage in the life of the Hamar,[27] one at the very beginning and one at the very end of the human life cycle, the Aari pot is used as a mnemonic device symbolically reconfirming the ritual bond between the two groups, the Aari and the Hamar.

This emphasis on the provenience of certain pots for specific ritual contexts was only articulated by the guests from Hamar, Banna, Bashada and Aari. The representatives of the other groups such as Arbore, Nyangatom and Maale[28]contrasted that the proveniences of pots used among them is not relevant, neither in domestic nor ritual context. As Kutsha from Arbore said,

> "We do not distinguish between Aari or Bashada pots. Not everybody knows which pot is from where. (...) We perform rituals with all pots (...). They could be pots from Konso, we would also use those. They are all the same to us" (pp. 15-16).

Nonetheless, all participants agreed that while clay pots are being slowly replaced in domestic use by the imported aluminum pot (*diski*) available for purchase on the markets, the traditional clay pots are still preferred by everybody for most ritual occasions. This is not necessarily because of any association with the group where the pot was manufactured or any other metonymical implications, but rather because they all cherish the clay pot for its flavor quality and the special taste

26 In the context of the child's naming ritual, if an Aari pot is not available, the participants explained that the pot here might be replaced by leaves of the *gali* plant. The person replacing the pot then will say, "It is my Aari pot" (Gude, p. 13). During the funeral ritual though, the Aari pot may not be replaced by anything else. It has to be an authentic Aari pot.

27 Every Hamar has to undergo a series of life-cycle rituals and only if all rituals are performed properly—this also includes the second funeral—will he/she be considered a legitimate and full member of the society and finally may become an ancestral spirit after his/her death. See Strecker/Lydall 1979 and Brüderlin 2005 for detailed description of these life-cycle rituals.

28 The guest from Maale, Ateme, did not know of any specific ritual significance of pots for his people. But he mentioned that, "The Maale people make pots for themselves. They do not sell them to other people. The Aari have their own. The Banna have their own. The Maale make the pots only for their own use" (Ateme, p. 15). In her thesis, Thubauville provides some more detailed descriptions on Maale material culture and also describes the variations in style and use of clay pots in Maale further (Thubauville 2004).

it gives to the beverages and food prepared in it. As Joseph from Nyangatom confirmed

> The coffee boiled in such kinds of pots [clay] is not the same as the one boiled in a *diski*. We say that the coffee boiled with this pot is sweeter than the one from a metal pot (p. 13).

During my own fieldwork among the Hamar and Ts'amakko I was told that the appreciation for the traditional clay pots is also related to its association with the traditional way of life, the way how things used to be before the introduction of new goods through the markets. Especially elder men repeatedly told me that the clay pots are the "right" way to make the foods and drinks.

By choosing the clay pot as the representative item of the Bashada for the museum, Bashiri lays emphasis on three aspects of Bashada culture that he considered to be essential to his people: First, the pot exemplifies the skill and knowledge of the Bashada women of their handicraft and the validation of their contribution to the economy of the Bashada. Second, Bashiri chose the *daa* to stress the great importance of inter-ethnic trade for the Bashada and the other groups of South Omo. The contribution of the participants showed that the dependency on certain goods produced and procured by the various groups in South Omo is not only important for the economic stability of certain groups, but that it is also a key for political stability within this region. Third, through the choice of object, as well as by his accounts, Bashiri accentuated the pride the Bashada take in the high esteem the Hamar hold for them.[29] The ritual connection between these two groups is obviously valued by both parties and is an intrinsic element of their definition of

[29] In this context I want to refer to the narration that Joseph from Nyangatom contributed later on in the workshop, as it further underlines the issue of pride felt by one group through the appraisal by another group. The Nyangatom have a rather hostile relationship to the Hamar, Banna and there have been many inter-tribal conflicts. This negative relationship, however, finds an interesting way to manifest itself, as the dialogue on the Nyangatom dance-bells, the *nidjeroi*, exemplifies.
Joseph: There are people in our country, blacksmiths, who produce the *nidjeroi*. Mostly they are made for dancing. The other people in South Omo have seen that and say: 'We want to dance like the Nyangatom!'
Walle (Bashada): The Nyangatom are the fathers of the dance!
Joseph: The best dancers are the Nyangatom, aren't they? Don't you say like that? Also you sing the songs of the Nyangatom when you dance in Hamar and in Daasanech, don't you?
Sago (Banna): Yes, that is true!
Joseph: Just like the best dancers came from Nyangatom and moved on to the other groups in South Omo, these nidjeroi came from Nyangatom and moved to the other groups. Also the names for the *errawak*, for the favorite oxen in Hamar, come from Nyangatom. They use Nyangatom names (…) (p. 72).
This dialogue shows that not only objects are exchanged, but that dances, songs and names and other intangible resources may circulate between the groups. This case is especially interesting as the appropriation of certain cultural expressions is not based on the positive connoted ritual closeness between these groups, but actually on an oppositional concept, on the rather daunting respect these groups have for the Nyangatom.

each other and of their close relationship and was prominently expressed during the workshop discussions.[30]

Wooden staffs, authority, legitimacy and control

A material commonality between numerous groups in South Omo are the various kinds of wooden sticks and staffs used in daily and ritual contexts.[31] Of the nineteen artifacts donated to the SORC during the workshop, four were staffs of different shapes and sizes brought from Arbore, Hamar, Bashada and Banna. These staffs are fine examples for the minimalistic, but sophisticated material expression cultivated among the groups of South Omo. A materialistic expression which is visually so minimalistic, that it serves well as example of the kind of object which rarely finds its way into anthropological or contemporary artistic-oriented anthropological exhibitions, as the object's own expressiveness is so subtle that it is hard to present them to an audience without extensive background information.

The four staffs given to the SORC are such rather sober artifacts, more natural than man-made, but of greatest ritual significance, as Gude states, "It is just a piece of wood, but it is something big for us, something important" (p. 62). To meet this emphasis laid upon this object category by the guests of the workshop, I chose to introduce the different kinds of staffs and some of the practices related to them in the following.[32] By listening to the accounts of the donors and participants about the artifacts, it becomes apparent that the staffs are not just a stylistic and material commonality of South Omo, but that the objects themselves share vital metonymical functions. All the four staffs discussed are—in diverging contexts—objects of communication. To explain the staff's communicatory attribution a bit more precisely, let me focus on some of the narrations provided which serve to clarify this specific object's characteristic. This helps to investigate how and when these staffs can be implemented as a non-verbal communicator of authority, mediation, legitimacy, and subliminally of wellbeing. The emic context provided on the variations of wooden wands, the *koli*, the *shunkurr*, the *micere* and the *parko*, demonstrate how these staffs are some of the most powerful and essential objects associated with the communication and negotiation of control and status within the societies of this region. We are told that the staffs may metonymically and even metaphorically stand for individual authority[33] such as the right to speak, to request, to bless and to

30 Within the culturally dense area of South Omo inter-ethnic relationship continuously chance though time. For a detailed analysis of the Bashada perspective and on historic changes of the Bashada-Hamar relation, see Epple 2010.

31 Similar kinds of wooden staffs are not only common in southern Ethiopia, but in most parts of eastern Africa. For a comparison see Best (1993) who describes various examples in the collection of the Frankfurt Museum der Weltkulturen.

32 It should be noted, that the contexts and their accompanying narration are only excerpts of the diverse and complex ritual practices related to the staffs.

33 In Hamar, Banna and Bashada, the traditional concept of authority is always and foremost based on the social status of the person demanding the authority. Social status

curse, and how in other contexts they are used to communicate communal authority, as described in the instance of the "rise" of the whipping wands.

The *koli*—the staff of the go-between

The first staff I want to turn to is the *koli*, a long and lean wooden[34] staff brought by Gude from Bashada:

> This object belongs to the tradition of our grandfathers. There are many rituals connected to this staff. I think this kind of staff exists in all different places. We marry women with this stick (p. 59).

Gude here referred to the fact, that the *koli* is used in Bashada during marriage negotiations for the bride, as well as in the subsequent ceremony in which the bride is given to her husband and later when the bride goes to collect cattle from her in-laws.[35] Gude is right in noting that this kind of staff exists in many different places and his account on the practice of the *koli* during the marriage negotiations parallels with the narrations provided by other participants from Banna and Hamar, as well as by Kutsha from Arbore. Kutsha brought a similar staff, but with a forked end, called *shunkurr*, which is used during the marriage negotiations in Arbore (pp. 46-57). The specifics of the negotiation process vary among the Hamar, Banna, Bashada and the Arbore, but as Gude and Kutsha confirm, both the *koli* and the *shunkurr* fulfill the same purpose within this process, as they both are the staffs of the go-between. The go-between, the messenger, sent by the future husband's family to ask for the girl will carry the *koli* with him.[36]It is by way of this staff that he has the right to ask for the bride on behalf of the man's family, and to negotiate the bride price. The staff defines and legitimizes his office as the mediator between the two families. As the narration about the process of the bride price negotiation continues, it becomes evident, though, that the *koli* is more than just a visual symbol of legitimacy, it is also a metaphor for communication as such.

Gude recounts a situation from Bashada in which the father of the bride did not want to accept the request for his daughter. The future husband therefore decided to abduct the girl he intended to marry and took her away into the bush. To settle the dispute between the families, the go-between had to repeatedly go to talk with the bride's family. The go-between tried to appease the father by saying, as Gude narrated,

and correspondingly, the authority associated with it, can only be achieved through the person's legitimacy to request it. Therefore, authority cannot be gained through any other means and the other members of the group will not acknowledge it, if it is not legitimized by the social and ritual order of the society (see Strecker/Lydall 1979).

34 The wood used for *koli* is taken from a certain tree called *baraza* in Hamar (Grewia mollis Juss.). The *baraza* tree is associated with the indigenous concept of wellbeing, called *barjo* and is therefore used in various ritual contexts in Hamar, Banna and Bashada (see Strecker/Lydall 1979 and Strecker 1988).

35 For detailed account on the bridal rituals, please see Brüderlin 2005: 42-66.

36 Kutsha in his account refers to the *shunkurr*, also with the Hamar name, *koli*(pp. 46ff).

"'Why do you send me away all the time? You should not do that! You should accept the *koli*. When you were young, why did you steal the mother of your daughter? (...) Do not quarrel! Do not be angry!' This is how the go-between will settle the conflict. Now the father will accept the payment, the conciliation."

Sago summarized the situation by saying, "The conflict will be settled by way of the *koli*." This story reveals how the *koli* is used as a means of positive communication and mediation.[37] Should the conciliation not be accepted though, the *koli* may be implemented as an instrument of sanction. It will be applied in a negative sense, as it can be used to curse the person who is not accepting the *koli*'s plead for conciliation. When the father says, "Do not bring the *koli* to me. I do not want to see you [the go-between] anymore," (Sago, p. 62) the dispute may escalate to the point where the go-between gets so angry, that he goes and breaks the *koli*. "By doing this, he curses the girl and she will not bear any children. If she has children they will die. (...) The community, the men of the community, they will say, 'Oh, the *koli* of this girl has become bad'".[38] Gude and Tsasi supplement Sago's account by pointing out that this curse will not only concern this specific girl, but all the daughters of this family, "they all have become bad. Nobody will want to marry any of his daughters anymore."(pp. 62-63).

These stories about the *koli* provided by the guests teach us that in situations such as these, the *koli* is more than just a visual symbol of the go-between's legitimacy of request, but that the *koli* is also a metaphor for the actual communication process in itself. On the one hand, Gude's statement that the father "should accept the *koli*" (pp. 62-63) implies that the father should respect the sincerity and legitimacy of the proposal for his daughter and that he should respect the appeal. Please note that rhetorically, Gude did not differentiate between the actual staff and the process of negotiation itself. The *koli* here is one with the communication process. On the other hand, the ritual implication of the *koli* is further amplified when considering the account on the bride's curse, when the go-between forcefully broke the staff as a reaction to the unsettled dispute. By breaking the *koli*, a metaphorical dimension is added to the staff as its physical condition is directly related to the prospect of the communication process.[39] By breaking the staff, the go-between

37 The *koli* may also be send to mediate in other occasions, for example, in a conflict situation if someone has been cursed by someone else, as Kolle tells, "...then the *zarsi* [the elders of the area who belong to one village] come and bring a *koli*. *Koli* is along stick, which is used for settling conflicts. If you have a conflict, you can send someone with a *koli*" (p. 23).

38 There is a double implication in Gude's narration here. During her bridal rituals the girl will receive a different *koli*, which she later will also use to collect cattle from her in-laws. In the process of becoming a bride and mother, the *koli* plays an important role and is repeatedly referred to as the girl's future children. In this context the *koli* is used as a metaphor for the girl's fertility and her unborn children. For more information on this use of the bride's *koli* staff, see pp. 63-66 in the transcripts, as well as Brüderlin 2005: 42-66.

39 I am hereapplyingHahn'sdefinitionanddistinctionoftheconceptsofmetaphorandmetonym,

negates the possibility of finding a common ground between the two parties and, as Sago said, also for any future negotiations concerning the daughters of this family; the *koli* has "become bad" (p. 63). Within the acephalous Hamar, Banna and Bashada societies respect and acknowledgment of status are essential for the traditional social and political organization.[40] The *koli* thereby is a means to regulate and communicate this continued process of affirmation and negotiation of traditional values and social principles. This staff may, respectively, also be applied to sanction any disruption of these processes, as this could put the social and political balance at stake and thereby would threaten the wellbeing of the individual as well as the group as a whole.

The *micere*—the whipping wand

Another object brought to the discussion round also connected to this process of communicating authority and legitimacy, is the *micere*, the whipping wand. The *micere* is a long, flexible wand, pulled off by hand from the *baraza* tree. The *micere* in the museum's collection was donated by Sago from Banna. His presentation of the artifact was again supplemented by stories from all other participants, as they confirmed that the same or similar kind of use of the whipping wand applies to their people as well.

In his essay, Strecker refers to the whipping wand "as an extension of the arm" as well as an "extension of voice" of the herdsman (Strecker 1993: 6). In reference to the results of the workshop, I want to complement Strecker's notion of "extension" by adding that the whipping wand itself, as well as the pain produced by it, is a physical manifestation, affirmation and communication of authority and social hierarchy. The *micere* therefore is an "extension" of authority, a communicative tool, which physically implements the rightful hierarchical social order onto the individual as well as the community. The participants in their narrations further allude that, respectively, the right to whip someone or something (e.g. cattle) is always based on the relationship of legitimate "dominance" in a sometimes guiding and educational sense.[41] The herdsman dominates the cattle, the husband dominates his

"bei Metapher und Metonym handelt es sich aber um verschiedenen Formen der Bedeutungszuweisung. Metonyme sind immer dann zu beobachten, wenn ein … Gegenstand für einen Sachverhalt verwendet wird. Ein metonymischer Verweis bedeutet das "Für-etwas-stehen" eines Teils für ein Ganzes. … es werden aber keine Eigenschaften des Objektes auf den Sachverhalt ... übertragen. Im Gegensatz dazu ist die … Metapher. Die Metapher bezieht eine Eigenschaft einer Sache … auf einen Sachverhalt. […] Hinter jeder Metapher steht also die Aussage eines metaphorischen Konzepts, das selbst nicht artikuliert wird." Hahn argues that a metaphorical object in contrast to the metonymical object actually applies its, for example, physical condition onto the other matter (Hahn 2005: 157-158). In this case, the broken staff therefore is a direct metaphor for the disrupted communication process.

40 For a detailed description of the social and political organization of the Hamar society and its particularities, see Strecker 1976.

41 Correspondingly, no one has the right to abuse the *micere*. Should someone use it to hurt someone without having a legitimate reason or right to do so, he will be sanctioned by

wife,[42] the future husbands dominate the females[43] and the elder men dominate the younger and so forth. In consequence, the *micere* and the act of using it affirm the status of its beholder and the pain felt when being whipped correspondently is the confirmation of the status of the pain receiver within this relationship. The whipping wand hence is an instrument for keeping the traditional social order in place, as is confirmed by Sago's account about the *banch'amo*, the ritual when the whipping wand "rises":

> In Hamar you have senior brothers. Those who sit here are my seniors. If I insult the elders, if I insult my senior brothers, they will get up and whip me. If I don't herd the cattle properly, if I just go to the dances they will whip me with this *micere*. Therefore, I listen to the words of my elder brothers. (...) In the case the younger men do not listen to the elders, in case they just go and kill enemies, if they don't work properly, if they insult the elders, then (...) the elders will say, 'The *micere* has to rise!' (...) Then the elders take their whipping wands. And they will go and whip the next junior brothers. And then these will whip ones junior to them. And these again will whip their juniors. (...) The ones who really were bad in the past and never listened to the words of the elders, these will be bound by their hands and legs and they will be whipped severely. (...) This is where all the other traditions came from. There are no other rituals connected with the *micere*. That's the most important one. (pp. 83-84)

Bashiri emphasized that there is no escape, no way to get away from the *banch'amo*,

> ...the men who run away will be followed even down to Jinka. They will find you. They follow the footprints. (...) They are whipped and then brought back to the Bashada where everything will be settled. When everybody has been whipped and everything is settled again, the elders will talk together. Then the *micere* will be put back in its place and there will be peace again. (p. 85)

By accentuating that there is no escape from being whipped, Bashiri implied that there is no way for an individual or a group to breakout from the conformity of the communal social order of the society they live in, in this case of the Bashada.

The subsequent discussion about the *micere* and its role in settling social order and punishing wrongdoers opened insights on the emic perspective onto the relationship of the people of South Omo and their traditional way of life and new juridical systems introduced by the Ethiopian government. Joseph asked the other participants of the workshop, "In Nyangatom we have the same tradition of whipping people who did something bad. Do you like the idea of putting wrongdoers into prison or do you prefer your tradition of whipping?" And the collective

other members of the family or community for his wrongdoing (Epple/Brüderlin 2004: ch. 1.3). In her article on childhood in Bashada, Epple elaborates on the quality of the *micere* as a device of blessing and guidance implemented within the context of child rearing, adding yet another level of interpretation to these specific objects (Epple 2009).

42 For more information on gender relations in South Omo, see Epple/Brüderlin 2004.

43 Here, reference is made to the ritual whipping of women in Hamar, Bashada and Banna, which is part of the male initiation rite. See Strecker/Lydall 1979: 71ff. for more information on this ritual.

answer given by all guests at the workshop was that they prefer the whipping. Gude explained why this is so:

> The towns are only in one place. We go very far when we herd our cattle, we go far when the sorghum has ripened. The elders are the ones who call the rain. The elders are the ones who make everything well. They are the ones who call *barjo* [blessing] for us. Still sometimes the younger ones will insult them! When the younger ones do something bad, in which prison should we put them? We are in the bush. We are far away. Where should we put them? So we whip them. (p. 87)

Kolle from Bashada phrased it even more precisely. He clearly distinguished between the values of the Bashada and the externally introduced rules and modes of life. He said,

> It is their tradition [the people from the highlands] to put people into prison. Our tradition is to whip people. It's not our tradition to put them into prison. Prison, what does it mean to us? It doesn't mean anything to us! It's good to whip! (p. 87).

The participants of the workshop here strongly articulated their distrust of these juridical methods implemented by the government even though they nowadays have to submit to these changes introduced to them from the outside. Gude further underlines this when he states that "The government puts people into prison; we herd our people with the *micere*!" (p. 87).

These accounts demonstrated that the *micere*, in contrast to the *koli*, also has the power to leave physical and visual marks on the people. By using it in a whipping, the *micere* is applied as a tool to implement and communicate the strength of authority as well as pain; thereby inscribing it into the skin, leaving visual references to the emic understanding of social and ritual order. The *micere* hereby can be understood as a tangible manifestation of authority.

The *micere,* however, is an object, which has "multiple levels of interpretation" that can apply without excluding each other (Hahn 2004: 117). It therefore is important to note that in other contexts, the *micere* is not so much a tool, but an object with strong symbolic implications. Gude retold the situation, in which the father hands a *micere* to his son. In this context, the "*micere* is given by blessing. When the father gets very old, he will pass on the *micere* to his son, spit on it and bless it" (p. 86). Here, the *micere* is a positively connoted symbol of passing on the responsibility for the cattle (and thereby also for the economic responsibility for and prosperity of the family) from one generation to the other.

The previous examples laid open how the here discussed artifacts emically are understood and applied as metonymical, metaphorical or even physical communicators, extensions and/or affirmation of legitimacy and authority. This emic concept finds its climax in the following account by Belaini on the *parko* staff, which he had brought to the SORC.

The Bashada *parko*—the land, the people and the stars

> The rituals connected to this stick belong to our family, to our ancestors. To the family of the *parko*, to my family.[44] In Hamar and Bashada you have the *bitta* and the *parko*. They are two very important ritual people. The *parko* is the one who makes the *bitta*, who initiates the *bitta* to be the *bitta*. This staff, which I brought, is the staff of the *parko*. (Belaini, p. 67)

Being the eldest son of the family, Belaini is the hereditary successor of his father's office as *parko* of Bashada.[45]He therefore had the right to donate this ritual staff to the SORC. There are two kinds of *parko* staffs, one resembling the kind given to the museum, made from wood and forked at the one end and another one, referred to as the *real* one. The latter kind is said to be made from metal with a golden ring on top. The metal one, however, "may not leave the place where it is. It is in Banna, where it originally came from[46]. But we can use this one [wooden kind] for the rituals, too. The metal *parko* staff has to stay in Banna in a house, which is near to the *bitta*'s house" (p. 71). Gude added,

> The stick is not kept in a real house; it is kept in a tree. Not far from the *bitta*'s house. It is hidden in the bush, in a tree. Nobody can see it. In case someone would see it and take it out, this person would die. If someone touches it, a snake maybe will bite him and kill him. It is also taboo to hold the stick—the metal one—like this, because if you walk with it like this with this fork pointing towards you, you will die. It is like the evil eye." (p. 71)

So again, another staff is associated with a controlling force capable of bringing physical consequences onto the people who are not obeying the traditional ritual order. The following dialogue describes this controlling force of the *parko* staff even further,[47]

> Sago: If he [the parko] stand at the ritual gateway with the parko-stick, then the people who have done something wrong—maybe they killed someone in former times or they slept with a relative or something—may not pass through the gateway.

44 The *parko* is a hereditary ritual office in Hamar, Banna and Bashada. There are various ritual responsibilities related to the office of *parko*, which are connected to the wellbeing and prosperity of the country. As recounted in Strecker/Lydall, the *parko* is supposed to be the one who "looks after the country" (1979: 29). At the time of the workshop there was only one *parko* left among the Hamar, Banna and Bashada and that was Belaini's father, Nakwa Dal'o, who was also present at the workshop.

45 Belaini's father is Nakwa Dal'o, who at the time of the workshop was already of a very high age, but still made the trip to Jinka to join the workshop. He since has passed away though, so that Belaini now holds the office of *parko* for the Bashada.

46 In her article, Epple also refers to the metal staff of the *parko*, but contrasting the information provided at the workshop, Epple mentions, that the metal staff is said to originally come from the Aari (Epple 2010: 58).

47 In contrast to the *micere*, the *parko* himself does not exercise any physical force; instead, it is the staff's intrinsic magical properties, which are said to have the ability to make the people sick.

Belaini: Only the ones who know, 'from the day I was born I have not done anything wrong. I have not stolen anything. I have not done anything wrong.' Only these ones will be allowed to pass through the gateway.

Sago/Shada: If you (...) still walk through the gateway you will start to vomit or you will have diarrhea or something. On the spot it will happen!

Gude: Or your nose starts to bleed!

Sago: This is true! All these people here have seen it happen! (p. 71)

In contrast to the previous mentioned staffs (the *koli*, the *shunkurr*, the *micere*), the dialogue above reveals that the capacity of the *parko* to serve as a regulative device is not based on symbolic, metonymic or physical attributions, but on actual magical powers, which the *parko* staff is said to hold. But again, the context of its implementation is similar to the previously mentioned ones, as the magical powers of the *parko* are also mainly applied to keep social order within the community. It does, however, extend even further as the *parko* is also empowered to ritually affirm the territory in which the Bashada inhabit when inaugurating the new *bitta*.[48] By doing so, the *parko* establishes the rightness of order and brings wellbeing to the land and its people. The *parko* thereby has the influence to positively affect the people and the environment they live in, but also to punish those who do harm and do not submit to the social and ritual conformity. But most significantly, the *parko*'s powers are said to be so grand that they even extend beyond the human realm.

The following narration shared with us by Belaini exemplified how the controlling and stabilizing power and authority of the *parko*, may find their greatest expression yet in the manipulation of the cosmic sphere.

There is one more thing, which is done by the *parko*. The *parko* moves the stars. When the stars move to a certain direction in the sky it means that it will become very hot. The elders of the community, they will come to the *parko*'s homestead and they will say: 'The stars have moved to a position, which tells us that the sun will become very hot. Move them back to their old route!' so before the sunrise, the *parko* will get up and take his staff and lead the stars back to their right position.[49] It is still night time. Nobody sees it. If the stars move to the position where the sun becomes very hot, it means there will be a drought. No sorghum will ripen and the fields will dry out. So that is why he does it. If

[48] The *bitta* (lit. 'the first', the highest ritual office) is a hereditary ritual office in Hamar, Banna and Bashada. The *bitta* is ritually responsible for the wellbeing of the land and its people. When a new *bitta* (ritual leader) is inaugurated into his office, the *parko* will ritually lead him along the border of (in this account) the Bashada territory. Together they encircle the land and call *barjo*, thereby affirming and blessing the land and its people. For a detailed account on this ritual and the ritual office of the *bitta*, please see pp.67-68 and Strecker/Lydall 1979: ch. 1.

[49] Thirty years ago a description of the same ritual was recorded from Baldambe in Hamar, even if Baldambe then claimed that the elders and the *parko* jointly redirect the stars by calling *barjo* together. Baldambe cited the plea of the *parko* as follows, "May the stars not go off course, bring them back with the forked staff. May the stars not go to the left, may they not go to Korre, nor to Borana. Bring them back, back towards Aari country, to the mountains" (Strecker/Lydall 1979: 30).

> they [the stars] go to the place where the rain falls, it will rain a lot. This is the ritual of the *parko*. (p. 76)

In the book "Baldambe Explains" by Ivo Strecker and Jean Lydall, the Hamar elder Baldambe describes this ritual of redirecting the stars as a collaborative effort by the elders and the *parko,* in which "the elders and the *parko* call together, and with *barjo* the stars come back for them" (Strecker/Lydall 1979: 19). Here, yet again, the significance of the emic understanding of collectiveness and responsibility as the keys to maintaining stability and thereby the welfare of the people and the country they live in, is accentuated. By redirecting the stars and enabling the rain to nourish the fields and the cattle, the *parko* and the elders secure the prosperity of the Bashada (and in this case the Hamar) people.

The staffs and situational contexts presented above illustrate how an object's metonymical, physical, symbolic or magical force might be applied to communicate and implement social and ritual order within the societies discussed and borrowing from Girke's and Pankhurst's suggestion on the role of rituals in South Omo, one might even say that the objects also serve as a means to "persuade" the members of the society to find convergence in certain situations (2011: 228). All four staffs have obvious controlling and regulative characteristics to them, whose positive potency finds a manifestation in establishing balance and stability in interpersonal relations and, as in the case of the *parko,* even in human-cosmic relation. As has been revealed through these descriptions, it would be a misinterpretation, to reduce these artifacts to their controlling regulative qualities, as all of them also have an empowering characteristic to them. In this sense they are also comparable with Strecker's interpretation of the rhetoric power of the Hamar *barjo aela* [blessing] for which he notes, that the collective blessing has two important implications, as "it allows the men to exercise control over others while inhibiting the control of others over themselves" (Strecker 1988: 72-73). Importantly, though, the objects presented here can be—and should be—approached comparably from various perspectives, as the *koli,* for example, provides an opportunity for the person, who seemingly is in a weaker position, to formulate a legitimate plea. The unmarried man may ask for a girl, and the cursed one may ask for reconciliation by way of the *koli.*[50] The *micere* affirms the status of the younger generation as successors of the ones who are now demanding their obedience and the women whipped during the male's initiation rite carry their scars as signs of their mental and physical strength and as symbols of their social belonging within the family and the community. But again, this empowering force is best exemplified by way of the *parko,* because the *parko* staff enables the community (represented by the elders) to jointly and actively take control over the people's faith and future by manipulating the environment they live in.

[50] In their article about the Arbore peace ceremony in 1993, Girke and Pankhurst describe how the *koli* was used in this context as a cultural symbol implemented by the Hamar elders to express authority and reconciliation within the process of the peace negotiations (2011: 236).

Conclusion

Returning for a brief moment to the imaginary storage space described at the beginning of this article, the question arises just what would become of the artifacts collected during the workshop "Convergence and Divergence" if they would be stored on a museum shelf without the additional data collected and contextualization? What would these objects communicate to a person, who did not know anything about the artifacts nor the people who made and used them? What and whom would these objects be able to "represent" if displayed in an exhibition? What would the visitor then learn about the originating communities from which these objects came from?

There were nineteen artifacts collected and presented during the above-discussed workshop and even though this article was only able to focus on very a small selection taken from this collection, I hope to have shown that artifacts cannot be reviewed as isolated entities, but that it is essential when working with material culture to thoroughly engage with emic perception, significance and concepts related to the artifacts. Only in such a way does it seem possible to fully unravel the multilayered expressiveness of material cultural and their significance for the originating communities. Importantly, it should be noted that artifacts and our relations to them cannot be analyzed as if the object itself is a "written narrative" (Pearce 1989: 27), or as if the artifact per se could be a witness of its own intrinsic meaning. To be able to unravel invisible relationships between the maker, owner and user of the object, its embedment into social and maybe political, or ritual functions a cooperation between anthropologists, museums and originating communities is a fruitful and necessary approach. This is well exemplified through the narratives shared by the participants of the workshop which clearly illustrate how they understand the objects donated to the museum to be references of their own identity and of their cultural particularities and most importantly, also commonalities of the various groups invited to the SORC. As the guests accorded to during a discussion on varieties of a similar ritual concept shared among them, "That is good! Our rituals are the same. Being different they are the same!" (p. 31). So even though the participants of the workshop came to the SORC as individual members of particular groups of South Omo, who might have had some skepticism and hesitation to interact with members of other groups with which they previously had negatively tainted relationships, the three-day workshop concluded in a dialogue about the similarities between the groups and the main emphasis was laid upon the commonalities between them, not on their differences. This result would not have been achievable without the interactive, dialogical space provided through the workshop setting. This process of creating a "spirit of agreement" and "commitment to create conditions of (...) joint self-esteem" through dialogue is in a sense comparable to the ritual and rhetoric processes discussed by Girke and Pankhurst in their description of the 1993 peace ceremony in Gondoroba, South Omo (2011: 245). The active process of creating situational commonality and dialogue thereby appears to be an essential part of the communicatory and social repertoire of the groups presented here and may also be applied to the dealings with material culture.

Human relations are of non-static nature and so are human-object relations non-static and may change throughout time. Artifacts therefore cannot be considered as static archives of cultures, but rather as possible dialogical spaces, which help us to understand the complexity of the human realm. And as such, the workshop, as well as the choice of objects, provided a unique way for the members of the various groups to share and discuss their image of Self, of their own perspectives, narrations and traditions while at the same time utilizing the opportunity to accentuate the image of the Others and of their relationship to each other. The potential for further material culture studies in the region of South Omo is great and hopefully this workshop and article will inspire some further investigation within this area of research in this region.

References

Abbink, Jon, 2000: "Tourism and its discontents. Suri-tourist encounters in southern Ethiopia". *Social Anthropology 8*, 1-18.

Ayalew Gebre, 1995: *The Arbore of Southern Ethiopia: A Study of interethnic relations, social organisation and production practices*. Addis Ababa: Addis Ababa University, Department of Sociology, Anthropology and Social Administration. (M.A. Thesis).

Best, Günter, 1993: *Marakwet &Turkana: Neue Einblicke in die materielle Kultur ostafrikanischer Gesellschaften*. Frankfurt: Museum für Völkerkunde Frankfurt am Main. Stadt Frankfurt Dezernat Kultur und Freizeit.

Brüderlin, Tina, 2005: *The Incorporation of Children into Society: Pre-and postnatal rituals among the Hamar of southern Ethiopia*. Mainz: Johannes Gutenberg-University Mainz, Department of Ethnology and African Studies. (M.A. Thesis).

Brown, Alison K. and Laura Peers (eds.), 2003: *Museums and Source Communities*. London: Routledge.

Bunten, Alexis Celeste, 2010: "More like Ourselves: Indigenous capitalism through tourism". *The American Indian Quarterly* 34, 285-311.

Comaroff, John and Jean Comaroff, 2009: *Ethnicity INC.: On Indigeneity and its Interpellations*. Chicago: University of Chicago Press.

Epple, Susanne, 2010: "Culture, Contact, and Identity. The multiethnic composition of the Bashada of southern Ethiopia". In: Christina Gabbert and Sophia Thubauville (eds.): *To Live with Others. Essays on cultural neighbourhood in southern Ethiopia*. Köln: Köppe, 47-67.

Epple. Susanne, 2009: "Whipping as Guidance and Blessing. Childhood and Socialization among the Bashada, Southern Ethiopia". In Gebre Yntiso (ed.): *Understanding Children and Childhood in Ethiopia: Children at Risk, Child Protection and Socialization*. Addis Ababa: ESSSWA.

Epple, Susanne and Tina Brüderlin (eds.), 2003: *Convergence and Divergence. The Diversity of Material Culture in South Omo. Transcription of the Workshop in the South Omo Museum and Research Center (SOMARC), Sept. 16.-18.2001*. (Electronic document: www.uni-mainz.de/Organisationen/SORC/content/view/58/41, last accessed 10.10.2011).

Epple, Susanne and Tina Brüderlin (eds.), 2004: *The Pride and Social Worthiness of Women in South Omo Ethiopia. The Transcriptions of the Intercultural Women's Workshop Held at the South Omo Research Center Jinka, Ethiopia October 4th-8th 2002.* (accessible online at http://www.uni-mainz.de/Organisationen/SORC/content/view/58/41/, last accessed 10.10.2011).

Flier, Thomas and Hermann Parzinger (eds.), 2009: *Humboldt Forum Berlin. Das Projekt—The Project*. Berlin: Theater der Zeit. 116-237.

Gabbert, Christina and Sophia Thubauville (eds.), 2010: *To Live with Others. Essays on cultural neighbourhood in southern Ethiopia*. Köln: Köppe.

Getachew, Hanna Amare 2010. *Tourism in South Omo. The case of the Mursi of southern Ethiopia: Perceptions of stakeholders and tourists.* Vdm: Dr. Müller. (MA Thesis).

Girke, Felix and Alula Pankhurst 2011. "Evoking Peace and Arguing Harmony. An example of transcultural rhetoric in southern Ethiopia". In: Christian Meyer and Felix Girke (eds.): *The Rhetorical Emergence of Culture.* Oxford, New York: Berghahn. (Studies in Rhetoric and Culture 4).

Girke, Felix, 2010: "Bondfriendship in the Cultural Neighbourhood". In: Christina Gabbert and Sophia Thubauville (eds.): *To Live with Others. Essays on cultural neighbourhood in southern Ethiopia.* Köln: Köppe, 68-98.

Girke, Felix, 2008: "The Kara-Nyangatom War of 2006/07.History, Ecology, and Rhetoric in the Tribal Zone." In: Eva-Maria Bruchhaus and Monika Sommer (eds.): *Hotspot Horn of Africa II. Approaches to make sense of conflict.* Münster: Lit.

Hahn, Hans Peter, 2005: *Materielle Kultur. Eine Einführung*. Berlin: Reimer.

Jolly, Margaret, 2011: Becoming a "New" Museum? Contesting oceanic visions at Musee du Quai Branly. *The Contemporary Pacific* 23 (1), 108–32.

Krieger, Kurt and Gerd Koch (eds.), 1973: *100 Jahre Museum für Völkerkunde Berlin.*Berlin: Reimer. (Baessler-Archiv, XXI).

Pearce, Susan, M., 1989: "Objects as Meaning or Narrating the Past". In: Susan M. Pearce (ed.): *Interpreting Objects and Collections*. London: Routledge, 19-29.

Phillips, Ruth, 2002: "Where is "Africa"? Re-viewing art and artifact in the age of globalization". *American Anthropologist, New Series* 104, 3, 944–952.

Phillips, Tom (ed.), 1999: *Africa: the Art of a Continent*. London: Prestel.

Salazar, Juan and Inés Domingo (eds.), 2008: *Mundos Tribales. Una visión ethnoarqueológica*. Valencia: Museu de Prehistoria.

Schildkrout, Enid 1988: "Art as Evidence: A brief history of the American Museum of Natural History African Collection". In: Susan Vogel (ed.): *Art/Artifact. African art in anthropology collections.* London: Prestel, 153-160.

Schildkrout, Enid and Curtis Keim, 1990: African Reflections. Art from northeastern Zaire. New York, Seattle: AMNH and University of Washington Press.

Simpson, Moira, 2001: *Making Representations: Museums in the post-colonial era.* London: Routledge.

Simpson, Moira, 2009: "Museums and Restorative Justice: Heritage, Repatriation and Cultural Education". *Museum International* 61, (1-2), 121-129.

Stanley, Nick, 2007: *The Future of Indigenous Museums: Perspectives from the Southwest Pacific.* New York: Berghahn.

Stanley, Nick, 2004: "Can Museums Help Sustain Indigenous Identity? Reflections from Melanesia". *Visual Anthropology* 17, 369-385.

Steiner, Christopher B., 1994: *African Art in Transit*. New York: Cambridge University Press.

Stelzig, Christine, 2004: *Afrika am Museum für Völkerkunde zu Berlin 1873-1919. Aneignung, Darstellung und Konstruktion eines Kontinents*. Herbolzheim: Centaurus.

Strecker, Ivo and Jean Lydall, 1979: *The Hamar of Southern Ethiopia Volume II. Baldambe Explains*. Hohenschäftlarn: Renner. (Arbeiten aus dem Institut für Völkerkunde der Universität zu Göttingen 13)

Strecker, Ivo 1988. „Some Notes on the Uses of '*barjo*' in Hamar". In: Fritz Serzisko und Marianne Bechhaus-Gest (eds.): *Proceedings of the First International Symposion on Cushitic and Omotic Languages*. Hamburg: Buske, 61-74.

Strecker, Ivo, 1976: *Traditional Life and Prospects for Socio-economic Development in the Hamar Administrative District of Southern Gamu Gofa: A Report to the Relief and Rehabilitation Commission of the Provisional Military Government of Ethiopia.* (Accessible online at: http://www.uni-mainz.de/Organisationen/SORC/content/ view /58/41/, last accessed 10.10.2011).

Strecker, Ivo, 1993: "Cultural Variations in the Concept of 'Face'". *Multilingua* 12, 119-141.

Strecker, Ivo and Jean Lydall (eds.), 2005: *The Perils of Face. Essays on cultural contact, respect and self-esteem in southern Ethiopia*. Münster: Lit.

Sobania, Neal, 1991: "Feasts, Famines and Friends: Nineteenth Century Exchange and Ethnicity in the Eastern Lake Turkana Region". In: John Galaty and Pierre Bonte: *Herders, Warriors and Traders: Pastoralism in Africa*. Boulder, San Francisco, Oxford: Westview, 118-144

Thubauville, Sophia, 2004: *Maale Material Objects in Their Social and Ritual Context.* Mainz: Johannes Gutenberg-Universität Mainz, Institut für Ethnologie und Afrikastudien. (M.A. Thesis) (Accessible online at: www.uni-mainz.de/Organisationen/SORC/content/view/58/41, last accessed 10.10.2011).

Turton, David, 2004: "Lip-plates and 'the People who take Photographs': Uneasy encounters between Mursi and tourists in southern Ethiopia". *Anthropology today* 20, 3-8.

Verswijver, Gustaaf and Hans Silvester, 2008: OMO. People & Design. Catalogue of the temporary exhibit (7th November 2008—3rd January 2010). Paris: RMCA and La Martinière.

Vogel, Susan (et al.), 1989: *Art/Artifact. African art in anthropology Collections.* London: Prestel.

Part III

Differential Perception of Social Boundaries

Knowledge, Identity and Epistemological Choices

Competing theoretical trends in Oromo studies

Thomas Osmond

A few months after joining the Social Anthropology Department of Addis Ababa University in October 2008, I presented my work on "*Qaalluu* regional leaders in Ethiopia" and their controversial links with the so-called "Oromo traditional religion". During this departmental seminar, I clearly noticed a kind of relative disappointment among the audience because my presentation did not focus on outlining the original form, essence and development of this "Oromo traditional religion".[1] I rather privileged dynamic and deconstructionist approaches, borrowed from postmodern perspectives, emphasizing the existence of plural regimes of historicity, regional multi-ethnic networks and competing identity projects. More than simply being subjective issues, outsiders' and insiders' positions in the field of Oromo studies directly question the deep epistemological consequences of my own theoretical approach, as a *ferenji* (foreigner) or European postmodern-made social scientist, and those approaches influenced by both Marxist and structuralist perspectives privileged by some of the students and instructors of Addis Ababa University present on that day. This epistemological divergence both reflects distinct interpretations of the social and identity stakes inherent to the present multinational institutional framework of the Ethiopian Federal Republic, as well as distinct final goals in social anthropology in general, and the field of Oromo studies in particular. Indeed, it strongly underlines the close entanglement of knowledge, identity and epistemological choices in our ways to conduct researches.

Becoming aware of this close entanglement in concrete terms entailed that I could not avoid dealing with central but also highly sensitive and intimate questions such as the following: for which purposes are we seeking knowledge about the Oromo social category? How do academic writers conceive Oromo identity (or identities), and how do they order their plural social expressions? How are various social researchers invested in this enterprise, in terms of political projects and social involvements? Finally, to which extent do the answers to these questions predetermine predominant epistemological choices and the promotion of one particular theoretical model in social contexts like inquiries, articles and direct confrontations during academic courses and seminars?

1 After the seminar, several Oromo students told me that I did not enough underline the existence of the 'original Oromo religion' and its perversion through historical contacts with what they called Christian and Muslim 'foreigners' or 'invaders'. They asked me whether I had already observed some remaining aspects of this 'traditional Oromo religion' during my different fieldworks. They expected arguments strengthening the promotion of this 'authentic Oromo religion' and its clear distinction from Christian and Muslim organizations.

This chapter is rather an essay than a research paper as it attempts to examine these views of "Self and Other" within the academic community involved in the scientific field of Oromo studies. This topic has so far remained under-discussed, even though these controversial views of "Self and Other" correlate with major current epistemological issues that cannot be neglected anymore if social scientists aim at providing a better understanding of current social phenomena, like the springs of political indigenousness, the rise of traditionalist claims, conversions to messianic Evangelical/Pentecostal churches, Muslim reformist trends or ideological developments on multi-ethnic nationalism. How shall such views of "Self and Other" within the field of Oromo studies be examined?

These diverse points of view implement a frontier, a set of distinctions or counter-appositions between each other, showing that they are all related to and embedded in the same social arena—of those who deal with the question: "what does being Oromo mean?"—as they tend to define each other through their mutual observations, relations and interactions. Nevertheless, each point of view is particular as it exposes distinct social interpretations or projects. I suggest here to present and assess the five main theoretical trends and their promoters within the field of Oromo studies. These are represented through the following ideal-types: (1) the official Ethiopian imperial historiography, (2) the anthropological work of European Christian missionaries, (3) the academic publications of Oromo social scientists, (4) the cultural productions of the Ethiopian Federal State, and (5) the studies conducted by contemporary Western social scientists.

It is almost impossible to deal with the numerous and by definition all unique points of view developed by individuals involved in the academic field of Oromo studies. This is even truer here, as I do not consider this "academic" field in the restrictive meaning of university studies. Under this field, I rather attempt to gather plural types of knowledge which all have in common that they are institutionalized in different forms: the official historiography produced during the imperial regime, the Christian missionary corpus, the official positions of the Ethiopian Federal State and the studies conducted by both Oromo and Western scholars, published in academic and associated contexts. Thus, instead of assuming that the five registers of knowledge production I attempt to investigate are real or do exist as such in reality, I rather adopt an ideal-type approach to be able to discuss them as idealized but operational representations of the main trends which have dominated the field of Oromo studies since its inception. None of these registers exists as such, but are of course in reality much more nuanced, heterogeneous and intermingled. Nevertheless, to posit them constitutes an attempt to summarize in terms of theoretical perspectives the main epistemological cleavages that have split academic knowledge on Oromo identity issues. The presentation of these ideal-type registers here has no other aim than pointing out historical backgrounds, presupposed ideas, political stakes, logics of counter-appositions and other objective conditions which tend to govern the plural perceptions and interpretations of Oromo identities.

These five ideal-type versions are discussed through the examination of the objective conditions that influence, for each of them, knowledge production, conceptions of identity and the resulting epistemological choices. The last part proposes to overcome the present tensions, related to competing trends in the field of Oromo studies, by repositioning them in the still controversial political history of what is today Ethiopia. Rather than defining one 'ethnic group', Oromo identity issues stage plural social statuses and regional political orders, involved in ambiguous relations with the two idealized Christian *Habesha* and Muslim *Sharifa* hegemonic networks.

Interpreting the Oromo identity framework

What does being Oromo mean today? Officially, the Oromo population comprises more than 25 million individuals,[2] distributed in a territory as large as France. Some are Muslim, and in quite various ways (being involved in *Sufi* or more reformist *Shafi* networks); others are Christian, and here again with clear differences (some are followers of the Ethiopian Orthodox Church, others are in Protestant and Evangelical churches, few are Catholics); others celebrate *Waaqa*, presented as the ancient almighty God of the Oromo. There are at least four official Oromo political parties, representing the officially established Oromo "nationality" within the Ethiopian ethnic federalism. These political parties are both present in the governmental coalition and in the opposition. In rural areas, modes of social organizations are various and reveal diverse historical and regional patterns.

These few remarks illustrate the difficulty to deal with Oromo identities. How can social anthropology contribute to interpret them? Though such social categories are epistemologically ambiguous, they are still promoted by actors, who produce discourses and perform practices in different contexts or social fields. Accordingly, the production of collective memory largely consists in recomposing the past within the economic and political stakes of the present social context. Unlike historians, anthropologists do not really discuss the historical veracity of the several competing versions over the definition of one cultural identity, but rather investigate the different social objective conditions which lead to the production of historical narratives, cultural norms and social philosophies mobilized in the ongoing (re)construction process of identity categories.

The process of knowledge production often involves relations of domination as it attempts to monopolize the legitimate discourse over one social issue, and imposes its own political project at the expense of others. However, politics is a set of relations, the place where social contradictions are expressed and confronted (see Balandier 1970). In social anthropology, the positive confrontation of different or even opposite theoretical models is welcome by definition, as permanent question-

2 According to the report of the 2007 population census, up to 25,438,344 individuals belong to the Oromo 'ethnic group', i.e. 34.5% of the total Ethiopian population (*Summary and Statistical Report of the 2007 Population and Housing Census*, FDRE Population Census Commission, p.18, December 2008, printed by UNFPA, Addis Ababa).

ing and challenging theories are a necessity in the comparative as well as generalizing study of human culture and social action. Definitions and representations of social identities are never uniform, inside or outside the social locations of power. They are rather social constructions embedded and reformulated in the stakes of the present. In this perspective, "authenticity is a view of mind".[3]

Again, this paper neither discusses all the various ways of being Oromo, nor aims to distinguish the "authentic" discourses from the "unauthentic" ones over this generally so-called "ethnic" group: this essay rather tries to unveil the main different historical, political and academic factors which tend to shape the main controversial perceptions and "regimes of historicity" (Hartog 2003) of this ambivalent social category.

The development of Oromo identity claims cannot be understood without clearly taking into account the political history of Ethiopia, the long dominance of the official imperial historiography on this issue, the role of Western Christian missionaries, the trajectories of Marxist-based movements (embedded in the historical developments of Ethiopian left-wing parties) and the revival of ethno-centered "traditional" identities. This complex history involves politicians but also intellectuals, clerics and scholars from Ethiopian and Western universities. Last but not the least, the official recognition of an Oromo Regional State and the promotion of an official Oromo language, history and sets of cultural items are not anodyne enterprises: since the implementation of federalism in the 1990s, the Oromo identity has become a state institutionalized category, but state administrations are not the only actors competing for the legitimate definition of what being Oromo means.

Ethiopian imperial historiography versus western missionaries' anthropological studies

Through the official Ethiopian imperial historiography, the Oromo category was systematically mobilized in pejorative terms to designate a population perceived as radical enemies of the empire. Opposing narratives have been produced since the second part of the 19th century by Western Christian missionaries, promoting the historical, cultural and religious unity of what they called the "Oromo nation". These narratives were actively used in the creation of positive Oromo fictions, countering the cultural hegemony of the Christian Orthodox *Habesha* kingdom.[4]

3 This question of "authenticity" can be understood as "a view of mind" to quote J. Derrida (1967: 9) [this is my English translation of Derrida's French expression '*une aventure du regard*' which literally means 'a looking adventure'] and his criticism addressed to the Western notion of "centered structures": the definition of one "authentic" norm is always an illusion which consists in producing an immutable and transcendental 'centre' which defines the nature of the 'structure', out of the structural 'game' (Derrida 1967: 410).

4 *Abyssinia* and *Habesha* are classical terms used to designate the northern regions of present Ethiopia and their inhabitants. Though their historical origins and linguistic geneses are not well known, these two terms are recurrent stereotypes mobilized to

Official Ethiopian imperial historiography

The Ethiopian imperial historiography drew a very negative portray of Oromo populations.[5] Since the 16th century, they have been indifferently called *Galla*, a general name—today used only to insult—designating the so-called "pagan" populations living across the symbolic southern boundaries of the Christian *Habesha* kingdom. Imperial chronicles and other related narratives present them as "hordes of pagans", "bloody conquerors" coming from the South to destroy the Christian empire (Ficquet 2002). Depicted as the radical Others, in opposition to the Christian 'civilized' *Habesha*, they were often associated with a kind of divine punishment. Following the war against the Muslim coalition of sultanates, gathered and commanded by Imam Ahmed Ibrahim Gragn, Emir of Harar, the so-called "Galla conquests" in the 16th century are described in imperial written sources as the main plague that had ever threatened the Christian *Habesha* kingdom (Bahrey in Beckingham & Huntingford 1954). However, some critical analyses of historical written sources reveal that several Oromo clans played a significant role within the royal kin groups themselves, through marriage links and alliance strategies (Ficquet 2002; Toubkis 2008). Recent historical studies have stressed that the notion of a monolithic empire is by itself a fictional construction, contrasting with the permanent negotiations between regional political entities, with unclear boundaries in what is today Northern and Central Ethiopia. Throughout its long history, Ethiopia has always given the impression of having a strong central state, the reality however, was a loosely controlled political system, punctually ruled by the *Negusa Nagast* (King of kings), with a significant element of devolved and regional power (Pennec & Toubkis 2004). The definition of common and so radical foes like the Oromo has probably participated, through the writings of imperial chroniclers, to consolidate the historical discourse on a united and immutable Ethiopian Christian Empire.

Here, knowledge production is based on a theological center, defining a political and historical doctrine emphasizing the quality of chosen people,[6] labeled on the ancient inhabitants of the present northern Ethiopian regions, and the sanctity of their kings, descents of Solomon, King of Israel, and Makeda, Queen of Sheba. The Ethiopian/*Habesha* Christian divine revelation supports a theory of knowledge based on hermeneutics, the interpretation of Christian texts (the Bible, hagiographies and other religious texts) reserved to a small part of the population, an elite composed by Orthodox Christian clerics who can read and write Ge'ez, the language of the Christian *Habesha* theological state. This elite is directly linked to the

stage the classical historical narratives promoting the mythic Christian Semitic monarchical basis of the Ethiopian state.

5 For a general discussion on this topic, see Eloi Ficquet, 2002, "La fabrique des origines Oromo", *Annales d'Ethiopie XVIII*, 55-71, Paris/Addis Ababa: La Table Ronde.

6 The word *Egzebeher*, which means God in Amharic today, is a combination in Ge'ez of two roots whose association can be literally translated as 'the people of God' or 'the elected people'. This etymological meaning reminds the Jewish claim but rather promotes the *Habesha* competing version.

political power as these clerics produce the official historiography and history, as well as all kinds of de facto official knowledge.

In this epistemological stance, identity is considered as immutable ascriptions, fixed by religious texts ordering individuals and groups. The main emerging social categories are the *Habesha* (the 'original' populations of the Christian kingdom, with several internal cleavages), the "Muslims" (both recurrent enemies and close commercial clients, socially considered as "Peoples of the Book"), the "Galla" ("the hordes of bloody pagan invaders", coming from the South) and the "Slaves" (war prisoners and dark skin individuals, especially those coming from the present southern Ethiopian regions). This conception of identity tends to reveal a kind of Ethiopian divine evolutionary paradigm, legitimating a political order dominated by the ideological *Habesha* Christian imperial pattern. Within this order, the Oromo comprise different southern groups labeled as "pagans". This religious label positions them among the lowest social statuses, at the bottom of the *Habesha* Christian political hierarchy: contrary to the more 'civilized' Muslim foes, they are imagined as primitive and dangerous neighbours, a sort of brutal, savage and natural threat.

Western missionaries' representations

The Christian missionaries were the first to actively deal with Oromo identity. They entered western and eastern parts of present-day Oromya Regional State in the second half of 19th century and began to produce important studies on language, history and religious practices. They were the first to use the word *Oromo* to designate these populations.[7] The Christian missionaries had to bypass the influence of the Ethiopian Orthodox Church, deeply rooted and influential in Abyssinia, to enter the southern Oromo margins. After years of tensions and failures, the missionaries finally settled among the Oromo populations. They considered them as an "African nation", and especially as descendants of ancient biblical prophets. Their religious practices were depicted as very similar to ancient Judaism. In short, the missionaries found them much more to their liking than the 'heretic' Christian Orthodox *Habesha*. Their putative close links with the Old Testament positioned them as stereotypes of an ancient biblical African nation, ready to be evangelized through conversion to Catholicism or Protestant churches. Several missionaries wrote a large number of books based on long fieldwork and local inquiries (Tablino 1980, Bartels 1983, Leus 1995). However, their approach was deeply culturalist, aiming to reveal and largely invent an ideal African-Cushitic population. In addition, missionaries built schools where this biblical interpretation of the Oromo was taught. They contributed to the training of local intellectual elites able to counter the *Habesha*/Christian—Pagan/"Galla" ideology through the promotion of discourses

[7] Christian missionaries were numerous. Some of the most influent ones were Johann Ludwig Krapf, Antoine d'Abbadie, Martial de Salviac, Gustav Aren, Ton Leus and Lambert Bartels. For an overview, see Ficquet 2002 and Osmond 2004b: 51-81.

about the 'oppressed', 'monotheist' and 'African indigenous Oromo democratic nation'.[8]

The evangelical work was mainly based on the fact that the conversion of indigenous populations would be really achieved once they would start praying the Christian God in their own Oromo language, mobilizing their own religious concepts and practices (Leus 1997). In this process, missionaries' studies largely focused on the Oromo "traditional" religion. As everywhere in Africa, this search for "original" African religions has often tended to produce partial constructions—or even inventions—promoting putative links with ancient Judaism and minimizing cross-cultural heritages and various religious influences. This process of "traditional" religion building, associated to the promotion of the historical existence of an "Oromo African Nation", has largely fostered Oromo nationalism since the 1960s, providing it with political weapons to oppose the perceived *Habesha* hegemony. Without any doubt, the early work of Christian missionaries constitutes one of the main influences and references of Oromo ethno-nationalist rhetoric (Getachew, Lande & Rubenson 1998; Ficquet 2002; Osmond 2004).

Largely embedded in Evolutionist views, missionaries' conceptions of identity reflect the idea that they were bringing "civilization" to the "primitive" populations. However, this view was mixed with a certain fascination for these "indigenous" peoples: Western missionaries were the first to use the "native" category to designate the Oromo with a positive connotation, distinguishing them from the imagery "pagan invaders" promoted in the *Habesha* imperial chronicles, as they linked them to the peoples of the Old Testament and thus to ancient Judaism. The Oromo were then perceived as populations ready to adopt modernity through their conversion to Catholicism or Protestantism. The identity of the Oromo seen by the Western missionaries is then the result of a biblical mystical interpretation, boosted by the project of subverting and circumventing the *Habesha* Christian 'heresy' and ending its monopoly over the 'chosen people' discourse in the field of Eastern African Christianity.

The epistemological choices were borrowed from the social anthropology of the time, and especially from Evolutionist views and neo-Marxist interest on "pre-capitalist" societies. These epistemological choices illustrate a quest for a "native/primitive" people, "untouched by Western influences". The missionary factor followed European colonization but has often provided the evangelized or colonized Other with intellectual resources and political tools to create African national liberation movements (see Balandier 1953; Corten & Mary 2001).

8 The German missionary J. Krapf wrote that "Providence destined [the Oromo], after converted to Christianity, (...) to fulfil the mission that God assigned to the Germans in Europe." (J. L. Krapf & C.W. Isenberg 1843: 72).

Politicization of Oromo identities since 1960s

Examining the Oromo ethno-nationalist register of the academic Oromo studies implies to deal with the politicization context of Oromo identities since the 1960s. This paper takes into account the historical developments of Ethiopian left-wing movements as well as the succession of three political regimes, concluded by the establishment of ethnic federalism in the beginning of the 1990s.

First Steps: the Cultural Association Network and the Oromo Liberation Front: The politicization of Oromo identity was mainly stimulated by cultural associations since the 1960s. The Mache Tulama Self-Help Association (MTSHA) is probably one of the most well-known. Founded in 1964 by Addis Ababa dwellers, socially well integrated, it gathered high rank civil servants, army officers and university students. The main objectives of the association were to improve health, education, job opportunities and general social life, but it quickly turned to promote political rights of the Oromo populations oppressed by the 'Amharization' policy conducted by Haile Selassie since the end of the Italian occupation.[9] Based in Addis Ababa, the MTSHA had also regional franchises. The growing radicalization of its political discourses led to the aborted coup d'état in 1966 attempted by Tadesse Birru, the president and founder of the association.[10] Since the establishment of the federal regime, regional associations promoting Oromo culture have developed and generally collaborate with the MTSHA that was also allowed to pursue its activities. The cultural associative network is neither globally structured, nor managed by a common administration or bureau. Nevertheless, it attracts many students and middle-class individuals in Addis Ababa and in major towns of Shawa and Wollaga. More recently, a new association named *Waaqeffannaa* (which literally means 'we celebrate *Waaqa*', the almighty monotheist God of what is presented as the 'Oromo traditional religion') emerged out of the MTSHA, which focused on the promotion of the Oromo traditional religion. Largely involved in the recent revival of *Irreeccaa* ceremonies around Horra Lake in the town of Debre Zeit/Bishoftuu, the Waaqeffannaa association was dissolved in 2004 as their members went on public demonstration to protest against the decision of the Federal government to displace the capital city of Oromya Regional State from Addis Ababa to Nazareth/Adaamaa (Osmond 2004a).

Created in 1973, the Oromo Liberation Front (OLF) still represents the main historical emblem of Oromo nationalism. Based on a classical a-religious conception

9 Ezekiel Gebissa (2007) rightly points out that the "Amharization" policy started to be implemented before the Italian occupation of Ethiopia, through the decision of Haile Selassie to remove the western regional dynastic leaders in Jimma and Nekemte. However, in other parts of what is today the Oromya Regional State, local rulers were not systematically replaced by northern of Shawan officials.

10 For a general and militant view over the Macha Tulama Association, see GammaccuTaye (1993).

of Nation-State, the OLF originally fought against the Amhara "colonization" of the Oromo nation and aimed at creating an Oromo independent State. Its popularity became important during the transitional period between the collapse of the Derg and the establishment of the federal regime. Its alliance with EPRDF broke up in 1992 and the OLF became illegal in Ethiopia. Since the 1990s, several other political parties, namely the Oromo National Congress or the Oromo Federalist Democratic Party, intending to represent the Oromo have emerged both within the ruling EPRDF coalition and among the opposition.

Let us sum up—somewhat provocatively—the points of view developed by the current Oromo intellectuals in the field of Oromo studies in terms of knowledge production, conceptions of identity and epistemological choices. As many of them frequented, at one moment or another, missionaries' schools, their theoretical models are mainly borrowed from academic social anthropology. However, they consider the social sciences first and foremost as a tool to counter the *Habesha* Imperial Christian hegemonic discourse and tend to privilege two main perspectives: the Marxist one (illustrated by their former involvement in the socialist movements fighting the imperial regime) and the field of "indigenous" studies, through the development of *emic* knowledge built by the "Natives" to promote an "indigenous", "original" and "authentic" form of African modernity.

In this perspective, social anthropology can be considered as a tool box mobilized in a political struggle against the *Habesha* Imperial cultural supremacy, by helping to shape an archetype of a "native", "indigenous" people close to ancient Judaism. Nevertheless, these epistemological choices mobilized to deal with Oromo identities do not totally escape from a kind of schizophrenic relation with its Western Christian missionary legacies.

Except for some notable exceptions and notable massacres, the incorporation of those regional Oromo political entities (or even states) within the imperial state ruled by Menelik II did not deeply change their organization.[11] However, the "Amharization" policy implemented by Haile Selassie in the 1940s, which was again boosted after the Italian occupation, entailed more acute transformations of the balance of local powers, through the removal of local rulers replaced by *neftenia* colonizers who were actively supposed to "amharize" the locals. Since this time, it is impossible to deny that the Oromo category has been used, in different circumstance, as a scapegoat, a pretext to political oppression. Many of the actors involved in organizations claiming political rights and better recognition for the Oromo populations have been jailed, killed or forced to leave the country. Though these individuals were oppressed due to their opposition to the successive Ethiopian governments, rather than for being Oromo per se, it seems clear that the recurrent political antagonist relations between the promoters of Oromo identity and the Ethiopian authorities have largely participated in fostering Oromo nationalism. In a

[11] As it was previously exposed, the imperial regime never fully controlled its empire and often negotiated with their powerful vassals rather than strictly ruled over them. For a regional example, see Triulzi (1986).

way that reminds of the construction of Western nationalisms during the 18th and 19th centuries (Anderson 1983), "being Oromo" is often perceived in urban areas as being politically and culturally oppressed by the successive Ethiopian central governments. This tendency is particularly expressed among Oromo scholars who migrated to Northern America and developed Oromo studies in American universities.[12]

The Institutionalization of Oromo Identity within the Ethnic Federal Regime: By 1990 three main liberation movements founded on ethno-national bases—all of whom had their roots in one form or another before the revolution of 1974,[13] brought about the military defeat of the Derg regime in 1991. A transitional Ethiopian government was established, Eritrea declared independence in 1993, and in 1995 a new constitution proclaimed establishing the Federal Democratic Republic of Ethiopia on an *État de droit* basis (Bahru & Pausewang 2002). The ethno-nationalist movements that were born in the 1960s emerged as the opportunities for local interlocutory politics at the interface with the imperial system were increasingly closed down. Though many local leaders remained minor relays of the Imperial authorities, major regional figures were removed and replaced by loyal representatives and promoters of the "Amharization" policy. The interruption of traditional interlocutory politics, breaking with the centuries-long logics of negotiation and 'indirect rule' which organized the relations between the *Habesha* Christian kingdom and its ambiguous vassals/clients/allies, went along with Emperor Haile Selassie's projects to centralize, modernize and nationalize government. Yet it was not the ethno-nationalists that overthrew the Imperial state, but rather a coalition of actors seduced by Marxist and Socialist ideologies. But it was left-leaning elements of this coalition who, a few years later, felt betrayed by the ultra-nationalism and authoritarianism *Derg* regime who went on to join the incipient peasant based ethno-national movements (Lewis 1996), which as a result, were imbued with a great deal of 'socialist' ideology including their concept of ethnicity and nationality (Young 1997). Ironically, it is only since the introduction of 'ethnic federalism' in the 1990s that the full flowering of 'pure' ethnic politics in Ethiopia has occurred, and whether actors believe in or bemoan this fact, none are above or indeed below 'playing the ethnic card'. Indeed as a historian of Africa has noted, like the early 'nationalist' parties in colonial West Africa, who organized primarily to take part in electoral politics (Iliffe 1996) many ethnic groups in Ethiopia seem to have been organized to take part in the new politics of ethnic federalism (Vaughan & Tronvoll 2003).

In this context, the official Oromo identity promoted by the Federal government is politically monopolized by the Oromo People Democratic Organization (OPDO),

12 See for example the productions of Oromo scholars in University of Tennessee, Georgia State University, University of Michigan and the role of the *Oromo Studies Association* and the *Journal of Oromo Studies*.

13 These liberation movements were namely the Eritrean People's Liberation Front (EPLF), the Tigrean People's Liberation Front (the TPLF) that incorporated other smaller ethnic fronts becoming the Ethiopian People's Revolutionary Democratic Front (EPRDF) and the Oromo Liberation Front (OLF).

the political party of the ruling coalition that is supposed to represent the Oromo nationality. Through state-controlled radios, television cultural programs and newspapers, it is constantly repeated that the Oromo people is now free, enjoying its own Regional State. Oromo traditional practices are largely broadcast in the "living museum of the fictional multinational Ethiopian community". Like other Ethiopian "nations, nationalities and peoples", the Oromo identity is promoted as folklore to celebrate the peaceful cohabitation of cultural nationalities within the Federal Democratic Republic of Ethiopia. Songs, rural everyday life and religious practices linked to the land and the elders constitute the main elements of this post-card looking folklore staged to promote a State-controlled Oromo identity fostering the multinational Ethiopian imaginary. One may also add that there exists a kind of informal rule which implies that the President of the Federal Democratic Republic of Ethiopia should be an Oromo. This title is purely honorific and apolitical, and may be understood as another ostensible "concession" of the Federal government to the "Oromo nationality".

Thus, the production of knowledge operated within the present Ethiopian ethnic federal regime has plural bases whose main ones are Marxist-Stalinist ideologies and African Renaissance think tanks, involving the promoters of the African Multinational State in Political Sciences (Tshiyembe 2003). Ethnic federalism is presented as the application of a political project that fully achieved the 1974 Revolution and the land reform. Knowledge production is also characterized by a state-controlled diffusion of "scientific" evidence to promote and foster the Ethiopian multi-ethnic federal imaginary.

Their conceptions of identity combine the European colonial and anthropological definition of "ethnic group" (considering these categories in substantivist, linear and biological ways) and the Marxist views on ethnicity, in which the word "nationality" tends to replace "ethnic group" to emphasize the struggle against imperialist orders. Modern non-*Habesha* identity in itself has come to be seen as a weapon to free Ethiopian populations oppressed by the imperialist and unitarian governments of the Ancient Regime and the Derg. This epistemological choice rejects or rather totally ignores more dynamic and postmodern approaches.

Western anthropologists in the academic field of Oromo studies

Western social scientists' positions within the field of Ethiopian and Oromo studies are historically heterogeneous. Early on, many of them have contributed to foster the classical imperial Ethiopian historiography, opposing the so-called "primitive" Oromo populations to the "civilized" Christian *Habesha* kingdom. Others have rather promoted the existence of an Oromo "people" and attempted to reveal its cultural and historical political unity, as well as the consequences of its incorporation into the Ethiopian Empire, in terms of acculturation and loss of its 'original' identity. More recently, an active postmodern minority of mostly German-Italian-French anthropologists have developed new trends in Oromo studies.

Theoretical prejudices of the ethiopianist discourse

Regarding knowledge production, academic studies conducted by Westerners on Oromo issues tend to be few in number in Ethiopia, compared to investigations in the northern regions of this country or on similar "ethnic" topics in Western African countries. One reason explaining this underdeveloped status of Oromo studies comes from the orientation of many Western academic publications in the 1950s-1960s that reactivated an ancient European fascination for Ethiopia inherited from biblical interpretations. This fascination has already been staged in the mainly Portuguese Jesuit literary genre promoting 'the kingdom of Priest John' (Pennec 2003) and depicting Ethiopia as an old and isolated Christian kingdom surrounded by Muslims and pagans. Following this European imaginary, some Western intellectuals, fascinated by this country that they considered as a natural ally of the West, have promoted the Great Narrative or Myth of Greater Ethiopia (Pankhurst 1955; Ullendorff 1965; Levine 1965 and 1974). The narratives produced by these Western scholars can be read as "a parallel version of a European *grand récit* about origins and historical mission: in this perspective the narrative of the Ethiopian 'other' can be seen as the tale about an African alter ego, with whom the Europeans share common descent and a common destiny" (Hultin 1996). In this view, these academic narratives were "both embedded in and contributing to the maintenance of the dominant group's hegemony", legitimating the political domination of the Christian *Habesha* kingdom over the Oromo.[14]

In terms of identity and epistemological choices, these Western scholars were trapped in evolutionist theories. Indeed, already the cultural construction of an Oromo 'other' in this Western academic tradition is deeply rooted in a stance which views the Christian *Habesha* kingdom as almost as 'civilized' as European societies, whereas the Oromo are classified as 'savage' populations, who have gradually reached to the 'Barbarian' stage thanks to their incorporation into the Ethiopian Empire. Contrary to the political threat incarnated by the Muslims, morally classified as 'civilized' populations, the Oromo were defined as "dangers outside human society ..., a kind of natural disaster" (Hultin 1996: 88). According to these evolutionist discourses, the Oromo turned to be "no longer 'nomadic tribes', savages living outside of the boundaries of civilization, in nature, but had 'learnt farming and settled living'. (...) They had reached a stage of development that made it possible to integrate them into 'Greater Ethiopia'" (Hultin 1996:87) at the time of Menelik II in the end of the 19th century. Through this interpretation, the Oromo are evacuated from Ethiopian history and labeled as picturesque folkloric groups, out of national political issues and differentiated from the "fanatical Muslim invaders".

[14] Through his deconstruction and textual analysis of these narratives, J. Hultin (1996: 82) writes: "In this [Western] scholarly genre, the cultural representation of the Ethiopian Self and the Galla Other can be read as an expression of a frontier cast ideology (Kopytoff 1987; Triulzi 1994) about a hierarchical arrangement of social roles and categories in the Ethiopian Empire. The representation of the 'Galla' in the Great Narrative of Ethiopia is part of a generalized and diffuse discourse about the right of northern settlers to rule over Oromo tenants."

As summarized by J. Hultin (1996:84), "the Oromo are virtually left outside of the narrative: there is no role for them to play. (...) The savage Galla of the past become the 'Invisible Man' of the present."

From structuralist approaches to postmodern perspectives

Opposing these scholars during the same period, other Western social scientists have rather promoted the existence of an Oromo "people" and attempted to reveal its cultural and historical political unity as well as the consequences of its incorporation into the Ethiopian Empire in terms of acculturation and loss of its 'original' identity. Historically, this trend has mostly been led by the English structural functionalist school, which has until recently dominated this field of researches (with some notable exceptions).[15] Since the 1990s, one has to mention the inquiries conducted by an active postmodern minority of mostly German-Italian-French anthropologists (Schlee 1994; Bassi 1996; Gufu 1996; Ficquet 2002). The Structural Functionalist group was vaguely related to British colonial administrations (as illustrated by the strong historical influence of UK in Ethiopia) while the second one is more freelance, mostly sponsored by institutions largely involved in fundamental research and rarely appears among the priorities of their respective embassies.

Today, these Western academic contexts of knowledge production are strongly challenged by social work and NGOs consultancies, privileging 'developmentist' issues like food security, water/electricity networks etc. Thus, in both Europe and America, fundamental and independent social anthropology tends to be out of—and sometimes against—state political agendas.

Regarding conceptions of identity, the structural functionalist approaches applied by mainly English anthropologists till the end of the 1980s entailed that the study of Oromo identities was divided into two categories: the first one aimed at revealing the "original" ones, like the cradle land of Oromo peoples or the "authentic" forms of their political and religious systems. The second category is composed of "corrupted" versions, linked to far distances separating some Oromo from their "original" homelands, entailing contacts with other non-Oromo groups and confrontations with other cultural and political hegemonic regimes. More recently, anthropologists privileging dynamic, situationist and postmodern perspectives in general, consider identity as the staging process of social stereotypes, bearing different and competing political projects. Embedded in identifiable and mostly political and economic stakes, these social stereotypes are manipulated by different actors proposing answers to different social issues, through the production of idealized social interpretative models. Identity is an ongoing arrangement of competing interpretations of plural social relations and representations, punctually fixed or crystallized by the implementation of one point of view or one center. This dynamic

[15] These English Structural Functionalists are mainly P.T.W. Baxter (1978a, 1978b) and H. Blackhurst (1978). One has to mention the work of H.S. Lewis (1990) and K.E. Knutson (1967) and their attempts to apply American Interactionist models and German comprehensive sociological ones.

approach of Oromo identities directly fights the classical substantivist and fixed theoretical anthropological models by promoting plural identities and regimes of historicity. It neither adheres to nor rejects the identity projects developed by Oromo intellectuals or the Ethiopian federal authorities. This approach rather questions them, mobilizing different theoretical and methodological anthropological tools (Schlee 1994; Ahmed 1997; Osmond 2005).

The epistemological choices of classical structural functionalist studies tend to follow those developed by the current "indigenous" promoters of Oromo nationalism, aiming to isolate the cultural nucleus and the basic social structures of the Oromo people. For the second postmodern group, their epistemological choices aim to reveal the inner working of and the actors behind the plural Oromo identity narratives expressed in the present federal regime, questioning potential gaps between the general discourses on the "nationality" category and regional configurations. In this approach, the weight of ethnicity is moderated by the study of other types of social solidarities and regional forms of affiliations.

Reinterpreting Oromo identities in the historical dynamics of the Horn of Africa

Having presented the main epistemological registers in the field of Oromo studies, one may legitimately ask, and then, what shall we do? Are those positions irremediably bound to oppose each other and saturate this academic field? I do not think so as new theoretical perspectives may unlock the debates. Regarding epistemological choices, it could be scientifically fertile to apprehend Oromo identities less as "one people" but rather in terms of social statuses, regional orders and political projects, shaped by the political historical dynamics of the Horn of Africa.

From one people to ambivalent regional constructions

Almost all academic theoretical frameworks have considered the Oromo categories in substantivist perspectives, presupposing the founding existence of an original unity and one unique centre. However, the centre of this fictional structural game[16] or, here, the predominant epistemological prejudice that determines the theoretical field of Oromo studies dwells in considering the Oromo as "one people" in diverse biblical, biological, culturalist or national romantic registers of interpretation. In this context, the main meanings of this expression or sign, "one people", gather the cursed or blessed biblical interpretations of the historical trajectories of "the Oromo people"(pejoratively called "Galla", produced by Christian *Habesha* clerics and Western missionaries), the "scientific" biological analogy operated by classical

[16] See Derrida (1967) and particularly the chapter devoted to the criticism of structuralist approaches in Social Sciences.

structuralist social theories[17] and the Oromo nation-state rhetoric ('one people, one nation, one State').

These predominantly substantivist descriptions contrast with the empirically present plurality of narratives on origins and regional memories in oral sources and traditions. Various studies in local areas clearly establish that the different kinds of discourses around the geographical and historical origin(s) of the Oromo populations designate different times, places and regions, oscillating between western, southern and even eastern parts of present-day Oromiya Regional State (Braukämper 1986). Though local informants generally agree today on similar genealogical frameworks, with two main branches (*Boraana* and *Barentu* (or *Bartuma*)) and several subunits which globally correspond to the present territorial repartition of the Oromo "kinship groups", the contents and meanings of these genealogical categories have not been yet fully investigated. The same remark is also relevant for the Oromo social categories and other terms like *Qaalluu, Abba Muuda, Ayyaanna*... Fieldwork conducted by several researchers indicates that oral traditions are deeply rooted in regional and not national configurations, shaped by various actors and trans-ethnic/religious networks. Concretely, the Oromo identity gathers regional identities with their own meaningful historical memories, which do not necessarily—and not predominantly—mobilize a pan-Oromo scheme to stage their existence.[18] Historical narratives emphasizing a pan-Oromo order are rare, whereas those which promote regional political entities, based on local leaders, religious organizations and Gadaa assemblies are numerous. Oral traditions recall the ancient existence of different states and political entities, governed by plural political systems involving "Big Men"[19] and hierarchies of rural religious leaders and Gadaa assemblies. These Oromo states were based on religious and political philosophies which largely differed from the two dominant Christian/Muslim orders, though long and plural influences and interrelations between these three political models cannot be denied. The regional networks of Oromo States constitute historical realities (at least since the 16th century) and have to be considered as a third political philosophy and set of discourses, beside the dominant Christian/Muslim orders.

[17] Historically rooted in biological reductionism to apprehend social phenomena, structuralist theories and Sociological Holism started to develop in the second half of the 19th century in the West. Besides German and American Comprehensive Sociology, it has deeply influenced all the classical theoretical (positivist) schools in Social Sciences until the 1960s.

[18] Till the establishment of ethnic federalism, Muslims living in Jimma or in Eastern part of Ethiopia did not use the term Oromo to define themselves. According to them, the term Oromo was related to the narratives developed by Christian missionaries (in Wallaga and Hararghe) and has designated since the end of the 19th century those who converted to Christianity when Menelik conquered their territories. They considered that being Muslim (in opposition to the Christian Amhara and in relation with trade Muslim networks) was more relevant to define themselves. See Lewis (1996: 40).

[19] *Mooti*: "the one who defeats, wins" in the Oromo language, refers to leaders of coalitions of kinship groups, economic networks and diverse associated religious communities.

Diffusionist temptations intending to reveal a cultural centre, led by the Oromo populations, among the Cushitic peoples, have not brought convincing findings till now. Though the populations gathered under the Cushitic linguist label (like the Oromo, Hadiya, Somali, Afar, some groups of Gamo...) present some similarities in terms of linguistics, conceptions of time, political and religious organizations (like systems of generation-sets or religious dignitaries), they also differ from each other on many issues (like kinship orders, livelihood or definitions of Self). Their several similarities do not prove (at least today) the historical existence of a Cushitic cultural or political order.[20] In addition, the words *Cush* and *Cushitic* are still unknown by the majority of the Oromo groups and many of them have developed closer relations with non-Cushitic populations than, in many cases, with other Cushitic or Oromo groups inhabiting the same regions.[21]

Questioning social statuses and political projects

Hidden diverse regional constructions

Let us agree that almost nothing is known about the populations who inhabited most of Eastern African territories before the 16th century, except that most of them spoke what has relatively recently been labeled Cushitic and Semitic languages. In terms of geopolitics, this eastern regional space of the African continent was roughly organized according to two main dominant political and religious orders, the Christian *Habesha* kingdoms and networks of Muslim sultanates.[22] Each order was founded on vertical hierarchies of socio-religious statuses. The Muslim one was ruled by the urban-*Sunna-Sharifa* ethic and its legitimate domination over heterogeneous regional rural and partially Islamized political entities. The Christian order promoted the *Ge'ez-Orthodox-Habesha* model and its legitimate domination over adjacent regional *Muslim* and *'pagan'* territories. Between—or rather among—these

20 The Cushitic label started to be popular among the Oromo nationalist elite in the 1980s-1990s. Originally, the Cushitic Biblical reference used by the linguists was not based on historical or sociological studies and did not bear any heuristic dimensions. It was rather a kind of frequent anecdotal reference to Biblical myths (like the 'Semitic' and 'Hamitic' languages), arbitrarily chosen to name populations sharing linguistic similarities and nothing more, or maybe some free speculations or phantasms emanating from certain linguists.

21 This is particularly true for some Oromo groups in Western Shawa and Gurage groups. See Fecadu (1986) and Osmond (2006).

22 In the 15th-16th centuries, the Christian Habesha kingdoms were roughly located in the present northern-western regions of Ethiopia. Recent archaeological inquiries, conducted by French researchers affiliated to the French Centre for Ethiopian Studies, tend to prove the existence of networks of sultanates at least since the 14th century. These sultanates were organized on three lines, marked by Muslim cities: one coming from the North (from Adulis and following the foothills of the highlands) and the second from the East (from Zeila to Harar). Both converged in Ifat, from where another line (or other lines) started in the South-West direction till the present Sudanese border (Ahmed 2007).

two dominant centres were located heterogeneous populations, including the Oromo rural federations.

These sets of populations occupied different positions both within and outside the two dominant Christian/Muslim orders. Indeed, depending on historical and regional contexts, they could be out of these two dominant orders, organizing themselves in autonomous local political coalitions and networks. In other historical configurations, these Oromo groups could be positioned within one of the Christian/Muslim order and shared ambiguous social statuses: mostly rural, illiterate and considered as almost 'pagan', these groups generally got lower social statuses than the political elites of the Christian *Habesha* kingdoms and networks of Muslim sultanates. However, they were at the same time powerful military allies and key economic clients. Whether they were outside or within the Christian/Muslim political orders, these groups composed the huge majority of the inhabitants of these two dominant political centers, and even their elites: all these populations were not culturally different by essence, but rather culturally differentiated through social distinctions in terms of religious, economic and political statuses, developed through complex historical processes.

Many definitions and speculations have been produced about the original meaning of the today very pejorative word "Galla". Very few studies have attempted to consider this term as a social stereotype, expressing social statuses related to both Muslim and Christian political orders. One of them formulates the hypothesis that "Galla" originates from the Arabic term designating long-distance merchants, camel herders, and its pejorative Muslim connotation of 'wanderers'.[23] Today, the word 'Gaala' (or 'Galla' in *Habesha* and Western sources) is still used in Hararghe in most Cushitic languages and signifies 'camel, dromedary'. Local oral sources and Egyptian administrative archives recall that, in the past, 'Gaala' was ascribed to these "unfaithful" separatist groups who rejected their former political affiliation to one pro-eminent sultanate after the defeat of Ahmad Ibrahim Gragn.[24]In these configurations, 'Gaala' expresses logics of distinction between political and religious models, from urban-Sharifa-puritan centers to more rural networks.[25]

23 Zitelmann (1996: 110-111) was the first to raise this hypothesis that tends to be corroborated by my own present inquiries around Harar. The Arabic word جوالة is pronounced *'jawaala(ta)'* in formal and some regional forms of Arabic. It means 'those who circulate, move from place to another and come back again', like itinerant merchants, breeders or wanderers. In Eastern Africa, *jim* (ج) is often not pronounced 'j' but rather *'gue'*. Thus, جوالةs pronounced *'gawaala'* from which Gaala/Galla probably come from. Nowadays, Somali speakers still use the word *'gaal'* to designate 'bastards' and the White Westerners, considered as non-Muslims and generally Christians (or rather atheists).

24 Other similar narratives that I recently collected around Harar about the term 'Gaala' argue that this name staged the refusal of the local rural leaders to meet the "foreign" Egypto-Turkish leaders who ruled Hararghe for almost ten years in the second part of the 19th century, before the coming of Menelik II.

25 This remark may be linked to some interpretations of the term Oromo: in several

Being Oromo is a reality, or rather social realities, and I do not doubt that 'Oromoness' exists. However, instead of trying to determine who was the first 'original' and 'civilized' people who inhabited the Horn of Africa (a question without scientific answer but whose formulation tells more than highly hypothetical answers), I propose to reconsider the social manifestations of Oromo categories since the 15th-16th centuries, emphasizing their social positions within and outside the major regional Christian/Muslim political poles of the Horn of Africa. The historical events of the 16th century reshaped political hierarchies and allegiances. The weakened Christian kingdom and Muslim coalition faced the rebellion of their internal and heterogeneous allies who established (or re-established) autonomous political entities and pluri-ethnic coalitions, based on plural political projects. These projects mobilized various trans-regional religious networks (through the cults of local Saints) and different social hierarchies based on norms like seniority (the *Boraana* scheme), monotheist—but non-Muslim and non-Christian—religious leaders (the *Qaalluu* title) and regimes of assemblies (the generation-sets of the *Gadaa* system and its local variations). Whereas these populations were very similar to those who ruled the famous sultanates and even, to a certain extent, the Christian *Habesha* kingdom,[26] their distinction was mainly social, through statuses and positions within the idealized political hierarchies of Muslim/Sharifa and Christian/*Habesha*-centered identities.[27] These regional entities were later reorganized through their incorporation into the Shawa kingdom and then to the Ethiopian State in the end of the 19th century. The 1974 Revolution deeply modified them. In the new ethnic federal framework, these rural and plural political entities are attempting to slowly reappear, but their former regional authorities are now challenged by numerous other actors and do not fit with the theoretical model of ethnic nationalities.

regions, local informants argue that Oromo comes from 'Orma' that literally means 'Stranger'. Instead of considering that the Oromo originate from another country (as claimed in Ethiopian *grand discourses*), one may suggest that Orma/Oromo are related to a common semantic field designating 'the peoples who are neither affiliated to the Christian Habesha nor the Muslim sultanates hegemonic orders'. This is of course a hypothesis that needs to be assessed.

26 Due to the lack of information before the 15th-16th centuries, I do not promote the existence of an original supremacy of a "Cushitic" order in the Horn of Africa. Nevertheless, it seems difficult to doubt the existence of cultural and linguistic similarities shared by a large part of its populations. For example, in the 11th century, the well-known Lalibela ruled the coalition of political entities that composed the Christian Habesha kingdom. Though the state language was Ge'ez, king Lalibela spoke a Cushitic language (close to Agew) in informal contexts. His name itself came from Cushitic and not from Semitic languages.

27 These numerous Oromo political entities are still understudied. Researchers involved in the field of Oromo studies have tended to neglect them as they did not fit with their quest for 'pure' and 'authentic' Oromo cultural frameworks. However, I strongly believe that these regional political entities constitute core issues whose investigations have to be developed in Oromo studies.

Following this epistemological hypothesis, I suggest to develop the following research perspectives:

—deconstructing 'Oromo' labeled key terms and concepts, mobilized in diverse social and regional contexts, through comparative and interdisciplinary perspectives. Structural functionalist readings have shown their limits in this field. *Oromo, Boraana, Barentu/Bartuma, Qaalluu, Gadaa, Ayyaanna* and many other terms are still to be examined as social categories.[28] Such investigations should unveil the role of dominant actors, staging political and social projects, to order regional configurations, shacked by historical contingencies and the plural influences of several external hegemonic models.

—reconstructing regional political histories by revealing and investigating the social networks (involving war leaders, sets of local assemblies, economic and religious networks, political alliances, etc...) which have played a predominant role since the 16th century. Their positions and relations within and outside wider political entities (like regional Oromo coalitions (involving non-Oromo groups), or the Christian *Habesha* kingdoms and networks of sultanates) should be evaluated too.[29]

—questioning more recent discourses and social expressions related to present ways of being—or claiming to be—Oromo. Pentecostal or Muslim reformist entrepreneurs and promoters of the *Waaqeffannaa* Oromo traditional religion are today among the main actors investing the field of 'Oromoness', challenging old assumptions by their involvement in more transnational networks and fostering the internal confrontation of plural reformist models and competing 'African Renaissance' projects).

Conclusion

In this essay, I have tried to raise questions related to different ways of apprehending Oromo identities in academic fields of research. Since the 1960s, their growing politicization is linked to different factors. Among them, the discourses produced by Western Christian missionaries for more than a century and the historical trajectories of Ethiopian left-wing movements have played a great role.

28 For example, many of them have probably been too arbitrarily classified into the classical structuralist 'kinship systems'. However, the natures and different regimes of historicity of these categories invite social scientists to consider clans and lineages rather in terms of economic corporations, trade unions or social lobbies gathering individuals sharing common interest in one particular socio-economic activity, and promoting common social and political projects. Genealogical narratives constitute the concrete expression of plural—and often competing—regional discourses over historical memories and political hierarchies, involving diverse Oromo political entities and ambivalent vassals/clients/allies social statuses.

29 In this process, links between urban and rural centres should be carefully examined case by case. Beyond classical centre/peripheries distinctions, urban/rural relations stage different discourses produced by plural regional centres competing for regional hegemonic positions.

Directly related to these two factors, the establishment of ethnic federalism has largely contributed to develop debates around the definition(s) of these plural social constructions dealing with 'Oromoness'. Various actors are now competing for the monopoly of the legitimate discourse over these identity categories. In the field of Oromo studies, clear tensions have appeared between different academic perspectives, confronting Ethiopian classical historical narratives and Western plural stands with insider Oromo constructions.

I suggest overcoming these obstacles by moderating the scientifically sterile distinctions between one "true", "authentic" knowledge over Oromo issues and "invented" statements produced by 'Others'. I am aware that the causes of these distinctions and associated conflicting perceptions are embedded in the complex and often painful political history of Ethiopia, whose layers are ancient and still highly debated in the present ethnic federal framework. I do not believe that the role of social scientists is to tell individuals what they have to think and do: identity is always a question of personal choice eventually. Researchers can bring their interpretations on one particular situation, question what seems obvious or controversial, and raise debates to encourage constructive discussions over complex and sensitive social issues. However, since the 1960s, social scientists have come to realize that quests for "truth" and "authenticity" are finally illusions or militant statements. All types of knowledge produce meaning and stage "truths". Rather, they attempt to convince that their form of knowledge represents the best interpretation on given issues. Current and more ancient identity claims on 'Oromoness' express rational political projects and philosophies, proposing versions of African modernity which are not more fictional than the Western theoretical interpretations and models produced since the birth of social sciences in the 19th century.

Within the academic field of Oromo studies, the five ideal-type registers of knowledge production presented in this paper have to be seen as mutually opposed discourses, interpreting historical and social facts through different epistemological approaches which highly determine the nature of their research object. As a social anthropologist, I can discuss these epistemological approaches and deconstruct their logics, various declensions, stakes and actors competing for the monopoly of the legitimate or dominant discourse over Oromo identities. Having proceeded with this methodological deconstruction, emphasizing the different contexts of knowledge production, conceptions of identity and resulting epistemological choices, I have come to the conclusion that the predominant apprehensions of 'Oromoness' as "one people" largely hinder the development of new trends in the academic field of Oromo studies.

To overcome this epistemological aporia, I propose to review Oromo identity frameworks in terms of political projects, regional networks and ambivalent social statuses which have contributed to shape the history of these eastern African regions since the 16th century.[30] The epistemological change brought by this

[30] I do not mean that the Oromo identities did not exist before the 15th-16th centuries. I simply argue that I do not have enough data to deal with them before this period.

approach does not entail that I reject former visions and the rich findings that a large number of excellent studies have produced till now. I simply intend to implement the first rule of R. Descartes' *Discourse on Scientific Method*: doubt, by challenging the theoretical roots of previous scientific studies and promoting other interpretations of what finally constitute the controversial political history of the Horn of Africa since the 16th century. Thinking in such terms seems more relevant to apprehend the complex differentiation processes which have historically ordered in plural and ambiguous categories stocks of populations who have shared similar cultural and linguistic patterns for centuries.[31] These "invisible" (Hultin 1996:84) Oromo regional entities have to be seriously investigated if one wants to overcome the present sterile ideological oppositions that hinder the development of Oromo studies.

I argue that major historical developments occurred during the 15th-16th centuries in the Horn of Africa and reshaped its regional political orders. After the bloody conflict opposing the Christian kingdoms to the coalition of sultanates led by Ahmad Gragn, their ambiguous Oromo regional vassals/clients/allies have (re)developed diverse regional political entities, philosophies and solidarities. Most of them were closely connected through several religious and economic networks. They involved different kinship coalitions, networks of Gadaa assemblies, religious actors like Qaalluu(s), Muslim saints or divine entities, represented by Big Men centralizing intermingled kinship networks, agro-pastoral unions and chains of spirit possession cults. The historical constructions of these regional social relays mobilized plural cultural registers, including ancient Sufi influences and more recent associations with Christian Orthodox saints. These plural registers and their concrete regional manifestations constitute the most numerous social sequences of Oromo identity frameworks. Unfortunately, their study has been unfairly neglected by many scholars searching for non-Muslim and non-Christian versions of a questionable 'pure'/'authentic' Oromo identity.

The different conceptions of 'Oromoness' tell us about points of view promoted by groups of individuals observing each other within the same social arena. Within those groups, individuals born in Ethiopia and who identify themselves as descents and heirs of the Christian *Habesha* Ethiopianist narratives, struggle against those who define themselves as survivals and legitimate representatives of the 'indigenous and monotheist Oromo democratic African nation'. In other groups, Westerners have interpreted in yet again a different way the Oromo people as 'pagan invaders threatening Holy Christian Ethiopia', or as the biblical stereotype of the 'democratic African people' compared to the peoples of ancient Judaism.

United by the inscription of their research topics within the controversial Ethiopian history, all these scholars stage their own insiders/outsiders' positions: through

31 For example, almost nothing is known about the differentiation process of the today labeled Cushitic languages. When, how and why did the current Oromo, Somali, Afar, Hadiya... languages emerge as distinct linguistic sets? Answers to such questions are still important missing parts of the Oromo identity frameworks.

the production of "scientific" discourses related to the field of Oromo studies, they perform their nuanced and often intimate relations with their scientific objects. Knowledge production and images of Self and Other remain inseparable. This is probably why epistemological debates and constructive confrontations of theoretical perspectives remain an absolute necessity in social sciences, defined as the art of interpreting human social constructions.

References

Ahmed Hassan, 1997: "State and Ethnic Relations in Northeastern Shawa (Ethiopia), 1912-1935". In: *Ethiopia in Broader Perspective (Kyoto, 12th-16th December, 1997), International Conference of Ethiopian Studies 13*. Kyoto: Shokado, 138-150.

Ahmed Hassan, 2007: "L'Islam en Ethiopie". In: Gerard Prunier (ed.): *L'Ethiopie Contemporaine*. Paris: Karthala, 204-226.

Anderson, Benedict, 1983: *Imagined Communities: Reflections on the origin and spread of nationalism*. London: Verso.

Bahrey, 1954: "The History of the Galla". In: Charles Fraser. Beckingham and George Wynn Brereton Huntingford (eds.): *Some Records of Ethiopia, 1593-1646*. London: Hakluyt Society, 111-129.

Bahru Zewde and Siegfried Pausewang (eds.), 2002: *Ethiopia. The challenge of democracy from below*. Stockholm. Elanders Gotab.

Balandier, Georges, 1953: "Messianismes et Nationalismes en Afrique Noire". *Cahiers Internationaux de Sociologie 14*. Paris: Presses Univers. de France, 41-65.

Balandier, Georges, 1970: *Political Anthropology*. New York: Random House.

Bartels, Lambert, 1983: *Oromo Religion. Myths and rites of the western Oromo of Ethiopia—An Attempt to Understand*. Berlin: Dietrich Reimer.

Bassi, Marco, 1996: "Power's Ambiguity or the Political Significance of Gada.". In: Paul Baxter, Jan Hultin and Alessandro Triulzi (eds.), 1996: *Being and Becoming Oromo. Historical and anthropological enquiries*. Uppsala: Nordiska Afrikainstitutet, 150-161.

Baxter, Paul, 1978a: "Ethiopia's Unacknowledged Problem: The Oromo". *African Affairs* 77, 308, 283-296.

Baxter, Paul, 1978b: "Boraana Age-Sets and Generation-Sets: Gada, a puzzle or a maize?" In: Paul Baxter & Uri Almagor (eds.), *Age, Generation and Time: Some features of east Africanage organization*. London: Hurst, 151-182.

Baxter, Paul, Jan Hultin and Alessandro Triulzi (eds.), 1996: *Being and Becoming Oromo. Historical and anthropological enquiries*. Uppsala: Nordiska Afrikainstitutet.

Blackhurst, Hector, 1978: "Continuity and Change in the Shoa Galla Gada System". In: P.T.W. Baxter & Uri Almagor (eds.): *Age, Generation and Time: Some features of east African age organization*, London: Hurst, 245-267.

Braukämper, Ulrich, 1986: "Oromo Country of Origin: A reconsideration of hypotheses". In: *Proceedings of the International Conference of Ethiopian Studies 6*, 25-40.

Corten, André and André Mary, 2001: *Imaginaires Politiques et Pentecôtismes*. Paris: Karthala.

Derat, Marie-Laure, 2003: *Le Domaine des Rois Ethiopiens (1270-1527). Espace, pouvoir et monachisme*. Paris: Publications de la Sorbonne.

Derrida, Jacques, 1967: *L'écriture et la Différence*. Paris: le Seuil (1978, *Writing and Difference.* Chicago: University of Chicago Press.

Ezekiel Gebissa, 2007: "Resistance, Political Consciousness and Incipient Nationalism: Oromo Reaction to the Italian Invasion of Ethiopia". In: Ezekiel Gebissa (ed.): *Contested Terrain. Essays on Oromo studies, Ethiopian discourse and politically engaged scholarship*, Trenton/Asmara: The Red Sea Press, 95-123.

Fecadu Gadamu, 1986: "Traditional Social Setting of the Kistane (Soddo) in Central Ethiopia." *Paideuma 32*, 15-44.

Ficquet, Eloi, 2002: "La Fabrique des Origines Oromo". *Annales d'Ethiopie* XVIII. Paris/Addis Ababa: La Table Ronde, 55-71

Gammaccu Taye, 1993: "The History of the Macha-Tulama Association."Addis Ababa: Addis Ababa University. (B.A. Thesis).

Getatchew Haile, Aasulv Lande and Samuel Rubenson (eds.) 1998: *The Missionary Factor in Ethiopia. Papers from a symposium on the impact of European missions on Ethiopian society, Lund University.* Frankfurt am Main: Lang. (Studien zur Interkulturellen Geschichte des Christentums 110).

Gufu Oba, 1996: "Shifting Identities along Resource Borders.". In P.T.W. Baxter Jan Hultin and Alessandro Triulzi (eds.): *Being and Becoming Oromo. Historical and anthropological enquiries*. Uppsala: Nordiska Afrikainstitutet, 117-131.

Hartog, Francis, 2003: *Régimes d'Historicité, Présentisme et Expériences du Temps.* Paris: Seuil.

Hultin, Jan, 1996, "Perceiving Oromo. 'Galla' in the Great Narrative of Ethiopia." In: Paul Baxter, Jan Hultin and Alessandro Triulzi (eds.): *Being and Becoming Oromo. Historical and anthropological enquiries*. Uppsala: Nordiska Afrikainstitutet, 81-91.

Iliffe, John, 1996: *Africans: The history of the continent.* Cambridge: Cambridge University Press.

Knutson, Karl, 1967: *Authority and Change: A study of the kallu institution among the Macha Galla of Ethiopia*. Göteborg: Etnografiska Museet.

Kopytoff, Igor, 1987: The African Frontier: The reproduction of traditional African societies. Bloomington: Indiana University Press.

Krapf, Johann Ludwig and Carl Wilhelm Isenberg, 1843: *Journals detailing their Proceedings in the Kingdom of Shoa and Journeys in other parts of Abyssinia in the Years 1839, 1840, 1841 and 1842.* London: Burnside & Seely.

Leus, Ton, 2006: *Borana Dictionary: A Borana book for the study of language and culture.* Addis Ababa: Shama.

Leus, Ton, 1997: "The Evangelisation of Cultures and the Inculturation of Faith in Boraana: A missionary perspective." *Ethiopian Review of Cultures* (Special Issue), 6-7, Addis Abeba, 119-131.

Levine, Donald, 1965: *Wax and Gold: Tradition and innovation in Ethiopian culture.* Chicago: The University of Chicago Press.

Levine, Donald, 1974. *Greater Ethiopia: The evolution of a multiethnic society.* Chicago and London: The University of Chicago Press.

Lewis, Herbert, 1990: "Gada, Big Man, K'allu: Political succession among the eastern Mech'a Oromo.".*Northeast African Studies*12, 1, 43-64.

Lewis, Herbert, 1996: "The Development of Oromo Political Consciousness from 1958 to 1994". In: Paul Baxter, Jan Hultin and Alessandro Triulzi (eds.): *Being and Becoming Oromo. Historical and anthropological enquiries.* Uppsala: Nordiska Afrikainstitutet, 37-47.

Osmond, Thomas, 2004a: "*Waaqeffannaa,* une Association Religieuse Oromo d'Éthiopie entre Nationalisme Ethnique et Idéologie Afrocentriste". *Politique Africaine 94*, 166-180.

Osmond, Thomas, 2004b: "Possession, Identités Régionales et Nationalismes Oromo: le cas des dignitaires religieux qaalluu en Ethiopie".). Université d'Aix-Marseille 1, France. (PhD Thesis).

Osmond, Thomas, 2005, "Jeux de Pouvoir et Référents Identitaires: Quel statut institutionnel pour Dire Dawa?". *Politique Africaine 99*, 63-82.

Osmond, Thomas, 2006: "Possession et Stratégies de Représentation chez les Oromo du Shäwa occidental(Éthiopie): Le cas du Mo'aata". *Les Annales d'Éthiopie 20.* Addis Ababa/Paris: La Table Ronde, 221-237.

Pankhurst, Sylvia, 1955: *Ethiopia. A cultural history.* Woodford Green: Lalibela House.

Pennec, Hervé, 2003: *Des Jésuites au Royaume du Prêtre Jean (Ethiopie).* Paris: Centre Culturel Calouste Gulbenkian.

Pennec, Hervé andDimitri Toubkis, 2004: "Reflections on the Notion of 'Empire' and 'Kingdom' in Seventeenth Century Ethiopia: Royal power and local power". *Journal of Early Modern History*8 (3-4). London: 229-258.

Schlee, Günther, 1994: "Islam and the Gada System as Conflict-Shaping Forces in Southern Oromia". In: Harold Marcus and Grover Hudson (eds.), 1994: *New Trends in Ethiopian Studies*. Lawrenceville, NJ: Africa World Press, 975-997.

Tablino, Paolo, 1980: *I Gabbra del Kenya*. Bologna: E.M.I.

Toubkis, Dimitri, 2008: "Des Confins du Royaume à la Conquête du Trône: les Oromo Face au Roi Chrétien d'Ethiopie (16th-18th centuries)", Université Paris1, Département d'Histoire (France). (unpublished manuscript).

Triulzi, Alessandro, 1986: "Nekemte and Addis Ababa: Dilemmas of provincial rule". In: Donald Donham and Wendy James (eds.): *The Southern Marches of Imperial Ethiopia. Essays in History and Social Anthropology.* Cambridge: Cambridge University Press, 51-68.

Triulzi, Alessandro, 1994: "Oromo Traditions of Origin". In: *Etudes Ethiopiennes, Actes de la Xe Conférence Internationale des Etudes Ethiopiennes*1. Paris: Les Presses de la Sorbonne, 593-601.

Tshiyembe, Mwayila, 2003: *État Multinational et Démocratie Africaine.* Paris: Karthala.

Ullendorf, Edward, 1965: *The Ethiopians. An introduction to country and people* (Second edition). London: Oxford University Press.

Vaughan, Sarah and Kjetil Tronvol, 2003: "The Culture of Power in Contemporary Ethiopian Politics. (Sida Studies 10). (Accessible online at: http://www.ihasa.org/documents/special-reports/SIDA-REPORT-ETHIOPIA.pdf).

Young, John, 1997: *Peasant Revolution in Ethiopia: The Tigray peoples liberation front (1975-1991).* Cambridge: Cambridge University Press.

Zitelmann, Thomas, 1996: "Re-Examining the Galla/Oromo Relationship. The stranger as a structural topic". In: Paul Baxter, Jan Hultin and Alessandro Triulzi (eds.), 1996: *Being and Becoming Oromo. Historical and anthropological enquiries.* Uppsala: Nordiska Afrikainstitutet, 103-113.

The Way to Shashamane

The Rastafari return to a fictive Ethiopia

Wolfgang Bender

Rastafari—a very short introduction

The Rastafarian movement developed out of the poor sections of Jamaican society from the 1930s onward. It is better described as a highly religious movement than as a formalized religion, and it is based on the Old Testament which hints at the strong Christian basis among the people of Jamaica.[1]

The Rastafarian movement came into existence through a number of factors. One line leads us back to the Jamaican-born preacher and organizer Marcus Garvey (1887-1940), who had dedicated his life to improving the living conditions of the formerly enslaved African-American populations. In 1914, he founded the Universal Negro Improvement Association (UNIA) in Jamaica which came to be especially successful in the US. "The Philosophy and Opinions of Marcus Garvey, or, Africa for the Africans" was first published in two volumes in 1923 and 1925, and the central demand he formulated was "Give the blacks a chance" (Garvey 1986: 83).

One of his prophecies was taken from the Bible and promised the liberation of the "black people" after the crowning of a king in Africa (see Barrett 1977: 67). When the nobleman Ras Tafari Makonnen (1892-1975) was crowned Emperor of Ethiopia in 1930 under the name His Imperial Majesty Haile Selassie I, he became the Messiah to the adherents of Garvey's prophecy. His followers continued to call him Ras Tafari, which is a combination of two Amharic words: "Ras" is the title given to a noble or a prince, literally meaning "head", and "Tafari", is a given name literally meaning "creator" or "one to be feared" (Niah 2012: 71). Themselves, they called accordingly "Rastafari". Subsequently, in Jamaica, prophets assembled followers around them and began to create "camps," where they lived together. Some of these settlements exist until today. But in principle anybody may become a Rastafarian.

There are not many features, which the Rastafarians share uniformly amongst themselves. Haile Selassie is recognized as the Messiah by most of them. Regarding their diet and clothing, many claim to be following biblical—even mosaic—rules. Examples include Rastafari men letting their hair grow (the well-known "dread-

[1] This paper is the result of literature research and fieldwork in done Ethiopia in the year 2002. Research was done in the context of the SFB 295 on "Cultural and Linguistic Contacts in North East Africa and West Asia" at the Johannes Gutenberg University Mainz, Germany as part of the subprojects "Cultural Contact, Respect and Self-Esteem in Southern Ethiopia". The present situation of the Rastafarians in Ethiopian and changes that have occurred in their relationship with the local people around Shashamene have been described in recent publications for example by Michael Barnett 2012, Giulia Bonacci 2010, 2011, Erin Macleod 2012 and Niaah Jahlani 2012.

locks"), but also dietary restrictions, such as an often vegetarian diet. Alcohol is banned, and women have to seclude from public during their monthly periods. Ganja, the "holy herb" marihuana, is specifically smoked on meditative occasions, known as the "reasonings", but sees wide use in general. Their "Back to Africa" program is central to the Rastafarians' self-understanding that they are in so many ways like the biblical Jews in Egyptian exile. To bring the exiled back to their home, a mystic vessel is instrumental: the Black Star Liner. While immortalized in the song "Seven miles of Black Star Liners" by Fred Locks, the main reference is yet again to Marcus Garvey, who had set up a shipping line called the "Black Star Line" which was originally supposed to trade with Africa and to bring back the former slaves to their land of origin.[2]

The heterogeneous character of the Rastafari customs and rules has over time slowly fed into the creation of different so called "houses", now more or less organized groups, like the "Ethiopian World Federation", "The Twelve Tribes", the "Ethiopia Africa Black International Congress" (also known as "Bobo Shanti"), or the "Nyahbinghi Order".

The main effect of Rastafari as a movement was the encouragement it provided for the average disenfranchised African-Jamaican person by offering to strengthen their low self-esteem. The Rastafarian man is one with god and speaks of himself as "I and I"—i.e., he himself and God are one. The "I" is taken from the imperial title: Haile Selassie I—the number "I", the first, read according to English orthography. The Rastafari as a person becomes deified, being one with God.

Rastafarians generally have refused and still refuse to be part of the society at large. They maintain a de facto parallel society, often either living off their garden products or practicing handicrafts and art. Rastafarians are also famous for Reggae music, which is playing an enormous role in spreading the faith. Special cultic music exists besides the commercial Reggae, and the latter is not seen by all Rasta as in line with their rejection of capitalism, which for them is part of their antithesis, "Babylon". Today, there are also Rastafarians who belong to the middle classes, and there are "beach Rasta", who sell themselves to tourists. People all around the globe have joined the Rastafarian faith.

The lost homeland and the spiritual context of repatriation

For Rastafarians, Africa, more specifically Ethiopia, is the lost homeland—a clear analogy to the biblical lost homeland of the Jews. It is the land Rastafarians long to return to and all and everything is oriented towards a day of return. The key question this chapter addresses, then, is whether the real return could ever live up to this mythological content. In the early years of Rasta, "the return" was wholly

[2] Later, Kwame Nkrumah (1909-1972), the first President of independent Ghana (the former Gold Coast), a "Garveyite" himself, named the national shipping line accordingly "The Black Star Line." And again, the flag of Ghana carries in its center a black star. Its background colors are taken from the Ethiopian flag: red, green and gold.

mystified and neither expected nor supposed to take place. Would the actual return not destroy the mystification of the fictitious land of origin for the Jamaicans, who have established and still now form the core of Rasta? One could argue that much of Rasta faith lives off the expectation never to be fulfilled, off the realization never to be realized. It is the longing for the fulfillment, the longing to overcome the historical separation that keeps Rasta going. It is out of this emotional state of mind that Rasta is creative, creative to its utmost possibility. Creativity becomes a goal in itself as an expression of this longing. This is the enigma of the Diaspora experience.[3]

This nostalgic character of Rasta does connect with the theoretic analysis of the movement: Rastafari is a messianic movement; it contains a millenarian aspect, which often is disputed in academia and can be seen as partly a revitalization movement of nativist character (Edmonds 2003:127-30). Nativism, which in its strict sense means to hold onto your own culture which seems under threat from the outside, does only apply to Rasta in so far as Rasta artificially holds on to an alleged "Africanness" and wants to defend it against all "Westernization", a central aspect of the specter Rasta calls "Babylon." This again indicates how above all, Rasta relies on the Old Testament and only partially on the New Testament. It is called a millenarian movement by some (if you consider the waiting for the Black Star Liner as a central issue), and a Zionist project by others: but Zion, the Rasta's New Jerusalem, is a Utopia. As argued above, this Utopia is only particularly valuable as long as it is not present. For the Rastafari, the imaginations of this mythic Utopia have turned out to revolve around Ethiopia.

It is said that there are as many versions of Rastafarian belief as there are Rastafarians (Naliwaiko and Bender 2005: 1-13), and with the concept of repatriation, it is the same. Is it the exile in Babylon, the expulsion to Egypt, or redemption—or all in one? The professor for religion Nathaniel Samuel Murrell (University of North Carolina) and the Kingston-based Baptist preacher Burchell K. Taylor argue for a reading of a "return home". But even that could be interpreted in various ways, as in the well-known euphemism "to return home" for dying:

> Africa (Ethiopia) is the Promised Land, Zion, or the New Jerusalem of biblical messianic expectation. Repatriation to the Promised Land is the goal of the liberation that the messianic promise and hope imply. It is not migration (escapism) but repatriation (a return to what was owned before). It is not the pilgrimage of a foreign spectator so much as a return home (Murrell and Taylor 1998: 392).

The easy switching between the world on this side (the very real repatriation) and the mythical beyond (the biblical expectation) seems at the first glance to indi-

[3] In another society based on a slave past, the Cape Verde Islands, "sodade" in Creole, stands for the same topic: longing, like the German "Sehnsucht"—in Cape Verde, it is the longing, a feeling of nostalgia, which became more and more dominated by the feeling to have been left behind by all those who left the Islands. Today, the Cape Verdes have more daughters and sons living abroad than there are people living on the Islands.

cate contradiction, or at least some confusion. But Murrell and Taylor explain it in the following way:

> Although the promised land of the messianic hope, Ethiopia, is beyond the bounds of Jamaica, for Rastas it is an actual historical location; it is the home of the Messiah-king, who is both divine and human. No dichotomy exists between the historical and the eschatological, the earthly and the heavenly, the natural and the supernatural, the present age and the future age, to make these mutually exclusive (Murrell and Taylor 1998: 399).

In Rev. Joseph Owens' words, who wrote the first in-depth analysis of Rasta in 1976, a similar thought is expressed: "Repatriation is the earthly redemption which the Israelites have long sought in vain—the blessed state of living in peace in the kingdom of Jah." (Owens 1976: 230) Thus, Rasta thought ends the conceptual splitting and abolishes dichotomies.

In the face of the idea of repatriation, it became a necessity to agree or compromise on one single land of origin for the Rastafarians, as the Afro-Jamaican population is composed of people of -as far as their African line of descent is concerned—diverse ethnic origin. Their "roots" are manifold. There is not anything like one "common root," unless one would take "Africa" as one whole entity—clearly impractical and divisive! "Ethiopia" is therefore a welcome reference point. It fits well because in present-day Jamaica, and in fact, in the Jamaica of the past centuries already, Christian belief based on the Bible has become the central unifying content for all the Afro-Jamaicans. Ethiopia is mentioned in the St. James version of the Bible as the land "beyond". At the same time, Ethiopia is definitely one region that most likely none of the slaves who eventually arrived in Jamaica originally came from. This inherent non-partisan negativity qualified it as a common denominator: as nobody came from there, it had the potential to offer roots for everybody. This is another part of the enigma of the repatriation to Ethiopia.

But where did the idea of repatriation to Africa originally come from? For the Rastafarians, they are following the teachings of Marcus Garvey. Ennis B. Edmonds, who teaches Caribbean Religion at Barnard College in the U.S., provides us with some answers:

Drawing on Marcus Garvey's 'Back to Africa' campaign, Rastas have always made repatriation to Africa one of their main tenets. However, there are divergent views concerning its meaning and means of achievement. To some Rastas, repatriation means the literal, physical relocation to Africa/Ethiopia. For others, repatriation means the psychological and cultural re-appropriation of their African identity and culture. Still other Rastas expect repatriation by divine intervention, which will occur either through some political action of the Jamaican or British government as a gesture of restitution or by means of Rastas' own rational socio-political efforts. (Edmonds 1998: 31)

Accordingly, at least some Rastafarians were pushing for physical repatriation already at the end of the 1950s. Horace Campbell[4] mentions the pressure and the threat exercised by Rasta:

> Rastafarians in Jamaica invested considerable energies in the efforts towards repatriation, leading up to the Nyabingi[5] of 1959, which was violently dispersed by the police. Using language which reflected their determination, Rastas in Jamaica called repatriation a human right, posing the alternative as *repatriation or rebellion* (Campbell 1985: 339).

Barry Chevannes from the University of the West Indies in Kingston, an authority on Afro-Caribbean religions and culture, describes the Rastafarian drive for repatriation as predicated upon the idea of divine action:

> Repatriation is viewed as a divinely ordained act, depending on the will and actions of God, not on humans. It is different from migration. In the August 1934 episode in which Leonard Howell told his people to prepare and await the ship for their repatriation to Ethiopia, people allegedly expected the sea to part, just as in the time of Moses—but this time only for those with a beard. Mass agitation for repatriation, when it did take place in 1958 and again in 1959-1960, came against the background of increased migration to Britain and renewed attention by old Garveyites to the possibilities of migration to Liberia and other West African countries. Interest in repatriation again heightened, particularly among the Rastafari, when an Ethiopian World Federation official visited Jamaica in 1955 and announced that Haile Selassie was making a small land grant at Shashamane in Ethiopia for the settlement of Blacks, in appreciation for their support during the fight against Fascist invasion of his country.[6] (Chevannes 1998: 60)

As mentioned in this paragraph, there have been at least two official missions from Jamaica to Africa with the express purpose of starting a dialogue between certain African governments and representatives of the repatriation movement. The second trip, beginning in 1963, led the mission to Ethiopia by end of 1964. There, the three delegates took up again the issue of repatriation and returned home in April 1965 with another assurance by the Emperor that Jamaicans and other Africans residing in the West were welcome to settle in the country and to support Ethiopia with their skills. After their return to Jamaica in May 1965, they formed the Rastafarian Brethren Repatriation Association (the R.B.R.A., see Mack 1999:145).

4 "Jamaican Horace Campbell, the well-known Walter Rodney scholar, political activist, and Pan-Africanist who taught in Dar-es-Salaam, Tanzania, since 1981..." (McFarlane 1998: 115).

5 The definite origin of the term Nyabingi is not known. It has been described as an East African colonial underground organization, and the name allegedly means "Death to all whites!" Nowadays a "Nyabingi" may also stand for a serious assembly of Rasta men (Barsch 2003: 93f).

6 The Ethiopian World Federation was founded in 1935, when the fascists began their war of conquests against free Ethiopia. Worldwide, people supported the struggle to liberate the occupied Ethiopia. As a kind of reward Haile Selassie I offered land to willing migrants. This had nothing to do originally with the repatriation request by Rastafarians in Jamaica.

Thus, a specific name took on special meaning: Shashamane, the site promised by HIM, Haile Selassie himself. Following up on the discussion above, this means that if Ethiopia was the pars pro toto for Africa, and its rhetorical function was the synecdoche, then just as well Shashamane stands for repatriation. As such, it would have to carry the burden of being considered at the same time the concrete territory of the land grant as well as mythical Zion. The critical question to be raised here will be whether this is, in fact, how the Rastafarian settlers feel, or how they view their daily struggle of survival in Shashamane? How far does their belief help them to cope with the daily hardships to provide a living? According to Christian teaching, life on earth is always determined by human insufficiency, human weakness and also by hardship, whereas heaven signifies the opposite. If Shashamane is Heaven on Earth, it is still very much Earth in character. How do the Rasta cope with their wider environment? For Rasta, work within the greater society is too much involved with "Babylon," i.e., with capitalism, bureaucracy, and—in a sense—alienation in general. Creative practice is less so -at least you work for yourself and avoid exploitation through others. But is this sufficient? The subsequent section continues to pursue the background of the land grant, and leads up to the recent and contemporary conditions in Shashamane.

His Imperial Majesty's land grant

Haile Selassie I is central to the picture of a mythic Ethiopia. His intervention into the Rastafarian spiritual world caused confusion and separation, which in Rastafarian terms (yet another case of "Babylon" showing itself) would be an argument to doubt the divine character of Haile Selassie—a true paradox. It is not on us to discuss the divinity of Haile Selassie, but we want to address this most problematic notion of a real repatriation caused by his invitation, the spiritual dimension he was surely ignorant about. The reproduction of the poster for the "5th Annual Shashamane On My Mind" for October 6th 2001 on a website gives us the basic background information about the land grant as it is seen by the Rastafarian organization called the "Twelve Tribes of Israel":

> Shashamane, Ethiopia is land which was given to the black people of the West by H.I.M. Emperor Selassie I in appreciation for the support given to Ethiopia during the time of the Italian invasion led by Mussolini. Since 1970 the 12 Tribes of Israel has been repatriating brothers and sisters to Shashamane, Et. fulfilling H.I.M. Emperor Haile Selassie I offer. At present we are collectively & independently building houses, school, library, hotel, guest houses, and a health center. This benefit is to assist and further develop the land. Thanks for your support. (http://www.angelfire.com/ny4/SoulJahs-Band, last accessed 21.11.2011).

The Twelve Tribes here do not mention the role of the Ethiopian World Federation in this offer by the Emperor. Barrett gives a more detailed account:

> ...the Ethiopian World Federation, Inc., New York, established in 1937 as a lobbying organization to solicit aid and goodwill for Ethiopian struggles against Italian colo-

> nialism. It was said to have been organized under the direct authority of Haile Selassie. As early as 1938, a branch of this organization was established in Jamaica. The aims of the EWF, as its preamble proclaimed, was to unify, solidify, liberate, and free the Black people of the world in order to achieve self-determination, justice, and to maintain the integrity of Ethiopia—which is the divine heritage of the Black race. We do not know whether the Rastafarian leaders knew of this movement, but it is quite possible that Howell might have been connected with it [...]. Our sources suggest that the success of the Jamaican EWF led to many schisms, each claiming to be the true organization. To this day, the Rastafarians are in close touch with the EWF group, sometimes combining efforts in their enterprises.

The great impetus came in 1955, when a leading official of the Ethiopian World Federation, Inc., visited Jamaica with an important message which was to energize the flagging Rastafarian movement. The *Daily Gleaner* of September 30, 1955, headlined the event as 'Large Audience Hears Message from Ethiopia.' Among the statements is the following attributed to Mrs. Mamie Richardson:

> 'The Emperor (Haile Selassie) is now engaged in building up a Merchant Navy... and the time was not far distant when ships from Addis Ababa would sail to American ports. There was the possibility too that ships would one day call here (Jamaica).'

But better news was just around the bend for the Rastafarians—news that was to develop their doctrine of inevitable repatriation. Soon after Mrs. Richardson's return to New York, the Ethiopian World Federation of that city informed the various branches in Jamaica that the Emperor had granted 500 acres of land to the Black people of the West who, through the EWF, aided Ethiopia in its time of distress. The rich and fertile land was the personal property of the Emperor and was being given on a trial basis. If used successfully, additional grants would follow. The letter stipulated the types of people who would best profit from the land grant were farmers, carpenters, plumbers, masons, electricians, and other skilled persons including nurses and doctors. The vision of ships and now land in Ethiopia created what might literally be called a religious revival among the Rastafarians. 'Repatriation Now!' was the cry of cultists (Barrett 1977: 89f).

This report by Barrett confirms that the land grant was not directed at the Rastas themselves, but was much rather a much more encompassing campaign started by Haile Selassie and aimed at supporters worldwide.

A new approach to repatriation emerged from the very real opportunities provided by the Haile Selassie I land grant. This shift was supported, on the one hand, by the advance of modern means of transport, allowing easier access to Ethiopia. On the other hand, the Emperor was pursuing material benefits as he was hoping to entice professional West Indians or Americans to contribute to the development of Ethiopia. However, the offer to repatriate people of African descent to Ethiopia made by Haile Selassie I was not intended to involve too many people, but was in many ways a political gesture in return for the veneration directed towards Ethiopia and the Emperor. The full mythical implications of the "repatriation" in Rasta terms he seems not to have envisaged. Once it seemed possible, however, repatriation had become a goal to be achieved. "Repatriation is a must" was the basis of the campaigns in the 1960s, and it was also the title of an issue of the Rastafarian journal JAHUG (Vol. 4): "The fullness of Repatriation is Blackman redemption" (Iah C n. d.:4).

One could argue here that the Emperor had offered the land due to his misunderstanding of Rasta or the "Back to Africa" movement. By actually offering a vision of how to make it reality, he inadvertently demystified repatriation. In the process, he also partly defused the powerful emotions that provided the energies for Jamaican Rastafarianism. In fact, the visit of the Emperor to Jamaica in 1966 had the effect of calming down the stirred-up sections of the African Jamaican population. At least for the time being, the Rastafarians felt honored and accepted by their government. What was even more important and revealing or even confusing the whole issue was something the King of Kings is supposed to have said at the time of his visit to Jamaica, namely"...that the Rastafarians should 'liberate themselves in Jamaica' before they repatriate" (Barrett 1977: 172). This was, according to Barrett, the origin of the phrase "liberation before repatriation", a phrase that came to be especially popular among the younger generation of more politically oriented Rastafarians who were prepared to enter into a struggle with the government (*ibid.*).

Later it was Bob Marley who took up the controversial question of repatriation and argued for repatriation "here" in Jamaica, a perspective which understood "Africanization" as to mean liberation in Jamaica. Bob Marley himself was a member of the Rastafarian association "The Twelve Tribes" mentioned above, and even though the Twelve Tribes are represented in Shashamane today, at the time they were more guarded with their endorsement of repatriation to Ethiopia: after their leadership returned from their visit to Ethiopia, for example, they decided not to repatriate but to instead invest more time and resources in developing Jamaica´s economy and culture (Murell/Taylor 1998: 398).

For Haile Selassie I, "Liberation before repatriation" might have well meant that Rastafarians should acquire first certain professional qualifications before coming to Ethiopia. Haile Selassie I was hoping at the time that in this way he would encourage trained immigrants to help with the building up of a modern Ethiopia and assist in the training of Ethiopians. This would have been one of the Emperor's primary motives to invite people from the "western" world to his country.

West Indians were well known in most of the Anglophone West African countries (Sierra Leone, Ghana, Nigeria) for their services to the communities, working as nurses, soldiers, or administrators. This would have required a completely different approach on the side of the Rasta immigrants, though, who did not and until today do not want themselves to be regarded as immigrants, but as repatriates. Instead of being accepted as useful expatriates they wanted to be repatriates without any responsibility towards their new community. Their "return" indeed was one to a fictive Ethiopia—to an Ethiopia not existing outside their own settlement.

For many Rastafarians, and especially in the period before 1955, repatriation had been something Rasta was hoping for, waiting for, but it lay in the hands of God the Almighty, as Joseph Owens writes:

> Most Rastafarians hold that repatriation is both in principle and in fact outside their control. It is redemption, and, as such, a divine act; it is up to Jah himself to work this great wonder. The Rastas feel no special need to work towards repatriation, except by way of preparing themselves spiritually and physically for the day of decision. Most Rastas condemn the idea of saving up one's money and then migrating to Ethiopia on one's own initiative. In the first place, such action would evince despair of God's saving power, and, furthermore in such a procedure, one could not envisage to be anything more than an immigrant. Despite the general consensus that the brethren must wait on God for repatriation, some Rastas are willing to admit that so great is the misery of Jamaica and so great is the glory of Africa, they would gladly go at their own expense: `I-n-I would like to leave now, even if it cause I-n-I to work and pay I-n-I passage, to work very hard and sweat and to save everything, to even starve I-n-I self—I-n-I would like to come out of Jamaica.(Owens 1976: 237f.)

If it is up to God to find the right time for repatriation, the offer of Haile Selassie I from 1955 could be seen by the Rastafarians as a divine signal. But at the same time, it is difficult to accept it as the "real" repatriation, which is seen in connection with redemption. It may be one of the tragic misunderstandings and tragic consequences of what Haile Selassie I said at particular times. Haile Selassie I, in the role assigned to him, representing the Messiah, made this offer which was interpreted as a call on repatriation by some Rastafarians. What was to be labor migration became in their eyes the fulfillment of the promised repatriation. But living in the mythical "Land of Glory" neither did nor does equal the experience of redemption, but rather constitutes a continuous trial. The Rastafarians stayed on Earth with rather earth-bound problems. Ethiopia was fiction, Shashamane became hard reality.

Settling in Shashamane, Ethiopia

Shashamane is a city south of Addis Ababa, located at an important intersection where roads crossing the country from East to West and from North to South meet. To the South, the road leads towards Kenya and ultimately to the port of Mombasa, where aid shipments would be picked up and taken onto the long route up to the Ethiopian highlands.

An earlier witness illustrates the roots of the present state, both in terms of infrastructure and demography:

> [By] the end of the sixties the settlement of Shashamane had between 40-50 Rastas and Afro-Americans, who had set up their community with a pharmacy, school, a small store and a number of modest dwellings. There were no efforts towards collective farming, hence the problems of individualism, competition and envy plagued the settlers, who eked out an existence. Petty differences between 'Jamaican' Rastas and Afro-Americans over the use of implements and over access to the Royal household simmered. These simmerings continued with the advent of the Twelve Tribes of Israel, who had begun their own scheme of repatriation. Fortunately, size, limited resources, and the struggle for survival ensured that none of the petty problems could fester into a

kind of armed confrontations which had taken place among the Liberian settlers in 1870-1873 (Campbell 1985: 343f).

But even before the 1980s, much had already happened to the settlers, little of it pleasant. According to the Rastafarian calling himself Ras Mweya Masimba, during the time of the Derg (the Socialist Government from 1977-1990 under Colonel Mengistu Haile Mariam), the Rastafarian population grew smaller, and probably their self-esteem as well: To celebrate Haile Selassie was not allowed then. It was forbidden to have buttons, pictures etc. of the former Emperor. If caught, the perpetrators were in danger of being imprisoned. The few Rasta who stayed on were taken under the aegis by the Twelve Tribes of Israel (Köppen 2002). Horace Campbell provides us with a more detailed analysis of what happened to the Rastafarians when the Ethiopian Revolution took place in 1974:

> Rastafarians in Ethiopia were confronted with the contradictory position of their beliefs when the Ethiopian people removed the monarchy in a popular revolution in 1974. This contradiction was posed for all Rastafari, but even more fundamentally for those who had settled in Shashamane, simply because their existence in Ethiopia was so closely linked with the whole dispensation of privilege by the Emperor. Land patronage and titles tied the regional landlords to the State and Church, so that the land grant to the Rastafarians was likened to the old practice of the monarch giving land to favored retainers. And some of the settlers did act as favored retainers for the administrators of the Shashamane settlement, they had access to tractors, seeds, fertilizers, and could sell their produce to the royal household, so that essentially the settlement was organically linked with the Royal Family, instead of with the people of the community where the settlement was based (Campbell 1985: 343).

This missing interest in the local population fired back in the end with the beginning of the revolution, ...

> ...when the people of Shashamane expropriated the land from the Rastas in 1975 as their own expression of opposition to the monarchy. Following the lead of the Derg, which had issued a land reform proclamation in March 1975, nationalizing all rural land, abolishing tenancy, and setting up of peasant associations, the poor of Shashamane seized all tractors, land and assets of the Rastafari and the E.W.F. settlers in Shashamane. Fortunately for the settlers there were elements in the Provisional Military Advisory Council who understood the sentiments of repatriation among Africans in the West, so after negotiations 44 hectares were returned to the Rastas who wanted to stay. It was inevitable that the elements who were closest to the Royal household from the administration of the settlement would leave, for the whole organisation of the previous form of capitalist intensive farming was broken down by the Ethiopian peasantry as part of the revolution. (Campbell 1985: 345f.)

It needs to be understood, then, that the Rastafarians coming to Ethiopia, to Shashamane, were strangers, they were regarded as *ferenji* and as strangers of a specific kind.[7] They also remained strangers. How did this in return affect the Rasta idea of having returned home—the home not recognizing them as their offspring?

7 Verbal communication with visitors to Shashamane in Addis Ababa 2001/2002

Did the ideology of the homecoming help to overcome the treatment as aliens? Might this not be one of the reasons why many Rasta are even today rather isolated in Shashamane?

The Rastafari settlers in Shashamane, like their counterparts in the Caribbean, went on the defensive, become passive bystanders in the whole process. Their continued support for the monarch placed them in opposition to the Ethiopian people. Unfortunately some of them continued to attempt to defy reality by sending stories back to the Caribbean that Haile Selassie was still alive. Inside the country they insulted their neighbors by insisting on putting up pictures of the deposed Emperor in their dwellings (Campbell 1985: 350f.). Again, the Rastafarian community was incapable of relating to the surrounding society. Social change it would have welcomed at home in Jamaica, here it did not want to have anything to do with it. With the new government after the socialist period, Shashamane became an attractive spot for Rastas from all over the world.

In several literary works, the African-American traveling writers described their surprise and shock, their disillusionment at being regarded as "Europeans" or even "Whites" despite being of dark complexion. This is, of course, not a unique experience, albeit surely shocking to many: a West Indian academic colleague visiting Nigeria for the first time was surrounded by children addressing her as "oyinbo," a Yoruba term for "European"; other children sang the rhyme "Oyinbo oyinbo pepe...", meaning "European, you are as red as pepper". As an example, the photographic visit of a Rastafarian photographer, documented in a book called "A Rasta's Pilgrimage. Ethiopian Faces and Places" by Neville Garrick, has to be taken as a source of a visual approach by a Rastafarian towards the formerly mythological land and now a real but foreign country. It contains all the characteristics of a tourist coming to Ethiopia. Similar to the experiences of West Indians or African-Americans visiting West African countries, the Jamaican photographer was seen as a foreigner as well—as a *ferenji* (Garrick 1999: 72). Though he writes the kids addressed him more often—as he is recognizably Rasta—as "Rasta, Rasta—Jamaica!" (Garrick 1999: 72). While Neville Garrick has not yet joined the repatriating brothers and sisters, he did include a visit at Shashamane in his journey through the country, and from him we receive an insightful Rastafarian journalist's description:

> Longing to connect with my Rastafarian brethren who now reside in Ethiopia, I embarked on a weekend excursion about 250 kilometers southwest of Addis Ababa to visit Shashemane [sic], the area that Haile Selassie granted to Western blacks who wished to repatriate to Ethiopia. Shashemane is in the Rift Valley area of the Sidamo region, which was the last region to be incorporated into the Ethiopian empire. [...]
>
> I arrived in Shashemane and rode in a horse drawn buggy called *gharri* to the Rastafarian community a few kilometers away. There I was given a joyous welcome by my Jamaican brothers and sisters who had fulfilled the dream of making Ethiopia their home. Some have been here for over twenty-five years, and speak both Amharic and the Oromo languages. I stayed for two days, and spent many hours discussing the present

> situation in Jamaica, the Rastafarian movement, and the Jamaican's history, struggles, and progress in Shashemane.
>
> I spent most of my time with Junior Dan and Flippins, members of the Twelve Tribes of Israel Organisation, one of the Rastafarian groups that settled in Shashemane. We knew each other from Trench Town days in Kingston, where this organisation began. We discussed their experience of living in Ethiopia for over twenty years and the treatment they have received from the government and the local people. Rastafarians are known supporters of H.I.M. Emperor Haile Selassie I and the legacy of the Solomonic Dynasty; Flippins and Junior Dan arrived in Ethiopia about a year after the military regime overthrew the monarchy. Yet the new military government had rarely bothered the Rastas during its seventeen-year rule. Flippins even remarked that on a national radio broadcast, Mengistu (the head of the military government) called the Jamaican Rastas more Ethiopian than native Ethiopians, because they were coming to Ethiopia while the Ethiopians were fleeing the country. My old friend told me of the love shown them by their neighbours, the Oromos. "They teach us their language and customs, and even help us with farming sometimes," said Junior Dan. "My children speak three languages. You think that would happen in Jamaica?"
>
> Although the land is bordered by rivers on either side, water is the main concern. However, the community is basically self-sufficient, with its own farms, shops, and other means of economic survival. Situated in one of the most fertile regions of the country, the Shashemane community has no fear of famine that plagues the northern regions. With economic support from the international Rasta community, we hope the Shashemane settlement will be a shining example for the repatriation cause. The time I spent amongst my brothers and sisters in Shashemane was an uplifting and joyous experience, and with Jah's help, I too hope to make Ethiopia my home some day (Garrick 1998: 15).

Despite this largely positive perspective, notably the marked amity expressed by the Oromo neighbors, there are different views as well. An online interview with the Rastafarian calling himself Ras Abel illustrates some of the local tensions and underlying problems (www.rastafaritoday.com/sitefiles/oneafrika.html, accessed on 26.9.2001, site no longer available). When asked, "You visited Ethiopia... how are people in Shashamane?", Ras Abel answered that in

> "Shashamane ... people today maintained nuff elements of Jamaican culture ... I see nuff positive things, and nuff negative things that can be worked out ...one of the negative things I saw that there were not unity among *The Houses*. There were certain groups that were not even willing to show me other Houses ... That kind of animosity defeats the purpose, because you have unity, you have strength ..." (http://www.rastafaritoday.com/sitefiles/oneafrika.html, accessed on 26.9.2001, site no longer available).

We see that Ras Abel is full of praise that the settlers maintained enough elements of Jamaican culture; what this very clearly implies, however, is that he did not find praiseworthy that they had adapted to local customs to a degree, as the text by Garrick reports. With what has been written above, though, this marked blind spot in the Rastafarian self-image is not really surprising: Rastafarians, coming from Jamaica, are in depth a Jamaican cultural product, and had little experience in dealing with other cultures. Garrick can be considered progressive in resolving this contradiction.

Ras Abel's reference to "quarrels" is of particular interest, as indeed unity is one of the central Rasta ideals. "Babylon" is—from the Bible onwards—a synonym for separation. While in Kingston it was the political parties that had divided the people so that one street fought the next, and Rasta propagated unity against this kind of "divide and rule" politics, in Ethiopia, there was no such party politics. There was no apparent need for unity against the common enemy. Instead, particularizm has begun to take over in the form of party politics among the different sections of the Rastafarian community. Each House claims to have the "right" path or, even worse, the "only" path.

More perspective is provided by the report "Rastafarians hope everything will be alright" (2005) by Matthew Lee, writing for the South African IOL News forum.[8] Lee makes some points worth quoting.

> Twenty-five years after reggae superstar Bob Marley visited fellow Rastafarians in Shashamane, residents of this dusty Ethiopian town are hoping the late music legend will put them back on the map. Having lived through decades of hardship and neglect, Shashamane's ageing and often wary Rasta community sees opportunity in the commemoration this month in Ethiopia of what would have been Marley's 60th birthday (http://www.iol.co.za/news/africa/rastafarians-hope-everything-will-be-alright.1.233185).

When in 2002, the author interviewed a member of the Rastafari community who had lived in Shashamane for thirty years, the man emphasizes that "We do feel it, we do feel forgotten." In the early years 2000, there seemed little sense of success among the Rasta of Shashamene, and equally little physical evidence could be observed. It gave the impression that the Rastafarians were not welcome by the locals, and the volatility of the political conditions since the settlers' first arrival up to then had severely handicapped the community's expansion:

Regarded with a mixture of curiosity and contempt by many Ethiopians and stung by the country's chronic poverty, instability and frequent natural disasters, Shashamane's Rastafarian population has never risen above 1 000, residents say. The euphoria that greeted the farming settlement among Rastafarians and proponents of Pan-Africanism in the 1940s, '50s and '60s, was tempered by the repression and isolation that Ethiopia's Marxist revolution brought in 1974. [...] And just as social and political conditions appear to be improving, there are fears the community's location along Ethiopia's main north-south highway will make it a prime target for government-backed commercial development. "They plan to make Shashamane the second city of Ethiopia", says 80-year-old Elda Solomon, an official with the Ethiopian World Federation who arrived in Shashamane from Jamaica in 1969. [...] "It's a problem we really resent now," he said. "It is the first priority for us." But any arrangement must be approved by the community, which is split into

[8] Too long to reproduce here in full (but see http://www.iol.co.za/news/africa/rastafarians-hope-everything-will-be-alright-1.233185),

at least four factions, each with its own interpretation of Haile Selassie's land grant, his religious stature and Biblical prophecy.

Perhaps a new approach is presently on its way. Since the establishment of an NGO by some settlers in the early 2000s, one might detect within the Rastafarian community an awareness of the importance of recognition by and interaction with the world surrounding it. The plan to establish Shashamane as "a model city of repatriation" may or may not entail a new conception of the "homeland," but seems a productive break with blind reliance on Rasta traditions and the rule of non-involvement. Be that as it may, the Centenary Committee of Rastafari, a UK-based association, has come to the following conclusion:

> Through the long years of settlement Shashemane came to represent for many blacks in the West, a glimmer of light in the darkness of Babylonian exile. The tenacity of a few has kept that hope alive for the many. If that hope is to bear real fruit it must be matched by a will and determination in the international Rastafari community to develop the Land Grant as a model city of return to the fatherland (Centenary Committee of Rastafari 1995: 11).

The idea of a "model city" seems to have caught on. To achieve this aim, a three-year plan was drafted according to Shangu Baku, a dramatist and poet from Trinidad:

> A three-year development plan is now being drawn up for the Shashamane area in consultation with organisations and individuals on the land. Its aim will be to transform the impoverished community into a model city of return and a center point for the regeneration of African culture and identity in the 21st century (Baku 1996: 11).

While the side remark about the "impoverished" community is worth mentioning, as it contrasts the repatriation rhetoric of arrival in Zion, it is actually more interesting to ask what "regeneration of African culture" is supposed to mean. If one does look around Shashamane—isn't there "African culture" alive today? Are the surrounding non-Rasta people not cultured? Maybe Rasta speaks here of regenerating his own lost African culture? Then the question arises which African culture is talked about? Obviously, there is no "African culture" as such, which is one of the most central mistakes of all diasporic concepts of Africa; additionally, it finds itself in the unpleasant ideological neighborhood of ignorant and even racist positions anywhere in the world assuming the existence of "African culture" and of an "African language" etc. To stress this point further, one could even ask what is "African" in Shoa province, where Shashamane is located. There is definitely "culture" in Africa, culture in parts of Africa like Ethiopia—but that doesn't explain to us what is the "African-ness" here. The "African" values which Jamaicans of African or partially African descent proclaim are mostly values declared as "African" for ideological reasons, but which might have their sources in the Old Testament or African-American myths on "Africanity." The most obvious example is the role of men in society, which in this context is always a patriarchal gender relationship.[9] This has been declared as a result of the emasculated male slave's attempt to regain self-respect only by setting himself superior to his wife or women in general, thus domestically reproducing the hierarchy which he suffered vis-à-vis his owner The role of men in Africa may have had or have today very specific and diverse forms, but these are unknown to the people in the Diaspora. Africa is a fictive place again.

Conclusion

Repatriation can be interpreted from different angles. From the political historical angle: the former slaves' return to Africa was organized by so-called philanthropists in Britain and the Americas on the pretext of bringing them "home." To bring them home where they came from (in most cases anyhow people did not know where they or their ancestors "really" had come from) is very close to our commonly known phrase by which racists attack Africans and generally foreigners: "go home, go back to where you came from." Repatriation might be seen as an internalized racist position by those who are made uncomfortable staying in "exile." The threat is transformed into a demand, a common effect oppression has on the oppressed. Before Rastafarianism helped to inseminate some pride and self-esteem into the majority of the Jamaican population, the Afro-Jamaicans could be called the most oppressed people on the island. For Marcus Garvey, who was so important for the idea of repatriation, "Back to Africa" was a slogan with a kind of magical effect. But it did appeal above all to the "black petit-bourgeois" (Garrison[10] 1979: 51). He himself did not show any deeper interest in repatriation:"Claude McKay,[11] writing in *Harlem: Negro Metropolis*, comments, 'Marcus Garvey himself had no intention of going back to live in some corner of the vast land of his ancestors'" (Garrison 1979: 51).

We have to repeat: Shashamane stands for the Rastafarian settlement. That there is, and has been for a long time, a city called Shashamane is never expressed in the Rasta texts. It is a hint to the relationship of Rastas in respect to the local population, and their involvement in the local conditions. Are they isolated, or are they isolating themselves? Do the Rastafarians care about the Ethiopian society today? After the experiences of the last four decades? It seems that nothing much has changed, then and now: First of all—they did not return there to have anything to do with the local population. They returned to their own homeland—fictitious as it was, as it is. That there is a local population may be disturbing, may create problems, but it was not part of their concept and prospect of the future.

9 This is expressed by values such as "righteousness", "justice", but also the proverbial "rod of correction", along with homophobia and unquestioned male domination.

10 Len Garrison: a Jamaican historian and educationist in Britain, 1943-2003. He founded the Black Cultural Archives in Brixton (1980), as well as the African and Caribbean Educational Resource (A.C.E.R.).

11 A famous Jamaican writer, 1889-1948.

"Shashamane" has by now become another term to replace Africa and Ethiopia. Shashamane has obviously been integrated into the mythological phraseology of Rastafari, a set expression which has made many appearances in song titles and lyrics. On the one hand, it represents the mystic return made real, and so constitutes the destruction of mythology. One the other hand, not all Rastafarians will have the opportunity to migrate to Shashamane, so for many it might retain the quality of a goal never ever to be achieved—a return one longs for, even if one is not in fact pushing for its realization. Most Rasta do not really want to "return" anywhere else. The demands "Back to Africa" and "repatriation now" remain largely what they were, namely, spiritual rallying cries rather than a concrete plan for action. The existence of the Rastafarians in Shashamane is more like that of expatriates than of repatriates. Shashamane has been from its very beginning a colony—its inhabitants may be quite metaphysical in their religious outlook, but are all too much exposed to down-to-earth problems of surviving.

Already in 1974, Walter Rodney from Guyana commented on the impractability of calling for repatriation in the era of national liberation:

> Some of us can get to Africa. The vast majority of our people will, in fact, not be able to go there, and struggle takes place where people live and work. That´s the locus of struggle. And in that sense, it becomes self-defeating for someone in the Caribbean or in the United States to suggest that Africa is the sole, or even the main, vehicle of black struggle. Black struggle must be universalized where black people happen to be (Rodney 1974).

Nowadays, regular international reunions of Rasta are held in Shashamane, and the town has become a focus of the globalized Rastafarian movement. Such tourism is a result of the global presence of Rastafarians, which is not even depending on race any longer, as it has come to integrate all kinds of people who self-identify regardless of their own origins with the basic tenets of Rastafarianism.

Accordingly, repatriation is not the only goal and cannot be the absolute basis for action any longer, except for a few selected people. Repatriation is obviously not the aim of the temporary visitors. Shashamane has become a Mecca for Rastafarianism and has to accept this role. It should indeed prepare itself for the future to become a major center for a worldwide Rastafarian pilgrimage. Even if the biblical "Ethiopia" has never been the real existing state of Ethiopia, and Rasta never included the historical social reality encountered by the settlers in its worldview, by such transformative future-oriented action, the mythic quality of Shashamane and Ethiopia might be maintained.

Epilogue

Presently, the Rastafarian community in Shashamane comprises around 400 to 500 persons half of which originally came from Jamaica and the other from about 17 other nations. According to Niaah (2012: 83), locally all of the Rastafarians in Shashamane are perceived as and referred to as Jamaicans When the author visited the place in 2002, they were living in a kind of loose community set up with separate private property. While some were living in original Ethiopian houses others were residing in partially fairly large villas. Nearly all the houses could be identified by their attached symbols from the repertoire of Rastafarian iconography (see Bender 1984, 1992, 2005). Increasingly, the Rastafarians of Shashamane have been trying to develop economic activities, including small businesses in the town itself, a tofu factory, as well as two flagship local hotels that are not only used by tourists but also locally for weddings, municipal events and conferences (Macleod 2012: 95). Individually, some Rastafarian households offer bed and breakfast to visitors, others, especially newcomers, engage in shop keeping, own small restaurants offering Jamaican food and juices, internet cafes and entertainment places. Others produce handicrafts and manufacture clothing. With increasing land investment large scale commercial development can be observed, mainly in the above mentioned hotels and in the production and processing of soya beans, places for entertainment and some internet cafes. The production and usage of *ganja* (Marihuana) is also on the increase (Niaah 2012: 84f).

Some humanitarian projects and development activities seems to have enhanced the integration of the Rastafari with the local community, such as the Jamaican Rastafarian Development Community School which offers good quality education for mainly Ethiopian students (Macleod 2012: 95). The school is being subsidized by the Jamaican Rastafari Development Community (JRDC). It has formally registered as an NGO in 2001 (Niaah 2012: 85). A rainwater harvesting project organized and supported by the EWA has also contributed to a changing perception of the Rastafarians by the local people. According to Macleod, as development agents and NGO workers the immigrants are locally much more accepted than as "returnees to a promised land" (2012: 100).

As the representative of the EWF in Addis Ababa, Ras Tagas King, resented, until today, even in the 2nd and 3rd generation the Rastafarians have not succeeded in gaining Ethiopian citizenship: "We have children born here, who have never left Ethiopia, and are asked to get Jamaican passports... "(Macleod 2012: 89). Instead, they have to live on tourist visa, business visa, or on resident permits (Bonacci in Macleod 2012: 90). The reason, as Macleod is stating, may be that Ethiopia is simply not prepared for immigrants and has no legal system in place to formally integrate them (*ibid.*)

Nevertheless, Rastafari culture is leaving its imprint on the Ethiopian society, also beyond Shashamane, and especially their music has gained prominence. According to Niaah (2012: 85), Bob Marley has become a hero in Ethiopia, and the first generation of Ethiopian Jamaicans has created a musical fusion of local Reggae called "Jam-haric" (*ibid.*) which is often to be heard on the radio. In the capital Addis Ababa and elsewhere, many young Ethiopians can be seen with dreadlocks. It seems therefore, that the strict boundary between Rastafarians and Ethiopians has become more permeable and is partly redefined, though in a different way that the migrants have may have expected before their arrival.

References

Baku, Shango, 1996: "Rasta Tabernacle Opens". In: *The Alarm No. 20,* September/October 1996, 11.

Barnett, Michael, 2012: *Rastafari in the New Millennium: A Rastafari reader*. New York: Syracuse University Press.

Barrett, Leonard E., 1977: *The Rastafarians. The dreadlocks of Jamaica*. Kingston: Heinemann.

Barsch, Volker, 2003: *Rastafari: Von Babylon nach Afrika*. Mainz: Ventil.

Bender, Wolfgang (ed.), 1984: *RastafariKunst aus Jamaika*. Bremen: Edition Con.

Bender, Wolfgang (ed.), 1992: *Rastafari Kunst aus Jamaika*. Bremen: Edition Con, Haus der Kulturen der Welt.

Bender, Wolfgang (ed.) 2005: *Rastafarian Art*. Kingston: Ian Randle.

Bonacci, Giulia, 2010: *Exodus! L'histoire du retour des Rastafariens en Ethiopie*. Paris: L'Harmattan.

Bonacci, Giulia, 2011: "An Interview in Zion: The life-history of a Jamaican Rastafarian in Shashemene, Ethiopia". *Callaloo 34*, 3, 744-758.

Campbell, Horace, 1985: *Rasta and Resistance. From Marcus Garvey to Walter Rodney*. Dar es Salaam: Tanzania Publishing House.

Centenary Committee of Rastafari, 1995:"Shashemane—A land grant". JAHUG4, 8-11.

Chevannes, Barry, 1998:"Rastafari and the Exorcism of Racism and Classism in Jamaica" In: Nathaniel Samuel Murrell and William David Spencer, Adrian Anthony McFarlane (eds.): *Chanting Down Babylon. The Rastafari reader*. Kingston: Ian Randle Publishers, 55-71.

Dhunjibhoy, Roshan, 2011:"Roshan-Memory Booklet" (Accessible online at: http://www.lannadog.net/blog/wp-content/uploads/2011/06/Roshan-memory-booklet.pdf).

Dizzy I, Ras, 1984: „Die Stimme der Rastas". In: Wolfgang Bender (ed.): *Rastafari Kunst aus Jamaica*. Bremen: Edition Con, 109-110.

Edmonds, Ennis Barrington, 1998:"Dread 'I' In-a-Babylon: Ideological resistance and cultural revitalization." In: Nathaniel Samuel Murrell and William David Spencer, Adrian Anthony McFarlane (eds.): *Chanting Down Babylon. The Rastafari Reader*. Kingston: Ian Randle Publishers, 23-35.

Edmonds, Ennis Barrington, 2003: *Rastafari from Outcasts to Culture Bearers*. New York: Oxford University Press.

Garrison, Len, 1979: *Black Youth, Rastafarianism, and the Identity Crisis in Britain*. London: A.C.E.R. Project.

Iah C (Carl Gayle) *JAHUG Vol. 4*

Köppen, Grit 2002. *Rastafari. Repatriierung nach Shashamane, Ethiopia*. Typescript/Ms. 6.

Kremser, Manfred (ed.), 1994: "Ay BoBo" Afro-Karibische Religionen. African-Caribbean Religions. Teil 3/Part 3. Rastafari. Wien: WUV Universitätsverlag

Linton, Ralph, 1964: "Nativistische Bewegungen". In: C.A. Schmitz (ed.): *Religionsethnologie*. Frankfurt a. M.: Akademische Verlagsanstalt, 390-403.

Mack, Douglas R.A., 1999: *From Babylon to Rastafari. Origin and history of the Rastafari movement*. Chicago: Research Associates School, Times Publications.

Macleod, Erin C., 2012: "Water Development Projects and Cultural Citizenship. Rastafari engagement with the Oromo in Shashamene, Ethiopia". In: Michael Barnett, (ed.): *Rastafari in the New Millennium: A Rastafari Reader*. New York: Syracuse University Press, 89-03.

McFarlane, Adrian Anthony, 1998. "The Epistemological Significance of "I-an-I". In: Nathaniel Samuel Murrell and William David Spencer, Adrian Anthony McFarlane (eds.): *Chanting Down Babylon. The Rastafari Reader*. Kingston: Ian Randle, 107-121.

Murrell, Nathaniel Samuel and William David Spencer, Adrian Anthony McFarlane (eds.) 1998: *Chanting Down Babylon. The Rastafari Reader*. Kingston: Ian Randle.

Murrell, Nathaniel Samuel and Burchell K. Taylor 1998. "Rastafari's Messianic Ideology and Caribbean Theology of Liberation". In: Nathaniel Samuel and William David Spencer, Adrian Anthony McFarlane (eds.), 1998: *Chanting Down Babylon. The Rastafari Reader*. Kingston: Ian Randle, 390-411.

Naliwaiko, Alja and Wolfgang Bender 2005. "An Introduction to Rastafarian Art". In: Wolfgang Bender (ed.): *Rastafarian Art*. Kingston: Ian Randle, 1-13.

Ras Dizzy, 1984: "Die Stimme der Rastas". In: Wolfgang Bender (ed.*): Rastafari-Kunst aus Jamaika*. Bremen: Edition Con.

Niaah Jahlani, 2012: "The Rastafari Presence in Ethiopia. A Contemporary Perspective". In: *Rastafari in the New Millennium: A Rastafari Reader*. New York: Syracuse University Press, 66-88.

Rodney, Walter, 1974: "Interview in "Black Scholar" Magazine, November 1974"*In:* Campbell, Horace, 1985: *Rasta and Resistance. From Marcus Garvey to Walter Rodney*. Dar es Salaam: Tanzania Publishing House.

Schmitz, Carl August (ed.), 1964: *Religionsethnologie*. Frankfurt a.M.: Akademische Verlagsanstalt.

Sherlock, Philip and Hazel Bennett, 1998: *The Story of the Jamaican People*. Kingston: Ian Randle Publishers.

Wallace, R.E., 1964: Revitalisations-Bewegungen". In: Carl August Schmitz (ed.) *Religionsethnologie*. Frankfurt a.M: Akademische Verlagsanstalt, 404-427.

Zips, Werner, 1999: *Black Rebels: African-Caribbean Freedom Fighters*. Princeton: Markus Wiener Publishers & Jamaica: Ian Randle Publishers.

Zips, Werner, 1999: *Gleiche Rechte und Gerechtigkeit. Eine ethnohistorische und rechtsanthropologische Rekonstruktion des Maroon-Rechtes in Jamaica im Kontext der afrikanischen Diaspora unter besonderer Berücksichtigung politischer Strukturen in Akan-Gesellschaften Ghanas*. Wien: Universität Wien. (Habilitationsschrift).

Zips, Werner, 1999 (with Anja Natmessnig): *Welcome Home. African Kingship meets the Diaspora in the Central Region/Ghana*. Wien: Institut für Ethnologie, Kultur- und Sozialanthropologie der Universität Wien(ethnographic film).

Zips, Werner (ed.), 2006: *A Universal Philosophy. Rastafari in the Third Millenium*. Kingston: Ian Randle Publishers.

Zips, Werner, 2006: "Repatriation is a Must'. The Rastafari struggle to utterly downstroy slavery". In: Werner Zips (ed.): *A Universal Philosophy. Rastafari in the Third Millenium*. Kingston: Ian Randle Publishers, 129-168.

Websites:

http://www.amazon.co.uk/Jahug-Rastafari-Nyahbinghi-Rastafarian-information/dp/0951981501/ref=dp_return_2?ie=UTF8&n=266239&s=books

http://www.iol.co.za/news/africa/rastafarians-hope-everything-will-be-alright-1.233185

http://www.angelfire.com/ny4/SoulJahsBan

EXTERNAL DESIGNATION VERSUS SELF-IDENTIFICATION

THE CASE OF THE BAYSO AND THE HARO PEOPLE ON GIDICCHO ISLAND, LAKE ABBAYA.

Susanne Epple and Fabienne Braukmann

At the Paradise Lodge in Arbaminch (Braukmann 2013)

Gidiccho: What is behind a name?

The term Gidiccho (also Giddicho, Gidicho, Gidicco) has appeared in many ethnographic, linguistic publications and official documents, mostly used for the biggest island in Lake Abbaya, Southern Ethiopia, but it has sometimes also been used for one or even both groups living on it. The inhabitants of the island today refer to themselves as the Bayso, a Cushitic speaking agro-pastoralist group, and the Haro, an Omotic speaking group of formerly exclusive hippo-hunters.[1] The Bayso and the Haro have been living in close and good neighborhood, but have always strictly observed a social boundary that is not only based on cultural and linguistic difference but also on concepts of purity and impurity.

1 The East Cushitic language of the Bayso has been classified as an own sub-group within Omo-Tana, Heine (1978) claiming it to be a Northern branch of Omo-Tana (The Sam languages) while Sasse (1975) is saying it was a Western branch together with Dasenech (also Daasanech, Dassanetch), Arbore and Elmolo (Brenzinger 1999). The languages Kachama, Koyra (Koreete), Zayse and Haro have been classified as one sub-group within East Ometo. The Ometo cluster itself belongs to the Western branch of the Omotic language family (Fleming 1976, in Hirut 2004: 2f).

The island and its inhabitants have been mentioned by early travelers to the region, and visited by several anthropologists, geographers and linguists. However, probably due to the very short times that all these researchers stayed, and also because the neighboring groups use many different names for the inhabitants of the island,[2] even in the most recent publications there exists confusion on the names and identities of these two very different people living on the island. Officially also (in Ethiopian national censuses, administrative documents) all inhabitants of the island and both languages are called 'Gidiccho '.

This paper intends to clear up the confusion existing literature around the name Gidiccho. It will answer the question how the inhabitants of the island define themselves, how they have been living on the island together, and, since several generations', also at the shores of Lake Abbaya. This article will also contribute to the sparse ethnographic literature on the Bayso and the Haro. The thematic focus lies hereby on their history of migration to and from the island, the sharing of space between the two groups and aspects of cooperation but also separation between them. It also looks at how locally, i.e. from the viewpoint of the Bayso and the Haro, the merging of the two very distinct groups into one is perceived and reacted to. As most of the data stems from the recent research of the authors among both groups, this paper provides the perspectives of both groups on the same questions.[3]

2 The Wolaitta, for example, call the Bayso "Haruro", and use the same name for the Haro and Get'eme (Brenziger 1995: 2). See also Haberland (1963: 682) for the different names used for the Haro and Bayso.

3 Since June 2012, the two languages and cultures are being studied and documented by an interdisciplinary research group in the Volkswagen funded DOBES project: "Documentation of Bayso (Cushitic) and Haro (Omotic): two Afroasiatic endangered languages of the Abbaya Lake in the Ethiopian Rift Valley." (see: http://www.volkswagenstiftung.de/index.php?id=172&L=1). Fabienne Braukmann and Susanne Epple are doing anthropological research among the Haro and Bayso respectively, while Graziano Sava, Endeshaw Wolde/Michael and Lemi Kebebew are is doing the linguistic research. Braukmann has already done research among the Haro in 2010 and written her M.A. thesis on their economy and adaption of livelihood practices in recent years (Braukmann 2012). The authors would like to use the opportunity express their gratitude to thank the Volkswagenstiftung and the DOBES program for financing this research. We would also like to thank our colleagues for the good cooperation, and especially Professor Mechthild Reh who is administering and supervising our project at Hamburg University and has been giving us valuable advice on many organizational and scholarly issues. Thanks also to our field assistants, especially to Nigatu Dubale, Maru Mota and Abdissa Ballamo, and especially to our friends and informants in the field. Ballamo Worba deserves a special mention as he is a kind of indigenous anthropologist of the Bayso who enlightened us on many linguistic and anthropological questions and introduced Susanne Epple to many other knowledgeable Bayso people in Alge. Among the Haro of Gidiccho and Alge the families of Tefari Borchesa, Alemayehu Woshere and Legesse Sesa, but also Wasihun Tada and Tola Asamenew should be mentioned here. They contributed immensely to Fabienne Braukmann's research since 2010.

Islands in Lake Abbaya and settlement areas on the shore

Gidiccho Island lies about 400 km south of the Ethiopian capital Addis Ababa in the Southern Nations, Nationalities and People's Region (SNNPR), about 60 km north of Arbaminch, the administrative capital of Gamo-Gofa Zone. With 32 km² Gidiccho is the largest of several Islands in Lake Abbaya (also: Lake Margherita). Other islands are Golmakka (also: Wollega) which was until recently also inhabited by Bayso people, and the Get'eme Islands (inhabited by the Get'eme people, who are closely related to the Haro) (Braukmann 2012: 2). Lake Abbaya, a sweet water lake, lies in the African Rift Valley at 1169 m above sea level. With its size of 1162 km² it is the second largest lake in Ethiopia (Bogale 2010: 3). The hilly island is rather dry and thick grass is mostly found along the shores and inside the villages. This is also where one can find some moringa and acacia-trees, while the other vegetation is rather thorny or succulent (Braukmann 2012: 2f).

The two groups who have shared the island for at least the last two hundred, living in three villages: the Bayso people in Shigima, at the northern tip, and Bayso village in the South of the island, and the Haro in the centre of the island in the village Haro (also Haruro). West of Gidiccho lies the smaller Golmakka Island, until recently also inhabited by Bayso people. In 1994 there were 292 inhabitants in Shigima and 250 in Bayso (Brenzinger 1995: 4).[4] In 2012, there were only 35 individuals living in Haro, and some of these were preparing their migration to the island in 2013.

Migration to the shore has begun several generations ago. Today, the majority of both groups have settled along the western shores of Lake Abaya, mostly in Alge, a village southwest of Mirab Abaya, which is inhabited mostly of Bayso people, but with an increasing number of Haro. Several hundred Bayso (Brenzinger speaks of a total of 847 in 1994) live mixed with other ethnic groups in the small villages of Wajifo, Worbe, Ch'ink'ile (also: Shingiko) and Jigeesa on the north-western shores of the lake (*ibid.* 1995: 5).[5]

According to Brenzinger in 1994 there were still 100 Bayso people living on Golmakka Island. In 2012 Epple was told that no one lived on the island anymore, but that some former inhabitants still had their beehives there and went to collect honey from time to time.[6]

4 As Epple has not visited the island yet a more recent census still needs to be done for Bayso and Shigima villages.

5 In 1955 Haberland (1963: 686) estimated the population of Bayso village to have 700 inhabitants. Today they do not exceed more than few hundred and the large number of abandoned houses prove the recent migration of Bayso people to the mainland. In 1995 Brenzinger was told that "the majority of Bayso people left Gidiccho islands 4 to 5 generations ago". A survey made by Epple in 2012 has shown that that most elderly Bayso people in Alge claim that they have been living in the third generation at the shore.

6 According to Brenzinger, in 1994 the population of Alge and Gólmakka together was 1,871, the total of all Bayso people being 3260 (Brenzinger 1999: 4f). The number of Haro on the island and at the shore does probably not exceed 150.

Politically, the Haro and Bayso are administered as one ethnic group. The island people and their migrants at the shores had asked the Ethiopian Government to be taken out of Gedeo zone and included into North Omo zone of the SNNPR. Carrying the common name "Gidiccho" together the two groups form one of nine additional minorities in the Southern Regions with special constituencies and are thereby represented in the council of the Southern Region since 1995 (Brenzinger 1999: 5). The Gidiccho Island constitutes its own *kebele* (smallest administrative unit) and belongs, like Alge village at the shore, to Mirab Abaya (also: Birbir) *woreda* (district).

(Fabienne Braukmann 2012: 3)

The common administration of Bayso and Haro under the name Gidiccho may have led to the fact that in different reports of Ethiopian government institutions on the cultural diversity on North Omo the Bayso and the Haro are also not differentiated.[7] During cultural festivals in Arbaminch (e.g. festival August 2012; Thousand Stars Festival on 13th -14th, December 2012) where the different ethnic groups of North Omo perform their dances and songs, it is also only the "Gidiccho" who appear. The Gidiccho dance groups then consist only of Bayso presenting Bayso dress, dances and songs, while the Haro are completely ignored and are even not aware of the festival.

7 The Authority for Research and Conversation of Cultural Heritage has published an "Inventory of the Intangible Cultural heritage of Twenty Nations and Nationalities of North Omo" (2009) in which the term "Gidicho" is used to refer to the Bayso people. The same is true for a publication made by House of Federations on "The profile of SNNPR" (EC 2001). Here, the Haro are considered as one of four "ethnic roots" (*yezergint*) of the Gidiccho people (page 361f).

Ethnic identity in contemporary Ethiopia

The multi-ethnic state of Ethiopia has long been dominated by the ruling classes of the centre. Especially the smaller minority groups at the periphery have not been represented and were not able to participate in regional and national politics. With the downfall of the socialist Derg regime things have changed and since 1995 the Ethiopian constitution guarantees equal rights and political participation to all ethnic groups, no matter how small in number its members might be. In its "cultural policy" (1997), Ethiopia promotes the respect and preservation of "languages, heritage history, handicraft, fine arts, oral literature, traditional lore, beliefs and other cultural features of the various nations, nationalities and peoples of Ethiopia."[8]

Article 39,5 of the constitution defines what is meant by "Nation, Nationality or People" as "a group of people who have or share large measure of a common culture or similar customs, mutual intelligibility of language, belief in a common or related identities, a common psychological make-up, and who inhabit an identifiable, predominantly contiguous territory."[9] This definition has been challenged for its resemblance with overcome primordial concepts of ethnic groups and identities in anthropology, and also as it seems questionable to what extent today's identified ethnic groups in Ethiopia really represent a "continuity of past forms of social organization" (Abbink 1997: 160). Abbink and others are suggesting that Ethiopian ethnic identities are presently "re-surfacing or re-created" (*ibid.*) and some examples of newly acknowledged ethnic groups are quite prominent in Ethiopia.[10]

The fact that two culturally and linguistically very different groups have been clustered together as one even though cultural and linguistic differences between them are known is unusual in contemporary Ethiopia, also that the individuals among them (all Bayso) who are aware of the new developments in Ethiopia seem to support the common labeling of the two groups, rather than insisting on separate identities.

Earlier visits of researchers and officials to the island and the shore

The Island and the shores of Lake Abbaya have been visited and mentioned by numerous travelers, and researchers. The first western scholars to mention the people on the island were the participants of the second Bòttego exploration

[8] CP, Objective 1 (http://www.ethioembassy.org.uk/fact%20file/a-z/culture.htm). For an extended discussion of the cultural policy see Epple/Thubauville (2012).

[9] Constitution of the Federal Democratic Republic of Ethiopia (accessible online at http://www.servat.unibe.ch/icl/et00000_html).

[10] A well-known example is that of the Siltie, who were formerly considered as a subgroup of the Gurage and have achieved acknowledgement as an independent "nationality" (Ismagilova 2006; Nishi 2003).

(Vannutelli 1899, cf. Haberland 1963: 678) who came to the area by the end of the 19th century.

The German Anthropologist Eike Haberland was maybe the first who actually spent several weeks on the Island in the mid 1950s (Haberland 1963: 679) during his second expedition to Southern Ethiopia. Having stayed there for several weeks he has provided an ethnographic outline of the Bayso people, and also briefly mentions the Haro. Haberland claims that the people who today refer to themselves as Bayso, i.e. the inhabitants of the two villages on Gidiccho island, Bayso and Shigima villages as well as the inhabitants of Golmakka island, do not have a name for self-reference, but rather refer to their villages when asked about their identity (Haberland 1963: 687). As they form a linguistic and cultural entity, he decided to refer to all of them as "Gidiccho", but distinguished them from the Haro, who also lived on the Island.

Paul Henze visited the area and the eastern shore when he late 1960 and early 70s when he was a member of the American Embassy in Addis Ababa. He did not travel to the island but met its inhabitants on what he refers to the "Gidicho market" (1977: 145) (i.e. the market at Melka). When he speaks of the "Gidicho" people (*ibid.*) he obviously refers to the Bayso, as he mentions that their language very similar to Somali (*ibid.*: 148). He also speaks of some "Gatami" (i.e. Get'eme) people having a village on the island, hereby probably referring to the Haro (*ibid.*: 146, also Henze 1974).

Matthias Brenzinger, a German linguist, visited Gidiccho Island in 1995. He wrote that all inhabitants of Bayso, Shigima and Golmakka as well as those who had migrated to the shore were referring their whole community as well as to their language as "Bayso" (Brenzinger 1999). The Ethiopian anthropologist Awoke Amzaye in his book on the *Mosaic Cultures and Peoples of Southern Nations, Nationalities and Peoples' Regional State* refers to the Bayso with the terms "Ibado Kabayso" (which literally means "the people of Bayso") and "Gidicho" (2007: 163). The German anthropologist Nicole Poissonnier visited the Island only very briefly while making an inventory of stone stelen in Southern Ethiopia. Though she stayed only few hours, she distinguished between the two groups and the distinct name for the island (Poissonnier 2001, 2005). Fabienne Braukmann noted that the Haro on Gidiccho Island use the terms Shigima and Bayso not only to refer to the villages but also to their inhabitants, so that in her M.A. thesis (Braukmann 2012) she wrote that possibly the Shigima constitute a different ethnic group.

When Susanne Epple began her fieldwork in 2012 in Alge village she noticed that the term "Bayso" was predominantly used by all people at the shore to refer to themselves and also their language. In some interviews she deliberately used the term "Gidiccho" to ask about the language, as one of her key-informants insisted this was the right term to use. Testing the reaction of the interviewees she observed that even though she had used of the term "Gidiccho" for people and language in her questions, the people still used "Bayso" in their answers.

Making place: Migration to an emerging island

In the existing literature on Gidiccho, different versions of the migratory history of Bayso and Haro to the island are provided. Enrico Vannutelli who visited the area in the late 19th century assumed that the Haro were actually a group of bandits having fled from different mountain people living around the lake (1899: 261). Eike Haberland (1963: 688f) also wrote that the island has always been a rather safe place for its inhabitant, but does not mention that these may have been deviants who needed to hide. He depicts that the first migrants to the island came on bundles of reed from a place called Gidiccho which lay in Darassa-land (today: Gedeo). According to him most Bayso clans have come from there, except two, *mulmal* and *danga.*

About Gidiccho he reported that the local people believe that it has not always been an island. The lake around it had filled up when a woman had forgotten to close the water well after she had fetched water and rushed home to her children. The flowing water had then quickly filled the lake. Borana people, who had lived on the elevated area of today's Gidiccho Island, had fled the place before the water became too deep to be crossed (ibid: 688).

The Bayso and the Haro have similar versions of how the lake and the island came into being, while their stories of how they migrated to Gidiccho are differing.[11]

Bayso oral history on migration to the Island

The Bayso people interviewed by Epple in 2012 and 2013 all shared the view that the name of the island refers to the first migrant, i.e. a man called Gidiccho who scared the Borana people living there away. During a group discussion several elders and former ritual experts (2 male and one female) of Bayso explained the history of the Bayso.[12] Chumburo Assefa[13], former ritual leader (*wonno*), described the arrival of the first settlers:

> Our people first lived in a place called Lalemicha. There were five brothers: Gidiccho, Darasse, Gujo, Ochole and Boroda. The five brothers spread into different directions, and one of them, Gidiccho, went to the place today Gidiccho Island. In those days the place was not yet surrounded in the water, but rather an elevation of the ground. During that time, Borana and Gemmi people lived there.[14]The man Gidiccho lived some time

[11] Brenzinger (1995: 1) referring to Wedekind (p.c.) stated that island's name Gidiccho stemmed from a Gedeo term meaning "small thing inside [the water]".

[12] The group discussion was held in Alge on the 15th of February 2013. Two male elders, Chumburo Assefa, and Molla Harkule and one female, Fallaye Buya, participated. The conversation was recorded and the next day translated with the help of Abdissa Ballamo and Ballamo Worba, who added some further explanations.

[13] Chumburo Assefa belongs to the Achegele clan of Bayso village. He has been a wonno (ritual leader) of Bayso village for 2-3 years. After him came two before the Bayso gave up their belief system and became Christians. He is today about 60 years old and a member of the protestant K'ale Hiwot Church.

[14] Often people mention only three brothers: Gidiccho, Darasse and Gujo. Also in the

with them and then killed a Borana man in a fight.[15] Having killed the man, Gidiccho sang killer songs that could be heard afar. When the other Borana and Gemmi people heard him sing, they left the place out of fear that Gidiccho and his friends might kill them too.

Gidiccho went back to his wife. She was fetching water when he returned and he told her not to close the well with the stone people usually put to stop the water form flowing.[16]When the spring remained uncovered, water continued to flow and the lake began filling up. When eventually the Borana came to take revenge for the murder they could not cross the water and reach the place which had now become an island. (...) Gidiccho had moved there with his family and then also other people started joining them

Chumburo's account makes clear that the rising water turned the place into a rather inaccessible island which made it attractive for the people to stay. This was also emphasized by Molla Harkule, former *woycha* (assistant of *wonno*)[17]:

The island was seen as a safe place, as enemies could not simply come and attack. To make sure that no one could identify the shallow spots in the lake, the island people assigned their youths to stand along the shore and throw stones onto birds, which stood in shallow water to catch fish so that no one could guess where the water was shallow enough to pass. The water served as a protection. Ochole, Donne, Gujo and Boroda (Gidiccho's brothers) started living around the shore.[18]

The decision to stay on the island and to protect it from enemies is said to have been an advice by the ritual leader of the Bayso, Chumburo explained:

Do you know who allowed us to go on the lake by boat? It was the *wonno* (ritual leader) who decided that people should stay on the island to be protected from enemy attack, and who advised them to build boats to be able to cross the rising water.

Ballamo Worba[19], a respected elder from Alge, added that the Bayso developed special ways to make sure no one could come to the island:

literature usually only these three brothers are mentioned. Darasse is said to have become the forefather of the Gedeo people (their former name was Darrasse), and Gujo of the Guji people. The believed common origin of these three groups and also the Ochole and Boroda (part of Gamo) were commonly mentioned as the reason for the prohibition to kill members of these groups.

15 In one version of their history, it is said that he deliberately killed the Borana man, while in another version it is told that the Borana man died in a competitive ring fight.

16 One version of the story tells that she was fetching water when he arrived. He told his wife not to cover the spring with the stone used by everyone to stop the water from flowing. Another story says that she simply forgot to cover it as she had a small baby and was rushing to return home.

17 Molla Harkule belongs to the Worji clan of Shigima. He has been the last *woycha* (assistant of *wonno*) of Shigima village and became an orthodox Christian about 18 years ago. Today he is about 60 years old.

18 They are believed to be the forefathers of neighbouring ethnic groups, i.e. the Ochole, Gedeo (formerly called Darassa, Guji and Boroda who are part of the Gamo). They are until today considered as relatives of the Bayso and there exists a prohibition to kill each other.

19 Ballamo Worba belongs to the Mulmalle clan of Shigima. He has three years of formal

> To be identified as an islander, the Bayso used secret names when travelling by boat: they shouted *"Hankalcho! Ferferra! (paddle)"* when they returned to the island instead of personal names.

The first people are believed to have settled in the North, in today's Shigima village, as there was a spring providing potable water. Later more and more people moved to the Island and the two villages of Shigima and Bayso were formed. Migrants to the island came from different directions and formed today's clans of the Bayso. In the village Shigima the following clans are found: Gondo and Achele (both with origin in Boroda-Malla/Gamo) Worji (moved from Bayso village to Shigima). The biggest and most well-known clan in Shigima is Mulmalle (origin "somewhere in the east").

In the Bayso village there are the clans of Achele and Achegele (named after their forefathers, two brothers from Boroda-Malla/Gamo), the clan Dhantu (from Arsi), the clan Fago (from "far away", possibly Guji), the clan Baala (from Guii), Maman-kat'ae'ae (from Boroda-Malla), Dhabootee, Dakartee and Worji (origin unknown). Those who settled on Golmakka Island formed a clan called Golmakka (originally from Boroda-Malla/Gamo).[20]

The territory on the island was divided between the two villages of Bayso and Shigima, each of which had its own ritual leader, the wonno, and his assistants, the woycha.[21] The villages lie at the Northern and Southern tip of the island. In the centre of the village lies the place called Haro. Here they identified a special place used for meetings. Fallaye Buya, the sister of an *oddobaddo* (ritual expert), explained during the group discussion:[22]

> The *songonn*, our meeting place, lies in Haro. This is the name of the place, not the people. The *songonn* is surrounded by trees that were planted there to give shade, and there are stones to sit on.

education and has served as soldier during the Derg regime for many years living outside of his community. He is himself interested in the history and culture of the Bayso and talked to many elders and ritual experts after his return to the area. He has become a kind of "native anthropologist". His relationship with the local community is ambiguous, i.e. he seems to be respected but also envied.

20 The information on the different origins of the clans were given by Ballamo Worba and confirmed during a survey conducted in Alge in 2013 during which individuals were asked about their clan membership. However, more research needs to be done on this topic.

21 The *wonno* was responsible for the well-being of his people, cattle and land in general, he had several woycha to assist him and was elected for 2-3 years only when the next one would take over. Though there is no space to go into detail here, it must be mentioned that the *oriwonno* (wife of the *wonno*) and the *maganencho* (wives of the *mochas*) played a central role in ritual life of the Bayso. Another important office was that of the *oddobaddo* and his wife, the so-called *abaddo* who performed rituals for women who has miscarriages. The traditional belief system has been given up in favour of orthodox and protestant Christianity only 2-3 decades ago.

22 Fallaye Buya belongs to the Gondo clan of Bayso. She is the sister of the last *oddobaddo* (ritual expert for women and fertility) in Bayso village. She is today about 75 years old and is a member of the protestant Mekane Yesus Church.

On the *songonn* both *wonno* from Bayso and Shigima got together from time to time, to discuss issues concerning both villages, and perform rituals together. Here, it was also decided how to divide the island between the inhabitants of Shigima and Bayso village. Ballamo Worba explained:

> When once the two *wonno* from Shigima and Bayso met to discuss how to administer the island, they decided to separate it into two equal halves. They met on the *songonn* (common meeting place) and agreed on the border. When the Shigima *wonno* encircled his territory he cheated and entered Bayso territory. People then started arguing about the demarcation and after some negotiation they finally agreed on the border being at place called Dhakaree (in the west of the island). Since then the greater part of the island was allocated to the Shigima people.

About the Haro people's arrival the Bayso say the following: at some point some hippo-hunters from Get'eme arrived at the island and asked to be given a piece of land to settle, as their hunting grounds were far from their original island and so the hippo meat was rotting on their way back. They preferred to stay closer to the hunting places and thus to be able to trade the meat and skin to other groups, keeping Gidiccho Island as their base. The Get'eme people were given some space in the centre of the island to build their houses, and later also some land to be able to cultivate. As the place where they settled was already called Haro, the new village of the settlers was then also referred to as Haro, and likewise extended to the people and their language. According to the Bayso, the original settlers at Haro were later joined by others from Gedeo, Ganjule and Golmakka, all of whom through eating hippo meat became one group. The Golmakka people, it is said, left their island and became refugees after a violent conflict with the Arsi people who had managed to cross the water, reach the island and kill many of them, including their ritual leader. Some survivors took refuge in Gamo, others went to Gidiccho and stayed in Bayso and Shigima villages. One family stayed with the Haro. As they started eating hippo-meat there they could not re-join their relatives who moved back to Golmakka after several years, as they had become impure.

The Bayso clearly consider themselves as first comers (after the Borana had left) and privileged to the Haro whom they generously allowed to stay and assigned some land. This was clearly expressed during public meetings held on the public meeting place near to the Haro village. Here, the *maga* (also *haromaga*; ritual leader) of the Haro, participated, but rather as an assistant and spectator, not as an equal. Chumburo Assefa described their relations as follows:

Only the *wonno* and the people from Bayso and Shigima are administrators of the island. The *maga* welcomed and received the *wonno* during public meetings on the *songonn* (meeting place), relieved them of their *cherfanna* (ritual staffs) and kept them for them until the end of the meeting. He was not allowed to sit next to the two *wonno* of Shigima and Bayso, as he has eaten hippopotamus meat and is considered impure.

The history of migration to the island from Haro perspective

While it was relatively easy to identify knowledgeable elders among the Bayso, there were very few Haro who could give a mythological explanation of the creation of Lake Abaya and the island. This may partly have to do with the very low population number of the Haro (not more than 150 individuals). The information Braukmann was able to collect in 2010 and 2012/13 is based on informal conversations with different people, and on interviews with two elders. Even though both belonged to the same clan (Hulma), the two men did not fully agree on one version of Haro history. Generally, Braukmann had the impression that oral history is not of much significance to the Haro anymore. Possible reasons for this negligence are the harsh and violent way the Haro were treated during the time of the socialist Derg regime and also later by missionaries which may have harmed the Haro confidence to talk about their culture. As Braukmann observed, the Haro rarely talk about the past or their origins so that during her research no shared perspective on the Haro migration history could be found. The Haro elder Alemayehu[23] gave a cultural explanation:

> Because we were ritual leaders—my family were ritual leaders' descendants—we don't talk about our culture or anything to our children. If we would tell, they would worry that we might die the next day, as when people are very ill, when they are close to dying, they tell their children about their experiences and the customs. This is the reason why people who are not severely sick do not talk about this to their children, as it might cause their death. [...]
>
> We get to know about our culture also by living together. I, for instance, even if my father did not tell me anything, I know everything. He did not need to tell me. But anyway, until the Derg came, it [culture, knowledge] belonged to the ritual leader, this is how we lived. When the Derg came they were hovering around my home, dressed in uniforms and screaming that I should get out. They forced me to leave the house but I refused. They even tried to burn my house. Finally I got out. [...] So it was not common to tell, but rather to live in it [culture]. Nowadays, the young people do not have any culture to transfer to the next generation. There is nothing, we just live, there is no ritual leadership. (Interview with Alemayehu, 24.08.2010).

From Alemayehu's account one can presume that not only the ritual, but also the historical and mythological knowledge had been in the hands of the *maga*, the ritual leader of the Haro, and that with the abandoning of the traditional belief system and the ritual office of *maga* several decades ago a lot of the knowledge got lost and seems to have become insignificant to the people.

[23] Alemayehu is one of the elders belonging to the Hulma clan. He was a ritual leader, a *haromaga* in Gidiccho for 5-6 years at an earlier age. Although he does not carry this office anymore, he was still respected and consulted by the community in Haro as Braukmann observed during her research in 2010. As the last elder among the Haro he migrated from the island to Alge in December 2012. Alemayehu had no formal education and is now about 80 years old.

The Haro share the same myth of origin on the creation of the Lake and the Gidiccho Island as the Bayso, though some details vary. The creation of the Lake is explained by a man who had forgotten to close a well not far from the elevated land forming the island today. When the water continued to flow the land was flooded and surrounded today's island. The first person to settle in Haro is said to have been a man from Ganjule Island in Lake Chamo. He had travelled to Gidiccho in order to sell hippo meat, but during his visit the water level rose so much that he was unable to return and forced to stay on the island. Another version told by Legesse,[24] a Haro elder and former *haromaga* (religious leader) speaks of a water hole dug by elders that was forgotten to be covered. The rivers known as Gelana, Gidabo, Bilate and Tafe also contributed in filling up the lake. Legesse had heard this from his father Sesa who claimed that Lake Abaya was created in the time of Legesses's great-great-grandfather Joche. At that time his clan Hulma was living in the Gedeo region east of the lake not far from the area of the island. The Bayso and Shigima people lived around the same area. When the lake began to fill, people rushed to the island to secure a plot of land. Thus the settlement areas of Haro, Shigima, and Bayso were founded and houses built there.[25]

While the Bayso associate the name of the Haro with the place where they were on given on Gidiccho Island to settle on, some elderly Haro people asserted that it relates to a water pond used by pastoralists when the lake was still grasslands. It was located between Gidiccho and Dila town and locally called '*haro*', a term that could etymologically be related to '*haré*', the Gamo word for pond.[26] Legesse stated that names for people generally stem from the places where they live:

> People are named after places. People have no common name. People from Alge are called Alge. When you speak in more specific terms, then people will refer to the place of origin [i.e. Haro, Bayso]." (Interview with Legesse, 13.04.2013).

The migration history of the Haro becomes manifest in their four clans: Hulma, Ga'ne, a Golmakka and Get'eme. Every clan owns a compound area with plots for gardening inside the village, grasslands next to the shore. These partitions are used for activities such as fishing. Burial sites equally belong to different clans. Only the Get'eme clan do not possess a burial place on Gidiccho, they bury their people in the Get'eme villages on the western shore of the lake.[27]

24 Legesse is a member of the Hulma clan. He took over the office of the *haromaga* from Alemayehu and kept it for eleven years. He was the last ritual leader of the Haro before formal religion was introduced by missionaries. He has no formal education and is today about 70 years old.

25 The land was given to them by the *Bayso* ritual leader and then distributed among the four clans (Braukmann 2012: 17)

26 All data stated here stems from a group discussion with several elders from different clans at the beginning of my MA research, 6th August 2010. All information gathered during that time was translated from Gamo and Amharic to English.

27 Non-community members living on the island, such as a Guji blacksmith or other Guji individuals are not buried within the Haro burial site but in short distance to it.

Some Haro have later also settled on the western shores in Shingiko, Wajifo and Alge for cultivation of cotton and maize. It is said that the first settlers left the Island before the rule of Emperor Haile Selassie. The migration to Alge is recent. Braukmann counted 11 Haro households of different clans in the settlements of Shingiko and Wajifo, while there are 32 Haro households in Alge. This is also where the Haro elders reside today.

The four Haro clans claim to have come from four different groups. The clan of the Hulma is said to have originated from Gedeo area northeast of the lake. Their migration to the Gidiccho Island can be traced back at least eight generations. The second clan, Ga'ne, ascribes its origin to Ganjule Island (Lake Chamo). They are also said to have come to Gidiccho in order to pursue hunting from there. The Golmakka clan traces back its origins to the mainland in the west and to a homonymous island in Lake Abbaya. Before coming to Gidiccho, they lived on apiculture and stock-breeding until they came to the Island with a few cattle about five generations ago. The 1970s political suppression of the socialist Derg government finally led the Get'eme to Ugayo and later to Mole on the western shore and at the same time to Gidiccho. The Get'eme originally are said to have lived in the Amaro Mountains in the area of today's NechSar National Park. They then shifted their habitat to the Get'eme Islands (Lake Abaya) where they began living as s hippopotami hunters (Haberland 1963, Henze 2001; Kuls 1958; Vannutelli 1899).[28] Previously having been weavers and hippopotamus hunters, they have lived in Gidiccho since 30 or 40 years.

The accounts Braukmann was given on the order of arrival of the four clans as well as their motivation to migrate to the Island varied. Alemayehu, one of the two most knowledgeable Haro elders living today explained the following:

> We (the Hulma clan) came first, from Gedeo. We have this place [Haro village] and we also took plots for farming. When the others (other clans) arrived, they also took a place. This means we are all one now, but we came from different places and then formed one group: Haro.
>
> When the Hulma first came, they were all hippo hunters. We, the Hulma, came for the hippo hunting. The Golmakka also came for hunting. Also the Ga'ne came for hunting. The Wollega [other word for Golmakka] man wanted to stay when he arrived. When his brother came and wanted him to return to Wollega (the Golmakka island), the guy said: "This place is best for me, it is good for hunting and for living, so I want to live here". And he stayed. The Get'eme arrived very recently, after I was born, I know that. It was only now. I have seen when they came and settled." (Interview with Alemayehu, 24.08.2010).

The other elder, Legesse, claimed a different order of arrival of clans on the Island and also gives some more information of the motivation to come. According to him, the Hulma clan arrived first, followed by the clan Ga'ne and the Get'eme.

[28] The Get'eme left the Island completely and settled in Ugayo on the south-western shores as a result of the resettlement provoked by the socialist *Derg*-regime and probably due to food shortage (cf. Brenzinger 1995).

> The grandfather of the Golmakka people went to the Haro [village]. Golmakka fled to Haro by his free will. People of Golmakka first fled from the Gamo area because they had a war from Ochollo and they went to Golmakka [island]. Hulma is the first clan coming for hunting. People from the Get'eme clan first came to the Melka market (at the eastern shore of Gidiccho) to sell *buluko* [scarves], there, they got married to a Haro and thus the Get'eme clan has been created. The Ganjule came from Lake Chamo: they were looking for a place to perform their rituals, a good place for their ancestor spirits. It was one man with his wife and their children. Their spirits followed them to Gidiccho. They were the first (of today's Ga'ne clan) to Haro, and then became bigger and bigger and are now a clan. They were hippo hunters before they arrived to the Island (Interview with Legesse, 13.04.2013).

In another version, a man from Ganjule Island became the first Haro man who stayed in Gidiccho. It seems likely that ancestors of today's Hulma clan have indeed arrived first, as the Hulma clan is the only clan whose members are able to become ritual leaders. Also, the arrangement of land plots in Gidiccho seems to confirm the early arrival Hulma clan being first.[29] A late arrival of the Get'eme people on Gidiccho seems to be supported by Alemayehu's statement that he could remember that they came when he was young. Aminu, an elder from the Get'eme clan tells the story of his grandfather and how he had settled in the Haro village:

> My grandfather he told us that he came from Get'eme; this is now inv Ugayo in Mirab Abaya. [...] he came here [Gidiccho] to visit his friends and his relatives, but he was also interested in hippo hunting. When he came he got married to a woman from here [Gidiccho]. After me and my brothers were born he and his brothers stayed here. At some stage, they went to their original place to visit relatives and to build a house there. (Interview with Aminu, 18.08.2010).

One reason why it is commonly believed by outsiders (for example the Bayso, see above) that the Haro have greatly come from Get'eme Island is that Haro language is closely related to the Get'eme language. Besides, the Get'eme livelihood practices are similar to those of the Haro, and both groups practice hippo hunting. When Braukmann asked why Haro language is so similar to that of the Get'eme if the alleged first comers, the Hulma had come from the Gedeo, Legesse gave the following answer:

> The Hulma stopped speaking their own and adopted a new language. (…). They started to talk the language of Get'eme. They did not want to go back to Darassa and so they started to talk Get'eme. (13.04.2013).

During a discussion with a Bayso man on Gidiccho (16th October 2013), Alemayehu's son Mersha[30] stated that the Get'eme have been *the* hippopotami hunters of Lake Abaya, even in the northern part of the Lake where they used to sell

[29] The land of the Hulma clan is closest to the village, that of the Get'eme the farthest. One could assume that those who settled first took the land closest to the village to cultivation.

[30] Mersha is the oldest son of Alemayehu. He belongs to the Hulma clan and is about 50 years old. Mersha has received four years of formal education.

the meat to the Gedeo people. Once a man came from that area to Gidiccho for the purpose of trading and adopted the Get'eme language as well as the art of hunting. Later on the Ga'ne, the Golmakka and finally the Get'eme followed and also settled on Gidiccho. "Haro" became their ethnic name, and so did the language's denomination. To this Alemayehu's statement fits well:

> "At first we spoke the language of the Get'eme, but we are Haro and we speak Haro."(Alemayehu, 12.10.2013).

The Get'eme elder Aminu[31] also confirmed that the Haro took the language of the Get'eme:

> [...] He [Aminu's grandfather] is Get'eme, but after coming to Haro and having lived here for a long time, he has become Haruro. By the way, the people who speak the Haro language they have been living in Haro. This language was taken from Get'eme. The people who live in Get'eme speak like the Haro, they have the same language. (Interview with Aminu 18.08.2010)[32]

The splinters of the four different groups have fused by intermarriage to one ethnic group and today form the four clans of the Haro and all speak the same Omotic language.

Social boundaries and areas of contact and crossing

Residence on the island was clearly regulated and space divided not only into three villages, e.g. Bayso, Shigima and Haro, but also among the different clans. In Bayso and Shigima, each clan had its own space for houses, for fields, for herding and even for burial. There were clearly defined places for rituals and sacrifice and the common public meeting place in between in the centre of the Island close to the Haro village. In proximity north of this village the shoreline is used as a landing place for local boats and floats. This part of land also offers the salty soil which contains minerals important for cattle. It is mainly exploited by Haro women, sometimes also by Bayso women, who prepare the salt bars for trade. West of this shoreline and to both sides of the so called hill *ferenji zuma*[33] lie the burial sites of the Haro and non-community members. Farther north of the shoreline towards Shigima the land of the different Haro clans is to be found. The land with its shoreline north of the landing place belongs to the Hulma clan. It is followed by a section that is

[31] Aminu is the eldest living member of the Get'eme clan in Gidiccho and is therefore highly respected. He was also the last member of his clan living on Gidiccho Island in 2010. When the DOBES-project started in October 2012, he had already abandoned his compound in the island and had moved to Alge. He has no formal education and is today about 70 years old.

[32] The way Aminu uses the term "Haro" shows that the ethnic name of a people refers to the place they live in.

[33] *Ferenji zuma* literally means 'foreigner's hill' in Haro language. Its name refers to the stronghold constructed by Italians next to the hill during their time of invasion. While Haberland (1963: 689) observed its ruins, today they are not visible anymore.

owned by the Golmakka clan, the next part is hold by the Ga'ne clan and finally the land the farthest away from the Haro village belongs to the Get'eme clan whose last members in Gidiccho abandoned his house in 2011 or 2012.

The Haro were traditionally living on hippo hunting, weaving and trading of salt bars, a saline soil found at the shore next to the Haro village. Several decades ago, fishing became a central part of the local economy while agriculture is only practised in the settlements onshore.

The Bayso see themselves as pastoralists and engaged in cattle and small stock herding (also at the mainland) on the island as well as some agriculture. Recently, some Bayso started also fishing and among those living at the shore some have started to engage in cash cropping.

Boundaries of pollution

As outlined above, the Bayso and the Haro have a different origin and history, speak languages from different language families and have very different livelihood activities.

Some of these differences are strongly emphasized as social boundaries that separate the two groups, while others are of less importance. The boundaries are emphasized in situations of cultural contact that demand close interaction or actual "mixing", for example when it comes to co-residence and intermarriage. The strongest boundary between the two groups is the perception of the Bayso that the Haro are *tune* (literally: 'impure') due to two factor: they hunt and consume hippopotamus meat and traditionally do not circumcise their men and women.

The Bayso use the term *monuma* for 'pure', and *tune*, for 'impure' referring to the status of human beings. *Monuma* are people called *ahamatsisamun lako giro* (those who are circumcised) and for *dullo lako amiro* (those who do not eat hippo meat). Some food is considered especially pure, such as milk, honey and meat, especially the heart, the liver (for women), and generally the meat from the right side of a cow (and sheep). These items are also commonly used in rituals and for sacrifices. The meat of the hippopotamus is considered as unclean and its consumption by the Haro has created the strongest boundary between the two groups.

The Bayso despise the hippopotamus and consider its consumers equally as impure. The impurity is linked to the feeling of disgust towards the meat, which is somehow extended to the consumers and renders them as a lesser kind of human. This leads to avoiding eating and drinking together, as anyone eating hippo meat turns also non-Haro into impure people. This is expressed in the local saying "*Sowunka cherrer guddata, harota?*"(Are you from Haro to salivate for every kind of meat?).

In the past, the impurity was believed to be inheritable, and also polluting to others. Therefore, the Bayso avoided eating and drinking together with the Haro. Haro were also not allowed to touch certain objects, such as milk containers. Nowadays, the Bayso say, though some Haro claim they have stopped eating hippo meat, they actually still do it, and the Bayso still say they would never, due to that suspicion, eat meat at a Haro house. Otherwise, eating together has become more common between Bayso and Haro.

Other products from hippopotamus, such as whips and cover for paddles (*ferfera*) made by the skin were commonly used by the Bayso and not associated with impurity.

A second aspect for impurity is the issue of male and female circumcision. The Bayso consider people who are not circumcised as impure.[34] Impure people cannot do certain things or touch certain objects. Central to the Bayso is the circumcision before marriage. When a Bayso male is about to be married people ask: "*Hiro ta horoko bera?*" (Has he been freed from the Haro trouser? which means here: 'Has he been circumcised?'). No Bayso man and no woman can get married before marriage. In addition, females should be virgins when they marry. The Haro, the Bayso say, have neither circumcised males nor females in the past, but only recently started this practice.

Areas of boundary crossing

According to the Bayso, they used to marry Haro women as only 2nd or 3rd wife. Also the *wonno* and *woycha* (ritual experts of the Bayso) were allowed to marry Haro women, as they performed their rituals together with their first wives only. Children born in such unions were fully accepted as Bayso and there was no hindrance for them to become *woycha* and *wonno,* as their descent was strictly traced through their father's line only. Nowadays, the Bayso say, things have changed and Haro women can also become first wives.

While accepting Haro women as co-wives, the Bayso in the past gave only females who had lost their virginity (considered a big shame) as wives to the Haro. Such girls would not find a Bayso man who marries them anymore. Once a Bayso woman had been married to a Haro man it was assumed that she would gradually begin to eat hippo meat and thus she was considered to have turned a Haro herself. Such women would still come to visit their original Bayso families, but her family would be reluctant to go to her new home, assuming that she might serve them hippo meat.

As Haro women were traditionally only married as co-wives by Bayso men, their original impurity did not matter too much as long as they would stop eating hippo meat anymore, also not during visits to her natal family. A ritual cleansing of a Haro wife is not necessary when she moves to her Bayso husband, but circumcision (also considered as an act of cleansing) of the girl is absolutely necessary.[35]

[34] There exist also other categories of impurity linked to certain prohibitions among the Bayso. Females who are having their menstrual period for example are not allowed to pass over a grinding stone or over leather.

[35] Braukmann was provided descriptions of the circumcision, stating males were usually circumcised in groups. On the day of circumcision the respective families prepared food and invited the *haromaga* (ritual leader of the Haro) and elders to join them. The *haromaga* blessed everyone, the children and family members, and then also the young men to be circumcised. Then all were eating together. The circumcision was then done

The Haro claim that they have always been circumcising their males and females, explaining that a circumciser could be from any of the four Haro clans, and even from outside Haro, i.e. from Bayso, though the Bayso do not accept circumcisers from Haro. They also stated towards Braukmann that intermarriage between Haro and Bayso has always existed since the Haro arrived to the island, and that many Haro women were married as first wives by Bayso. They also refuted the Bayso statement that only Bayso girls who had lost their virginity were given to the Haro as wives, and some Haro stated that also in their culture girls should be virgins when they get married.
Further research has to clarify how these two contrasting claims have to be understood. Among other ethnic groups belonging to the Ometic cluster, the virginity before marriage and/or circumcision of females is unusual. This means that the Haro either constitute an exception or that the practice of circumcision has been introduced lately due to an influence of the Bayso. Since the Bayso regard the Haro as impure, the Haro may have been motivated to assimilate to the Bayso practice of circumcision and hereby eliminate at least one of the boundaries of pollution that separates the two groups. The number of Haro engaged in hippo hunting, consumption of the meat and trading with the skin is also reducing. This has to do with the illegality to hunt and the stricter prosecution, but also with the conversion of the Haro to Christianity. Three of Braukmann's elderly key informants (two male former hunters, one female) explained that they had given up eating hippo meat due to religious reasons. During her fieldwork in 2010 and 2012/13 she met only three men who were still active hunters. However, she did not have the impression that the Haro were hereby trying to become culturally closer to the Bayso or merge with them into a common "Gidiccho" group.

Other areas of contact

On the island, Bayso and Haro did not interact regularly. Mostly they would meet on the public meeting place of the Bayso close to the Haro village where the *wonno* (ritual leaders of the Bayso and Shigima villages) met to bless their own people and also the Haro. They were welcomed by the *haromaga*, who, due to his perceived impurity was not allowed to sit or bless with them, but who could attend the meetings.

Between individuals, from Bayso and Haro there existed and still exist traditional bondfriendships. Many Bayso have *saati* (male bondfriends) and *rancho* (female

by a specialist called *áansi addá* (literally: "breast father"). About a year or two later after the circumcision the initiated men were ready to get married. For the circumcision of a girl only the *haromaga* was informed and only women participated in the ceremonial process. The circumcision was done by the so-called *áansi índo"* (literally 'breast mother') and also had to be done be before marriage (between one day up to one year before). Nowadays, the Haro are aware of the fact that female circumcision (also known as female genital mutilation, FGM) is prohibited in Ethiopia, but nevertheless they still practice it.

bondfriends) in Haro, and many Haro have their *laage* in Bayso. As bondfriends people assist each other during work parties, exchange certain goods and visit during funerals and childbirth.

Besides ritual and social commitments, a more practical common activity is the construction of traditional boats. Henze (1974: 93) stated that "The Gidicho [i.e. the Bayso] acknowledge having learned weaving, fishing and boat-building from the Gatami [i.e. the Haro] (...)." Haberland (1963: 695) also suggested that the Bayso may have learned the boat construction from the Gatami (Get'eme), he was not sure about it as the names for boat in Bayso and Haro are very different.

When interviewed in 2013 by Epple, several Bayso expressed to her that they invented the boats once they had moved to the island, and that the Haro learned the skill from them. Chumburo Assefa stated:

> When the water rose, new plants appeared, among these the tree from which the traditional boats (*wollabo*) are made. First people did not know how to build boats, and they threw different kinds of wood into the water to see which one would be floating best.
>
> They tried out many different ways of building boats, improved through time and finally invented the *wollabo* (group discussion, 15.02.2013).

Ballamo Worba added:

> It was through herding boys that finally the good quality of the *borbono* wood was found. They had observed how well it floats and played with *borbono* wood at the shore in the water. When some elders saw this, people started using *borbono* for building the first simple floats made from trunks. The Haro, who came to the island later, copied it from the Bayso. (16.02.2013)

The Haro today seem not sure whether it was them or the Bayso who first invented the boat. The fact that many of them originally came from hippo-hunting groups was used in conversations with Braukmann as an argument that it must have been the Haro who originally invented the boat.[36] Today, the construction of a boat is oftentimes collectively performed, which means that Haro or Bayso men build their boats in collaboration with their bondfriends from the other group who also know how to build a boat. After the construction, the navigation of a boat is shared: those men who constructed one boat will also use it together.

Recent changes and the blurring of boundaries

As indicated in some places above, the relationship between the Bayso and the Haro has been changing in the last decades, possibly due to some external influences: the introduction of Christianity (orthodox and protestant) and complete conversion of both groups in the last 2-3 decades, and the outmigration of Bayso and Haro to the

[36] On a boat trip from Alge to Gidiccho (30th January 2013), Braukmann asked the crew consisting of married Haro men who had invented the local boat. They were not sure about it but assumed in a joking and self-confident way that it must have been created by the Haro people.

mainland. On the island, territory was clearly divided between Bayso, Shigima and Haro (including clearly defined spaces for residence, farmland, grassland, burial sites, ritual and public meeting places etc.), but on the mainland, people are settling where they wish or are assigned by the *kebele*. This has led to a mixing of clans and also of Haro and Bayso some of which live now together as closer neighbours. Haro and Bayso are members of the same associations (such as savings clubs, *equb* and *idir*) and modern cooperatives (fishing cooperatives, saltbar cooperative) and their children go to the same schools. From Bayso perspective, intermarriage restrictions have been partly lifted as Haro wives are nowadays also married as first wives by Bayso men and Bayso girls more often given as wives to the Haro. The Haro have, again from Bayso perspective, also eliminated a boundary by introducing the circumcision of males and females. The conception of impurity associated with hippo meat consumption has not disappeared yet but has found a new justification: it is nowadays confirmed by the prohibition of its consumption in the bible.

Further research needs to be done to clarify existing contradictions on the two groups' narratives on their origin and cultural practices, for example the question whether the Haro have recently adopted the practice of circumcision or not, and if they have, whether this is a strategy to become more "Bayso" or simply to be more accepted. It also needs to be observed whether in the future an increased political awareness of both groups would lead them to insist in separate acknowledged ethnic identities or whether they would unite—in whatever way—and willingly accept the common label of "Gidiccho". What seems clear at the moment is that as long as the Haro continue hunting and consuming hippos, a merging of the two groups is unthinkable.

References

Authority for Research and Conversation of Cultural Heritage, 2009: *An Inventory of the Intangible Cultural Heritage of Twenty Nations and Nationalities of North Omo, Southern Nations, Nationalities and Peoples Regions (SNNPR) Ethiopia, (Vol. 2).* UNESCO.

Awoke Amzaye Assoma, 2007: *Mosaic Cultures and Peoples of Southern Nations, Nationalities and Peoples' Regional State.* Awassa: Department of Culture, Bureau of Information and Culture.

Bogale Gebremariam, 2010: *Basin Scale Sedimentary and Water Quality Responses to External Forcing in Lake Abaya, Southern Ethiopian Rift Valley.* Siegen: Universität Siegen.

Bottego, Vittorio, 1895: *Viaggi di Scoperta nel Cuore dell'Africa. Il Giuba Esplorato.* Roma: Ermanno Loescher and C.

Braukmann, Fabienne, 2012: *Nilpferdjäger, Weber, Salzhändler. Wirtschaftliche Strategien und soziale Organisation der Haro Südäthiopiens im Wandel..* Köln: Institut für Ethnologie, Universität zu Köln. (Kölner Ethnologische Beiträge 41).

Brenzinger, Matthias, 1995: "The 'Islanders' of Lake Abaya and Lake Ch'amo: Harro, Ganjule, Gats'ame and Bayso." *Survey of Little-known Languages of Ethiopia.*

Linguistic Report 26, 2-36.

Cavendish, H. S. H., 1898: "Through Somaliland and around and south of Lake Rudolf". *The Geographic Journal*, 11 (4), 373-393.

Cerulli, Ernesta, 1956: *Peoples of South-west Ethiopia and its Borderland.* London: International African Institute.

Fleming, Harold, 1976: Omotic Overview. In: *Bender, M.L. (ed.): The Non-Semitic Languages of Ethiopia.* Michigan: Michigan State University, 298-323.

Gamo Gofa Zone, Communication and Culture Affairs, 2004: *The History of Gamo Gofa until 1974.* Arbaminch: Cultural Studying Group

Haberland, Eike, 1963: "Die Gidicco". In: Eike Haberland: *Galla Sued-Aethiopiens.* Stuttgart: Kohlhammer, 678-717.

Henze, Paul, B., 1974: "Patterns of Cultural Survival on Islands". *The Ethiopia Observer* XVI, 2, 89-96.

Henze, Paul, B., 1977: *Ethiopian Journeys. Travels in Ethiopia 1969-72* (2nd edition). Addis Ababa: Shama Books.

Hirut Woldemariam, 2004: *A Grammar of Haro with Comparative Notes on the Ometo Linguistic Group.* Universität zu Köln. (PhD Dissertation).

House of Federation, 2001: *The Profile of SNNPR.* Hawassa: Culture, Language and Heritage Department.

Kuls, Wolfgang, 1958: *Beiträge zur Kulturgeographie der südäthiopischenSeenregion.* Frankfurt am Main: Kramer.

Levine, Donald Neville, 1974: *Greater Ethiopia. The evolution of a multiethnic society.* Chicago: University of Chicago Press.

Poissonnier, Nicole, 2003: "Bayso Ethnography". In: *Encyclopedia Aethiopica Vol 1.* Wiesbaden: Harrassowitz, 509-510.

Poissonnier, Nicole, 2005:"Gidicco". In: *Encyclopedia Aethiopica Vol 2.* Wiesbaden: Harrassowitz, 790-791.

Vannutelli, Lamberto, Citerni, Carlo, 1899: *L'Omo. Viaggio d'Esplorazione nell' Africa Orientale.* Milano: Hoepli.

Voigt, Rainer, 2003: "Bayso Language". In: *Encyclopedia Aethiopica Vol 1.* Wiesbaden: Harrassowitz, 508-509.

Websites:

http://www.ethioembassy.org.uk/fact%20file/a-z/culture.htm).

http://www.volkswagenstiftung.de/index.php?id=172&L=1).

Contributors

Wolfgang Bender is social anthropologist with a special interest in popular African music, arts and literature. He did research in many west and east and South African countries, as well as in the Anglophone Caribbean. Besides numerous publications on historical and contemporary African music and arts, he organized many exhibitions within and outside of Germany, established collections and archives of music and arts at three German universities and published many musical records and CDs with traditional and contemporary African music and oral literature. Currently, he is associated visiting professor at the Iwalewa-House of Bayreuth University.

Bosha Bombe has a BA degree in history from Bahir Dar University and got his MA degree in social anthropology from Addis Ababa University in 2013. His research interest focuses on historical and contemporary practices of slavery, exclusion and inclusion of social classes, ethnic identity and interethnic relations, conflict and social boundaries. Presently, he is employed as associate researcher at Arbaminch University, and continuing his research in Ganta with financial support of the French Centre for Ethiopian Studies (CFEE) in Addis Ababa.

Fabienne Braukmann is a social anthropologist. Since 2010 her regional focus has been Southern Ethiopia where she has been conducting fieldwork among the Haro. She took her M.A. degree from the University of Cologne, Germany and is now continuing her research for her PhD. Currently, she is employed as a researcher in a language documentation project at the Asien-Afrika-Institut, University of Hamburg funded by the Volkswagen foundation. Her research interests include culture and environment adaptation, mobility, marginalization, minority groups, cultural change, globalization and urbanization.

Tina Brüderlin is a social anthropologist with a special interest on material culture and museological representation. Between the years 2000 and 2009 she has conducted various fieldworks among the Hamar and the Tsamakko of South Omo and was one of the early anthropologists involved in curating the first exhibits at the South Omo Research Center Museum in Jinka. She was Curatorial and Collections Assistant at the Department for North American and African Anthropology at the American Museum of Natural History in NYC and Research Associate in the cooperative research project "One History—Two Perspectives..." of the Freie Universität Berlin and the Ethnologische Museum Berlin. She is currently Head of the Ethnographic Collection of the Museum Natur und Mensch Städtische Museen Freiburg.

Susanne Epple has MA and PhD degrees in social anthropology from Mainz University. She is presently employed as assistant professor at the Department of Social Anthropology, Addis Ababa University in Ethiopia, and an associated researcher in a culture and language documentation project located at the University of Hamburg in Germany. She did extensive fieldwork in Southern Ethiopia among the Bashada (since 1994) and among the Bayso (since 2012). Her focus of interest lies in the areas of pastoral societies, gender and age, social discourse and identity, material culture, belief systems and conversion, cultural and legal pluralism, human rights.

Gebre Yntiso Deko is associate professor in the Department of Social Anthropology at Addis Ababa University (AAU). He earned his BA in Sociology and MA in Social Anthropology at AAU and did his PhD in Anthropology at the University of Florida. His research interests include population movement, diaspora and development, culture and development, urbanity, inter-ethnic relations, conflict resolution, civil society organizations, and disadvantaged groups. He published journal articles, book chapters, and monographs on many of these topics.

Yvan Houtteman has an MA degree in Philosophy and Comparative Studies of Knowledge Systems from Ghent University and did his PhD in Comparative Sciences of Culture at the same University. Currently, he is lector in philosophy and intercultural studies at Hogeschool Gent. His general interest lies in Adventure therapy and their effects on behavioral problems of adolescents. Between 1995 and 1997, he did extensive fieldwork on body and social identity among the Daasanech for the Museum of Middle Africa in Tervuren and wrote his PhD on Daasanech rituals. Presently, he is planning to resume his research among the Daasanech focusing on their confrontation with globalization.

Thomas Osmond has a PhD in Social Anthropology from Aix-Marseille University in France. Presently, he is working as an associate researcher at the French Centre for Ethiopian Studies (CFEE) in Addis Ababa. He is also affiliated to the Centre d'études des mondes africains in France (CNRS/Université d'Aix-Marseille). Previous employments included assistant professorships at Addis Ababa University and Haramaya University in Ethiopia. His research topics are related to political, religious and historical issues. He has conducted extensive fieldwork on Oromo identity in several parts of Ethiopia for more than ten years.

Nicole Poissonnier is a social anthropologist currently working with "Engagement Global" in Germany. Until October 2013, she was with EIRENE—Internationaler Christlicher Friedensdienst e.V. in the Civil Peace Service Program in Bukavu, Democratic Republic of Congo. She did her MA in Social Anthropology at the University of Mainz, and her PhD in the same field at the University of Goettingen. She has done fieldwork in Ethiopia among the Bashada from 1994 to 1999 and among the Konso from 1999 to 2005. Her interests lie in the fields of conflict, conflict transformation and concepts of violence, cultural aspects of communication and expression of emotions, "maleness" and virility and material culture. Her regional focus is on southern Ethiopia and eastern DR Congo.

Sophia Thubauville is research fellow and head of the library at the Frobenius Institute, Frankfurt. Earlier she has worked at the University of Mainz, the South Omo Research Center in Ethiopia and the Max-Planck Institute for Social Anthropology in Halle. She has done ethnographic field research in Ethiopia among the Maale and Ongota of Southern Ethiopia as well as on Indian academics. She co-edited the volume "Cultural Neighborhood in Southern Ethiopia" and the focus issue "Cultural Diversity in Ethiopia" in the journal Paideuma. Currently her writing is devoted to gender, questions of time and identity, cultural policy, migration and higher education.

Yeraswork Admassie is Associate Professor of Sociology at Addis Ababa University. He obtained his BA and MA degrees from the Swedish University of Lund, and his PhD from the University of Uppsala, Sweden. He has extensive research experience and has written on matters relating to the social dynamics of forestry, land degradation and conservation, rural development, as well as on urban phenomena and urban issues in Ethiopia. He published/co-published three books and numerous articles and research manuscripts and rendered 30 research related consultancy services to international organizations, civil society organizations and government organizations. He was one of the founders of the Forum for Social Studies (FSS) and the first President of the Ethiopian Society of Sociologists, Social Workers and Social Anthropologists (ESSSWA).